Sasha Fenton's
Moon Signs

Sasha Fenton's
Moon Signs

Discover the Hidden Power of your Emotions!

ZAMBEZI PUBLISHING LTD

Published in 2009 by
Zambezi Publishing Ltd
P.O. Box 221 Plymouth, Devon PL2 2YJ (UK)
web: www.zampub.com email: info@zampub.com

Text: copyright © 2009 Sasha Fenton
Cover design: copyright © 2009 Jan Budkowski
Text sketches: copyright © 2009 Jonathan Dee
Certain images/part-images, on cover and within:
with much appreciation, courtesy of NASA.

Sasha Fenton has asserted her moral right
to be identified as the author of this work in terms of
the Copyright, Designs and Patents Act 1988.
British Library Cataloguing-in-Publication Data:
A catalogue record for this book is available from
the British Library

Typeset by Zambezi Publishing Ltd, Plymouth UK
Printed and bound in the UK by Lightning Source (UK) Ltd
ISBN-13: 978-1-903065-74-7

About the Author

Sasha became a professional consultant astrologer in 1973, but had to tail off her consultancy business once her writing took off. She has written over 120 books, mainly on mind, body and spirit subjects, with sales of around 6.5 million copies to her credit, and translations of some titles into a dozen languages. Sasha wrote the stars columns for several British newspapers and magazines, and contributed a chapter to "Llewellyn's Sun Sign Book" every year for ten years.

Having broadcast regularly all over the UK and in several other countries at times, she has also lectured widely, including festivals in various parts of the UK and Sydney, Melbourne, Johannesburg and Cape Town.

Sasha has been President of the British Astrological and Psychic Society (BAPS), Chair and Treasurer for the British Advisory Panel on Astrological Education (APAE), and a member of the Executive Council of the Writers' Guild of Great Britain.

Sasha's first husband, Tony Fenton, died of cancer and diabetes related problems. She met her second husband, Jan Budkowski, in South Africa and their first home was a tent on the banks of the Zambezi River in Jan's country of birth, Zambia. They married and settled in the west of England, where they now run Zambezi Publishing Ltd. Sasha has two children and two granddaughters.

Dedication
To Maggie Hyde and Geoffrey Cornelius. Thanks for many years of encouragement and kindness.

Acknowledgements
Thanks to Jan for editing, typesetting and for many of the illustrations. Also to Malcolm Wright, Jonathan Dee for more illustrations, and Roy Gillett and Solar Fire™ for Moon sign data and charts.

Other books by the author

Astrology
Sun Signs
Rising Signs
Moon Signs
Understanding Astrology
How to Read Your Star Signs
Astrology... on the Move!
Astrology for Wimps
Reading the Future
Astrology for Living
The Hidden Zodiac
Astrology: East and West
The Planets
What Time Were You Born?
Understanding the Astrological Vertex
Ten years' contribution to Llewellyn's Sun Sign Book

With Jonathan Dee
The Moon Sign Kit
Your Millennium Forecasts
Forecasts 2001
Forecasts 2002
Sun Signs Made Simple
Six sets of twelve Astro-guides – from 1995 to 2000

Palmistry
With illustrator, Malcolm Wright
The Living Hand
Hand Reading
Simply Palmistry
Modern Palmistry
Living Palmistry
Learning Palmistry
The Book of Palmistry

Tarot
Fortune-Telling by Tarot Cards
Tarot in Action!
Super Tarot
Elementary Tarot
The Tarot

Chinese
Elementary I Ching
Chinese Divinations

Feng Shui for the Home

Psychic and Fortune Telling
The Fortune-Teller's Workbook
The Aquarian Book of Fortune Telling
The Book of Spells
Star*Date*Oracle
(with Jonathan Dee)
Body Reading
The Fortune Teller's Handbook
Tea Cup Reading
Dreams
(with Jan Budkowski)
How to Be Psychic
Dream Meanings
Fortune-Telling by Tea Leaves
Simply Chakras

Money and Business
Prophecy for Profit
(with Jan Budkowski)
The Money Book
(with Jan Budkowski)

Health
Diabetes: An Everyday Guide

Upcoming New Titles
The Love Tarot
The Flying Stars

Upcoming Revised Titles
Sasha Fenton's Rising Signs
Sasha Fenton's Planets

Contents

This Book's Natal Chart

(i.e. its publication date)

Plymouth,

09:00, 3rd April 2009

Introduction

Thanks to Merlin

My first book was on the subject of Tarot and the second was on palmistry, and then I decided to write an astrology book. I was mulling over what approach to take when the annual *Festival of Mind, Body and Spirit* came around, and I went off to do my stint on the stand belonging to *The British Astrological and Psychic Society (BAPS)*. During one of my breaks, I gravitated to the wonderful bookstall run by a guy who we called Merlin. I told Merlin that I wanted to write a book on astrology but that I hadn't yet come up with the right area to choose, and I asked him if he had any ideas. Without a moment's hesitation, he said, "Moon Signs." Apparently, it was something that the public regularly asked him for. Moon Signs was published a year later and it sold very well for several years. Eventually, it went out of print and after a certain amount of wrangling, I managed to take the rights back. I decided to update the original book and change the name to *"Sasha Fenton's Moon Signs"*, to differentiate it from the original.

I left much of the writing as per the original book, only taking out things that are obviously outdated or that wouldn't work in today's world. I have added sections at the end of each natal Moon sign along with several small chapters of completely new material. Some of this is due to my additional quarter of a century of astrological experience since writing the first book, and some is down to the massive advance of computerisation and software, as this has rendered techniques that were impossibly difficult once extremely easy now.

One of the things that made the original book so successful was the Moon Sign table at the back of the book, which meant that readers didn't have to wait until they could visit an astrologer before finding their natal Moon Sign. They could even progress their Moon Sign and check out the Moon's transits on the spot. I decided to leave those tables in place and to update them by adding another couple of decades rather than direct the reader to tables on a website.

Printing methods have changed massively over the years, so alterations and additions are no longer prohibitively expensive. This means that I can continue to update tables and other features as time goes by and keep this book, and others like it, in print on a permanent basis.

And so, with renewed thanks to the now retired Merlin (a.k.a. Brian Mountford) here is the new book. I hope the new generation of readers enjoy it as much as their predecessors did.

Moon Data

The Moon's average distance from the Earth, surface to surface, is 376,284 kilometres, or about 233,812 miles. It takes 27.32 days for the Moon to travel round the Earth and also 27.32 days for it to rotate on its axis, therefore it always has the same "face" pointing towards the Earth. Its diameter is 3476.6 kilometres and its temperature varies between plus 101° and minus 153° centigrade. The interior of the Moon is still hot enough to be made of molten rock and there are about 3,000 moonquakes per year. The surface of the Moon is fatter on the side that faces the Earth, and it's also warmer on the Earth side.

The Moon and Earth were both formed when the solar system came into being, roughly 4.5 billion (4,500,000,000) years ago. The Moon became attracted to the Earth's gravitational field and formed a double or binary planet system. Double planets spin round each other, rather like children swinging around each other on a rope; in this case, the relative sizes of the Earth and Moon mean that the Moon does most (not all) of the swinging. The first Moon landing was at 2.56 UT on the 20th July, 1969 by Armstrong, Aldrin and Collins in Apollo 11.

The Moon is about a quarter of the size of the Earth and its surface area is about the size of Asia. Nevertheless, its mountains reach 8,000 metres, which is higher than any on earth. There is no atmosphere on the Moon; therefore meteorites collide with it without being burned up by friction on their way down.

The Phases of the Moon

The Moon does not shed any light of its own, only the light that is reflected by the Sun. The phases of the Moon depend upon its position between the Earth and the Sun.

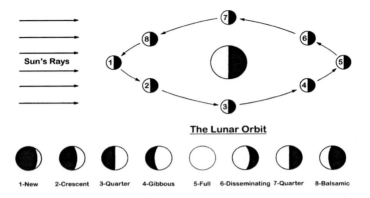

The Phases of the Moon

Eclipses

Eclipses of the Moon occur when the Earth is between the Moon and the Sun, and only when the Moon is full. Eclipses of the Sun occur when the Moon is between the Earth and the Sun, so this only happens when the Moon is dark or new. There are an average of two lunar and two solar eclipses each year, but not all can be seen from the same country and most of them are partial. Eclipses can last for a period of a few minutes to about an hour.

Lunar Eclipse

Solar Eclipse

Occultations
These occur when the Moon is directly between the Earth and a planet.

Tides
There are two high tides a day, and these revolve round the Earth in line with the Moon. At the time of the new Moon and the full Moon, when the Sun, Moon and Earth are in line, the tides are higher.

The Ecliptic or Zodiac
Until the discovery of the way that the solar system works, it was thought that the Sun orbited the earth and the line that the Sun appeared to take around the Earth is called the ecliptic. Interestingly, both astrologers and astronomers still use this "apparent" trajectory of the Sun to find their way around the sky. The constellations that make up our familiar zodiac are sited along or very close to, and touching, the ecliptic. The word zodiac comes from the Ancient Greek word for "animal" and is linked to the words "zoo" and "zoological".

Declination
The orbit of the Moon and the planets takes them above the ecliptic and below it as well.

Signs of the Zodiac

The Moon in Astrology

Emotions

When I give a lecture on Moon signs, I start by asking the audience members what they think the Moon represents, and they invariably answer, 'emotions'. I then ask them what emotions they think the Moon might represent; for instance, are we talking about rage, jealousy, lust or hatred? The audience members often look puzzled while they mull this over. The problem is that *all* the planets in astrology represent emotional states of one kind or another, and here are some suggestions that show you what I mean:

PLANET	EMOTIONS
Sun	Joy, success, children, happiness, achievement, day to remember.
Mercury	Ideas, things that excite the mind. Pleasure or stress from studying.
Venus	Love, jealousy, heartbreak, happiness, top of the world or bottom.
Mars	Jealousy, hatred, attack, sexuality, lust, wanting everything now.
Jupiter	Expansiveness, happiness, desire for justice, desire to explore.
Saturn	Depression, loneliness, sadness, fatigue, disappointment
Uranus	Desire to break out of restriction or boredom, desire for change.
Neptune	Love, kindness, obsession, confusion and loss.
Pluto	Rage, resentment, jealousy, need for security.
Chiron	Seat of pain, sickness, pleasure from arts or combat.

Old astrology books tell us that the Sun represents action and the Moon represents reaction, so the Moon can only offer an emotional reaction to any situation. The reasoning that used to be given for this is that the Moon cannot create any light itself but it can only reflect the light of the Sun. I may not be the biggest brain in the world of astrology, but it strikes me that none of the other planets do their own shining either, and they produce all kinds of effects, so that argument falls rather flat, doesn't it? Certainly the Moon represents a more emotional side of our nature than most of the planets, and it can show how we react in certain situations.

Inner Motivation

To some extent, the Ascendant and the Sun represent the outer manner or obvious nature of a person, but the Moon represents the inner, hidden side. Thus someone who appears soft as butter but is in reality hard as nails, has a Moon that is very much at odds with the outer manner. Alternately, someone who appears happy-go-lucky on the outside can be hurting badly inside. Also, if you want to see what a person really values and feels to be important, take a look at the Moon's sign and house.

Nurturing

Here are some old ideas and several newer ones about the Moon, motherhood and nurturing:

Old astrology books state that the Moon represents the mother and the Sun the father.

Most modern astrologers see the Moon as the mother and Saturn as the father.

Bruno and Louise Huber suggested that Saturn represented the mother, as it was she who disciplined the children and saw to it that they had proper food, clothing, education and good manners, while the indulgent, lunar father turned up from time to time, took them out and spoiled them.

Is that what fathers do? In our world, many fathers vanish over the horizon, into the mist, so one could suggest that fathers can be better represented by Neptune!

Frankly, I see the Moon as the maternal or nurturing influence. It may be the mother that gives the children the attention, love and care that they need, but it could come from the father, or both parents at once or both in turn at different times. Sometimes the main influence in a child's life is another relative, someone outside the family or even different people at different stages of the subject's life.

The Moon sign can sometimes symbolise the experience that the mother herself had during her life. It can show what she is like as person, and it can also demonstrate the influence she had on the subject.

However, you can't limit this to the mother herself, as it shows the experience of being mothered – or neglected or maltreated or loved - by whosoever happened to take on this role.

The Moon in some signs shows a deep attachment to the mother or to a mother figure, while in other signs it denotes a friendly but detached relationship, while it others it can symbolise, disappointment, dislike and disapproval.

The following table is a kind of quick rundown of the way in which adults tend to look at their mothers.

Moon Sign	Feelings for Mother
Aries	Fondness, but irritation, and sometimes a burden.
Taurus	Some love, but the mother may be considered a burden.
Gemini	Friendship, shared intellectual interests, but not living out of each other's pockets.
Cancer	These two can cling to one another, or get on each other's nerves.
Leo	The child will try to love the mother, but will eventually give it up as a bad job.
Virgo	The child finds the mother a complete pain.
Libra	A casual and friendly relationship, but some irritation.
Scorpio	Superficially close, but with much resentment and sometimes hidden stores of rage and hatred.
Sagittarius	The child is dutiful, but with little or no real love on either side.
Capricorn	The closest relationship is to the father, but the mother is also deeply loved.
Aquarius	At best, love and a friendly, and even a respectful relationship. At worst, no real contact.
Pisces	A close relationship with much to talk about, but they often irritate each other.

Family Life

Just as the Moon can show one's feelings about the mother, so can it show one's attitude to family life. Some subjects will make considerable sacrifices for their families and especially for their children, while others only focus on themselves and leaving their relatives and even their children to find nurturing elsewhere.

Women

The Moon represents the feminine principle, so it often refers to women or to dealings with women, especially when it comes to trends and events.

The Home, Property and Land

The Moon rules the home, and in particular the kitchen, cooker, fridge and everything to do with the preparation of food. The Moon sign can indicate a greater or lesser interest in these things. If you are looking into the value of your property, whether to buy, sell move or speculate on property, it's worth checking out the natal Moon and the progressions by the Moon and to it, and the transits to the Moon. Also check the condition of the nodes of the Moon, natally, by progression and by transit at the relevant time. Land is also a lunar interest, although it can connect with other planets depending upon circumstances – such as with Venus for ownership, and with Mars and Pluto if an inheritance is involved.

Providing What the Public Wants

This covers a wide area of operation, but the general idea is of the provision of goods and services that the public makes use of.

Farming and Food Production

Everything related to foodstuffs comes under the realm of the Moon. It can come under other planets too, especially Venus for a plentiful harvest and both Mercury and Jupiter for small animals and Jupiter on its own for large ones. The asteroid, Ceres (among others) also has something to say about harvests, crops and foodstuffs. Of all these items, the Moon is especially concerned with dairies, cows, dairy products and even mad cow disease, foot and mouth and so on.

Prince Charles has Moon rising in Leo – so he has his own farm and his own business producing and selling the "Duchy" brand of high quality, organic products. The Moon in Leo likes things to be the best and therefore, more expensive than similar products.

Shops, Businesses

The Moon rules the kind of small shop that an individual can own and run independently, as a franchise or linked to a buying organisation, so this might range from your local bookshop, the local shoe-mender/key cutter business, a Wimpy café or a Spar grocery shop. The Moon rules as pubs, restaurants, dairies, farm shops and convenience shops. One could ague that the Moon also rules a massive supermarket, because it provides goods that the public need, but the business as a whole – e.g. all the supermarkets in the chain, the shareholders, finance, distribution and much else are not lunar matters.

The Moon rules small businesses of all kinds, especially those that people run from home, thus astrologers and astrology writers who work from home are at least partially ruled by the Moon – along with other planetary influences.

Attitude to Money
Money is an emotive issue, so the natal Moon sign and progressed Moon can show the attitude towards money and even the financial situation at any time. The need for security is a lunar issue, so this also relates to money.

Travel and the Sea
Before the discovery of Neptune in the middle of the 19th century, the Moon was considered to be a restless planet that was connected to the sea, and by extension, to travel, so it was always associated with restlessness, and with an inability to settle down. It's interesting that so many aspects of the Moon deal with family life, parents, homes, property and land, farms, shops and businesses, which are all things that tie us to people and places. Old time astrology told us that the Moon was restless. It changes it shape and even disappears completely from time to time, thus it symbolises a desire for change and for getting away from things. The Moon can represent novelty, changes of scene, days out by the sea, the desire to roam and general foot-looseness. The Moon also rules changeable moods, a need for a new perspective and the urge to get away from it all once in a while. When we are desperate for a change, the Moon can move into just the right position to bring it along.

I haven't noticed the Moon being especially important in the charts of those who work on the sea, but others might know of such a connection. As far as the travel trade goes, there does seem to be a preponderance of people with the Moon in Gemini.

Mind

We forget that older forms of astrology associated the Moon with the mind, so it can show whether a person's thinking is quick, slow, original or traditional. It can show whether the mind is temporarily filled with obsessive ideas or flitting from one thing to another.

Career

Although not really associated with work, the Moon shows how we like to spend our days and what we feel is important to us and to the world. It can show talents, and it can point to certain types of interest, careers and hobbies.

Health

This is important. Transits, returns and progressions of the Moon are important indicators of serious health problems, and the Moon's movement can act as a trigger for these. In itself, it rules the chest, breasts, breathing and fluids in body, and being 'cold and wet' by tradition, it rules arthritis and fluid in or on the lungs and heart. It can rule mental sickness, due to its unstable nature.

Reflections

The Moon can borrow some of its nature from the sign directly opposite to the sign which it occupies, so here is a table of the signs and their opposites.

SIGN	OPPOSITE SIGN
Aries	Libra
Taurus	Scorpio
Gemini	Sagittarius
Cancer	Capricorn
Leo	Aquarius
Virgo	Pisces
Libra	Aries
Scorpio	Taurus
Sagittarius	Gemini
Capricorn	Cancer
Aquarius	Leo
Pisces	Virgo

The Zodiac

We know that the earth orbits the Sun, taking a year to complete the orbit, but it appears from earth as though the Sun goes around us, and the path that it takes is called the 'plane of the ecliptic' or the 'ecliptic'. It's also called the zodiac.

Genders, Elements and Qualities
Each alternate sign is masculine or feminine, which is a bit like the Chinese idea of yang and yin. There are also three signs in each element of fire, earth, air and water, and there are four signs in each quality, of cardinal, fixed and mutable.

The Gender
This has nothing to do with sexuality. Some astrologers call these signs positive and negative but their energies are perhaps better expressed as extrovert and introvert or yang and yin. All fire and air signs are masculine, while all earth and water signs are feminine.

Sign	Gender	Element	Quality
Aries	1. Masculine	1. Fire	1. Cardinal
Taurus	2. Feminine	2. Earth	2. Fixed
Gemini	1. Masculine	3. Air	3. Mutable
Cancer	2. Feminine	4. Water	1. Cardinal
Leo	1. Masculine	1. Fire	2. Fixed
Virgo	2. Feminine	2. Earth	3. Mutable
Libra	1. Masculine	3. Air	1. Cardinal
Scorpio	2. Feminine	4. Water	2. Fixed
Sagittarius	1. Masculine	1. Fire	3. Mutable
Capricorn	2. Feminine	2. Earth	1. Cardinal
Aquarius	1. Masculine	3. Air	2. Fixed
Pisces	2. Feminine	4. Water	3. Mutable

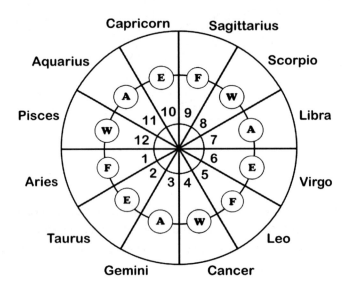

The Elements
Fire= F, Earth= E, Air= A, Water= W

The Fire Group - Masculine
Aries, Leo, Sagittarius

This group is associated with speed, quick thinking and fast responses. People with the Moon in fire signs don't lack initiative and they can get things off the ground quickly when they want to. They may lack patience with slower people, so it doesn't take much to irritate or anger them and they don't stand fools gladly. These subjects can concentrate on a project if it interests them, but they soon become bored if it doesn't. There are times when their self-centred attitude can make them appear arrogant, but they are not as confident as they look and they can be subject to sudden fits of depression. They need a steady partner who they can rely upon.

They are generous and good hearted as long as others don't take advantage of their generosity. As long as there is no heavy emphasis on earth or water signs, these people can be somewhat overgenerous when it comes to their own family. This is partly because they have faith in their ability to earn more money in the future, and partly because they want their relatives and friends to like them, admire them and approve of them. They dress well and put on a good appearance generally, with a nice home and a nice car and all the right accoutrements, and they splash money around in order to achieve all these aims. Having said this, the Moon is different from the Sun, and wherever it's placed, it adds a certain amount of thrift or carefulness. Unless the Sun and other planets are also in fire signs, the person is unlikely to be a complete 'spendaholic'.

The Moon is associated with a water sign, so it may not be comfortable when placed in this group. Sudden enthusiasms may not be all that easy to carry through, and the person's changeable emotions may confuse those around him. The subject himself can be confused by his own nature, because fire gives him a fast and logical mind, while the Moon gives him an emotional and intuitive heart.

Childhood experiences may not be all that comfortable or happy and this leads to a certain lack of self-confidence. The subject may cover this up by having the latest and best car, the trendiest designer clothes and the smartest house, or by looking more confident than he or she feels.

The Earth Group - Feminine
Taurus, Virgo, Capricorn

When the Moon is in an earth sign, there is a certain amount of practicality. These people like domestic life and they enjoy entertaining in the home. They tend to be thorough, careful and capable of dealing with details and there is a certain stubbornness here that helps them to finish what they start. On the other hand this can tie them into a job, relationship or some other situation longer than is good for them. These people fear poverty, so they work hard for their money and they hang on to what they have, to the point of becoming tight-fisted. Some worry unnecessarily over money matters. They are dutiful to their parents and good to their offspring but their work is also important to them. They may define themselves by their successes or failures at work. The Moon is quite comfortable in earth signs, but this element can make it hard for people to adapt to new circumstances.

As a child, this person would have had at least a reasonable relationship with his father. The mother would have been a powerful figure who either made unreasonable demands upon the child or was very loving. She may have been so contradictory that it confused the subject.

The Air Group - Masculine
Gemini, Libra, Aquarius

Air signs are mainly concerned with logic, a strong mind and intellect. This Moon placement adds intelligence and speedy thinking, but it can make it difficult for these subjects to cope with upsetting issues or with their own feelings. Some of these subjects avoid emotional situations by burying themselves in work or studies, while others find themselves at odds with partners who may be more emotional. A few of these people can be unrealistic, with dreams far above what life can hope to offer.

Saving and spending or giving and taking can be a problem for these people. They are inclined to be extremely self-indulgent, but they can be peculiar when it comes to dealing with others, either being over-generous or unnecessarily tight-fisted. Some give freely to one person while keeping others on a tight leash. Just like their confusing financial ideas, their emotions can be equally confusing, especially to themselves.

Childhood relationships are pretty reasonable and their parents will have done all they could to give these subjects a good education and plenty of intellectual stimuli.

The Water Group - Feminine
Cancer, Scorpio, Pisces

The Moon is supposed to be most at home in water signs, but this can put too much emphasis on the emotional and intuitive nature, making these individuals subject to elation at one time and depression at others – not to mention angry outbursts. Part of the problem is that they are quick to pick up on atmospheres and surrounding emotions. They absorb the feelings of those who are around them and sometimes get upset as a result. These sensitive people love deeply but they also hate with equal passion. Where practicalities such as money are concerned, they fear poverty but they may have to cope with this at some point in their lives. Water signs tend to be thrifty and careful at the best of times, and the watery Moon in a water sign adds to this tendency, so unless there is a preponderance of fire in the chart, this person can become tight-fisted and an advantage-taker.

The childhood can be difficult because these youngsters are not altogether on the same wavelength as those around them. This may put them at odds with their parents, siblings, schoolmates, teachers and so on.

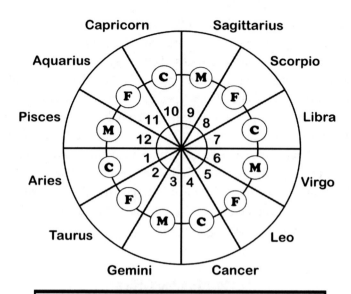

The Qualities of the Signs
Fixed = F Cardinal = C Mutable = M

The Cardinal Group
Aries, Cancer, Libra, Capricorn

These people try to maintain equilibrium in their lives but their destiny tends to force them to cope with quite profound changes in circumstances. They may move house several times, change partners or live through sudden bereavements or sudden career changes. They can think on their feet when they have to, and they can be extremely successful and wealthy at some points in their lives – sometimes due to a lucky marriage or an inheritance. Cardinal sign people cannot live under someone else's rules and they are perfectly capable of ignoring the demands of others. They like to make their own decisions and sometimes live only by their own rules.

The Fixed Group
Taurus, Leo, Scorpio, Aquarius

People with the Moon in fixed signs form their opinions when they are young and they find it hard to change these later. They aren't flexible and they find it hard to see a variety of ways of solving problems, so they become disappointed and depressed if their plans don't work out. They go after what they want in a dogged manner, sometimes by sheer hard work, but sometimes by freeloading. They can be self-absorbed. They are usually reliable and faithful in love relationships, and they are very attached to their families and those who they love. Some of these people are extremely emotional while others find it almost impossible to deal with emotions - even their own.

These people find it hard to let go of pain that is left over from their childhood or their past, so these things can haunt them and affect the way they react to things throughout life. In a more material sense, those who have the Sun, Ascendant or Moon in a fixed sign find it hard to throw stuff out, and they can end up living in a very small and cluttered space, due to the amount of junk they hang on to.

The Mutable Group
Gemini, Virgo, Sagittarius, Pisces

These people can attract lame ducks, and some of them are lame ducks themselves. They may sacrifice themselves for the sake of loved ones and even for strangers, so they need to be discriminating in their choice of friends and colleagues. They should try to avoid jumping in and offering help too quickly or taking on too much. Their own fluctuating moods make them difficult to understand, and they can suffer from chronic ailments, especially when unhappy or when they feel that their lives are out of control. These individuals make good friends and they are sympathetic, but they can be neurotic, nervy, emotional, stingy and inclined to pick fights over small matters when tired or stressed.

Dignity, Exaltation, Detriment and Fall

You will notice these strange terms cropping up in this book. They come from ancient forms of astrology that considered certain sign and planet groupings to be good and others to be less good. Some of these are easy to understand, such as 'dignity', which simply means that the planet is in the sign that it rules. The detriment sign is the one opposite the dignity one. Exaltation and fall don't have any common sense reason for their existence, but they probably have something to do with the astronomy of the signs and their position at certain times of the year according to ancient astronomers.

The houses act in similar ways to the signs because each house links to a sign, but these concepts are now called 'accidental'. Needless to say, every planet has this same system going for it; but this book is about the Moon, so as far as we are concerned, the table below shows how the system affects the Moon.

Sign	Moon's Condition	House	Moon's Condition
Aries		First	
Taurus	Exaltation	Second	Accidental Exaltation
Gemini		Third	
Cancer	Dignity	Fourth	Accidental Dignity
Leo		Fifth	
Virgo		Sixth	
Libra		Seventh	
Scorpio	Fall	Eighth	Accidental Fall
Sagittarius		Ninth	
Capricorn	Detriment	Tenth	Accidental Detriment
Aquarius		Eleventh	
Pisces		Twelfth	

Moon in Aries

Ruled by Mars

The sun shall not smite thee by day, nor the moon by night.
 Psalm 121

The sign of Aries is masculine, positive, fiery and cardinal whilst the Moon, through its association with the sign of Cancer, is feminine, negative, watery and cardinal. This Moon position gives its owner an underlying need for power and a desire for leadership. This may lead you to reach for the top in your career or to become the leader of whichever group you find yourself in. Women with this Moon placement face emotional conflict within their personality due to their highly assertive inner nature, and they frequently resolve this by choosing weak partners so that they can reverse the traditional man/woman roles. One such woman is Bernadette.

Bernadette is a hard working and successful businesswoman who travels far and wide to earn the money that her family needs. Her sensitive and artistic husband has a rather humdrum job in a local garage and he is super-supportive and caring towards their children! 'I didn't choose this way of life,' says Bernadette, 'it just seems to work out better this way. David cannot take too much hassle and he is really much better with the children than I am.'

Some choose single life and a demanding career in preference to housework and motherhood. Carol is now in her late thirties and is running a successful public relations business of her own. She has had long-term lovers but has never married. 'Some years ago I debated whether to have a child and bring it up on my own because I knew by then that marriage was not for me. In the end, I decided to stay as I am, but I'm not always sure that I took the right decision even now.'

Both sexes have an inner power pack of energy, forcefulness and courage. The cardinality of this sign means that you rarely allow the grass to grow beneath your feet, and if faced with a problem you would rather sort it out immediately. You may actually get others to do this for you, but help is appreciated when it's given. Your mind is highly original and, given other encouraging factors on your birthchart, you may be able to turn your ideas into moneymaking projects that could give you the means to get yourself up the ladder of success. However you may be so idealistic and enthusiastic as to be unrealistic. You have a tendency to do things on too large a scale on some occasions, while over-optimism can cloud your brain and make you unrealistic in your expectations. You need an element of risk in your life that may be reflected in the job you do or in your personal life.

Being quickly responsive to any situation, you can be relied on in a crisis; the sight of people who are in trouble does not embarrass you – indeed you will do what you can to help them. Your emotional reactions are fast and instinctive and your behaviour can be over-impulsive, but time and experience of life may soften some of the rough edges. Care should be taken not to be critical and impatient with those who see and do things differently from you, as this can lead you into a narrow-minded and bigoted stance. You quickly become irritated and may have difficulty in keeping your temper due to the combined blanketing effect of the watery Moon and the fiery impulsiveness of the sign of Aries. This tension may be released in sudden outbursts of temper and biting sarcastic remarks. If there are some Aquarian traits on your chart, your energy could make you an energetic social reformer. You prefer other people to be forthright and honest in their dealings with you and unless there is a very good reason for secrecy, you prefer to be direct and honest yourself. Your excellent sense of humour gets you out of a lot of trouble and you have the ability to take a joke against yourself.

Your ability to put ideas into action can be an inspiration to others; also you can motivate people by your optimistic outlook and your faith in the future. You know instinctively how to raise the spirits of others. However, you sometimes plunge into action without weighing the consequences, and therefore you need to cultivate a sense of proportion. Be careful not to override the feelings of others when you are in the throes of a new idea, although it's never your intention to hurt anyone. You have little patience with people who withdraw into their shell, sulk and won't tell you what's the matter with them; your own hot temper can make you insensitive at times, but you don't hold a grudge. The lunar Arian heart is warm and you are the first to help and comfort those who are in trouble. You respect the beliefs of others and are happy to preserve their independence; your broad mind makes you able to relate to people of all classes and colours. You really cannot stand neurotic people who whine for nothing. You will help anyone who has practical problems but have little patience with emotional doubts and worries and you tend to avoid having them yourself.

You are more of a city person than a country type, but you like to get away into the fresh air, and love being in the sun. It's a fact that many lunar Arians are excellent sportsmen and sportswomen. The fiery quality of Aries indicates a need for excitement and change. A monotonous job may pay the bills, but won't satisfy you for long. This need for excitement can also make steady relationships appear unappealing, and this may even lead you to choose unreliable partners. Some of you, on the other hand, seek to steady your own inner nature by marrying a much more placid and reliable personality than yourself, while a few of you may even destroy a relationship simply because it has become boring. I have a theory that Moon in Aries subjects of both sexes prefer a younger partner, as this suggests that you would enjoy moulding them to your own design.

Many of you choose a partner who is careful with money because you can't trust yourself not to overspend. You enjoy the pursuit of love and fall in love fairly easily but the flame can also burn out quickly. A relationship based on friendship is more likely to be enduring than a swift passion, but there must be excitement, sex and warmth or it will not work at all. Women with the Moon in Aries have a touch of masculinity at their core; that is not to say that they are all budding lesbians, just that there is dissatisfaction with the traditional feminine role. Whatever your gender, if you have this Moon placement, you may be hard to live with at times, because you can fall into the habit of being picky and fault-finding due to unreasonable fears based on imagined threats to your independence.

You can be quite a good homemaker as long as you have time and money to spare, but if you are short of both, you will ignore your surroundings. You enjoy buying gadgets for the home and you can put up with noisy or messy major alterations going on in the home better than most people can. However, when the atmosphere at home becomes unbearable, either for practical reasons of too many builders around the place or due to relationship stress, you find a good reason to get out of the house for a while.

You are a caring parent, but unfortunately you could belittle any child whom you considered weak and silly. You do your best to see that your children have all that they require and will move heaven and earth to get them a good education. You may not actually wish to spend too much time with your children, and the parent/child relationship works better if you have a fulfilling job and can direct some of your energies away from the home situation. You will never hesitate to spend money on your family's appearance because you consider that good clothes give a good impression.

Sexually, your attitude should be straightforward but you may wish to dominate your partner and control him or her. Talk of sex excites you but background music during lovemaking may put you off! You enjoy fun and laughter while making love but you need friendship and appreciation from your partner as much as you need sex.

Many of you love the arts, especially music and dancing, some of you will find your way into an artistic career, certainly you need a measure of creativity in your work. Many subjects with the Sun, Moon or Ascendant in Aries have a lifelong desire to study music or art but somehow never quite get around to it; perhaps the fear of failure is too great.

Career

The position of the Moon on a birthchart rarely determines one's actual career, but can show inner motivations. You are happiest in a job where you can make your own decisions and may prefer to be self-employed. If not too impatient, you can rise to an executive position in a large and well-structured organisation. You enjoy wielding power and should make a sensible and benevolent manager or employer, you have the ability to delegate tasks to others and then leave them to get on with the job. Taking orders from someone you don't respect is impossible for you and you would respond very angrily to anyone who tried to bully you; however you, in turn, must try not to bully or to laugh at others.

You need to be able to use your initiative; you would find it impossible to work for a wet blanket type. Work in the military or paramilitary field might appeal to you as might work as an engineer, in the electronics field, teaching or any kind of work that influences the public. You may enjoy working in the media and being in the public eye so that you can receive open adulation. Marketing, promoting and thinking up new ideas comes easily to you. Your Achilles' heel may be that you are susceptible to flattery. If there are other indications on your birthchart, you could make quite a good teacher. Your love of mechanics and vehicles makes you a good driver and even a good pilot and you are quick to grasp IT concepts. You could make a living from sport or dancing, possibly as a teacher.

Parents and Background

This Moon position shows a difficult relationship with the father, you may have loved him and hated him at the same time and you may also have tried to emulate him. Whilst growing up, you probably found yourself in a number of nose-to-nose shouting matches with him. There is a fight for emotional supremacy in this relationship with the father seeing the child as being unrealistic and the child seeing the parent as being overly restrictive or unhelpful. Sometimes the father actually shows contempt towards the child. Your mother may have been cold towards you or just too busy to take much notice of you. The family itself may be attached to a large and very structured organisation such as the armed forces or the civil service. The Aries Moon child may follow his parents into the same organisation but he would only be happy in that environment if he quickly gained a position of rank and decision-making.

Your parents encouraged you to stand on your own feet at an early age. They would have applauded and encouraged any physical activity (sports, swimming, dancing) and wanted you to do well at school. You don't have much attachment to the past or even to your own family, this is especially true if you feel that they don't appreciate you.

Your mother might have had to face some kind of circumstances where she was forced to leave you to cope alone. This was probably due to problems at that time; however it's possible that she was vain, selfish and all too easily bored by the tasks of motherhood. The Moon sign sometimes jumps back a generation, so some of the circumstances given here for your childhood could actually apply to your mother's experience when young. There may even have been jealousy and bitterness between you and your brothers and sisters.

Health

In so far as the Moon sometimes reflects continuous or chronic health conditions, any trouble in this case would be in the area of the head, eyes, nose, ears (upper) teeth and throat. Your impetuosity may lead you to have silly accidents such as cuts, burns and possibly bruises as a result of dropping things on your feet.

Additional Information

Maybe other astrologers have a different experience to me, but I haven't come across as many lunar Arians as other Moon signs. This could mean there are fewer lunar Arians, but on the other hand, it could indicate a lack of interest in astrology.

Sun, Moon or Ascendant in Aries folk have soft speaking voices, and some males with this Moon placement dislike their voices because they are slightly high, but many of them have good singing voices, so perhaps this offers a little consolation.

There is a fondness for culture but this can be hidden under a very ordinary exterior, so a lunar Arian can be a rough, tough engineer or businessman who loves literature, art and music.

You have to take care not to bully or shout down others.

Moon in Aries Celebrities

Jose Maria Carreras
John Cleese
Divine
Bill Gates
Jennifer Lopez
Martina Navratilova

♈

Moon in Taurus

Ruled by Venus
(The Moon's exaltation)

Ah, Moon of my Delight who know'st no wane,
The Moon of Heaven is rising once again:
How oft hereafter rising shall she look
Through this same Garden after me - in vain!
From The Rubaiyat of Omar Khayyam.

The sign of Taurus is feminine, negative, earth and fixed, while the Moon, through its connections with the sign of Cancer, is feminine, negative, water and cardinal. The Moon is fairly comfortable in Taurus, adding a measure of stability to the personality and bestowing an uncomplicated response to sensual pleasures. Older forms of astrologer called Taurus the sign of the Moon's exaltation. You enjoy eating, drinking, making love and listening to music. The feminine aspect of this placement prevents you from being much of an initiator; indeed you prefer to spend your life sailing along on a steady course than for it to be full of storms and disruption. The fixity of Taurus stabilises the natural restlessness of the Moon and makes you very purposeful and determined, particularly when it comes to getting what you want or hanging on to what you have. You try at all times to maintain the status quo; you may find that the circumstances of your life force you into this position. You might even find yourself putting up with a long-term lifestyle that is not of your choosing.

The Moon is said to be exalted in the sign of Taurus and this gives an inner sense of strength and resilience. Lunar Taureans are noted for their robust health and their ability to obtain practical results in all that they undertake. People who have the Moon in an earth sign love the natural world, which means that you can make a hobby out of botany or animal biology. You could become involved with some scheme that seeks to preserve the countryside. Even if you aren't actively involved with these pursuits, you will love getting out into the fresh air and into your garden. Many lunar Taureans choose to work as representatives or even milkmen, so that they can be out and about and thus keep in tune with the seasons. You have a strong need to build for the future and create things which will be useful and long lasting, this could be reflected in your choice of a career. You like the sea, but not with the same intensity as solar or lunar Cancerians, and you wouldn't have any great urge to run off and join the navy. Your affinity with nature could lead you to take an interest in ancient religions, such as paganism and Wicca.

You don't enter into relationships lightly, because the fixity of Taurus, along with your inner urge to build and preserve, leads you to take any form of emotional commitment very seriously. Most astrology books tell us that this Moon position leads to possessiveness and jealousy and to some extent this is true. Possessiveness is more of a problem than envy or jealousy but this is a rather subtle concept to grasp. You don't envy the things that other people have or the relationships that they enjoy but if your partner were to leave you for another, you would be very upset indeed. A woman with this Moon placement can become taken in by a man who promises to leave his wife at some future date, and then doesn't. In these situations, it's hard for you to give in gracefully and accept defeat, especially in the face of betrayal. As you can see, your tenacity and endurance are both strengths and weaknesses of this particular Moon Sign placement. Your tendency to be stubborn can lead you into psychologically damaging and obsessive relationships.

Your senses are strong, especially touch, smell and hearing. You love the scent of flowers and the feel of velvet. Your musical taste is well developed. One Moon in Taurus lady told me that she hates the sound of a 'murdered song' but loves the sound of laughter. Obviously this sensuality leads to a love of sex with all its scents, textures and passions, although relating is more important to you than sex for its own sake. You love to be cuddled and stroked in both a sexual and an affectionate manner, and ideally all this snuggling should take place within marriage.

You prefer to be faithful to your partner but if for some reason you find this impossible, then you would try hard to wait for your children to grow up before actually leaving the family home, so you try to do your duty for however long it takes. Oddly enough, you are quite a flirt, but this is 'social' flirting that is not important. You don't flirt in order to make your partner jealous; you do it just for the fun of it. You can annoy a partner by asking where he or she is going and when they intend to return, but this is not intended to irritate them or to show any lack of trust on your part, you just need to make sure that your family is safe.

You take to parenthood easily, you love your own children and you have patience with those of others. If you marry someone who already has a family, you cope with this very well. You take a responsible attitude towards those who depend upon you without making heavy weather of this. You are very loving and caring and really enjoy looking after those you love but you become understandably resentful if this care is taken for granted and not appreciated. You are good with sick people as long as there is not too much mess to clear up; the one thing you really hate is the sight of blood (especially your own). You are good at attending to practical needs but you may be less keen on attending to your partner's psychological needs, and you may forget to validate a partner or a child. Sometimes you just can't see what others want of you. I remember a friend called Jennie, who is an otherwise intelligent and sensitive woman, saying that she could never figure out what her ex-husband really wanted from her.

Some women with this Moon placement marry exciting types, but these types are too exciting to be good family men. This may propel the woman into an exciting career due to the need for financial survival, while she looks around for a less exciting man to come along and relieve her of the necessity to work all hours of the day and night.

Your deep attachment to your family, and your occasional misplaced pride in them and desire for them to be the best can make you over-critical and even tyrannical at times, especially when you are in a bad mood. You respect strength in others and you can walk all over those who you consider weak. You aren't over-competitive, so you will help a partner or workmate to get ahead. Above all you need a stimulating partner who has similar interests to yourself. You are emotionally habit-forming, not keen on too much change or excitement, and you must beware that monotony does not seep into your sexual behaviour. You are attracted to beauty and people who have cheerful, pleasant natures. Your pet hates are fatness, ugliness and people who wear dirty, tatty clothing. Both the people around you and your own surroundings must be clean and attractive.

You like your bills to be paid on time, so you are careful with money, and you like to have some savings to fall back on. You can earn good money but you can't make it by get-rich-quick schemes. You aren't particularly lucky with money and a confidence trickster can take you in because there are times when your judgement deserts you.

You control your feelings very well and are adept at hiding them from others probably due to childhood training, but being a feminine and emotional sign this can lead to moodiness. Occasionally your patience deserts you and you can also cut your nose off to spite your face. You may break out in a sudden angry response when something upsets you, but on another day, the same thing wouldn't bother you at all.

Being naturally rather cautious, you prefer to allow new acquaintances to do the talking, it's only when you know people better that you can relax and open up. You aren't above a bit of manipulation in social circumstances but you generally use it in the form of humour to defuse a tense situation. You usually guard your tongue well and rarely run off at the mouth. Once you have formed an opinion it's hard for you to alter it, and you can have the rather unfortunate habit of laying the law down to others. Your worst faults are laziness and a tendency to sit back and let others do the work for you or keep you in style at their expense.

Attitude to Career

You are undoubtedly ambitious for yourself and your family. Women with this placement seem to be given the message by their parents that they should stick to the old-fashioned idea of the feminine role, so they often start out as secretaries, nurses, cooks or children's nannies. All the lunar Taurean women to whom I have spoken tell me that they resented this bitterly, and also resented the associated implication that they were not as bright or as important as their brothers. They have all subsequently drifted towards less overtly feminine forms of work.

In common with the other earth signs of Capricorn and Virgo, Taureans of both sexes often have to put aside their dreams and ambitions for the sake of practicalities, and they may never bother to revive those dreams, which is rather a shame. One lady told me that she always dreamed of carrying the Olympic torch. Many of you dream about being a musician, dancer or singer, and with a bit of luck from elsewhere on your birthchart, you may just be able to make it into show business. Your practical side leads you to supply people with the things that they need, therefore you may deal in food, and furniture, household objects or even the things that help people make themselves and their homes attractive. Other typical Taurean trades are building, architecture, farming, market gardening, make-up artist, musician, artist and dancer. Because it's the Moon that we are dealing with here, you will not necessarily follow a Taurean trade at all but the need to be useful, get out and about and help to create something that is both durable and pleasing to the eye is a strong motivating force. You aren't drawn to speculative ventures which is just as well, because you are neither a lucky gambler nor particularly good at handling business crises. You aren't keen on sending memos or making up office reports - for one thing, you hate anything to be too cut and dried – but if you have to produce these, you will do them thoroughly.

You finish practically everything that you start and you can deal with details without becoming bored. Your persistence makes you good in the field of sales, and your creative flair can lead to a career in marketing (especially luxury products). A lot of this depends upon the rest of the chart, as a touch of Pisces, Aquarius or Sagittarius would add the ingredient of imagination. You hate to be rushed, and you can cope with anything when left to work at your own pace.

Parents and Background

According to most astrology books you should have enjoyed a happy and peaceful childhood, but my experience as an astrologer tells me that this is not so. Whenever the Moon is in a fixed sign there is at least one parent who has a bullying or intransigent attitude or who may also take advantage of the subject. This may be due to the fact that the parent has had a hard life and has subsequently developed an unsympathetic outlook. This leads to a hidden fear of parental disapproval then can develop into a fear of authority figures or an approval-seeking attitude.

It seems that one of your parents grew up in deprived circumstances, which may have been due to poverty and lack of opportunities, although a shortage of love might apply too. This parent is left with the feeling that things are safer than people and that one must obtain goods and money in order to survive. Therefore you may have grown up in a home where your practical needs were supplied but where real care, consideration and love was missing. You may have had a strong mother and a weak or ailing father who you loved by also looked down on.

Health

Insofar as the Moon influences health on a birthchart, an afflicted Moon in Taurus would bring problems in the area of the lower jaw, ears, throat, voice and tonsils. There may be thyroid problems and possibly diabetes. You may have that famous Taurean tendency to gain weight, but this will be mitigated if there is a lot of air on your chart. Some of you love food too much, while others can live without much food, but tend to drink too much.

Additional Information

Sometimes these people get a bee in their bonnet that makes them focus on one thing at the expense of everything else. I have known women with this placement who fall for a married man and then wait years for him to leave the wife, even though it's patently obvious to everyone else that this is never going to happen. I have known others who are mad keen on some sport or interest, to the point where it absorbs all their money and spare time. There are others who hate a particular race or group of people for no logical reason.

This subject appears to be close to the parents, but if you scratch the surface, you will find resentment. One such Moon in Taurus woman's mother accused her of having an affair with her sister's husband. The so-called evidence was so flimsy as to be a joke, but nothing would persuade the mother that this wasn't true. It's probable that the villainous mother got a lot of fun out of breaking up both her daughters' marriages by this ploy.

Some lunar Taureans take care of elderly parents out of a sense of duty, and they never let the parent down.

On a lighter note, lunar Taureans are always nicely dressed. Not outrageously, like some solar Taureans, but well turned out on all occasions.

They love going to the sales and picking up a bargain, and females really do know how to look good without breaking the bank. They enjoy gardening, and many grow vegetables and salad for their family.

Moon in Taurus Celebrities

Joe Biden
Bob Dylan
Elton John
Monica Lewinski
Meryl Streep
Dionne Warwick

Moon in Gemini

Ruled by Mercury

When they got there, the West Wind asked him if he could tell her the way
to the castle that lay East of the Sun and West of the Moon.
From a book of old Norse legends

The sign of Gemini is masculine, positive, airy and mutable, while the Moon, through its association with Cancer, is feminine, negative, watery and cardinal. The Moon is not really comfortable in this sign, and this may lead to some conflict within the personality. The instability of Gemini plus the fluctuating nature of the Moon could make your emotions a little too changeable and your nerves jumpy. If you have something steady, such as Leo or Taurus as your Sun or Ascendant, then the Gemini nervousness will be confined to bouts of irritability. You are impatient with whiners you can't cope with those who are chronically ill. Your own health is not particularly good but you try to ignore bouts of illness and you hardly ever take time off work to recover or recuperate.

The mutability of this sign makes you interested in new people and places, and this may lead you into the kind of job where you continually come across new people or where you move around. You like to be in the swing of things and you hate to miss anything that is going on. Your private life is probably less changeable than your working life but you certainly have many friends and can often be found on the end of a phone somewhere.

Women with the Moon in Gemini like to go out to work and some have an underlying nature that is ambitious and rather calculating. Both sexes like the home to be clean and orderly, and many can make a nice home with very little money. Both sexes like to look nice, and feel confident if they go out knowing that they are well dressed. You have strong dress sense and a good eye for matching up an outfit, although your taste is formal rather than flashy. Your mind is very active and you like to keep up to date. You may have had very little formal education, but you will educate yourself by reading a great deal and perhaps by taking courses later in life. Your mind (unless Mercury is badly placed) is very quick and acute, and you have a fine, fast sense of humour and a gift for making amusing and witty comments. The reverse of this coin is that you may become sarcastic if irritated.

Lunar Geminians think fairly deeply and they are less likely to be content with surface knowledge than are Sun-in-Gemini subjects. In addition to this depth of thought, you also have a dustbin-like mind full of rag-tag bits of knowledge. Although chatty and superficially friendly, your strongest relationships are with your family and a few close friends. Your moods change quickly but you don't sulk, and you have no patience with those who do. Your attention span is strange, because people who moan about their problems or go on at length about their pet subject bore you, but an interesting book or TV programme will hold you rivetted for ages. Your thought processes are logical and you learn in an orderly fashion, but you can blend this logical approach with instinctive or even psychic awareness if there is help from other areas of your birthchart.

There is a kind of Peter Pan aspect to this Moon position, which may also apply to the other air signs, Libra and Aquarius. Somehow, you never quite grow up and you can display quite babyish behaviour when away from the outside world. The reverse side of this coin is that you keep your youthful looks and a young outlook on life far longer than most. You have creative, artistic ability and you may paint, make ornaments or interesting clothes, or you may enjoy model-making or computer-aided design. Many of you are into music and you may play the guitar or even a banjo. Gemini rules the hands, so using them to play music or fix things is a common trait.

You learn to drive a car while you are in your teens, then you explore your own neighbourhood and start to travel the world as soon as you can. Cities appeal to you more than the countryside, and you particularly enjoy visiting interesting foreign cities. You are resourceful and you can usually find a way to solve practical problems.

Although not a social reformer, you hate racism and ill treatment towards those who can't stand up for themselves, and you may become involved in some form of politics, especially the kind that involves getting a fair deal for some underdog group of people. You may be very fond of animals and you may want to do something to help them as well.

As a parent you make quite sure that your own children are well treated, but you don't want to spend all your time looking after them, because you must do something to keep your brain active. Your worst fault is a certain inner coldness and a sharp and hurtful tongue, or a habit of switching off and even of disappearing for hours when others get you down. While you can work for the community or give practical help to those in need, in a personal sense, you can't cope with those who wish to lean on you or use you as a victim, so you can give the appearance of having very little depth of concern for others.

The Moon in Gemini doesn't make you flippant where relationships are concerned, so once you have made your choice of partner, you stick to them pretty well. Having said this, I have come across one or two folk with this Moon placement who stay free so that they can play the field. You rarely fall head over heels in love or become so obsessed with someone that you end up getting hurt – indeed, you go to great lengths to avoid getting yourself into an emotional mess. In some cases, lunar Geminians can appear to be caring and loving, while actually not feeling very much of anything. Most do have a heart and you try your best to make relationships work; this is particularly admirable, as you tend to choose difficult people to care about. You might be tempted to marry for money, but this wouldn't last, any more than marrying someone for their looks. It's intelligence that you value more than anything because you are a communicator, and if you can't bounce ideas off a partner and help them with theirs, there isn't much to glue you together.

Some of you delay marriage or parenthood until you feel that you are sufficiently mature, but when you do take the plunge, you are quite serious about it. You make a delightful parent; you never quite grow up yourself, so you relate easily to children. You will break the bank to provide them with a good education, and your children will never be short of books, materials or any other kind of mental stimulation. You try to remain close to your grandchildren too, because you value family life.

Oddly enough, you can suffer from depression at times, and you can become very downhearted. This is most likely due to overwork and exhaustion, because you have few reserves of energy to call on, and you have the habit of going beyond your limit if something needs doing. Prolonged stress, overwork and worry will make you ill. You might keep busy in order to hide a deep well of unspoken unhappiness.

You could attract (or choose) a weak, dependent partner, who would be drawn to your inner strength – remember Gemini is a positive masculine sign – but you are better off with one who can stand on his or her own feet. You may need to get in touch with your own feelings before being able to handle those of others. You could be a theoriser and, as far as emotions are concerned, you may prefer to read about, and to rationalise emotional matters, than to feel them. To some extent, this derives from a mistrust of the opposite sex and possibly a lack of sexual self-confidence. You don't like to be emotionally fenced in.

You don't suffer from jealousy if you see other people making a success of themselves and, like most of the lunar masculine signs, you measure your own successes against your achievements. Not being jealous or possessive yourself, you resent being on the receiving end of this behaviour by others. You are proud of your achievements and also proud of your family; you will encourage (perhaps push) your children educationally, and you will make sacrifices for them.

Sex has to start in your mind and if you aren't careful, it can stay there too, as you may be happier fantasising about sex than actually indulging in it. If you find a compatible partner who encourages you to relax you can bring all that sexuality down from your mind to reach the parts that the other beers cannot reach, then you could become the lover you always wanted to be. You are easily put off by coarseness. Your nerves are sensitive, therefore a quiet atmosphere, an amusing lover and a couple of drinks will work wonders. You may experiment with bisexuality and you may privately enjoy rude books and even blue films! Oddly enough both solar and lunar Geminians are tactile. They enjoy hugging, touching and being touched as long as they are not smothered or held too close.

Attitude to Career

The position of the Moon will not indicate a specific career, but will show inner motivations. People, mental activity, words and travel are essential to your working life. You may work in telephone communications, marketing or sales. Writing, especially journalism, may appeal; also all forms of teaching, possibly job training, sports or dancing. You are generally respected, both for what you know and for your pleasant way of handling people. You may work for the public good in general, as in banking or in the political arena.

Travel appeals to you, especially air travel, and many lunar Geminians work in the air force or the travel industry. You love driving and may be able to fly a plane as well. You have a quick grasp of new ideas and you communicate them well to others, so you are very good at handling people and you make a wonderful manager. You can be canny and crafty in business, and you love wheeling and dealing, but some of you may not always be a hundred per cent honest. You are at your best when teamed up with a practical partner. As this sign rules the hands and arms, you could be a super craftsman, printer, manicurist or even a palmist.

Oddly enough, religion and mysticism may interest you, but in a kind of one-step-removed fashion, as you are unlikely to take up a religious lifestyle yourself. You may enjoy the social side of a religious group rather more than the deeper elements of its philosophy. Another slightly odd thing about this Moon sign is an interest in military life or in history, and especially in military history. Some of you also like to read fairly bloodthirsty books as well.

Parents and Background

The chances are that you had one parent, probably your father, who tended to lay down the law or who was held up to you as a paragon of virtue. Your childhood home was probably filled with books and educational aids, and your parents will have been quite happy for you to have tuition in practically anything. There would have been stimulating conversation and interesting visitors in your home. You should have been born fairly easily and you may have been the youngest child in a small family or the only one of one sex among a family of the opposite one. There is some evidence of deep unhappiness in childhood and a sense of not fitting, and this may have been within the family or at school. You may have been suffered racial or religious prejudice! You may have been compared to some other brother or sister or even to a dead parent and made to feel that you didn't measure up to them.

An unusual mother is indicated for you. She may be a career woman, highly intellectual or just plain eccentric! Your mother would have shown you, either by direct reference or by example, that women must be able to stand on their own two feet in life. This will influence females to follow a career and males to choose a career woman for your partner. Your mother may have been involved in charity work if she didn't have a career as such.

Health

Your lungs may be weak also there could be problems with your hands and arms. Some lunar Geminians suffer really horrendous accidents that affect their arms, hands, teeth and faces, leading to bones and features needing to be rebuilt! You can suffer allergies and may have asthma, eczema, rheumatism, migraine, psoriasis, ulcers, colitis or some other autoimmune ailment. Your nerves may be your worst enemy. You need to find an outlet for your nervous energy, such as sports and fresh air pursuits, along with doing anything that makes you relax. People with the Moon in Gemini shouldn't smoke cigarettes or take too many over-the-counter pills.

Additional Information
Traditionally speaking, Gemini rules siblings, so you probably have brothers, sisters, cousins, step or half brothers and sisters, other relatives of around your own age, or friends who are as close as siblings who you care very much about. You make the effort to keep in touch, even if they don't always bother to make the trip over to your place.

According to tradition, you probably work fairly near to where you live, so you make lots of short journeys back and forth. You like to have goods delivered to your home, so you shop online quite a bit, and you love receiving mail. You also prefer to live near shops, perhaps in the centre of a city so that you are at the heart of everything that is going on. Although not a great drinker, you like to visit the pub to meet up with your friends and catch up on the local news.

Lunar Geminis are not stupid about money, so you probably have a savings plan in place and you don't get into debt the way that solar Geminis can. You like nice things, but you will wait until you can afford them.

The worst problem with Geminians is that they can moan, whine and go on and on about something that has annoyed or upset them.

You like to dress well and always look good, but you aren't extravagant when it comes to spending money on clothes.

You may travel a lot and have good friendships with foreigners. You may even marry a foreigner and have strong connections with your partner's home country and family; you may even emigrate after marrying a foreigner.

Moon in Gemini Celebrities

Noel Coward
Edwina Currie
Kirk Douglas
Goldie Hawn
Barack Obama
Claudia Schiffer

Moon in Cancer

Ruled by the Moon
(The Moon's dignity)

It was the lovely moon - she lifted
Slowly her white brow among
Bronze cloud-waves that ebbed and drifted
Faintly, faintlier afar.
It was the lovely Moon, by John Freeman (1880-1929)

The sign of Cancer is feminine, negative, watery and cardinal. The Moon rules this sign, so it's quite at home here. Like those with the Sun in Cancer, your reactions to people and places are very strong, and this is taken into account in any decisions that you make. Your feelings are very sensitive, which means that you link very quickly to other people's feelings, to the point where you can feel if they are unhappy or in pain. You can sense a 'funny' atmosphere as soon as you walk into a room.

Unless there are conflicting forces on your chart, you should have the Cancerian ability to listen sympathetically. In business, your intuition usually gives you an instinctive feel when a deal is about to go wrong - or go right!

The negative side of this coin is over-sensitivity. Like the other feminine water signs of Pisces and Scorpio, you can take things too personally, brood, sulk, lose your temper and shut yourself off. Some of you appear very even-tempered, but hurts and worries tend to go inwards and these can make you ill. They say that Cancerian moods change with each tide, and in some cases this is true. Moodiness, sulking and sometimes sheer nastiness from being in the wrong frame of mind are your worst faults.

Women with the Moon in any of the water signs are susceptible to period problems and hormone-related mood swings. The very worst aspect of this placement is that you may indulge in emotional blackmail by shutting off from others and sending out disapproving vibes. On a very bad day, you might be beset by feelings of paranoia or rage, and you can be critical and faultfinding on occasions. This kind of behaviour is rare because you are much too kind and thoughtful a person, far too receptive to the needs of others to be this unpleasant for long. You are one of the most generous people in the zodiac, and you put yourself out to help others even when you are hardly in a position to help yourself. You don't feel threatened by the success of others, although you would like to have a bit of it for yourself as well.

You are able to adjust yourself to your surroundings and fit in fairly well with other people (water signs find their own level). You may complain about the situation you find yourself in but you will make the best of it, and will often find a way of changing and manipulating the circumstances to suit yourself. Remember Cancer is a cardinal sign and the Moon represents one's instincts. Your instinctive reaction is to put things right and create a better atmosphere. Some people are starters and others are runners. The ability to initiate projects and to see them through depends upon a variety of factors in your birthchart, but your instinctive reaction is to set things in motion and then encourage others (or find someone else) to see them through. If you are really stuck for an answer to your problems you can always look a bit pathetic in the hope that someone will take pity on you and help you.

You are considerate towards others, especially your family, and it would be almost impossible for you to desert them, and you would only do so under extreme duress. I think that you would try several times to put things right before giving up on them for good. You have patience with children and young people and you are probably very fond of animals. You aren't entirely selfless, it's only when you are settled and satisfied that you can relax and give sustenance to others. Your greatest requirements are for emotional security, such as a partner you can rely upon, harmony in the home and friends who help build up your confidence. Lack of confidence in your own abilities and feelings of relative worthlessness are your worst enemy and it's these that can make you feel jealous and resentful towards others, often quite without justification.

You like children and enjoy having them around you, not only being good to your own children but kind to other people's as well. However, you greatly resent having other people's children being dumped on you. Your gentle inner nature responds to the vulnerability and honesty of children. You may remain close to your own children after they have grown up, but in some cases, lunar Cancerians want them to be independent but can't get rid of them! Alternatively, your own mother may cling to you after you have grown up! It may be difficult for you to forget your own childhood as you have a slight tendency to live in the past.

There is a tendency for you to attract parasitic people who hang themselves on to you and make demands. This is most evident among those of you who have your Sun or ascendant in a steady earth sign or an enthusiastic fire sign. Fortunately for you, you are astute enough to be able to spot these people before they get their claws into you, and to off-load them quickly. When you care for someone, you do all you can for them and you can become worked up on their behalf if you think that someone else is hurting them. Unfortunately, unless there is a lot of strength elsewhere on the chart, you won't actually do anything practical to help.

You might be sensual but you aren't greedy. You don't have a large appetite for food; you prefer small amounts that are well cooked and presented. Your sensitive stomach may reject spicy foods. (One Moon in Cancer friend tells me that he cannot eat raw onions.) You probably enjoy good wines but there is no evidence of this Moon placement leading to overindulgence. You may be a good cook yourself but this will depend upon other factors in your birthchart, along with your lifestyle. You can put up with any amount of chaos around you at work but you need peace and harmony in the home. Your senses are all strong, especially that of hearing, you really hate discordant noises. The senses of smell, touch and taste are well developed and you could be long-sighted. Sexually, you absolutely come into your own. The whole concept of an experience that involves all the senses plus love and affection is just too much for you to miss. Being basically kind and thoughtful, you should be a considerate - even a practised - lover. The fact that you are the faithful type works against variety in sexual experiences. Two of my friends who happen to be married to Moon in Cancer subjects tell me that their partners are good lovers.

You may have the Cancerian trait of collecting things, ranging from valuable antiques to junk. You don't like losing anything or anyone. You enjoy the company of new people and visiting new places but also you have an attachment to old ones. You enjoy gossiping almost as much as your Gemini cousins do. You have a habit of observing the behaviour of others, and in a way this is a form of self-protection. Being emotionally cautious, you are slow to fall in love and open yourself to the prospect of hurt and rejection. Others may fall in love with you because you listen to them and you understand their problems. You seem to know others psychically. If the one who falls for your sympathetic attitude expects you to continue to be an unpaid psychotherapist for them will be disappointed.

Being cautious, you may react in a slightly hostile manner towards new people. If you have something very outgoing, such as Sagittarius, on your Ascendant, there will be an open, confident attitude, however the caution will still be there hidden away underneath. You are basically honest and you can be trusted in any kind of confidential situation and with any kind of information. However, one less pleasant attribute is that you can occasionally display a touch of smarminess, flattering those whom you wish to get round or to make capital out of. This is a successful ploy in most cases, but it won't wash when dealing with people who are particularly perceptive.

You can be slightly mean in small matters, as the case with all who have the Moon in water signs. Both solar and lunar Cancerians find it hard to get rid of anything. Once in a while you decide to turn out the cupboards only to put almost everything back again. There is too much sentiment attached to your junk for you to be able to throw it out. You need a base to operate from, therefore, not only your home but also your office are important to you and you don't want these to be disturbed or cleaned-up too much. Unless there is a strong dose of Libra or Virgo on your birthchart, you aren't over-fussy about the appearance of your home, and you can make a home anywhere.

You have courage in odd places where others lack it. For instance, you are adept at asking questions, probing, finding out what makes people tick and keeping up to date with the local gossip. You aren't above giving a gentle form of third degree. Lunar Cancerians have a long memory, therefore, you can hold a grudge if you are hurt, but you also remember those who have helped you. Being rather sentimental, you remember birthdays and anniversaries and you feel peeved if yours are forgotten. Your intuition is very strong and this may just be a helpful tool in everyday life, but you can also be drawn towards psychic work of some kind. Quite a few lunar Cancerians have paranormal or psychic hobbies. Because you can be trusted with secrets, you could work as a psychic consultant of some kind because these people listen to people's confidences.

You like the countryside and really love the sea. If a Cancerian Moon is very prominent in your birthchart, you could choose a job on or near the sea. Another of your interests is the past, so you may study history or collect things that have been around for a long time such as antiquities.

Attitude to Career

The Moon will show how you approach the idea of work rather than give specific career guidance. Unless there are other factors on the chart, you will be an efficient and conscientious worker but you need variety in your work or you will become bored and walk away from a job. Your inner nature leads you towards the kind of job where you can be helpful. Many lunar Cancerians work in hospitals, schools and with the elderly, while others are attracted to the world of business. Some of you are drawn towards the field of antiques, rare coins, stately homes or genealogy Insurance may attract you because of its protective image, and some may work in estate agencies. Many of you retrain later in life if your original career ceases to be viable or if you find that you lack certain qualifications that would help you to get up the career ladder. Many of you run small businesses, shops and small agencies. Being good with your hands, you could work as a plumber, carpenter etc. Lunar Cancerians also make excellent teachers.

Your sensitivity means that you could make a good salesman or business executive, personnel manager or counsellor. Politics may appeal, as could accountancy, and you have a theatrical side to your nature and might be drawn to the world of entertainment or sports. The drawback to this is the irregularity of work and the general uncertainty of this field; being a worrier, you would probably be happier in a secure job while singing and dancing during your time off. You would be a good partner for a very go-ahead person, as you don't seek to hold others back.

Parents and Background

The Moon in this position suggests that your mother gave birth to you easily. The parental home will have been comfortable and the relationships there will have been reasonable, at least on the surface. The chances are that you are the eldest child in your family (although this is much more likely if the Ascendant were in Cancer). The background and history of your family is important to you and you may try to trace your family tree. The family may travel a bit and you would have travelled with them, but you wouldn't have moved house a lot during childhood.

Your mother may have been traditional and ordinary rather than eccentric. You would be close to your mother throughout life, you may love her very deeply and be really close to her. You could be best friends as well as mother and child. However, you may not actually want to be that close to your mother, but she may demand that you are part of her life and that you spend time with her and put up with her even though you don't really want to.

There may have been something very wrong with one or other of your parent's health or state of mind. I have known some people with this Moon placement whose mothers were extremely neurotic and even one whose mother committed suicide. The mother will have been the strongest influence, as the father may have been perceived as weak, either because his health was weak or because he lacked character and backbone. The mother may have spent years propping him up, but if he dies and leaves her a widow, she will became very despondent. The mother might have been older than the father.

Health

This Moon position suggests strong health with good recovery from illness and operations. The weak areas are the chest, lungs, breasts and stomach. There is no reason to suppose that you are any more susceptible to the dreaded disease of cancer itself than any other sign.

Additional Information

There may be a flare for foreign languages, or a connection to those who spoke different languages, due to the family background. Religion or mysticism can play a part, either because the subject becomes interested in these things or because they marry someone of a different religion or due to the family background. They may decide to be different from their parents, espousing a different religion to theirs. Avoid stirring things and deliberately upsetting or hurting others.

Moon in Cancer Celebrities

Janis Joplin
Liza Minelli
Sharon Osbourne
Franklin D Roosevelt

Moon in Leo

Ruled by the Sun

Or when the moon was overhead,
Came two young lovers lately wed;
I am half sick of shadows said
The lady of Shallot
     By Alfred Lord Tennyson

The sign of Leo is masculine, positive, fiery and fixed, while the Moon, through its associations with the sign of Cancer, is feminine, negative, watery and cardinal. At first sight, it doesn't look as if the Moon would be very comfortable in Leo, but in many ways it is. For the sake of convenience, astrologers call all the bodies in the Solar system planets, but the Sun is a small star whilst the Moon is a satellite of the Earth. These two objects dominate our view of the sky and their movements dominate the lives of every being on the face of the Earth.

The main differences between the Sun and the Moon from an astrologer's point of view are in the attitudes to relationships, especially inter-generational relationships. The power of the Sun seems to dominate the Moon, permeating the deepest layers of the personality with Leonine characteristics that then bubble their way up to the surface. If you have this Moon placement you are basically kind, generous and honourable with an instinctive need to encourage others. There is a real touch of Leo nobility deep down inside of you. It's worth remembering that many members of the royal family have the Moon in Leo. Being naturally dignified, you would find it hard to behave in a callous or a crafty manner and you are far

Ω

too proud to scrounge off others. Your need to appear honest and honourable may not reflect reality; but if you are caught out in a cowardly or underhanded act or if it becomes obvious that you harbour jealous feelings, you can react in an angry and aggressive manner. You can get on your high horse if your dignity is pricked. The fixity of the sign gives you the determination to see things through and to finish everything that you start. It's possible that you may dig your heels in too much and try to lay the law down to others. You could be stubborn and unbending at times.

You sometimes appear to behave in a distant and superior manner, this is your shield when you are in unfamiliar situations. When hurt, you retreat into something that you see as dignified silence and others see as the sulks; however, under normal circumstances you are cheerful, friendly and open. You occasionally have doubts about your own self-worth, but also occasional feelings of intense superiority. The emotions are always held under control when the Moon is in a fixed sign, but they may break out strongly from time to time. You could become quite aggressive if pushed, or if you are on the receiving end of aggression from others. If others hurt you, it makes you suffer from jealousy, anger and resentment.

Lunar Leos can be surprisingly self-sacrificing towards loved ones but heaven help them if the loved one doesn't appreciate their sacrifices. You place the objects of your love on a pedestal and feel hurt when you discover that they are only human. Your intense feelings give you a longing for excitement, drama, romance and passion, and with a bit of luck you will find this within a steady relationship; but if not, you will look for romance, passion etc. elsewhere. You may even create tension within a relationship to keep it alive. You also need an exciting career, as you can put up with an insecure one but not a boring one. Too much contentment bores you.

Your mind is broad and you are unlikely to follow any of the more fanatical religious or political beliefs. You may have a religious and philosophical outlook that is different from that of your parents but this should not be a big problem in your life. Although not in any way bigoted, your opinions are formed early in life and you may find it hard to change your mind later.

The Moon is associated with the home, so yours will be attractive with an interesting sort of decor. You are very fussy about your own appearance and may even be vain (men with this Moon placement are actually worse than women). The one thing that is the bane of your life is your hair. You may consider this to be too thick, thin, wiry, curly or if male, too bald! You may be vain about your body and even your sexual performance. One lady who is married to a very nice Moon in Leo guy tells me that he doles out sex as if it were a treat! As a lover you could be bossy and demanding but you could equally be comfortable, relaxed and kind. Being romantic, you enjoy dining out, giving and receiving presents and remembering birthdays. You are fussy about your choice of partner, nothing less than the best will do for you. You have a strong sex drive but couldn't cope for long with a relationship based on sex alone. You need romance; passion and above all, you need love. Life without love, in all its applications would be too cold to contemplate. Your senses are strong, therefore everything about sex appeals to you as long as you can retain a certain amount of decorum.

You may feel a need to attach yourself to some source of power. You may work with powerful and successful people or even with large and powerful animals, but you might also be fascinated by the power of magic and the spiritual world. This would enable you to enjoy risk-taking at second hand. Your courage, fire and enthusiasm could lead you to learn how to wield power by copying powerful people who are around you.

You will do anything for those whom you love but you need your generosity of spirit to be appreciated. Being a fixed sign, you resist change and find it hard to admit defeat in any situation, therefore, you would find it difficult to cut your losses and start again. You can put up with the wrong job for far too long and also hang on to a rotten relationship long after the time has come to end it. You are possibly a little too good at maintaining the status quo, especially in emotional situations. You may be self-centred emotionally and possibly inclined to hang on to those you love - this applies to your children as well. For example, Laura, a gentle and skilled palmist now in her mid-forties, recently left her paranoid and violent husband after many years of abuse, but she still feels that she is unable to make the final break and divorce him.

Unless there are very different characteristics in your Sun and Ascendant you are sociable and enjoy being entertained but being much shyer than the solar Leo, you can only entertain others in a quiet way. Sports and the company of young people appeal to you. You might become involved in some organisation like the Boy Scouts, Girl Guides, the Territorial Army or the Red Cross. Your fondness for looking and feeling good means that you don't only join a gym, you actually use it.

There is no need for you to be the centre of attention in the world outside, but you do like to be in the centre of things within your own home. If you found yourself in the spotlight, you could cope with it but you don't seek it consciously. You like to know where the various members of your family are and to make sure that they are all right, you have an inner need to organise them and keep them on the right lines.

Your inner nature, unless you are feeling hurt, is playful, sunny and friendly which makes you popular in a quiet kind of way. You appreciate beauty, creativity and art and have an instinctive sense of style. You are proud of your loved ones and even of your friends, and you prefer not to be surrounded by dirty down-at-heel types. You never forget a hurt but your strong loyalty means that you remember those who help you too. You need to belong somewhere and you may be attached to a particular set of bricks and mortar or to an area of the country with which you feel a particular affinity. Needing space, you hate cramped surroundings; you love to get away into the countryside and to take your holidays in a warm and pleasant place. You need holidays and breaks because you tend to put a lot of effort into your job and into life itself. Your vitality is never drained for long as you have inner reserves of strength.

You make an excellent parent, often treating your children as young adults and always preserving their dignity. You don't seek to hang on to them when they grow up. You are able to teach and encourage them through play, but you may not be too patient with them at times; you can be relied on to give them a cuddle whenever they are down-hearted or ill.

Attitude to Career
The position of the Moon does not indicate any specific career, but will show your inner leanings and drives. Both solar and lunar Leo subjects learn more easily after leaving school than before, and you may become qualified for something long after leaving school. You lack confidence in your abilities, so achieving something of this kind can only help you. Even if you don't have much formal education, you understand people and learn well from life. You have an inner need to be in an executive position, and if your circumstances are against this, you could be self-employed, so that you are the king or queen of your own world.

You make a good employer, as you understand the need to preserve the dignity of others. You are career-minded and with your good concentration and good organisational skills, can climb the career ladder in a steady manner. Your ability to make the right impression could lead you to the fields of marketing, personnel work, the display of works of art or antiques. You could have big dreams but you may be too lazy to make them come true. You want to be at the top of your field but are strangely uncompetitive, being too self-centred to worry about the status of others; your own high standards give you enough to compete against.

You are good at calming people down and dealing with touchy situations. You may choose to work with troubled youngsters. Your attraction to glamour might interest you in some form of show business. Being drawn towards children and young people, you could be a teacher but you might prefer to be a nursery nurse or probation officer. Your love of the good things in life could make you a good restaurateur or hotelier but you might be best employed out in the front as the maitre-de, as under no circumstances would you want to be the one to do the cleaning and cooking. You are competent, efficient and capable as long as you are allowed to work at your own pace but you detest being hassled and put under pressure.

Parents and Background

There is probably something wrong here, and there are many possible scenarios. One possibility is that your father was autocratic, authoritarian or just unable to relate to children, so you probably got on much better with your mother. Your parents may have expected more from you than you were able to produce, especially if you happen to be shy and not outwardly successful or pushy. At the worst end of this spectrum you may have been afraid of your father or made to feel that you couldn't live up to some impossible image of perfection. He may have been a very successful man himself or he may have achieved a great deal while he was still young, but lunar Leos are far more likely to succeed later in life. You need parental love, encouragement and appreciation and if you get this from at least one parent or from brothers and sisters, but you may have been made to feel undervalued, or that your sister or brother was more important than you or that their needs came ahead of yours.

The background may have been traditional, even religious, involving rituals and certain kinds of behaviour.

♌

Health

The Moon is not the only indicator of health problems on a chart, but it might point out any underlying chronic condition. There doesn't seem to be a real problem with this Moon placement, but Leo rules the spine and heart, so keeping your intake of food and drink down and taking exercise can only help, as would keeping the stress level down.

Additional Information

Childhood hurts linger in your mind and can never really be forgotten.

You dress in a formal but highly fashionable style, and you may spend a lot of money on designer clothes. Males with this Moon sign fuss and worry about losing their hair.

You might fall out with some members of your family and lose touch with them. It's possible for you to lose complete touch with your children due to a divorce situation.

You like high-status people, places and things, and you would find poverty a real drag.

Moon in Leo Celebrities

Mohandas K Gandhi
Clint Eastwood
Ringo Starr
Seve Ballesteros
Winston Churchill
Steven Fry
Margaret Thatcher
Martin Sheen

♌

Moon in Virgo

Ruled by Mercury

Pale moon doth rain, red moon doth blow
White moon doth neither rain nor snow
      Proverb

The sign of Virgo is feminine, negative, earthy and mutable, while the Moon (through its association with Cancer) is feminine, negative, watery and cardinal, so there is an uneasy alliance between the sign of Virgo and the energy of the Moon. You may find it very difficult to shape your world the way that you would like, it seems that the cardinality of the Moon (cardinality implies action) is halted in mutable, negative Virgo.

If you cannot make your job work for you, create the right kind of environment or find the right partner, you could retreat into fiddling about and fidgeting. You may never quite finish decorating your home, you may try out one partner after another or you could become your own worst enemy at work. If thwarted, you will develop a tendency to meddle, criticise, ruin, lose or destroy the very things that you most need. You could over-analyse yourself and everything around you then hide your fears and phobias under a layer of fussiness. Be careful not to fall prey to a psychological need to organise every detail, prepare for every eventuality so that you programme out not only life's unexpected problems and but also its pleasant surprises.

Virgo brings an inner need to serve people in a practical way, so you prefer to work in a field where you can be useful to others. You feel more comfortable in the workplace than in a social setting, especially if your talents are being used to the limit. Being dutiful and caring towards your family, you show your love for them by helping them in a practical way or by giving them material things, rather than by open displays of affection or even of verbal love. You are especially helpful and understanding if your loved ones or your friends are ill. You are reliable, businesslike and efficient in all that you do, and being loyal and trustworthy, you would never betray a confidence. Most lunar Virgoans are more alert in the morning than in the evening, and this also gives an impression of dutiful energy. Compare this to our belief that those who are not morning people are lazy layabouts.

Your mind is very clear and logical, your thinking is usually realistic and you prefer to think before acting. Your imagination works best when harnessed to some kind of structure, such as, writing poetry, making a garden or computer-aided design. You enjoy debating when you are among people with whom you can relax, and you never swallow what you are told without verification. Be careful not to spend too much energy on details and miss the main point. Also, you should try not to let problems revolve round in your head growing out of all proportion. Some lunar Virgoans are vigorous social reformers, but others just talk about what should be done without doing much about it. You can take practical decisions almost instantly and will go anywhere at the drop of a hat; when decisions have an emotional content, this is not so easy. Oddly enough, although the mind is quick, your bodily movements may be slow. Female lunar Virgoans are good homemakers, often loving their homes, but they need an intellectual outlet and to work in an interesting job. Although your thought processes are logical, you can also be very psychic. There is an acceptable logic to psychic matters that you seem to grasp more easily than many other people. Religion may not interest you overmuch and blind faith is never acceptable to you.

Virgo being a mutable sign suggests that you can fit yourself in to almost any type of company. You are unlikely to be prejudiced about race, religion etc. because all people interest you. You are shy at first but very sociable when you feel that you can relax. Although hardly likely to be the life and soul of the party, and even less likely to get drunk and make a fool of yourself, you enjoy socialising, especially in the company of witty and interesting people.

I very much doubt whether you see money in terms of the power it may give you, and you have little desire to waste your hard-earned pennies on flashy things. Virgo as a sign is supposed to be careful with money, but it seems to polarise either way, with some of you being very careful indeed and others being happy to max out their credit cards.

Being an earth sign, gardening appeals to you, especially growing your own fruit and vegetables, along with filling the house and garden with sweet-smelling flowers. Your senses of taste and smell (and your stomach) are easily upset; therefore good, homegrown produce is a favourite with you. Reading and listening to music provide you with a passive form of escapism. One active form of escapism that is very popular among both solar and lunar Virgoans is acting, because this is where you can forget yourself for a while and take on a completely different personality. This gives you the opportunity of behaving outrageously without having to risk being taken seriously.

Relationships can be a minefield for you, because you tend to make yourself useful to your partner and then wonder why you are being used. In a way, the most successful relationship is with those who have important and interesting careers, where you can help to smooth their path for them. There must be a mental rapport between you and your partner, so shared interests or work in common will help. You are prepared to make an effort in a relationship. Some of you attach yourselves to a glamourous, glittering personality and enjoy being a part of their life while not having to suffer the embarrassment of taking centre stage yourself. Any relationship based solely on sex wouldn't hold you for long. Many astrology books suggest that solar and lunar Virgoans are sexless but this is just not true, however there can be problems associated with sex and sexual relationships. You are easily embarrassed by the apparent ludicrousness of the sex act, and you find it hard to relinquish your dignity and make the necessary adjustment that enables you to surrender to your feelings. A second problem is that you may be ashamed of your own capacity for passion, possibly due to early childhood influences and incidents. You may fill up your time with work in order to avoid dealing with the whole relating and sexual scene. Shyness doesn't help here, but most of this can be overcome if you find yourself a kind and encouraging partner. Coarseness puts you off immediately. Criticism will squash you, not only sexually but also in every other way. However, Virgo is a very critical sign, so you must endeavour to avoid criticising others, even when you are angry.

If a relationship goes wrong, you can become desperate. You can be so insecure that you actually decide in advance that a relationship won't work out, and this becomes a self-fulfilling prophecy. On the other hand, you may go too far the other way - keeping your emotions on such a tight rein that you never allow yourself the luxury of love and romance, and this is a shame because you need a partner and a family.

You may find it hard to relate to your own children, so you may pay too much attention to their practical and educational needs and not enough to their need for love and affection. On the other hand, children maybe the ideal outlet for your love, giving you the opportunity to give and receive affection unreservedly. You may be able to romp, roll around and act out parts for their amusement in a way that you could never do with adults. Teaching comes naturally to you, so you enjoy opening your children's minds to the world of books, museums, nature.

Given a secure and loving partnership, you will gain confidence and really begin to blossom. You have an acute sense of humour that so often is able to save you from much of the unhappiness associated with this sign. If you can find an intelligent partner to laugh with, then you are really made. You are loyal and you have high standards of behaviour, so with a bit of luck, you can be very happy. You need to be hugged and comforted, especially if things are not going well for you. You need validation that you are a worthy person, and a feeling of solidarity in your relationships that shows you that your family circle will stick together and stick up for each other against the world.

Attitude to Career

You have a creative side that can be expressed in sewing, carpentry, cooking or writing because you like problem solving and bringing together separate parts in order to make a whole. Skills such as typing, driving and accounting come easily to you. You make an exemplary office worker, being neat, efficient, quiet, clean, practical and helpful. If your Sun and Ascendant are in an outgoing sign, you may enjoy a life in a skilled branch of the armed forces because technical matters would hold no terrors for you. The downside is that you do become bored once you have worked out how to do the job, and you can't cope with repetitive work. You need variety.

Lunar Virgoans make good nurses, doctors and dieticians, while some work in the field of disease prevention or medical research. You may be a hypochondriac, but this is far more common among those who have Virgo as an Ascendant. You may be drawn to a career in teaching. Maths, scientific subjects or business studies suit you but languages may be a problem, because while you can learn and teach the grammar but you may be too inhibited to throw yourself into speaking.

It may be difficult for you to be a manager, because delegating requires confidence both in your own leadership qualities, along with confidence in others to do a good job. Your tendency to become critical may not do you any favours. You get angry when you see others displaying an attitude of uncaring inefficiency. You may not be overly ambitious, but you like to do things well and to be appreciated for it.

Parents and Background

At best, your childhood would have been a fairly cool affair, at worst, it may have had nightmarish qualities. 'Nightmarish is just about right,' said Pamela, an elegant, divorced systems analyst. 'I used to study my father to judge which rules I should be playing by and just when I got the hang of the game, he changed the rules. I could never win, my place was always in the wrong'.

There may have been a great emphasis on being on time for meals, washing behind your ears and doing your homework. You may have been compared to other children in the family or even at school and criticised for not being clever, pretty, tall, sporty etc. as them, or perhaps you were not born into the preferred gender. If you were a diligent child who was naturally tidy, quiet, organised and clever at school, you would have pleased your parents and therefore have had an easier time of it. You may have only been able to win their approval by achieving success in exams or winning medals at sports or dancing. Some of your self-esteem problems result from being afraid of your parents and finding them impossible to please. You may even have been a timid child whose boisterous parents valued boldness. You didn't need harsh discipline at home or at school as you were easily ashamed and embarrassed at the very thought of doing something wrong and you strove not to make mistakes.

There is always the possibility that the Moon's position reflects the mother's youth, so the interpretation could be an indication that your mother had a hard time while young, rather reflecting your own experiences.

Health

Both solar and lunar Virgoans are strong and healthy, but the nervous system is delicate. Ailments include migraine and asthma, allergies, skin conditions and stomach ulcers. Tension and overwork is your enemy, so you must take exercise in order to relax. Severe health problems that sometimes arise are appendicitis, typhoid, peritonitis and anaemia.

Additional Information
Many lunar Virgoans have parents who go 'funny' at some stage in their lives, and this can lead you to rush into an early marriage. Virgo is an earth sign, and therefore both obstinate and determined, so you have an inner level of toughness that is not often obvious on the outside.

Some of you are very tidy while others are quite messy, but you know where to find things, and you resent other people trying to tidy up your stuff.

You have a good head for details, which could lead you into work that requires analysis and a good memory as well as being able to discriminate.

Many lunar Virgoans have secret love affairs that go on for years, or they have lovers who refuse to commit.

Virgo is a highly critical sign, and while this is great for a film or book critic, in relationships it can destroy everything it touches, and even the lunar Virgoan's children will eventually drift away because of this. Other lunar Virgoans are self-critical and too ready to blame themselves for everything that goes wrong.

Moon in Virgo Celebrities

Dustin Hoffman
John F Kennedy
Madonna
Michelle Pfeiffer
Gordon Ramsay
Robert Redford
Joanna K Rowling

Moon in Libra

Ruled by Venus

Fly me to the Moon
Let me play among the stars
Let me see what Spring is like on Jupiter and Mars
　　　Sung by Frank Sinatra

The sign of Libra is masculine, positive, airy and cardinal, but that most feminine of planets, Venus, is its ruler, so Libra is already a mixed up sign, without adding the lunar equation to the pot! The Moon, through its association with the sign of Cancer, is feminine, negative, watery and also cardinal. The cardinality is the most important factor here because even if the Moon is not really at home in such a strong sign as Libra, its cardinality will give you the inner dynamism to put things into action, albeit slowly. Being an air sign, your thought processes are logical, and provided you have a fairly active Sun sign, you could achieve a high position in life.

Libra is a cardinal sign, which means that when you decide on a course of action or when you decide that you want something, very little stops you from getting there, so you never lose sight of your objectives, and you never give up on a goal. You are more ambitious than your outer manner may suggest. Your mind is fair and balanced and you hate any form of injustice, so some of you will take up a cause that champion the underdog. You object strongly to any form of racism. When others argue, you seek to be the peacemaker but you can argue like a Jesuit when the mood takes you. You're always open to new ideas but will not swallow what others tell you without proof.

Whenever the Moon is in a masculine sign, the native is naturally competitive and a high climber but is only really impressed by his own measurements of success. With the Moon in Libra, you could have a similar 'what right do they think they have to tell me what to do!' attitude as you would expect from Moon in Aries. Although charming most of the time, you can be extremely sarcastic and hurtful when provoked, showing a grasp of vocabulary worthy of any solar Gemini!

You seem to need a touch of glamour in your life and could be drawn to work in some kind of glamourous or luxurious trade. You make sure that both your home and your working environment are comfortable and attractive with a pleasant peaceful atmosphere. You have no patience with ugliness in any form, and you loathe ugly or dirty people. Being fussy about your personal appearance you are also rather inclined to be vain about your own looks, and while you are young, your partners may be chosen for their looks or appearance of glamour rather than talent or personality.

Your nerves can sometimes let you down; therefore you need peace in the home environment. Both sexes of this Moon placement are good homemakers you're both attached to your own plot of land and house. You enjoy doing things around the home, but a life made up purely of housework would stifle you. Your good taste will ensure that your surroundings are always comfortable and elegant. Some subjects are musical or artistic, and you may have a nice speaking and singing voice. You certainly enjoy listening to music and you hate discordant noises. All your senses are strong but sight could probably be the strongest, because if something doesn't look right, you couldn't live with it.

Being an air sign, you need the stimulation of meeting new people and you are usually welcoming towards newcomers. Travel is liked, as long as you can do it in comfort, you feel perfectly at home in the world's nicest hotels and watering places. Although you enjoy your own company from time to time, you really don't really want to live or work alone for long. There is a need to keep in touch with the world and to keep your mind stimulated with new people and up-to-date experiences. You enjoy being part of a group, and seem to need the approval of your peers but you wouldn't necessarily wish to lead the group. Unless there is Leo or Capricorn on your chart, you prefer to be fairly near the top so that you could delegate the more distasteful chores to others.

You are excellent in a crisis, but unable to give sustained help, because you quickly become bored with other people's problems. You have no patience with fools, although you often hide your irritation under a layer of urbanity. Your mental responses are surprisingly fast and you can be quite calculating when necessary.

Your pet hates are loud discordant noises and, according to my lunar Libra friends, being travelsick! Perhaps this is because you have delicate eyesight and hearing (through the reflected association with Aries). You like the sea and the countryside but are really a city person at heart, because you like to be where it's all going on. You may travel a lot for business and you certainly will do so for pleasure. With luck, you may have a holiday home in some exotic location.

You aren't always easy to live with, as you can be critical, fussy, demanding and occasionally downright childish. However, you need to love and be loved; you also need friendship with people of both sexes. Some of you are strong in business but weak and henpecked at home. You can be capable of using, even of manipulating others, but you need to be needed, therefore you also allow yourself to be used by those whom you love. As a young person you can be inconsistent in emotional relationships, wanting the challenge and excitement of new faces practically each week. You enjoy the opening phase of a romance more than the later stage of commitment, because you don't like to be emotionally fenced in.

You love children and you want emotional security, so sooner or later, you will settle down into domesticity. Even so you will always be a flirt! Apart from the need for an attractive partner, you need one you can take anywhere. Your partner should be the kind of person who can be relied upon to be the genial host or gracious hostess who will help out with the social side of your career. You need someone with a gentle and gracious as you hate coarseness or hurtful remarks. I have actually seen Moon in Libra subjects become ill because they were unhappy at work or home. Men with the Moon in Libra have a curious split in their personality which, on the one hand, gives them a somewhat macho image, while at the same time endowing them with an almost feminine gentleness, especially when it comes to caring for young children. There is no evidence of you being an animal lover, but you couldn't hurt an animal or see one hurt by others. Your gentle manner with those who are weaker than you adds to the attractiveness of your personality.

Lunar Librans are very clever with intricate machinery, and like the other air signs, they all seem to have a love affair with vehicles and with speed. You respect the dignity of others and treat them with tact and charm. Those of you who have a strong Sun sign may hide strong feelings and opinions under this charming exterior, but those who have an unassertive Sun sign may need to develop your own point of view and learn how to make a stand.

Sexually speaking you could turn out to be one of the best lovers in the Zodiac! This, of course, depends upon other factors in your birthchart. Your sensual nature cannot be denied, and with a bit of luck you will find fulfilment within marriage, but if it doesn't work for you, you will move on and seek fulfilment elsewhere. You could actually relate well to a difficult partner who keeps you on your toes, so you may choose to live with someone unpredictable enough to give you a few lively arguments and passionate enough to satisfy your strong sexual needs.

Knowing instinctively when your partner is ill or unhappy, you rise to the occasion and do all that you can to make them feel better; you don't really like to see anyone downhearted. You are good at providing little treats but you can't always be relied on to remember anniversaries etc. this is because your giving is spontaneous rather than organised. Lunar Librans need to give and to receive affection, tenderness and sympathy. If you have the Sun or ascendant in fire signs, you could be a little too dependent on the approval of others. Some lunar Librans can be easily influenced and swayed by others but most of you have a mature outlook and can make up your own mind about life, most of you try to keep your emotions under control. You consider yourself to be cool and logical, but this may be something of an act, because your emotions and fears can be powerful, but you don't want to be controlled by them or for them to become obvious to others.

Attitude to Career
The position of the Moon alone is unlikely to suggest any specific type of career but it can show one's inner motivations. Firstly you will want a job which gives you scope to express your creativity and this may be in an artistic genre such as architecture or fashion. You are persuasive enough to make a good salesman, but unless there are strong factors elsewhere on the birthchart, you would not have the kind of sustained energy which selling requires. Public relations and marketing would be

better as would being a buyer, due to you talent for selecting the right goods for the job.

The world of catering might appeal; certainly glamourous hotels and restaurants are your natural habitat. Being good at calming others and even better in a crisis, you could make a good negotiator. You have a talent for arbitration and your quick mind and sense of humour can be used to defuse potentially dangerous situations therefore you might succeed as a union negotiator or as a particularly urbane politician. Personnel and recruitment are also possible career ideas. You can appear to be lackadaisical while working furiously behind the scenes. You are a good listener, so long as the person who is doing the talking doesn't go on too long. You enjoy money for what it brings, and while you don't need to have power, you do need a largish income to really enjoy life; therefore you will aim for the top anyway. The only thing you really cannot do is rough and dirty work among coarse people. You get on well with workmates and colleagues. With your logical mind, you would make a good engineer. Driving and even flying come easily to you. Finally, you could earn a few pennies as a spare-time musician if needs be, and more than a few pennies as a professional sports person. You are naturally sporty and competitive, so you are probably good at a number of sports and games. You certainly enjoy watching these.

Parents and Background

There is some evidence from this Moon position that you were born easily. You may have had a father who pushed you educationally and possibly a rather peculiar mother! This does not mean to say that you were unhappy as a child, you seem to have been loved and understood by your parents and even overindulged a little. Your charm, even as a baby, will have got you everywhere. Your mother was probably ambitious, clever or even eccentric, she may have forgotten to feed you or wash you on occasion but she never forgot to love you. The home was a stimulating place full of books, conversation and interesting visitors. This means you grew up without having to develop a suspicious attitude or a strong shell to hide behind. Nevertheless you are happier to be an adult – possibly because your schooldays were not a very happy time for you, maybe because schools and exams test what you know rather than the power of your personality.

Health

You are generally strong but may develop diabetes, cystitis or skin problems. You need to take exercise and keep your weight down as you gain it very quickly. You may eat too much rich food and you could definitely drink too much. Smoking is dangerous for you, as is working in a dusty environment, as you could develop both chest problems, such as hay fever and farmer's lung. You may eventually suffer from arterial or arthritic problems. Childhood health problems in childhood leave a legacy later in life.

Additional Material

You are lazy until something grips your interest, then you become self-motivated, which leads you to a high position in life. Your strange mix of laziness and hard work is due to the Moon's restless nature. You can be moody and sulky at times.

You will live and work in more than one country and while you love travel for business or pleasure, it has to be in comfort, so no camping for you!

You are independent and you solve your own problems. You can't stand clingy or self-pitying types.

Some Moon in Libra subjects make enormous sacrifices for their children, and even a divorced father will do his best to maintain a close relationship with his children.

Moon in Libra Celebrities

George Bush Senior
Leonardo DiCaprio
Mel Gibson
Patti Hearst
Derek Jacobi
Sylvester Stallone

Moon in Scorpio

Ruled by Pluto and Mars
(The Moon's Fall)

She's got some cruelty,
See it in the dark of the Moon,
Brother take her cruelty, face it
With her beauty and show it.
        Pagan Easter by Seldiy Bate,
        by kind permission of Temple Music

The sign of Scorpio is feminine, negative, watery and fixed whilst the Moon, through its association with the sign of Cancer, is feminine, negative, watery and cardinal. This would suggest that the Moon is comfortable in Scorpio but it must be remembered that this is the sign of the Moon's fall and therefore, it projects some of the most difficult aspects of both the sign and the planet. Scorpio's influence on the Moon adds intensity to the nature, also tenacity, capability and strong resistance to disease. It endows its natives with a strong instinct for survival along with an attraction to the more dangerous aspects of life. If this is your Moon placement, you have a tremendous ability to bounce back from illness, disappointment and even the door of death itself.

There are two quite separate needs within your personality and, bearing in mind that these needs hidden under the more outward and obvious aspects of your nature, so this can make you very hard for others to understand. You seem to require challenge and excitement on one hand plus constancy and security on the other. Like all fixed signs, Scorpio Moon people want to maintain the status quo. You prefer to stay in a job with which you are familiar, occupy the same house for years and remain with the same partner even when the partnership is no longer viable, but he other side of you cries out for the brink, the edge, the place where you can test your strength. Some lunar Scorpions become involved with risky or even illegal business interests while others involve themselves in risky romances or strange sexual encounters. You seem to have the feeling that you are invincible, bombproof: and you are probably right! A constructive way of dealing with this might be to have an interesting and risky hobby, such as a part-time attachment to a paramedical or paramilitary organisation. You may find yourself up against difficult situations without actually going out and looking for trouble. One lunar Scorpio friend of mine has a daughter who, after twice becoming involved with the shady side of the law, turned up at her house one day eight-and-half months pregnant!

Emotionally speaking, you have the ability to go at two speeds at once. When you meet a new attraction, you are cautious, watchful and apt to sit back and see what transpires, despite the fact that you are perfectly able to psychically sum up anyone who is likely to become important to you within minutes of meeting them. You can be manipulative towards others, but often only for their own benefit and you are as caring towards your family and friends as any solar Cancerian. Like all Moon in water people, you can occasionally be emotionally wearing, but you hate others being emotionally demanding towards you. You are perfectly willing to come to the aid of someone who is in a state of crisis, but if they continue to demand help and support after the immediate problem is solved, you become bored with the whole thing. Moon in Scorpio subjects all have a built-in bullshit detector and therefore are quicker than most at spotting a phoney. Sometimes the emotional sufferings of others make you feel helpless and powerless. Your worst fault emotionally is a tendency to become jealous and possessive towards others, and regardless of how secure lunar Scorpio subjects are, they don't seem to get life without most of these unpleasant feelings surfacing at some time.

Your home must be peaceful, clean and attractive. Your taste runs towards the antique rather than the modern and you will spend a considerable amount of time and money on furniture and fitments. You probably spend even more time and money on your garden because your love of beauty and strong sensuality draws you towards the beauty and scent of flowers. You enjoy the countryside and outdoor pursuits. The sea is attractive to you and you love to feel both its power and its peace. You are probably a very good swimmer.

You keep a tight grip on your own emotions and you tend to bottle up anger and allow your feelings to seep inwards. This can result in angry outbursts that may affect your health. On those occasions when you do become ill or suffer from some setback in life, your first reaction is anger. If you can't do something right away to solve the problem, you become silent, withdrawn and depressed. An athletic hobby would make a good outlet for your considerable energies. You can usually spot the feelings and motives of others quickly; you're able to find their weak spots and then use this information to help and encourage them or to wind them up and throw them off balance. You conceal your own feelings from others so that they don't get a chance to make use of you. Many of you hide your true feelings under an outwardly jolly manner.

Neither solar nor lunar Scorpios like officialdom, but you seem to have an uncanny knack of 'working the system' when you need to. You are persistent in pursuit of a goal, and when faced with opposition you will either find a way around it or as a last resort, force your way through assertively. You rarely consider asking others for help, seeing that as an admission of weakness.

You enjoy family life and make a reliable parent as long as you can step back a little from your children and let them be themselves. Many of you seem to have difficult or sickly children to care for, but you handle these problems better than most. You must be careful neither to smother your children nor try to mould them too forcefully, and you should allow them to develop their own individual personalities. Many of you are wonderful with animals and you love them more than people, so you may be a vegetarian as a result of this. Alternatively, you may just be funny about food, possibly due to a weight problem, but possibly because there are only a few things that you really like to eat. You may also prefer to eat alone than in company.

If you find something that interests you, you can be a hard worker. You try to finish everything that you start, and you dislike being interrupted. Preferring to work slowly and thoroughly, you hate being rushed or placed under a lot of pressure. If there is a little help from the rest of the birthchart, you can be surprisingly artistic. Both solar and lunar Scorpios have a strong sense of structure, an eye for detail and a well-developed sense of touch. This leads to a natural ability to handle materials in a creative manner. You could make an excellent sculptor, potter, design engineer or design dressmaker. Other structured interests such as dancing and sport appeal to you.

Your sexual feelings are intense and, if not fully gratified, you can become extremely irritable. Your deepest need is for a stable relationship with a reliable person who has as high and interesting sexual drive as you have. If you do not find satisfaction within your marriage, you will look for it on the outside. Your compelling nature makes you a pretty exciting lover but you are also sensitive enough to tune in to the needs of your partner and give as much pleasure as you like to receive. Depending upon your mood at the time, you can be extremely receptive to the needs of those around you or surprisingly dense. This depends upon your mood and the state of your health at any one time. You mustn't try to reform your partners but learn to accept them as they are. It would be better if you could pour your energies and reforming drive into the outside world if you can. There is some evidence of homosexuality and bisexuality associated with this Moon sign or of being attached to others who are gay.

You have strong intuitive and even psychic gifts and may be drawn to discover more about these aspects of life. Being mediumistic and clairvoyant, you may take a further interest by studying the occult in all its forms. You seek deeper meanings in everyday events and may consider them to be omens of some kind. Many of you feel that other people block your progress or even cause you to have bad luck instead of accepting that things do go wrong from time to time. You may be superstitious and inwardly fearful when faced with new circumstances and unknown factors in your life. Many of you are drawn to the arts of witchcraft and magic that give you the opportunity of linking into group energies and earth energies. The Qabala is another potential interest. The healing and caring aspect of psychic work attracts you. You have the potential to change the world, by politics, science or even by means of war.

Attitude to Career

The position of the Moon in a birthchart does not show one's actual career but the inner motivations that may affect one's choice of job. You are a slow, methodical worker preferring to stick to a job that you are accustomed to. You have an exceptionally pleasant voice and manner which makes you a natural for dealing with people, and your enjoyment of new and interesting people both at work and in a social setting, gives you the potential to be a good salesman or woman. You can inspire others to get things moving, but you should strive for success yourself as you can become resentful of the success of others if you don't. You can learn from others and can encourage them and guide them, but you don't have enough patience to become a teacher. Medical matters appeal to you and the sight of blood does not easily upset you, your patience and eye for detail would make you a fine surgeon, but psychiatry would also come naturally to you. Any work that brings you to the heart of matters is right for you, so you could become involved in the legal, forensic or political fields. In business you can make spectacular gains and even more spectacular losses. Many lunar Scorpios love the sea and can make their living on it as sailors, fishermen or swimming and diving experts and also, of course, in the navy. A life in the armed services appeals to many of you, as it requires the kind of skills and dedication that come so easily to you.

Parents and Background
Many lunar Scorpios are born into an inconvenient situation and are adopted soon after birth. On the other hand, some of you are born to families who already have a number of children and don't want any more. There is no doubt that you are on a different wavelength (possibly even a different planet) to that of your parents, and you will have been constantly misunderstood as a child. Your experience may have been poor because you were not really the type of child that they were hoping for or because you were compared unfavourably to another child in the family. I've come across two lunar Scorpios who had clever older brothers who were the favoured ones. You may have been successful at school or at sports, or you just about got by. There doesn't seem to be any real problem at school.

At the worst end of the spectrum, your parents may have bullied you, subjected you to violence, sexual abuse or just made to feel thoroughly inadequate. They may have given you the impression that you could never live up to their exalted standards. Negative attitudes die hard in fixed signs and you can go through life never shaking off the hatred and anger of your childhood. You may still feel yourself to be a nuisance to others and wonder why they put up with you. Nevertheless many lunar

Scorpios do love their somewhat inadequate parents very much and take a really caring if rather dutiful attitude to them later in their lives.

One peculiarity associated with either the Sun or the Moon in Scorpio is there could be a death in the family at the time of your birth or soon after.

Health

Although usually very fit you can worry over your health. Your weak spots are your arteries and veins and you could suffer from high blood pressure later in life. You may suffer from headaches and migraine, or allergies such as hay fever. The main problem seems to be in the reproductive organs as many women with this placement have terrible periods or an early change of life, and many end up having a hysterectomy to solve the problems.

Additional Material

You are highly intelligent but you may not make much headway in a career, as you are probably happiest when helping people or when caring for animals. You could make a living as a psychic medium or healer.

Some of you have peculiar parents. I have even met one whose mother was a prostitute, and while the lunar Scorpio child was completely protected and never saw anything unpleasant, there must have been a funny atmosphere in the home.

Many of you care for a partner whose health is poor or relatives or children who are mentally or physically handicapped.

You love deeply and you hate just as deeply.

You are outraged by injustice.

Moon in Scorpio Celebrities

Dwight D Eisenhower
Bette Midler
Bob Monkhouse
Katie Price (Jordan)
Steven Spielberg
Elizabeth Taylor

♏

Moon in Sagittarius

Ruled by Jupiter

Underneath your dreamlit eyes
Shades of sleep have driven you away
The moon is pale outside
And you are far from home
From "When Tomorrow Comes",
sung by the Eurythmics

The sign of Sagittarius is masculine, positive, fiery and mutable, while the Moon, through its association with the sign of Cancer, is feminine, negative, watery and cardinal. Neither the planet nor the sign have anything in common with one another, therefore each will work against the other in some way. Problems that result from this will be felt in the area of your emotions and in your relationships with others.

You probably didn't receive much physical affection from your parents, especially your mother, perhaps because they weren't the kind who went in for touching and cuddling, or because you yourself pushed them away. It's possible that your parents had to work hard and didn't have much time to spare for you. Being unaccustomed to touching or being touched by others, may make you in turn shrink back from being touched by others when you become an adult. However, any physical problems that you may experience are more than made up for by the excellence of your mind. Everything interests you but you accept nothing at face value. You enjoy reading and you enjoy television programmes that have something to say. Some of you are deeply philosophic in your manner of thinking. You may have been brought up in a religious family, rejected the ideas and later found others that suited you better.

You need personal freedom and independence as you need to be in charge of your own life rather than being under someone else's thumb and you must be able to come and go as you please. You cannot be cooped up anywhere, and you may even suffer from claustrophobia when travelling in a lift or in the back seat of a two-door car. New faces fascinate you and you need plenty of friends because you become bored if you have to spend every day in the same company. Sagittarius being a mutable sign, you can adapt to most situations and enjoy all kinds of people. You are broad-minded and never racist or bigoted.

Like most mutable sign subjects, you need to get away on your own from time to time in order to think and to recharge your emotional batteries. You have exceptionally clear vision and can see to the heart of a problem when others can only see muddle, and you are resourceful enough to solve most problems both for yourself and for others, although you do appreciate a helping hand when it's offered. You will help anybody who is in trouble but you can end up being used. You are sensitive to atmospheres and you can walk into a room and know right away if there has been an argument going on in there. You may over-react to people who show hostility towards you. Your temper is explosive and your tongue sharp and articulate; therefore you could make an unpleasant adversary. However, you don't hold a grudge and prefer to forget bad feelings and look towards the future with optimism.

The Moon is associated with the home and Sagittarius is a dextrous sign, therefore you should be good at do-it-yourself jobs and cooking. You don't like mess and dirt and cannot stand living in chaotic surroundings, as you need peace and calm in the home in order to rest your delicate nervous system. Your most important traits are your absolute honesty and your sense of humour. You can diffuse difficult situations with humour when necessary. You don't use honesty to hurt others, so you are perfectly happy to use little white lies for the sake of diplomacy, but you aren't a crook and you can be relied upon to do what you say you will.

You enjoy sports and you may be a good swimmer, and you are too active to spend your spare time sitting about so any form of sports or dancing would appeal to you, as this also brings out your competitive spirit. Although you may be a little on the shy side, you enjoy singing, music or artistic hobbies. Your active nature makes you choose work where you have the chance to move around and meet people and also where you are up on your feet rather than sitting about. Your pattern of working may alternate between manic activity and apparent laziness, because you aren't good at keeping to a regular routine.

If you have to leave your home for any reason, you would set about making another attractive place for yourself as soon as possible. Being attractive and rather vain about your appearance, you enjoy buying nice clothes and you may tend to spoil yourself while conveniently forgetting that there are bills to be paid. Your appearance and your body are very important to you, as activity is so much a part of your nature.

As with most of the mutable signs, there is a strange duality about you. You want something passionately and then go off it once you have got it. You need security but you also need freedom. This can make you appear irresponsible to others, but somehow you always find an answer and seem to be able to pull the irons out of the fire when things go wrong. You are no stranger to debts but you hate to be in debt. You can soon put other people's problems in perspective for them but you may be hopeless at sorting out your own muddles. A friend of mine, who is just about typical of this lunation, is responding to the fact that her husband has left her by giving up her job and spending money on clothes and luxuries when it's the last thing she ought to be doing. This is a reaction against facing reality - because reality right now is too much to face!

There is another split in your attitude to personal relationships, because you need and want to love and be loved, but you may find it hard to be faithful because there are so many interesting people out there. You could appear to promise much and not really deliver anything at all! You may actually prefer friendship to affairs anyway, and you certainly are an excellent and most reliable friend. You cannot cope with someone who lays the law down to you and under those circumstances, you assert your independence and probably walk away.

You are two sided in the world of work too. You are highly ambitious but not necessarily money-minded. You need money to pay the bills and to have money for fun, but not for power or to impress others. Women of this lunation like to control their own finances. You need to work at something that you enjoy and which keeps you in touch with people. You can appear lazy because you have a habit of preparing your work at home either before or after your normal working hours, thus hiding the actual amount of effort that you put in. Even if you love your job, you need to relax and socialite and you aren't a workaholic. You are what a well-rounded person.

Women of this particular sign can become wrapped up in causes, and this can bring problems on the domestic front as there will sometimes be too little time left for the family. Being slightly bossy, a woman with the Moon in Sagittarius would needs a very understanding husband. She is normally wise enough to find the right one for herself, and if she doesn't do so the first time, she will have another go. Both sexes love children, but spending your days looking after small children wouldn't stimulate you enough mentally. Many of you are brilliant with older children and may involve yourself with the scout or guide movement or something similar. Lunar Sagittarians make excellent teachers.

Your sense of adventure means that you could take up anything from hang-gliding to mountain climbing and you enjoy every experience that comes along. This is the sign of the traveller, and the Moon being associated with travel (especially on or over water) means that you take every opportunity to travel at the drop of a hat. Desert and mountainous areas where you can stand tall and see for miles fascinate you.

Anyone choosing to live with you would find you a happy and optimistic partner, as long as you have the freedom to do your own thing. You cannot stand people who try to dominate you or control your actions, and neither could you live with a partner who whines and nags. You hate those who criticise you while considering themselves perfect. Your intense need for freedom and independence means that you spend time away from the home, possibly travelling around in connection with your work. You would be happy to be married to someone rather like yourself, as you wouldn't seek to tie him or her down either. If you have an ambitious partner, you will help them to get ahead in their career. You are generous and kind, but your unpredictability can be hard to live with. You may choose a partner who is out of the traditional mould, for instance someone older or younger than yourself or of a different racial or religious background.

You may strongly attract repellent people, drinkers or drug addicts and you can put up with their behaviour because somehow, you aren't as repelled by them as others are. It's hard to find someone who is right for you mentally, physically and spiritually, so friends tend to fill some of the gaps. I discovered while researching this book that lunar Sagittarians have many connections with mental illness, either through senile parents, a schizophrenic child or a depressive spouse. There are times when you are so busy trying to adapt to their unrealistic behaviour that you begin to wonder just who is the dotty one! An alternative to choosing difficult people as lovers and partners is to take up humanitarian work on behalf of those who drink, take drugs, live on the streets and so on. This makes sense, as there is an inner need to help others and to do God's work. Another alternative is helping sick, injured or unwanted animals. Even if you do nothing to help animals, there is at least one animal in need of a good home that will find its way to you somehow or other.

As a parent you are proud of your offspring and will do all you can to help them get on in life. You respect their need for space and a separate identity and also their need for dignity. There is a possibility that you could live apart from them for some part of their childhood, either due to work that takes you away from home or as a result of a divorce.

Many of you will have parents who were born in a different country from the one in which you live. This may, to some extent, explain some of the splits in your personality, as you may have been educated in a different manner from those around you. Your parents may have a different religion from those of their neighbours or they may have spoken a different language at home. One such person told me that her parents moved around Europe when she was a child, so she was always the new girl at a school where she either didn't speak the language, or spoke it with the wrong accent.

Attitude to Career
The position of the Moon on a birthchart does not show which career you choose but it can show your inner motivation. In the case of Sagittarius, your greatest need is for freedom of action and the ability to communicate with others, possibly on a rather large scale. You are a natural teacher and if you don't work directly in education you would still enjoy helping and guiding others and passing on the knowledge that you have accumulated over the years. Most of you are surprisingly modest about your work and your achievements and tend not to promote yourselves very well, therefore, it's only when one gets to know you better that we learn just how knowledgeable you actually are.

You would enjoy a job in broadcasting, publishing or even as an entertainer. Many of you are good actors and singers, but shyness may hold you back. You are adaptable enough to get on with anyone and to work anywhere, but you have high standards and a strong sense of your surroundings; therefore you couldn't do anything that was really downmarket, under-handed or that involved working in dirty, messy surroundings. You are determined enough to finish what you start, but you may start too many projects and then become worn out from trying to do them all at once. Your amazing memory and your sense of humour and timing could give you a successful career in comedy.

The travel trade would attract you, as you love to expand your horizons in a practical sense as well as in a mental one. Some of you can work on dicey projects that involve intuition and the ability to guess right. This could be something like the futures market on the stock exchange or some business connected with gambling. Being over-optimistic at times, this could occasionally run you into trouble. Whatever you do, and even if your own confidence deserts you at the wrong moment in your career, your great sense of humour will always see you through. Lunar Sagittarians are excellent salespeople as long as they believe in the product they are handling.

Parents and Background

In many cases, the relationship with your parents was good but distant, possibly because they were busy or because they didn't encourage closeness. 'I just couldn't keep my parents' attention,' says Joe. 'My father led a busy life that took him travelling and my mother was always preoccupied with cronies at the church.' You may replicate your parents' lack of closeness when it comes to your own children.

Health

You could suffer from some of the Sagittarian ailments of leg and hip problems, varicose veins, phlebitis, rheumatism and blood disorders. Women of this lunation may have period problems followed by a hysterectomy.

Additional Information

Your pleasant appearance and friendly, open attitude makes you popular, as does your sense of humour.

You ensure that you have a nice home that is not built on a pile of debt. You may appear to have values that are more spiritual than material, but that isn't really true, as you appreciate the good things of life and want them for yourself, but you aren't afraid to work for them. Sadly, some of you can be stingy and penny pinching.

Not all of you travel that much in reality, so it may be your mind that does the travelling by being full of interesting bits of knowledge. You are bound to get a good education one way or another, either by doing well at school, going on to further or higher education later, and always by reading a great deal and by studying the many things that interest you.

A downside is that you can be self-indulgent, which means that you may escape into the world of drink and drugs or overeating perhaps, when you feel pressured.

You will very likely have luck in property dealings when buying, selling or inheriting property

Moon in Sagittarius Celebrities

Simon Cowell
Danny DeVito
Charlie Sheen
Mary Shelley
Justin Timberlake
Oprah Winfrey

Moon in Capricorn

Ruled by Saturn
(The Moon's detriment)

The first time ever I saw your face,
The Sun rose in your eyes,
The Moon and Stars were the gifts you gave
Sung by Roberta Flack

The sign of Capricorn is feminine, negative, earthy and cardinal, while the Moon, through its association with the sign of Cancer, is feminine, negative, watery and cardinal. The planet and the sign are quite compatible but the Moon is said to be in its detriment in Capricorn because the sign is opposite the sign of Cancer, which is the Moon's natural home. This means that the emotional side of your life could be a little suppressed.

Whatever you appear to be on the outside, inwardly you are sensitive, vulnerable and shy, especially where your personal feelings are concerned. The earthiness of Capricorn endows practicality, so if you find that an idea works for you, you will use it, otherwise you will reject it. You are very shy when you are young but later in life you hide your lack of social confidence with a layer of polish. Nevertheless, inwardly you are rather deep and somewhat unfathomable. You resist serious illness and have, in addition to bodily strength, considerable strength of character. These strengths enable you to survive almost anything, plus giving you the kind of tenacity and determination that allows you to finish whatever you start. You rarely take time off from work, even when you're ill.

♑

Many of you go into business for yourselves thereby giving yourself the opportunity to create something of your own which will stand the test of time. You learn self-discipline early in life and feel inwardly that life is a serious business. You have the feeling that you should work to build up your finances while you are young so that you can relax and enjoy the result later on. You will probably live to a ripe old age, so you are right to think like this. Another reason for self-employment is the fact that you enjoy being in a position of responsibility and you carry authority well without throwing your weight around.

Your careful attitude to money may simply ensure that you have a roof over your head and money in the bank, but it can also lead to stinginess or constant unnecessary worry about money. You aren't a great candidate for self-employment, as the income is too up and down for comfort, but you like doing your own thing, so you often end up with your own business, despite worrying about it all the time. I have known a couple of lunar Capricorns who have demanded readings on a monthly basis to reassure themselves that they wouldn't run short of money. One sensible thing that you do is to invest in property, and this can both be the property that you live in and property that you buy as an investment. At the very least, you probably have some bolthole that you can retreat to if a relationship fails.

You need security, because your idea of hell would be to be dependent upon others, and you hate the idea of being a burden or having to suffer the embarrassment of having to ask for help. You are resourceful and hard working but you could be a little scheming and just a touch dishonest when chasing a goal. Your serious nature is relieved by a delightfully dry and witty sense of humour. You don't make hurtful jokes about others but just see the world in an offbeat way, and those who share your sense of humour will find you very funny. You enjoy the company of humourous people too.

You learn well and may be academic but practical subjects really suit you best. You can think and plan on a large scale and in a structured manner, rules and methods come easily to you, whether they are mathematical, engineering, or the pattern made by a series of dance steps. You prefer not to gamble on life but to plan your course, moving forward and then consolidating your position. Although your values are material rather than spiritual, the most important aspect of your life is probably your relationship with your family. You are very caring and you take your responsibilities towards them very seriously. You are dependable and faithful in marriage and you will try to make almost any kind of situation work. Your work may occasionally come between you and your family but if they are ill, they get all of your attention immediately. Oddly enough you really enjoy hearing all the local gossip, and not just family gossip either, and you can really get your teeth into a nice juicy piece of scandal but you yourself would hate to be in the middle of it yourself!

As a parent you are gentle and caring, and although you would be unlikely to join in rough games with them, you will do your best to teach them, and to open their eyes to the possibilities which life has to offer. You may be a little old-fashioned in your approach when they reach their teens but you will try to see things from their point of view. At least you would always be aware of your children's need to be treated with dignity.

You exert considerable control over your own inner nature in order to prevent your feelings from getting the better of you. Your somewhat formal manner protects your vulnerability; for example, it would be impossible to imagine you getting drunk and making an ass of yourself. It takes a lot to make you lose your temper but when you do so you can go over the top and cut your nose off to spite your face. You may expect too much from your friends, relatives and partners, and this means that you inevitably get let down and hurt. All those who have the Moon in cardinal signs like to get their own way, and you can also be bossy; although you would argue that you only boss others around for their own good. The Moon in earth signs can make you stubborn and blinkered, which makes it hard for you to see someone else's point of view. If you allow your attitudes to become too entrenched, it will ruin your relationships and friendships and destroy your chances of happiness.

Making friends is a slow process, but you do keep your friends for years. In a way, you are better able to adapt to new places than to new people and can fit in almost anywhere. Your pet hate is to be embarrassed and humiliated. For example, a spell in a hospital that is staffed by insensitive people would be dreadful for you. Another pet hate is coarseness or vulgarity of any kind. You have a love of beauty and grace in all things and a hatred of any kind of ugliness, from an ugly appearance to ugly behaviour. Being reserved, you don't readily reach out to touch people but you love to be held and touched by your partner and you love to cuddle children. Earth signs are sensuous, and this could show up in your case as a love of flowers, music or the seasons of the year. You may love art, music, design or literature but you can also be very heavily into spiritual matters. Many lunar Capricorns derive much benefit from meditations and from joining New Age interest groups, including those concerned with astrology.

You are kindly and helpful towards other people, especially in a work situation and you would make a good financial adviser or a good teacher on a small group basis. You need a strong and independent partner who can, to some extent, protect you. Your hidden sensitivity can give you nervous ailments such as skin problems, asthma, rheumatism or a tendency to have colds. You can be a hypochondriac. You listen to any advice that is offered to you but in the end you prefer to make up your own mind.

Where sex is concerned you improve with age, and also with the overcoming of your shyness and inhibitions. You are fastidious and very particular both in your choice of partner and in your behaviour. One-night stands are not for you! The feeling of closeness while making love is as important to you as the act itself. You may choose to marry someone who is older than yourself but whoever you choose, whatever their age or appearance, you will feel protective and caring towards them. You even like to work with a partner so that you can share the same problems. One problem is that you either choose difficult people as partners or you nit-pick and cause arguments, so relationships may be a major problem area for you. You don't always realise what a strong personality you are or how much you seek to control others.

One relationship that you will always keep going if at all possible is the one you have with your parents. If a parent needs financial or practical help, they have only to call on you and you will be there, even if the parent is feckless or a loser, you will do all you can to help, and you will never stop doing so. You may resent this a little at times but your love for your parents is strong, so you don't really mind.

You need to get away from time to time, and you really appreciate a holiday. You may not be a footloose traveller, but you may travel quite a bit in connection with business. You aren't very experimental with foods and you don't have a large appetite. You may be a vegetarian, however, you enjoy eating well cooked and presented foods in pleasant surroundings. You aren't much of a drinker, but you enjoy the little that you do drink. Comfort is a necessity for you when travelling, and you aren't likely to be found on a camping site.

There could have been some conflict between you and your father, and this may account for your slight air of watchfulness when around new people. A very frequent scenario with this Moon is poverty. There may have been too many other children in the family, or a parent may have had to struggle alone to bring you up. Your parents may have been slightly insensitive or critical of your schoolwork, or you may have had critical teachers who made you feel small. However, you were a quiet and obedient child, so you did well at school and gave the teachers no problems. Health problems may have made sports difficult. Many of you go on to further education, especially of a practical nature.

Attitude to Career
The position of the Moon on a birthchart does not necessarily indicate your choice of career, but it can show your inner motivations. Lunar Capricorns prefer to do something useful; this could be anything from structural engineering to making medical supplies. You may be happy to work in a large, international organisation that moves goods around the world. You have a good head for maths, and money matters come easily to you, so you could work in banking, the stock exchange, accountancy or insurance. The civil service and government departments are also good areas for you. You prefer being in a position of management. Computers hold no fears for you.

Travel and transport or working for a chain of shops are possibilities too. You can get everything done, but you need to do so at your own pace, and you get upset and disconcerted if someone starts to push or hassle you. Being thorough and efficient in all that you do, you become annoyed by petty inefficiencies in others, and you can get worked up when the bus is late or paperwork has not been properly done. You may be an early riser. Whatever you do, you are ambitious and will climb slowly towards the top of your career.

Parents and Background
There is something strange here. You begin by being very close to your mother and then losing your idealised picture of her. There may even be tragic circumstances involving death of a family member or a spell in a children's home due to illness or divorce in the family. As you grow up you may realise that your mother is a loving woman who did her best under the circumstances. Here is a situation that a client called Peter explained:

'My parents were very caring, but there was just too much for them to cope with. My father never got over being shot in the war and my mother had to work hard to keep us. The love was there, but they were getting old and up against it. I felt it would be wrong to make too much noise, and too disruptive to bring other, noisier youngsters into the house. I doubt whether they would have stopped me, but I would have felt bad about it.'

Health

Your weak spots are the bones, especially the knees; therefore you could have rheumatism later in life. Hearing problems are a possibility, especially tinnitus. You may have skin problems and you may be shortsighted. If life gets difficult, you will suffer from nerves. Generally speaking you should live a long and healthy, if rather hard-working life.

Additional Information

You are ambitious and you don't mind putting in the hours to achieve your goal. You like status and status symbols. You like to live in a nice area and drive a nice car. You may join some prestigious club or group such as a golf club, but you probably won't become a committee busybody.

You may marry someone much older or younger than you are.

You have a good head for details, and when you add this to your good memory, you could become an expert in something like hallmarks, numismatics or antiques.

Your clothes are never flamboyant but they are right for the circle that you move in. You prefer to own a few good things rather than a wardrobe full of tatty rubbish, and you don't follow fashion too much.

You don't get fat, but if you do gain a bit of extra weight, you have the self-discipline to lose it again quickly. Indeed, you may tend to lose weight too easily and to be too thin.

You may be a good teacher.

You probably enjoy gardening, cooking and do-it-yourself work.

Many of you have an unpromising start in life, perhaps having grown up in a very large family where there was little time for you and your needs.

Your parents may have been poor, and your childhood experience so deprived that you became determined to succeed in life, and to avoid poverty at all costs.

Moon in Capricorn Celebrities

Johnny Depp
Michael Douglas
Elizabeth Montgomery
(Samantha from Bewitched)
Ozzy Osbourne
Jimmy Perry

Moon in Aquarius

Ruled by Uranus

When the moon is in the seventh house
And Jupiter aligns with Mars,
Then peace will guide the planets
And love will steer the stars
This is the dawning of the Age of Aquarius
From the musical *Hair*

The sign of Aquarius is masculine, positive, airy and fixed, while the Moon, through its association with the sign of Cancer is feminine, negative, watery and cardinal. The power of the Moon is rather muted in this sign, the greatest effect being to reduce the feeling element from the emotions. Inwardly, you are detached, independent and rather cool. Although controlled and possibly a little bottled up at times, you like other people to show that they need and want you.

When meeting people for the first time socially, you are pleasant and affable if a little shy; meanwhile you weigh people up in a slightly watchful manner. You have a strong inner sense of self that allows you to take a calculated risk in a career or even in a relationship. Although sensible, you aren't over-cautious; therefore you accept most of life's challenges whether they put your finances or your feelings at risk. This ability to inwardly weigh and measure confuses those who fall in love with you because although you can discuss feelings in an articulate manner, one wonders just how much you really care.

Your inner nature is offbeat, you could find yourself travelling in a different direction to everyone else. Like your solar Aquarian cousins, you are educationally minded and will choose a career where you can stretch your mind and also broaden the minds of others. You are kind, helpful and humanitarian but this goodness may be directed more towards the world in general than to those who are closest to you. Although helpful in practical ways, there could be an element of embarrassment and helplessness when faced by the sight of other people's emotional pain. You fear that if you allow weak people to latch themselves on to you that they will drain your energies or worse still, bore the daylights out of you! Your general outlook is balanced, optimistic and cheerful, and to all except the most neurotic you would be a good friend.

Your mind is excellent, and whether you are educated and academic or shrewd and streetwise, your thinking processes are fast and your intuition is strong. You possess a dry and intelligent sense of humour. Your ideas are often excellent and you have the ability to put them into practice. Being strongly independent, you prefer to cope alone with your own problems, however harrowing they may be, and you may reject outside help in case it makes you appear weak and incapable. One Moon in Aquarius friend of mind wouldn't allow anyone to go with him when he went into hospital for a major heart operation, and he only allowed his family to see him once he was better.

You don't like people who try to own you or to manipulate you, although you can be adept at manipulating others. Another pet dislike is of being falsely accused - you are willing to admit to your own errors but will not carry the can for others. Your friendliness is universal and you wouldn't reject anyone due to colour, age, race or religion. Many lunar Aquarians belong to clubs and societies, and many of you enjoy hobbies that are sociable and charitable, such as Masonry, the Rotarians, the Federation of Small Businesses or youth work.

You can take any amount of chaos going on around you at work but you need peace in your home, where you can be in control of your own environment. You enjoy visitors but you don't appreciate people who dump themselves upon you. Many of you are clever at do-it-yourself, enjoying the challenge of working on your home and garden and often finding imaginative and original ways of solving practical problems, and you may be a very good cook. There is evidence that you wouldn't be so happy if the hobby was a particularly noisy one because you hate loud discordant noises.

Your memory may be strangely selective, easily recalling things you find interesting but tuning out things that you consider irrelevant, but you don't duck really important issues, as you have high standards of honesty and integrity. You don't go in for petty jealousy and neither do you make mountains out of molehills. If your pride is hurt, you can be quite spiteful and very sarcastic, and you really do need a creative or useful outlet or you can become bored, gossipy or aloof. Some of you are lazy and easygoing while others can be truly very eccentric. You have a strong ego, so criticism brushes off you. Indeed, you consider that everyone is entitled to his or her own opinion but you don't have to take any notice of it, and anyway, you are never going to change your ways in the face of criticism anyway.

In close personal relationships you are kind, pleasant, thoughtful and passionate, and you could even be rather romantic. Aquarius being a fixed sign suggests that you don't easily walk away from situations, so you may stay in the same house, the same job or the same relationship even when it's clear that you should really move on. However, if the day comes when you do move on, you can do so in a decisive manner, looking mentally forward rather than backward. You can wait years for the right person to come along, if this paragon does not appear, you are happy just to have lots of friends. If you become bored with a partner, you may look outside the relationship for change and excitement.

If you fall in love with someone new while you are still married, and especially if you have children, then you will be terribly torn between the need to be loyal and the need to be with the one you want. However, your famous Aquarian detachment comes to your aid here and allows you to work out logically what would be for the best. There is no doubt that you need an interesting and stimulating partner, along with shared interests and mutual respect, as without shared interests, the marriage can drift into failure and loss. There is just a suspicion that lunar Aquarian males might find a very successful career-girl type of wife too much of a good thing, as there could be just a tinge of jealousy creeping in here. Either sex can be strangely blind to both the needs of your lover, and you may never really get to know your lover on a deep level. This lunation does produce amazingly sexy people, as your combination of action, imagination and stamina seems to bring something special to the act of love. Your partners are chosen to some extent because they have the right appearance. Fatness turns you right off, as does dirt and mess.

The relationship between lunar Aquarian parents and their children is pretty good, as long as the child isn't the clingy, needy type. There is a natural sensitivity to young people and you offer help without making undue demands upon your children or smothering them. It's just possible that you could expect too much of a very timid child but for the most part you make a successful parent. You are always ready to stump up cash for education or hobbies but you might be a little absent-minded about some of the practical details, such as making sure that they have a clean shirt for school.

Your temper can be a problem when you are young but if you are hurt, you lash out verbally. You will only go so far in order to fit in with the wishes of others, and you take the view that other people ought to take or leave you just as you are. Needing a pleasant home and a nice garden, you have no special preference for the town or the country. I think you would make the best of it wherever you were, as long as you aren't isolated from people or fenced into a very small space. Money is not your god, but you need to feel comfortable and you aren't afraid to work, so you put your back into ensuring a decent standard of living for yourself and your family.

Attitude to Career

The position of the Moon on a birthchart rarely determines one's actual career but can show one s inner motivations. You take work seriously and don't like chopping and changing jobs, preferring to find a career that you can settle into. You are interested in ideas and willing to learn; therefore you do well at school and continue to learn later on. Certainly your parents encouraged you to progress, but like all lunar masculine signs you are inwardly quite goal-orientated, you enjoy work that is useful to the community and you also like making things that are needed. You can pursue a goal.

Working with children might appeal to you and you have the patience to deal with difficult ones, so you might take up youth work. You take well to challenges and can ride out most problems without falling apart, therefore the armed services or police may appeal to you. Your incisive mind may lead you into the legal sphere, or medicine, psychiatry or even astrology. Being impatient with fools, you find delegating difficult. You usually learn from your own mistakes and are fairly forgiving towards others for theirs, as long as the mistakes do not occur too frequently or are not too obviously stupid. You solve problems in an original way, but you must learn to keep lists, because your memory is actually a forgettery!

You seem to be happiest when working in large enterprises, so you may wind up in the civil service, a large commercial firm, a bank, the teaching profession or government. Computers, maths and science are your forte, so you may find a job in some specialised area of programming. Some aspect of astronomy or space may interest you and it's possible that you will travel and work in space some time in the future. You are capable and inventive and will give the whole of your attention to the task in hand, therefore you can create some highly original and very workable methods of production, so designing comes easily to you. You don't like being pressurised by others, preferring to work things out in your own way and to do things slowly and thoroughly.

Some of you enjoy being attached to some kind of glamourous or powerful enterprise where your own dynamism can come to the fore. Although ambitious while young, you are prepared to settle for something comfortable later in life. Most solar and lunar Aquarians have a need to do something worthwhile and to put something back into life. One lunar Aquarian friend of mine raises money for handicapped children, but he does this very quietly despite being one of the most prominent members of this country's civil service, and another is in the scouting movement. Needless to say, politics is a natural arena for you, especially as the sign of Aquarius actually rules local government and local politics.

One occasionally runs across the type of Moon in Aquarius subject who is languid, arty, and who lacks ambition and self-discipline. There are a few others who may be theorisers who never quite able to put their theories into action. Some are just too eccentric to fulfil any ordinary kind of role. Most of you enjoy a challenge though, and you get a kick of making something succeed. Some of you are drawn to the arts of the world of drama and if there are other encouraging factors on your birthchart, writing and editing may come naturally to you.

Females of this lunar sign are unlikely to be homemakers unless you have loads of outside interests, especially humanitarian interests or the kind of interests that revolve around caring for animals.

Parents and Background
On the face of it you had a good childhood, certainly your practical needs were attended to, and if you came from a background where there was little money to spare, your parents would have made sure that you had enough to eat and were dressed and equipped in a clean and decent manner. Your mother may have been a busy career woman or she may have poured her energies into some personal interest. One lunar Aquarian friend of mine had parents who were actively involved in the church. You may have had religion rammed down your throat in childhood that put you completely off formal religion later in life.

It's possible that you loved your father but inwardly considered him weak. He may have had poor health. (Oddly enough, many Moon in Aquarius subjects have fathers who suffered from stomach ulcers). Your mother would have been the more organised and capable parent, especially as far as money is concerned. Your parents discouraged you from making scenes or allowing your emotions to become a nuisance to others. It's possible that you were never really close to your parents or that you loved one and ignored the other.

Your parents probably took a reasonable view of your educational needs; they encouraged you to learn but didn't push you unduly. They may not have been so accommodating when it came to hobbies and interests, possible due to lack of money.

Health
You are basically very strong. Blood pressure could be a problem especially for women during pregnancy. Allergies such as hay fever, asthma, eczema, psoriasis and hives can occur, also migraine, menstrual problems in women, rheumatism and diabetes are possibilities. The weakest part of the body is the lower legs and ankles, which could involve problems with veins, phlebitis and thrombosis, also leg ulcers later in life.

Additional Information
You can have a bee in your bonnet or some fixed idea of how things should be. For instance, some of you may be animal lovers who become incensed at those who hunt, while others may be so into green issues that you oppose road building and so on. Some may have particular political views that take you well to the right or left of others, and you may sit-in at military bases and so on, while others may be so right wing that you

actually run the military base! I have even known people of this Moon sign who are deeply into playing chess or bridge, so that all their spare time is taken up with this.

You could be extremely good looking or unusual looking in some nice way. You certainly like to look nice and you spend a fair bit of money on your appearance, and you can be quite vain.

Many lunar Aquarians are sporty in a quiet way that doesn't involve heavy teamwork. Some enjoy fly-fishing, badminton, tennis, horse riding, ten-pin bowls or outdoor bowling and some play snooker.

Your love of independence means that many of you are self-employed and self-motivated; happily, you are also dexterous and clever in your line of work.

Moon in Aquarius Celebrities

Cary Grant
Larry Hagman
David Koresh
John McCain
Sarah Palin
Princess Diana
Britney Spears
Denzel Washington

Moon in Pisces

Ruled by Neptune

I am the star that rises from the sea
The twilight sea.
I bring men dreams that rule their destiny.
I bring the dream-tides to the souls of men
From The Worship of Isis

The sign of Pisces is feminine, negative, watery and mutable while the Moon, through its association with the sign of Cancer, is feminine, negative, watery and cardinal. This would make the Moon appear comfortable in Pisces but to some extent the mutability of Pisces weakens the active, cardinal nature of the Moon. Pisces is an emotional water sign, so this person's feelings run deeply.

If this is your Moon position, you will spend some part of your life searching for answers to deep and indefinable questions. You will contemplate the meaning of life and the possibility of an after-life and you could even be drawn to a religious or quasi-religious way of living. Your energies to some extent will be directed towards trying to improve the quality of life for others and to introducing people around you to a gentle and healthy understanding of their minds, bodies and spirits. Life may disappoint you, as it may never match up to your idealistic dreams and indefinable yearnings. Yet, somehow, life must go on and you will probably wish to live it to the very full. Therefore a particularly Piscean form of practicality often seems to combine with your desire for perfection, and the requirements of the hereafter.

You can be surprisingly ambitious. This ambition may take the normal route of upward mobility in the working and the suburban community or it may take a totally private form. You could push yourself to improve your performance in a creative capacity. Either way, you have the long-term patience to achieve your goals. You also have the gift of creative visualisation. The only real drawback to you reaching your goals is your lack of confidence and your fear of making other people angry with you for competing with them. A sarcastic remark can wound deeply and it's never forgotten.

On a more mundane level, you can be sensitive to the needs of others and some of you are extremely kind and considerate. Some of you have to stop and analyse your feelings from time to time to ensure that they are your feelings and not those of the people around you. You should also note that it doesn't always do to rush in and smooth the path of others, as it might be better to allow them to solve their own problems from time to time. Not everybody will want your intervention - although, human nature being what it is, most people will take advantage of free help when given the chance. If you become a permanent listening ear for neurotic friends and relatives, you will become worn out, depressed and even physically ill. There are people who don't actually want their problems solved because this would stop them from attracting the attention and sympathy of others. You must make a special effort to avoid the truly mad, bad and sad, even if it means abandoning some of those who call themselves friends.

You have an inner streak of resilience and you can usually find a way round your own problems. If absolutely pressed, you can stand up for yourself very well and dish out a surprisingly devastating dose of criticism. People tend to forget that just because you are so ready to sympathise and to understand their needs, that you also see their faults and inner motivations. If you are wounded you withdraw into your shell but if the problem is too great, you can be very spiteful and destructive.

Some lunar Pisceans are really horrible. They take the attitude that if there is the slightest chance that others may criticise them, it's best to strike first. This means that they extremely unpleasant upon meeting people for the first time. They don't hesitate to be hurtful to their partner's families or to others who they fear might judge or criticise them, even when these people have absolutely no intention of doing so, and they have no concept of being pleasant for the sake of peace or even for the sake of their partner or loved ones. They attack all those who come near them in order to deflect any possibility of criticism. Another unpleasant trait is stinginess and penny pinching in small ways and moaning about small expenses, and some of you are penny-wise and pound-foolish. You are always broke but you usually manage to do all the things that you like doing.

Other lunar Pisceans are the polar opposite of the nasty ones, being kind to everyone and generous to a stupid degree, even to the point of taking in lame ducks and having the house full of relatives who take advantage of your good nature – and of the contents of your fridge! If you belong to this type, you won't tolerate injustice in any form, and you value loyalty above all things and hate to let anyone down. Friendship is terribly important to you and you can be far too caring and giving towards those who you consider friends.

You are creative, many are artistic and you need to express this creativity somewhere in your daily life. You work at your own rather strange pace, often going at it like a dervish for a month at a time and then switching off for a week to recharge your batteries. Most of you enjoy some kind of sport. Swimming is probably high on your list, also dancing, tennis and walking the dog. Every lunar Piscean that I have come across is a naturally good dancer, and some become champion ballroom dancers. Some will become serious athletes if there are competitive elements elsewhere on your chart. Those of you who have a very ordinary job will probably have a creative interest on the side. Some work in the psychic field or become involved in Wicca or traditional witchcraft and it's likely that the people at your normal place of work having any idea of this other interest. You may be superstitious and fearful of unexplainable dark forces that sometimes seem to gather around you. Even the most practical among you can feel patterns in events.

You aren't as changeable in your moods as most astrology books would suppose and when you get upset, the feelings go deep. You are able to hold a grudge forever but you are equally apt to remember those who stand by you in times of trouble. If someone hurts you gratuitously even in a minor way, you will never quite be able to trust or really like them again. In some ways your apparent moodiness stems from your inability to get the whole of your life together at any one time. It seems that if your work is going well, your love life will be in a state of collapse and vice versa. Even if everything is going well, you can be discontented due to boredom!

Your home is your haven and it may be a private place that nobody else is allowed to invade, but it can equally become a centre or haven for a good many other people. Many of you work wholly or partially from home, and this can involve people coming to your home. The place is also permanently full of friends and neighbourhood children. Lunar and solar Pisceans are supposed to be loners but I have yet to see any evidence of that, as your phone and your doorbell are always ringing. Many of you literally don't bother to shut your door as there are so many people pounding in and out. Your home is attractive and comfortable but not over-decorated or cleaned to the point of sterility. You love warm colours, interesting textures, pictures, music and loads of books. There will be novels, books about the occult, history, psychology, health and magic on your shelves.

You can be so adept at hiding your inner nature that your kind heart might be buried under a shield of efficiency, toughness or even sarcasm. You are slow to reveal your own inner feelings and it takes some time for you to get to know and trust someone. Some lunar Pisceans even go through many years of marriage without their partner ever really being let into their innermost hearts. You can be a little manipulative at times, either to prevent yourself from hurt or in order to benefit those around you. When you are entirely comfortable with someone you can be surprisingly bossy in a rather mother hen way.

You probably make a mistake with the first marriage, but when you find the right partner, you are supportive and loving. You can live alone, but you far prefer to have someone to love. Not receiving the love and understanding that you need in childhood, you actively chase after it in adulthood. Some of you are so shy and repressed that you never get the love you want and then you retreat into a life of daydreams and illusions. Your powerful imagination is both your most valuable asset and your greatest weakness. If you can channel this into creative pursuits, spiritual development or work in the counselling field, you will be happier. Your greatest fault is of over-sensitivity to criticism and attacking those who you think might take it upon themselves to hurt you. This probably results from your low self-esteem.

You make an excellent parent because you understand the needs of children and are happy to spend time playing with them, and you respect the dignity of children. You could be so busy teaching them about the universe, the world around them and giving them all the love that they need that you overlook their need for clean shirts and breakfast cereal. Don't worry, they will survive your dottiness and love you all the more for it.

Although you are friendly and non-hostile in your approach to new people, if you really fancy someone, your first reaction may be to run in the opposite direction, because you fear rejection, ridicule and loss. You are afraid to become close to people, in case you learn to rely on them and then lose them again for some reason or other. Love relationships make you nervous because you are aware of your great need for emotional sustenance and of your vulnerability. Adolescent relating can be very painful, and although you eventually learn some protective techniques, you still fear rejection. Being incredibly romantic, you appreciate little presents, birthday cards, and candle-lit dinners and shared memories. You have a stock of romantic melodies and catch phrases that you link to your lover.

Your nerves are delicate and often over-stretched, so sex gives you a tremendous release of tension. A pal of mine tells me that he is 'horribly romantic' and couldn't enjoy sex without love. There must be affection and fondness, if not outright adoration, for you to be able to really relax and enjoy yourself. You need affection and cuddles even more than you need sex, and you need to be able to have a laugh with your partner. Oddly enough, you don't much like to be touched by strangers, so you need to keep a little distance from them to protect your sensitive aura. Some of you escape into alcoholism or drug addiction or both, while others of you attract these as partners who you try to reform. You can be too serious at times and you should let your friends encourage you to let your hair down and have some fun.

You like fresh air and the countryside, but not in cold weather. Finally, you need good clothes and you may be fussy about the shoes you wear.

Attitude to Career
The position of the Moon does not suggest any specific career but can show one's underlying motivations. You are creative, inventive and easily bored, therefore a routine job will not satisfy. Not having endless reserves of strength, you tend to work in fits and starts, so you need a job where you can work at your own pace. Many of you have an urge to do something useful, so you find work in hospitals or even in prisons. You can be found in the world of music, acting, dancing and art. Creative work obviously appeals; floristry and cookery are typical interests. glamourous work such as fashion interests you, as does the more up-market kind of public relations work. Many of you are skilled engineers, electricians, telephone engineers and precision sheet-metal workers, because the work is detailed, creative, requires problem-solving techniques and involves drawings.

I belong to an organisation called the British Astrological and Psychic Society and we have always had more than our fair share of lunar Pisceans involved in the society and particularly on the committee. Among the collective skills are astrologers, palmists, tarot readers, numerologists, clairvoyants, healers, complementary therapists, trance mediums, aura-readers, graphologists, sand-readers and much more. All lunar Pisceans are natural psychics and healers, and many are drawn to work in the field.

Parents and Background

You may have been born with difficulty and could have been the youngest child in the family or perhaps an only child. At least one of your parents was not particularly interested in having a child at that moment in time, possible due to having other problems to cope with. One way or another your childhood was rather lonely. Some of you felt yourself to be 'different' in some way, possibly being the only artistic and sensitive child in a household full of very rugged and practical people. Even with nothing tragic or 'out of gear' in the childhood, there was a need to withdraw into your imagination, to get away and spend time on your own, reading, drawing and thinking.

You may have been badly bullied at school or badly treated by your family. Some of you will have grown up in a home or boarding school of some kind. You may have felt embarrassed by your appearance, thinking yourself too tall, short, fat, thin, etc. You found it hard to relate to your parents and may have been afraid of them or afraid of other people around you. There may have been an over-emphasis on a particular kind of moral or religious observance, or too much emphasis on passing exams. Your natural inclination was to please your parents and teachers but you may have found this impossible to achieve. Some may have become rebellious.

You developed a watchful approach to adults and learned how to gauge their moods and how best to please them. This could be carried into adult life making you adept at finding out just how to please people. You learned to turn yourself into a whole variety of things that you aren't, in order to please others or to keep them off your back.

Adolescence is likely to have been a minefield as you learned to adapt to one person after another, not learning about your own realistic needs and making them plain to others. Pisces is a sign that is associated with illusion, but you eventually learn to channel your illusions into artistic or creative work and you learn to find people to love and who love you back. Eventually, you become settled and less of a victim.

Health

You could have been weak as a child and you may have spent a good deal of time alone or in hospital due to illness. Later in life the legacies of your childhood have a habit of lingering on. Your energies are quickly depleted and your nerves are delicate. The traditional problem area for Pisces is the feet, also the lungs. Heart trouble is a possibility; also skin allergies, migraine or asthmatic problems. You may retain water or have blood disorders. You may need counselling and comforting at some point in your life if you are to stay balanced.

Additional Information

Both the Moon and Pisces are associated with the sea, rivers and lakes, so you may prefer to live by water. I have the Moon in Pisces, and at one point in my life, I lived on an island in the Thames; I now live a few hundred yards from a river and two miles from the sea. Pisceans also travel quite a lot, possibly due to having relatives in other countries, but also due to their work or just for the fun of it. You enjoy travelling.

Mutable signs are associated with movement, so you may do a job where lots of people or things pass through your hands. I have come across electricians, teachers, psychics, engineers, hoteliers and festival organisers who have this Moon placement.

Lunar Pisceans are often accused of being 'psychic sponges' because they pick up on the moods of others. I don't know why we are denigrated for this in so many astrology books, because to my mind, it's not much fun being so easily upset and depressed when others are unhappy. We certainly pick up on moods and atmospheres very easily.

Moon in Pisces Celebrities

Hillary Clinton
Diana Dors
Catherine Zeta Jones
Piers Morgan
Paul Newman
Robert de Niro
Michelle Obama
Elvis Presley

Find Your Ascendant

Here are some useful ideas for finding your Ascendant (Rising Sign).
  Make a note of the exact place and time of your birth – or as near
    as you can get to the right time.
Ask an astrologer to make up a birthchart for you, and note down a
    list of the planets' positions and houses for you. As long as
    he or she doesn't have to interpret the chart, the charge should
    be small.
Send off to a computerised astrology service.
Buy the software and make up your own charts and reports for both
    natal and predictive purposes. Take a look on Amazon.co.uk or
    Amazon.com, as they often sell really useful astrology software
    at an amazingly low price – at the time of writing, you can get a
    useful program for less than £10.
Currently, www.astrodienst.com is one example of a very good,
    all-round site that also offers basic free chart services.

Meanwhile, here is an easy Ascendant Finder to help you to find your
Rising Sign, and even discover the houses that your natal Sun and Moon
occupy. It isn't as accurate as a fully drawn natal chart, but it does cover
most situations.

Speedy Ascendant Finder
Place your Sun in the house corresponding to your time of birth, and then
add the sign of the Zodiac that lies on the cusp line (house division).
    For example, if you were born at 2.30 am on the 14 April, place your
Sun in the 2 am to 4 am space, then write "Aries" on the 4 am line.

Place the remaining eleven signs of the Zodiac on the cusp lines around the chart in an anti-clockwise direction.

Place your Moon in the appropriate sign. This will give you your Rising sign and the house placements for your Sun and your Moon.

1	Aries	♈
2	Taurus	♉
3	Gemini	♊
4	Cancer	♋
5	Leo	♌
6	Virgo	♍
7	Libra	♎
8	Scorpio	♏
9	Sagittarius	♐
10	Capricorn	♑
11	Aquarius	♒
12	Pisces	♓

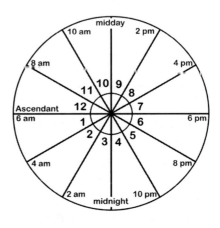

The Sun and Ascendant in your Horoscope

The Astrological Houses

House Systems

A house system is a way of dividing up the chart into twelve segments. There are various house systems that astrologers use, with Placidus being the most common in the UK. All but the Equal House system divide the chart into unequal segments. These systems are not easy for a beginner to use, so I always recommend the Equal House system to beginners.

N.B. Angular Houses are those that come immediately after the lines made by the Asc, IC, Dsc, and MC. Succedent Houses follow those, and the houses preceding a new cusp line are called Cadent Houses.

First House
Angular
Similar to Aries
Ruled by Mars

This shows how you appear to others, how you present yourself and your normal manner of expressing yourself among people who are new to you, so this can be your outermost personality. Obviously, this shows the first impressions that you give, but also the first impressions that you receive, so it can show what initially attracts you in other people. This house represents your childhood experiences, the parental home and the attitudes to be found in it along with early school experiences, early actions and reactions. It shows how you tackle new ventures. As this also contains information about your physical body and health, it might have a bearing on your appearance but other factors, especially the Sun sign, must be taken into account here. Any planets found here are very important, especially in respect of one's early experience of life.

Second House
Succedent
Similar to Taurus
Ruled by Venus

This house concerns your own possessions and anything of value, also investments and the ability to earn money, along with personal funds and personal debts. Personal and moral values can show up here, also personal requirements such as freedom versus security or the need for personal fulfilment. To some extent, this concerns partners and relationships, especially where money and goods are involved. It symbolises, matters related to property, farming, building, gardening and the land, along with artistic and musical abilities or interests, if any. To some extent this rules the way you give and receive love, and your attitude to beauty.

Third House
Cadent
Similar to Gemini
Ruled by Mercury

This rules the local environment, matters under negotiation and in some cases, papers to be signed. Messages, phone calls, correspondence of both a business and private nature. Local journeys, methods of transport. Brothers and sisters, neighbours, colleagues, sometimes nephews, nieces and friends. Business matters related to buying and selling. Education, training and retraining, foreign languages and writing of all kinds. Some sports and games. It shows the way you think.

Fourth House
Angular
Similar to Cancer
Ruled by the Moon

The home, property and premises of all kinds. Small businesses. Domestic life, roots and background, the basis from which you grew up into adulthood. The mother or any other person of either sex who nurtured you while you were young. The beginning and ending of life, also how you are viewed after your death. Your attitude towards family commitments. Security.

Fifth House
Succedent
Similar to Leo
Ruled by the Sun

Children, young people and their education, even pregnancy. Fun, holidays and leisure pursuits of all kinds. Games of chance, sports, dancing, singing, writing, entertainments and any aspirations to glamour or show business. Creativity and personal projects, even a business of one's own, as long as it offers the possibility of making a personal statement. Also publication, politics and social life - especially if influential. Traditional and religious attitudes, along with lovers, love affairs and fun, games, gambling of a sort and leisure pursuits.

Sixth House
Cadent
Similar to Virgo
Ruled by Mercury

Duties and day-to-day service to others; usually related to work, but includes those taking place in the home. Employers and employees, superiors and subordinates. Everything related to health, doctors, hospitals and hygiene. This could apply to the types of health problems you will encounter yourself or among your family. Your clothes and how you wear them. Details and analytical methods, meticulous work, analytical thinking and even changes in your way of thinking. Aunts and uncles. Healthy eating habits. Food and nutrition.

Seventh House
Angular
Similar to Libra
Ruled by Venus

Open partnerships and relationships, husband, wife, live-in lover. Open enemies. The giving and receiving of co-operation. Colleagues one is closely involved with, business partners. Work in a glamourous or attractive field. Creative and artistic endeavours that are done in partnership or a small group. Attraction to places, things and people, therefore, to some extent even sexual attitudes and exploration. The kind of person one looks for to work or live alongside who fill in the gaps in your character. To some extent documents related to partnerships are indicated here. Land, farming and gardening involving co-operation with others.

Eighth House
Succedent
Similar to Scorpio
Ruled by Pluto and Mars

Beginnings and endings. Birth and death. Sexual matters. Money involving other people, e.g. spouse's income, mortgages; taxes, wills, legacies, banking and insurance. Above all, partner's assets or lack of them. Shared feelings, feedback of other people's feelings (especially if they are intense). Crime and investigations and the police. Surgeons and surgery, also some illnesses. Hidden assets, secrets. The occult. A sense of commitment to anything or anyone. The things we really need from other people. The ability to regenerate or recycle anything. Deep feelings, deep thinking and such things as deep resentment and anger are to be found here.

Ninth House
Cadent
Similar to Sagittarius
Ruled by Jupiter

Expansion of one's horizons e.g. travel, higher education, new environments. Foreigners, foreign goods and foreign dealings. Legal matters, important legal documents and court cases. Religious and mystical matters, including the philosophical and spiritual side of psychic matters. On the one hand, science, and on the other hand, intuition, dreams and visions. The church and the clergy. Sports and games that are taken fairly seriously. Outdoor pursuits. Gambling (especially on horses). Interest in or work with large animals. Need for personal freedom. Teaching and learning of a high standard also ethics and some aspects of public and political opinion. In-laws and grandchildren.

Tenth House
Angular
Similar to Capricorn
Ruled by Saturn

Aims and aspirations, your goal in life, your professional reputation and standing in the community. This may represent one's career, but also political ambitions, creative aspirations and future success - or lack of it. The ego and its chances of being satisfied. Your employer if you work for a large organisation. Authority figures of all kinds, including governmental and public authorities. Achievements, fame and personal promotion. The organisation of the church or any large organisation. The parents, especially father, or father figures. Status, your standing in the world. Responsibilities and visible commitments. Self-promotion.

Eleventh House
Succedent
Similar to Aquarius
Ruled by Uranus and Saturn

Social life, friends and capacity for friendship, clubs and societies. Detached relationships but also love received, even the affection of friends. Intellectual pursuits and hobbies. Hopes, wishes, desires and goals and the chances of achieving them. Conversation, learning for pleasure. Teaching and learning of the usual kind, also instruction at work, political or philosophical training of a specialised kind. Money from one's job, especially if there has been training involved. Eccentricities, unexpected changes and circumstances. Stepchildren and adopted children.

Twelfth House
Cadent
Similar to Pisces
Ruled by Neptune and Jupiter

One's inner thoughts and feelings also secrets and secret worries. Suffering, sorrows, limitations, frustration and handicaps. This house can show whether you are your own worst enemy or not, it also shows inner resources and inner weaknesses or anything which is too painful to face up to. Hidden talents, hidden thoughts, hidden love, hidden angers. Also inhibitions, restraints, secret enemies and hidden danger. Any association with hospitals, mental institutions, prisons and other places of confinement, even exile. Any tendency to escapism, or things that we seek to hide from others. Your subconscious mind, plus karmic or spiritual debts. Self-sacrifice, love and help freely given (and possibly received). Also public charity and kindness, given and received. Inspiration and insights. Illusions, meditations and daydreams. Hidden friends and enemies. Here is where one could reach the stars - or mess one's life up completely.

The Moon through the Houses

Moon in the First House

You love your home and family and you don't want to live alone. Your nature may appear quiet and introverted but you have an inner desire to be recognised. You will do much to help others but you're not prepared to make too many sacrifices on their behalf. Your mother was a strong influence on you and she may have been an exceptional woman in her own right, so you could find yourself walking in her shadow. You may choose a motherly type of person as a partner or perhaps a childlike one who you can mother. The sea calls you so strongly that you may choose to live and work by or on it. You may be physically restless, finding it hard to sit still, or you may love travel, preferably with your family along for the ride. You may be drawn to hobbies or even work in the field of food and nutrition and could be a vegetarian possibly due to your love of animals. It comes naturally to you to support the underdog wherever you can. This placement suggests a need to work for the public in some way, either before them as some kind of celebrity or, more likely in a humanitarian or welfare capacity. Being finely tuned in to your own body you usually know if you are going down with some illness. You must try not to allow your moods to dominate your personality.

Moon in the Second House
(The Moon's accidental exaltation)

Material things matter to you, because you need the security of money and possessions. There is a suggestion that these may be hard to obtain or to keep hold of. You need emotional security, possibly as a result of a materially or emotionally deprived childhood. There is a shrewd and slightly calculating business head on your shoulders but your pleasant approach to others hides this well. Women will be involved in your personal finances in some way and women could help you, possibly by inheritance or through family connections. You will probably take an interest in Taurean pursuits such as cooking, dancing, building, music, the arts, gardening and the creation of beauty.

Moon in the Third House

You need to communicate which could lead you towards a career in travel, the media or education. You are restless and curious but possibly lacking in concentration and easily bored. You pick up knowledge casually from those who you brush up against, and your parents might be clever and bookish. Throughout life you will keep learning and then passing on information to others. You have a natural affinity to the telephone and also to vehicles.

Moon in the Fourth House
(The Moon's accidental dignity)

This is the natural house of the Moon due to its association with the sign of Cancer that is ruled by the Moon. You prefer to work at home or at least to do your own thing, preferably in your own business. You may be nervous of the big wide world and have a habit of scuttling back home when the going gets rough. You are sympathetic towards those who are weak and helpless and you are especially fond of animals. You could be strongly attached to your parents or separated from them by circumstances beyond your control. It's possible that you lack confidence or feel insecure due to childhood problems. You need love and affection and should try to avoid hurting yourself further by forming relationships with destructive types. The past attracts you and this might lead you to work in the field of antiques or history. You are patriotic. You enjoy being by the sea.

Moon in the Fifth House

You like children so you might work as an infant school teacher or become involved with young people's sporting activities. Your emotions are strong and you seek fulfilment on both a practical and a romantic level in relationships. You could have a number of affairs if marriage does not work out for you. You have a good deal of charm, you are good to look at and you keep a youthful appearance throughout life. You could work for or in a theatre or in marketing and public relations. A creative outlet is an emotional necessity for you. You would make a good teacher, writer or publisher. Be careful not to cling to your children

Moon in the Sixth House

You have a strong urge to serve the needs of others, so you may work in some kind of caring profession, especially medicine. You could be drawn to a career that involves the production of food or something that helps the public to stay in good health. Your career will have to appeal to you on an emotional level, and you can even walk out of a job if the atmosphere or the people there didn't suit you. You need variety, so you could be better suited to having a couple of part-time jobs rather than one full-time one. You are considerate to others and would be a caring employer.

Moon in the Seventh House

You get on with most people because you need company and companionship. Where relationships are concerned, you will bend over backwards to make them work even at the expense of giving in to others for the sake of peace. There is a feeling that while young you aren't quite sure who you are, so you may look to others to validate you. You prefer to work in co-operation with a partner or in a small group, and you may be drawn to work in an agency of some kind. You are politically minded and you have a good grasp of office politics. Glamour appeals to you, drawing you towards the world of fashion and music and this could become part of an interesting hobby. Your partner may be moody and difficult, but it's possible that you could understand him or her where others just don't.

Moon in the Eighth House
(The Moon's accidental fall)

Women will be instrumental in helping you to gain money or prestige. You could work in trades that cater to women's needs or work mainly among women. You have an interest in psychic matters and you will be drawn to the mediumistic and spiritual side of these things. Your clairvoyance could be prodigious, but it will depend upon other factors on the chart as to how this is directed. There is a feeling that love, affection, sensuality and sex are important factors, and you could have your greatest successes in life in partnership with someone who inspires you both mentally and sexually. You can be devious, hurtful and destructive to others and even to yourself, even to the point of destroying your career or your future chances of success if you feel thwarted. The Moon and the house are both involved with instinctive and reactive behaviour.

Moon in the Ninth House

Religion and philosophy will be an important part of your life, and you will go on some kind of inward journey in order to find your way forward. You think deeply and will turn to a consideration of the deeper things of life. You are a natural psychic with the ability to see and feel beyond the boundaries of this Earth. Travel will be an important part of your life, as will any dealings with foreigners or foreign goods and you may marry a foreigner. You are a natural teacher. You could find yourself attached to slightly crazy people because they are more interesting than ordinary ones.

Moon in the Tenth House

(The Moon's accidental detriment)

This gives you an inner urge to shine before the public in some way, or to help humanity on a grand scale. There is evidence of an emotionally impoverished childhood during which something went wrong. Your parents (especially your mother) could have been super-achievers whom you seek to emulate. You will change jobs a few times until you find the right road for you. Your achievements will lead to acclaim, or if the Moon is badly aspected, to public scandal and ruin. You are drawn to a career that seeks to supply the needs of women or which is traditionally carried out by women. Sales, marketing, domestic goods and women's literature are a few possibilities. Your standing in the community, especially your career standing, is of paramount importance to you and even to others who are around you. You will be known and remembered by many before your life is done. To some extent this is a compensation for insecurity deriving from your difficult childhood, and a somewhat arid personal life.

Moon in the Eleventh House

You enjoy the company of others and could be heavily involved in some kind of club or society. Being extremely independent, you hate to be told what to do. Your family are sometimes left in the dark as to your plans and feelings but there is a possibility that you may find it hard to understand yourself. Your aims in life may change dramatically from time to time due to circumstances. Friends, especially female ones, are very helpful to you, and you have a strange kind of luck that brings them to you in times of trouble. You are well organised and able to manage others, but you can on occasion misjudge people and be taken advantage of by more astute and crafty types.

Moon in the Twelfth House

You seek to hide away from the world from time to time and to work in seclusion. Certainly you are happiest doing your own thing and working from your own home. Women will be an important part of any achievement, while men tend to interfere with your life, particularly with your career. You need to get away from time to time to recharge your batteries because too much stress will make you ill. You could be very creative as you have a rich imagination but you find it hard to bring your ideas into being. Your instinctive need to care for others may lead you to work in the field of nursing, childcare or working with animals. You may be too ready to sacrifice yourself for others. There is a secret side to your life and you may have to keep the secrets of others.

The Progressed Moon

The progressed Moon is an invaluable tool for predicting the future. To find the progressed Moon position, look for your natal Moon's position in the table at the back of this book and make a note of it. Now work out how old you are, and add as many days as there are years in your age. Therefore, if you are now twenty-five years old, add twenty-five days to your date of birth. If you are forty-three years old, add forty-three days to your date of birth. For instance, if you were born on the 3rd of December and you are now 20, your progressed Moon date would be the 23rd of December. Next year it will be the 24th of December, and so on. Now all you have to do, is to look up the table and find the new progressed Moon position. This is very easy to do, but you can choose to visit an astrologer or approach someone who runs a computer chart service and ask for a progressed chart to be made up.

When you have established the position of the Moon for the year in question, check out the progressed Moon information in this book to see what kind of year you are going to have. If you have sufficient astrological knowledge to know what house your progressed Moon is traversing, then use the house information too. Remember, the sign will show the kind of mood or circumstances surrounding you, the house will show what you are doing.

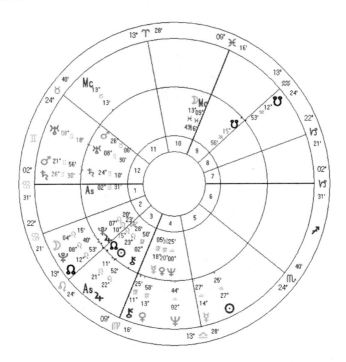

Robert de Niro's natal & progressed chart: January 2009

Robert de Niro's progressed Moon shows that he is about to embark on a busy and eventful phase during 2009, and while some of the experiences will be lovely, others will be much less pleasant. This exciting phase kicks off with a life-changing progression to natal Pluto, followed a month later by a slightly less traumatic one when the Moon crosses progressed Pluto.

The Moon progresses forward at roughly one degree per month. As there are thirty degrees in a sign, you can see that the Moon spends roughly two-and-a-half years going though each sign. It's strange how this two-and-a-half year time scale seems to affect our lives. When I worked as an astrologer, I often heard clients saying that a particular situation, relationship or a job lasted for about two-and-a-half years.

When looking at the progressed Moon, see whether it has just entered a new sign, if it's in the middle of a sign or if it's wending its way to the end of one. Sometimes it takes a while for the effects of the Moon being in a new sign to make an impression, but at other times, the effect kicks in right away. Once you have established the actual degree of the progressed Moon at the time of the reading, then simply move it forward a degree for a month to see what the year ahead will bring. See whether the Moon passes another planet on its journey, or whether it makes an aspect to planets elsewhere in the chart. A typical situation would be if there was a planet at 18 degrees of Scorpio and the Moon reached 18 degrees of Cancer, thus making a pleasant trine aspect between the Moon and the other planet.

Progressed Moon in Aries or the First House

Aries and the first house are symbolically associated with birth and with all that is new and fresh. When this progression is in operation you will find that your emotions seem to take on a life of their own, you feel more passionate in every way, and even the most placid among you will become excited and enthusiastic. Being more moody than usual, you could find yourself involved in a series of family arguments; in fact your home could become something of a battleground that starts to resemble a nest full of egomaniacs. There will be problems with regard to your mother or other older females, and you will have to take extra responsibility for them in some way.

Your energy level is high and you are ready to take advantage of the new opportunities that will begin to present themselves to you now. Even without your intervention, you will find that events move quickly. This is the time when you could find yourself a new and more challenging job or make a start in a business of your own. You will take chances with your money and may borrow money without thinking too deeply about how you will be able to pay it back.

The Moon in astrology often refers to the home, therefore you may move house, relocate yourself in another part of the country, or even move right out of the country and spend a few years in another part of the world. There will be new family groupings resulting from marriage, childbirth or divorce, and if you have been sitting in a marriage that has long been worn out, you will find the courage to do something about leaving. The familiar patterns of your life will change quickly now perhaps of their own volition or with your help. If you have been assessing your potential and making plans while the Moon was in Pisces or in the twelfth house, you will put those plans into action now. You have to guard against losing your temper in the wrong place at this time. Also guard against letting all the new contacts go to waste, or allowing your new enthusiasms to fizzle out. Short-term projects will suit you better than long-term ones, but you will need to find a way of expressing yourself rather than just following other people's leads.

You may realise that your moods are more changeable and your behaviour more impulsive. The Moon, of course, rules the emotional response, therefore, while it travels through Aries or the first house, the Moon's power will be at a peak. Women may be able to blame their sudden attacks of over-sensitiveness on an increase of pre-menstrual tension, men will have to look for another excuse! You may eat and drink more in order to cope with your extra energies. There is a feeling of Arian greediness for all that life has to offer.

The lunar influence could bring you into a closer connection with the sea or with work that involves liquids, there could also be an interest in mechanical and engineering projects. Women will feature in your life now and they may inspire you or encourage you to reach for the stars. Women who have spent years as housewives may go back to work under this influence, while others will give up work and have baby. You will take the initiative, find new methods and forge ahead with your life. Many of you will make an effort to identify and then to satisfy your own needs. Your sexual energies will increase and you may change your outlook and your requirements with regard to sex under this influence. If you meet a new love there will be a strong chemistry between you. If there is a child conceived at this time, it should by all astrological theories be a boy. Another unproven astrological possibility is that Aries-type people may figure strongly in your life at this time.

Progressed Moon in Taurus or the Second House

When the Moon moves into Taurus or the second house your emotions become more settled and comfortable. The projects that were begun in a blaze of enthusiasm while the Moon was in Aries or the first house should be well under way by now. This is a time of consolidation in all things and of steady and controlled growth. Material matters move to the top of your priority list now, so your attention will be firmly focused upon your personal income and your financial base. This would be a good time to buy a decent property, especially if it has some land or a garden. If you aren't buying a new property, you might refurbish the one you're in.

If you have been in the habit of living for the moment you will begin to think ahead, no longer allowing your credit card debts to grow. You will be reluctant to lend your money to just anybody, only making loans to those whom you can trust to pay you back in a prompt and orderly manner. If you are challenged about your newly materialistic attitude you will become defensive and awkward, while at the same time demanding a ten per cent discount! You feel instinctively that this is a good time to put personal savings schemes into operation but a bad time to risk money on nebulous or speculative ventures. If you buy anything expensive it must be durable, and the same goes for projects that are started at this time. When the Moon is travels through an earth sign, the prospects are good for long-term projects. Goods, especially luxurious or artistic ones that are bought at this time, will increase in value and business transactions will be carried out in a spirit of pragmatism rather than of overexcited speculation. You will find yourself dealing with businesswomen, and they could become an important part of your financial or working life. There is a danger that there could be too much emphasis on materialism at the expense of other aspects of your life.

This is a good time to form durable business partnerships, especially with women. You could soon find yourself signing leases on premises or land related to your work, and there will be a strong connection to people in the building trades. Emotional partnerships may be formed now but they will not have the explosive chemistry that they did when the Moon was in Aries or the first house. Relationships that have been recently formed will become deeper and more reliable, while new ones will be based on emotional security and possibly also financial security. Your sexual drive will be strong and all your senses will be heightened because Taurus and the second house are both earthy and sensual in character. You will be far less changeable emotionally and will be possibly less inclined towards sexual experimentation at this time. You will be more interested in settling down than in voyages of exploration. Be careful not to become too set in your ways, as you don't want to bore your partner to death. You will set the patterns for your future life now; certainly you will be reappraising your values and priorities. If you form a new relationship, your partner will be attractive, quiet and reliable.

You might find yourself involved with the production of food, and you will certainly do more shopping. This will be a highly developmental time for all artistic or musical interests and you could learn to appreciate art, dancing or music for the first time. All in all, this should be a peaceful and settled period that you can relax into and enjoy.

Progressed Moon in Gemini or the Third House

This will be a very busy and rather restless year for you. You will be moving around your neighbourhood more than you did in the last progression, and if you haven't learned to drive, this is the time to do so, because you are going to need the freedom of your own transport.

This will also be a year for mental exploration, so you could take courses at your local college or at evening classes. The best subjects might be connected with language, communication or computer studies. All studies, whether they are taken for a specific purpose or just for fun will be successful, and you shouldn't have much trouble in passing examinations. You may need to give more attention to your children's education or to their out-of-school hobbies and interests. You need all your communication skills as your work will involve you in activities such as typing, telephone and customer liaison, probably also in selling and advertising. There will be more than the usual amount of meetings and discussions with colleagues and there could be some kind of brochure or catalogue to be made up. You will travel around visiting different departments at your place of work and you will deal directly with clients either at your location or at theirs. You might take a series of temporary jobs or travel around your area carrying your skills with you. This will be an especially interesting time in your life because you will be meeting new people and will begin to become known outside your immediate circle. One simple example of getting around for commercial purposes would be that of a youngster taking a job delivering newspapers or groceries on a bicycle for a local firm.

You will become more than usually involved with neighbours and also with local issues. Although you might want to redecorate or otherwise change the appearance of your home and your garden, this would not be a particularly good time to make major changes or to make a move of house. There will be more visitors to your home than is normal and you will also spend more time visiting friends and family. Party-plan selling with friends and neighbours is a possibility. Gossip and trivial conversations on the phone are all an important part of your life now and you might find other people affecting your thinking in some fairly profound way.

Your own thought processes are more intuitive and instinctive than usual, and in some cases you could find yourself feeling more nervous and jumpy; however when you focus your mind on work or on studies your concentration will be good. There will be letters and parcels to be sent in the post, also possible are rental agreements and other minor documents to be signed. There will be more than the usual amount of dealings with females, and it's possible that products or services that cater to female requirements or that capture the imagination of women could be important in some way. You will be involved with mechanical and inventive ideas and you will have to learn new methods, so your dexterity will increase now. If you have been away from work for some time, you will return now.

This is not a particularly romantic time, but if you become involved with someone new, you will find that conversation and greater understanding are the keynotes to the relationship. If you are experimenting socially or sexually at this time it would be best if you didn't commit yourself too firmly to one person as your heart will be a little fickle. Romance will involve outings to restaurants, theatres and other local events, and even to sporting events. You should become involved in some kind of sport or hobby, which gives you an outlet that helps you to contend with your restlessness. You will tend to over-analyse and intellectualise your feelings.

Progressed Moon in Cancer or the Fourth House

The Moon rules the sign of Cancer, therefore when it travels through this sign or through the fourth house, one's lunar characteristics will make themselves strongly felt. This may make you more moody, emotional and 'Cancerian' or it may emphasise your own natal lunar position. Regardless of your basic nature and outlook on life, you will act and react in a far more emotional manner and will become more interested in the private and personal aspects of your life.

Your home circumstances are going to play a major part in your life this year, and this may include a move of house, building work to be done, decorating or buying new furniture and fittings. The definite domestic slant to this progression will temporarily anchor you firmly to your home and family. You will take on more responsibility for relatives, and this could be a source of irritation or a great comfort to you depending upon the prevailing circumstances. There will be more dealings with your mother and with other female friends and relatives, especially those who are older than yourself. Feelings of family loyalty will strengthen, and you might spend some time researching your family history and background. There will be a need to identify with a specific group on the basis of family, race, religion or nationality and you will experience some kind of patriotic or group identity.

You may need to retreat from the outside world and to sink back into comfort and security, having little desire to meet new people and preferring to stay close to reliable old friends. You will want some novelty in your life, but this will come in the form of new domestic interests or learning how to use new gadgets in and around the house. You could work from home at this time or even start a small business from your own back room. The sign of Cancer is associated with shops; therefore you may take a job in one or even open a shop of your own. Whatever sex you are, you will be more concerned with daily chores than you have been in recent years, and the reason for this could range from retirement to setting up a family. Antiques are associated with the sign of Cancer, also history and genealogy, therefore you could find yourself delving into the past for a while or even searching for your roots. You will be over-sensitive, especially over family issues and you could even become unaccountably possessive towards those around you. You may feel alienated, neglected and superfluous, so your moods could vacillate between wanting to be alone and fearing loneliness.

Friends could cling to you now or you could cling to them, and old friends that you haven't seen for years could suddenly come back into your life now. Some of you could start to work with liquids. The sea could prove to be a pull, urging you to live and work on or near it. Travel on or over water will be especially pleasant at this time. Cancerian-type people may influence you at this time and, due to the active femininity of the sign, a child conceived now should, by all accounts, be female.

This time is a time of gradual change where you spend time looking inside yourself and revising your needs and attitudes. Old habits could now be seen as being inappropriate to your present and future way of life.

Progressed Moon in Leo or the Fifth House

During this progression you will be dealing with children and young people. This is often the time when a mother is at the height of her involvement with a growing family. Whoever you are, you will enjoy a more youthful attitude possibly joining in sporting activities and youthful pastimes. Interestingly, when my daughter's progressed Moon moved into Leo, she got a job in a firm that makes jigsaw puzzles and children's board games!

The sign of Leo (and the fifth house) is concerned with creativity; therefore you will embark upon projects that are close to your heart. You should develop the ideas and the determination at this time to make something of yourself and to create something which will stand the test of time, but you might have to wait until the Moon progresses into Virgo before you gain the ability to focus your attention and to get on with the job.

Travel will be important now but it might prove something of a trial to you, as you may have to cart restless and difficult children around with you. Another possibility is that of business travel, which is often less glamourous than it seems. However, this sign is associated with leisure, pleasure and time off, so travel for fun and relaxation is also possible.

There might be some connection with work in a glamourous field, so you may join some branch of show business. You might take up attractive or amusing hobbies now, skating and dancing are possibilities, also light and interesting sports. This is a good time to give attention to your personal appearance, to keep your figure trim and be prepared to go out and knock 'em in the aisles, because it's going to be important for you to look good. This may be the time when you emerge from your shell and find yourself in the limelight; it's even possible that after years of being held back you find yourself breaking out with a vengeance. You may even become the stronger partner in a relationship after years of having been kept down. This is definitely not going to be the time to keep your light under a bushel but to discover the power of your own personality and to enjoy expressing it.

Your feelings will rise to the surface and will be hard to hide and they may even be difficult to control. All your relationships and friendships will be re-evaluated and some changes may be made soon. You could become more aware of and more wrapped up with your own feelings. Sexual feelings will also be high and there might be an affair of the heart (or body) now. None of this may last too long but you will learn a lot about yourself, other people and life generally. You may sometimes appear to be wasting time and energy on frivolities, but this will all be part of the learning process.

The sign of Leo (and the fifth house) is associated with children and you will find yourself dealing with and enjoying the company of children. You might help out the local boy scouts or girl guides, become involved in the activities of the local dancing school or in some other way find yourself in charge of children. You may start your own family now or you may find yourself responsible for someone else's children.

All dealings with women will be good, your mood will be generous and happy a good deal of the time and you might gamble a little, either literally or figuratively as this can be a time of great gains, but also there may be surprising losses.

Progressed Moon in Virgo or the Sixth House

Work will be important to you now, and you could find that either your normal job becomes more interesting or that you begin to do something new and highly satisfying. You will have to cope with paperwork, bookkeeping, correspondence and record keeping; computers and word processors might become an important feature of your life now. You will perform precise and delicate tasks whilst analysing and checking your own work carefully, and these jobs could include do-it-yourself work, home dressmaking or gardening. You might take a course at your local evening classes. If you do take lessons, these would be in useful and practical subjects such as car maintenance or cookery. Whoever you are, you will be dealing with household chores and, if you aren't skilled at these types of job, you will soon learn the ropes. If gardening becomes important now, you will concentrate on producing fruit and vegetables.

You will fall into a sensible routine of work this year and may find yourself following a strict set of directions. This is the time to establish good work habits and you will find reliable and efficient colleagues to work alongside at this time. Women may pose problems on the one hand but they can turn out to be of great benefit as well, perhaps one group of women will give you trouble while another will help enormously. All this talk of duty and effort may seem a bit dull, but the resulting rewards will make it all worthwhile. This is not, strictly speaking, a great time for creative pursuits but writing would work out well, especially if it involves specialised research and analysis.

You may become involved with hospitals now, either because you yourself need treatment or people close to you may be sick. It's possible that you could work in a hospital at this time, but either way, you will take more notice of your own state of health and will try to improve it in any way that you can. You may become interested in alternative or complementary therapies now. You will concentrate on your diet and appearance and could even go a bit overboard by becoming too clean and tidy or by developing hypochondria. There will be some irritating nervous ailments to put up with which, although not dangerous, could make life difficult at times.

Your behaviour under this progression might irritate others, as you will try to over-rationalise or over-analyse everything. You must guard against playing the martyr, taking on unnecessary chores and then moaning to everyone about this. Guilty feelings will plague you even though you really have nothing to feel guilty about. You must make time to rest and enjoy life because you will be ill if you don't.

This is hardly the best progression for romance but it's possible that you could meet someone special through your work. Relationships that are formed under this progression should be steady and relatively trouble free, if rather dull. On a brighter note, this is a great time to buy new clothes; perhaps this is a consolation prize result of all that hard work.

Progressed Moon in Libra or the Seventh House

Partnerships and relationships are going to be of paramount importance to you this year. Whether you are at the dating stage or even contemplating the end of your present partnership, new relationships made will have an air of freshness and a strangely experimental feel about them. It appears that you will be searching around for the right person rather than making a serious commitment. This doesn't mean that you won't settle down with your current date, just that you need to keep your options open now. Not all your relationships will be pleasant as there could be some major confrontations especially with women at this time. The seventh house (and the sign of Libra) are supposed to represent one's first marriage, but I have found this progression to be more concerned with forming and breaking relationships of all kinds.

Your emotions will be strong at this time that will cause you to overreact, so you will find it particularly hard to be detached and objective. You may require both security and freedom at the same time, wanting your partner to be faithful while you yourself slip off the leash. There will be an element of sexual exploration and experimentation.

You should become drawn into the world of business, and if you have no business knowledge, you will have to acquire it quickly. The communications side of business will be important, and you will need to keep in touch with current ideas and methods. Although you will not necessarily be directly responsible for the sale of goods and services, you will have to deal with marketing and public relations, which means finding ways to advertise and to present your organisation's image in an attractive and modern manner. There will be a good deal of interaction with other business people and also with the general public. Libra is a cardinal sign (the seventh house is a cardinal house) therefore, you will be much more decisive and dynamic now than ever before. You will have to present yourself in a stylish way in front of others, therefore your appearance and manner of dress will become more modern and interesting now.

There will be interesting new beginnings and new working relationships in which you meet inspiring and dynamic people. You will spend far more time in cities than in the countryside but you will probably see something of the countryside as you travel through it on business. Your self-esteem will take a few knocks, mainly due to the fact that you will be working in an unfamiliar field and you will inevitably make errors.

There is some evidence that you will find others trying to manipulate you and you may react angrily when you discover what is going on. On the other hand, people could validate and value you, thus boosting your self-esteem. In the areas of both your work and in your domestic life you could find that your finances and your financial decisions are inevitably wrapped up with your emotions.

Progressed Moon in Scorpio or the Eighth House

You will make the changes that will set the pattern of your life for many years to come. If you have been experimenting with friendships and relationships during the past couple of years, you may settle into marriage now. However, on the other hand, if you have been travelling towards a potential divorce, this is when you might bring it about. There will be major beginnings and endings that might include setting up a home or dismantling one. You could start a family now or find yourself at the stage when your children are leaving the nest. Your children may soon start their own families, or there may be births around you in other branches of your family or among your friends. Unfortunately, there could well be a funeral or two to attend as well.

You will either make a fresh commitment to your present job or make a change for one that will stand you in good stead in the future. A young woman may give up work for a couple of years in order to stay at home with children. Whichever way this progression works for you it will mean transformation, rebirth and a redefinition of your goals both within and outside the home. You may become interested in conservation and recycling. You will spend money on your surroundings now.

Work changes could take you into the farming or food production industries. Another possibility is some kind of professional contact with the police, private detectives or hospitals. Health or legal matters might enter your private life too. You will be more aware of the mystical and psychic elements of life and you might have some kind of psychic experience, possibly for the first time in your life. This progression will make your intuition and hunches strong and you might even go as far as to develop mediumistic qualities.

Financial matters that involve other people's money will become important now also their attitude to financial matters. This could include alimony, legacies, mortgages, taxes, joint accounts and business finances. You must guard against too great an emotional response to legal and financial matters. Joint properties and joint possessions can be sorted out at this time, but you must guard against feelings of greed and covetousness. There may be family or business wrangles, especially over property. These problems would be typical of a divorce, the ending of a business partnership or after a death in the family. The structure of your life will be transformed in some way.

Some activities will be deeply satisfying, and these could fulfil a variety of instinctual needs. These could include almost anything that makes you happy but I would have to put sex pretty high on the list, along with settling into a happy home or a more comfortable way of life. New habits will be formed, probably resulting from a new understanding of your inner needs. Your instinctive side will overshadow your logical mind and you could experience an almost compulsive pursuit of your objectives.

There are some mighty awful problems that could emerge under this progression, and the intensity of your intense feelings could spill over into jealousy and passion of a particularly lustful or obsessive kind. You could become trapped or manipulated into a situation that under normal circumstances you would avoid, or conversely you may seek to possess or manipulate another. The abnormal over-emotional response will take some living with and it could cause you to act in a manner that is totally out of character. This would be the right time to delve into the bottom of a long-standing mess and finally sort out the reasons for it, even if it means bringing a few skeletons out of the cupboard. You might feel as if you are in an emotional mincing machine now but you will emerge at the end of it as if reborn, salvaged from destruction.

Progressed Moon in Sagittarius or the Ninth House

The key idea behind this progression is the expansion of your personal horizons. You might travel overseas for the first time or you could take the time to really investigate a particular part of the world that you have always fancied visiting. Your work could take you away and you might enter into a business venture that involves overseas goods, services or property. You may have to sell to foreigners, thereby learning about them and their way of living. Your family may move to another country or there may be people entering the family who are from a different cultural background and this could be the cause of some of your long distance journeys. Some of you will fall in love with a person who comes from a different country or a different cultural background now and this may cause you to review your own religious or philosophical outlook.

You may be subjected to economic or cultural changes in conditions around you that affect your private or your business life. There is even a chance that you will have to deal with people whose views are biased or even bigoted regarding race and religion.

There might be increased dealings with institutions such as schools, colleges and churches either personally or as a matter of business. You could go back into training or just study for fun at this time. The subjects you choose will be philosophical or mind broadening rather than purely practical, but you may learn a foreign language as a means of meeting a larger range of interesting people or in order to progress in your career. You will find ways to overcome mental stagnation and boredom at this time. School connections may take you into teaching or training others and you may have to give lectures on a special subject. You may go into publishing or you may use the Internet to broadcast information. You could soon create brochures or trade journals for your company.

There is a feeling that the end of a phase in your working life is on the way now and you could finish this progression with a determination to do something quite different. This may be a high point, a culmination of all that you have worked for; alternatively, you may reach the bottom of a pit of unhappiness with regard to your work and decide to change direction for good and all.

You should be able to enjoy life and have some fun. The chances are that you will become enthusiastic about a number of new ideas, hobbies and pastimes, and sports could be high on the list. There will be more chance for you to get out into the fresh air, and you may become interested in the world of large animals, especially horses. Gambling on horses is a possibility, or just taking a chance or two on life. This should be a time of increased fun and a sense of adventure. Your level of confidence will be high, maybe too high, but this might just begin to wane as the progression moves towards the cusp of the tenth house.

Sometimes there is an increase of activity concerning legal matters under this progression, but it's usually the tail end of outstanding problems rather than new ones rearing their heads. This may be a detail or two that is still hanging on from a recent divorce settlement, or some kind of family or business matter that has still to be put to rest. Sagittarius and the ninth house is concerned with second marriages, therefore this may be the time when you meet a second partner or when you decide to marry for the second time.

Progressed Moon in Capricorn or the Tenth House

This is a time of hard work but also of ultimate achievement. This progression may start with a monumental setback in your life or just a feeling that you cannot go on any longer in the same old way. The chances are that the frustrations and the problems that are affecting your working life will spill over into your personal life as well. You will receive a great deal of useful help from others at work now. Those who help you may be in positions of seniority or they may be equipped with some kind of specialised knowledge that they are willing to pass on to you. If you are selling a product or a service, buyers will be more receptive now, and one interesting point is that women are likely to be particularly helpful to you.

You will want to make improvements in your techniques and methods, and if you aren't used to working in a structured organisation, you will learn how to do so. Alternatively, you might go from one sort of structure to a completely different one that runs by a different set of rules. It's important that you are honest in all your dealings, whether they are in your working or your private life and you should find yourself among decent and honest people. You will need to be seen as being respectable both in your public and family life as this is a time when secrets and deceptions might emerge in an uncomfortably embarrassing way.

Your work will bring you into contact with the public and you will perform services for people both individually and in large groups. You will need to dress the part of a successful and competent person, as both you and your work will be highly visible at this time. Sales and promotional work will be important and you will have to make public appearances, possibly even give lectures or make speeches from time to time.

Colleagues will be more sympathetic to your aims than before and you, in turn, will be more responsive to the needs of others. It's possible that you could be temporarily short of money, maybe because you are investing fairly heavily in a project or because your job offers training and future possibilities rather than present financial rewards.

You will take a sensitive attitude towards those you work with and will be careful not to tread on their egos. There will be responsibility now attached to the work that you do and you may well also be responsible for the efforts of others. This is the time to build a team of juniors or a sensible framework of method and experience that will follow you into the future. Delays and setbacks in your career will be followed by success, and good things will come out of bad ones. Your work will need a conventional attitude and old-fashioned skills and there will be the need for a structured and practical outlook. You may find yourself reviving the spirits of a flagging company or institution, which will require you to be responsive to the moods and feelings of groups around you, possibly in the form of union negotiations. Time keeping will be important, either in the form of working hours or of timetables of one sort or another.

Your professional and personal relationships may become a bit blurred as you could turn towards someone who you work closely with or alternatively, you could begin a work project with someone you love. This is not, truthfully speaking, a romantic time. Your feelings may be dampened or you may be forced to keep them on a tight rein. However, if you do meet someone, it's likely that this will happen through your work.

In personal relationships you will be shyer than usual and also very slow to commit yourself. There may be some strangely public displays of emotion either directed towards you or coming from you. Angry scenes could take place where others can see and hear or feelings of loving and caring which you have been keeping dark might also emerge in a somewhat public manner. Domestic life will have to take a back seat now but the work that you are doing will go to make the domestic scene nicer and more comfortable later on.

Progressed Moon in Aquarius or the Eleventh House

This is a time when friends will be extremely important to you, you will have to rely on them to help you and you will in turn, be a good friend to others. There will be an involvement with clubs and societies, and you will definitely feel the need to become part of a group. This group identity may be political or work related. There may be spare time activities with a sports team, people who are interested in artistic pursuits or some kind of intellectual grouping. You will make achievements as part of a group or a team. At work, you will have to work in co-operation with, and possibly in charge of, others; you cannot achieve much on your own now.

Friendships with women will be important and you will become slightly less attached to your family, finding that your time and attention is diverted by outside considerations. Even in the realm of friendships there will be changes as you move on to newer, more dynamic or influential people. Both you and your associates could try to achieve something that would be of benefit to humanity. Your attitude will be idealistic but possibly rather impractical at times. It would be wise to guard against being drawn into specific and fixed ideologies that don't leave room for differences of opinion.

It will be necessary for you to learn new methods that arise from your work or as a result of a change in your way of life. If, for instance, you were to move house at this time, you would have to get to grips with decorating or making a garden even though you have never done these things before. You may learn to sew, drive a car or bring your work skills up to date. If you have school-aged children, you will be dealing with educational matters on their behalf and you may be drawn into some of their school activities. It's possible that you could return to college or even become a teacher yourself. Retirement at this time would give you an opportunity to learn new skills or take up new hobbies. You may have to deal with very modern methods and computer techniques.

You will redefine your personal goals and ask yourself what you want out of life in general terms. By investigating your own hopes and wishes you will change the direction of your thinking in some radical way. One instance may be a person who has thus far, never wanted children deciding that he or she wants them after all, another person who had always been lazy might suddenly become ambitious. New goals and values will replace outworn ones now.

There can be a surprisingly disruptive element in this progression that could change your outlook or your life completely. You might re-emerge soon with a new career. You will almost certainly have a new home soon, possibly even with a new set of personal relationships. This is the time when you revolutionise your own life or that you find that it's being revolutionised for you by bringing a complete breakdown in your present status quo.

If someone else wants to move on and leave you behind, you will learn about feelings of rage, jealousy and rejection. You may react by becoming possessive in an attempt to hang on too tightly. What happens depends upon your circumstances at the time of entering the progression and your particular way of handling change.

If you went through difficult times during the previous progression through this house or sign, you will find this a surprisingly good progression this time round. Money will come your way, gambles come off and your dreams begin to come true. There is no doubt that this is a phase where anything could happen - and it frequently does. Try to keep a strong grip on reality as events around you might become tinged with fantasy or even a subtle form of lunacy. Remember to keep in touch with friends, as they will help you through both good times and bad ones.

Progressed Moon in Pisces or the Twelfth House

This will be a time of reflection, possibly even a time of retreat from the hurly-burly of life. Events seem to be in the hands of fate, and there doesn't seem to be much you can do about it. You may have to suppress your own personality for a while, possibly until your progressed Moon crosses over the Ascendant into Aries. In addition to having to keep a good many of your feelings under wraps, there could be work projects carried on in secret. One example might be of preparing to set up a small business of your own while still carrying on at your usual job. There may, of course, be a secret relationship going on, such as keeping in touch with a 'black sheep' relative that the rest of the family ignores. This progression may mark a sad and depressing time, as you seem to be working through some kind of karmic programme. The outcome will be a change in your consciousness leading to a renewal of life and hope, plus a completely new direction.

It's important to keep some kind of hold on reality during this progression, as it would be only too easy to slip into a strange state of mental limbo. Some aspect of your life will be insecure, probably on the emotional level, and you may find it hard to face the facts that confront you. It would be easy to slide into a state of disillusion or even despair worse still; you could try to chase illusion, exacerbating the situation by the use of drugs and drink. It would be best to keep away from opiates at this time, especially sleeping pills.

There is a much more positive side to all this and it's the opportunity for you to learn how to relax, meditate and travel on a series of inward journeys. One way or another, you will be spending much more time alone than you have before and while you are looking inwards, you may discover talents and abilities which you never knew you possessed. The benefits of this progression tend to be recognised only in retrospect. Artistic and creative abilities will come to the fore, but you should be able to enjoy quiet pleasures like reading, listening to the radio and gardening. Photography, filmmaking and art or music is possible too.

If you are naturally rather moody, this aspect of your personality will be accentuated but you may find yourself on the receiving end of someone else's moodiness at this time. Your intuitive abilities will develop and you should follow any instincts that you feel. Being more sensitive and shyer than usual, you may find others strangely difficult or even unsympathetic to your needs and wants. It's possible that psychic or mediumistic abilities will become noticeable now and you might begin to take a serious interest in these subjects. There could even be a revelation, a kind of 'gateway that thrusts you forward into spirituality.

Typical Piscean or twelfth house circumstances would be that of a young woman finding herself at home with small children at the very time when her husband is having to make the maximum effort at his job and therefore, is being less supportive than before. Another reason might be the beginning of retirement with its inevitable change of perspective. One unfortunate reason for this situation might be a period of illness, or possibly of having to take care of somebody else who becomes ill or incapacitated. There may well be a connection with hospitals, even mental institutions or prisons at this time, either because you yourself are directly involved or through those close to you. You could even find yourself working in one of these places. You will have an uncanny ability to link with the moods of others and to give real help and understanding to those who need it.

One of the nicer possibilities is of travel. There maybe a move or a drift towards water for you now and, depending upon circumstances you could buy property by the sea, rent a holiday villa on the coast or become involved in the world of boats. Some people go cruising when the Moon is in Pisces.

If you are working, you will be better off as a backroom boy now than out in front. You may find it hard to trust others either in your private or your working life. Relations with women could be particularly difficult or even peculiar now, and you may have to face a change in perspective regarding the women in your life at this time, probably due to factors that are outside your control. An easy way to grasp the idea behind this progression is to think of a seed spending the winter lying in the soil waiting to come to life in the spring.

Strange and subconscious forces affect your moods as the axis of your previous way of life subtly shifts. This is truly a time to recharge your inner forces by retreat and reflection in readiness for the 'first house breakout' which will surely, surely come.

Other Predictive Techniques

Transits

The first predictive technique that anybody who gets into even the most basic forms of astrology learns is transits. This method is used in newspaper astrology and in every normal type of astrological reading. While progressions uses a day-for-a-year technique, transits mean finding the current location of any planet, noting the sign and house it occupies and seeing whether it's making an aspect to any other planet. Although astrologers do this by looking at charts on computer screens or in an ephemeris (book of tables), you can go outside and do this by looking at the sky This is because we are dealing with the actual planets in the actual sky, rather than just a mathematical calculation.

The following illustration shows a natal chart on the inner ring and the transits on the outer ring.

It's always worth seeing whether a planet is making a transit to the Moon, as it has such a powerful effect on so many areas of one's life. For instance, I recently spent a few weeks feeling quite depressed for no reason that I could account for, and I eventually took the sensible step of looking at the transits. I saw immediately that Saturn was sitting opposite my Moon and that it had been doing so for several weeks. Nothing terrible was happening, but life was dull, the weather was awful, I had too much work to do and I was tired.

The Moon moves so quickly that its transits are not normally worth bothering with, but there are times when they are. If you have some important date or event looming, it's worth looking at the transits, and especially the position of the Moon beforehand, as that can give you some idea as to the likely outcome.

There is a closely related form of astrology, called 'electional astrology' because it involves electing (selecting) the best time to do something. For instance, Jan and I look at all the transits, including the position of Moon, before we submit a book to the printers. If the situation doesn't look good, we'll wait a day or two until it's better.

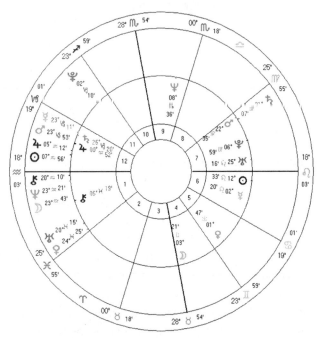

**Natal & Transit chart of
USA President Barack Obama,
just after his Inauguration**

Combining Methods

Professional quality astrology software allows the astrologer to make up a triple chart that has the natal chart in the centre, the progressed chart surrounding it and the transiting chart on the outer rim. This allows an astrologer to look at the transits and progressions in one go, but the very quantity of information on the page can make it hard to handle.

Void of Course Moon

There are some astrologers who won't make a decision or do anything when the Moon is 'Void of Course'. The word 'Void' in this situation means empty, and the word 'Course' refers to the track or orbit of the Moon.

A 'Void of Course' Moon means that the Moon cannot make an aspect to another planet (using zero orbs) before leaving the sign that it's moving through. The following example shows all the planets, apart from the Moon, below 25 degrees. Thus, the Moon will be Void of Course for the next few hours

Many astrologers won't agree to anything or do anything important until the Void of Course period has passed.

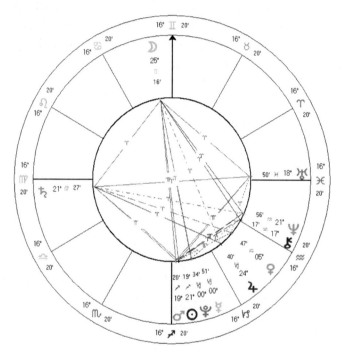

Void of Course Moon

Solar and Lunar Returns

A solar return chart is made up for the moment when the Sun returns to the exact point that it was in when a person was born, which happens once a year. Every time we wish someone 'many happy returns' on their birthday, it's the solar return that we are unwittingly referring to!

Naturally, a solar return can refer to any kind of anniversary.

Not all astrologers use solar returns, and even fewer use lunar returns, after all they are nothing more than a picture of the transits at the particular moment in time. I find that they give a sense of the atmosphere at the time in question, and that can sometimes be useful. I don't usually look too deeply into these return charts, but a quick glance will show the rising sign, and thus the emphasis of the year or month in question. For instance, if the Ascendant was in Aries, with Mars rising in the first house, I would surmise that the subject of the chart would have a fight on his or her hands during the coming period.

Even a quick scan will show the house that the Sun or Moon or other significant planets occupy and whether they are being afflicted by nasty aspects or helped by nice ones. It's worth checking out the position and aspects to and from the planet that is associated with the Ascendant. For instance, if the solar or lunar return rising sign is Taurus, it's worth seeing what Venus is up to.

My friend Jon Dee says that in his experience, the events shown in a lunar return chart won't necessarily kick in at the start of the lunar month, but often only when the month is three-quarters of the way through.

Moon and Planet Conjunctions

A lunar transit will only last a day or so, but a lunar progression will last for a few weeks. The effects will be felt before the Moon reaches the planet and perhaps for a little while after it has passed by. When the Moon approaches a planet or object, it makes an 'applying' aspect, then it becomes 'exact' and finally a 'separating' aspect. Professional software expresses these as 'A', 'X' and 'S'.

Moon/Sun Conjunction
There may be events concerning children, also this is a time of increased self-confidence or even of personal triumph. Fun, holidays, speculation, games, sports, will become part of your life now. You could fall in love with an exciting person and have an affair to remember. There is a possibility that you may buy yourself a holiday home, a house in the sun. There should be some good times with older relatives now. You might find yourself dealing with more than the usual number of Leo type people at this time.

Moon/Moon Conjunction
Domestic matters come to the fore, there could even be a move of house or you may take out a lease on business premises. Travel is a possibility especially over or near water and you may revisit the place of your birth. There will be some special dealings with females, especially mother figures. Your emotions will be stronger now. There could be a connection with the provision of food or domestic goods. Things that have been kept secret may suddenly be revealed. You may have more dealings with Cancerian people now.

Moon/Mercury Conjunction

Communications with the family characterise this progression. There may be documents to be dealt with in connection with property and premises. There could be a new vehicle for you now or you may simply change your method of daily commuting. Paperwork will be important. Any educational courses undertaken now will go well, exams can be passed at this time, as can the driving test. There should be friendly dealings with neighbours, friends and relatives of your own generation or a bit younger. You could take up a new sporting interest in company with others. Groups of friends may begin to meet in your home. You will begin to think about diet and food values and could make plans to alter the appearance of your home. There may also be a rethink about your methods of working and improvements in the methods you use. You may begin to write for publication. You may have more than the usual amount of dealings with Gemini or Virgo people now.

Moon/Venus Conjunction

Family affairs come to the fore; you will get on well with the women of the family. There could be public relations involving women, or even a business partnership with a woman. This is a good time to decorate the house or to have a celebration in the home. Food and catering, diet and appearance will occupy you now. There could be a new romance; certainly you will begin to feel more attractive and more romantic. There may be some involvement with artists and with artistic work at this time. There will be an increase in business opportunities and good new contacts. You may find yourself dealing with more than the usual number of Taurus or Libra people now.

Moon/Mars Conjunction

You will experience a high level of energy and drive, and you could develop sudden enthusiasms for work projects or energetic hobbies. There will be some kind of fresh start now. There could be a working partnership with a young man and you will have a more energetic and youthful attitude to work matters. If you are in a competitive field or are playing in competitive sports you should be able to win. Your ambition level will be high and opportunities will suddenly come your way. This is not a great time for dealing with women and you will have to watch your temper now, as all your feelings will run high. You may become ill, feverish or even have an accident (especially in the home). If you change vehicles now, the new one will go faster than the previous one did. Your sex drive will be high but you could also fight over emotional and sexual matters. For women, this transit is almost bound to bring a man into your life; probably young, certainly sexy and energetic. You could be dealing with more than the usual number of Aries or Scorpio people now.

Moon/Jupiter Conjunction

You might rethink your religious and philosophical views now. There will be an interest in travel and dealings with foreigners, possibly in connection with work. There is a feeling of optimism and change for the better although it may not be apparent immediately. You will make new and useful contacts and could have unexpected opportunities at work. Money should become easier to find and doors will open for you. There might be an involvement with legal matters at this time and, if so, you will come out on the winning side, especially if property is involved. This is a good time to deal with women in regard to financial matters, also to invest in property. Domestic matters should go well and you will be given the opportunity to expand your horizons and even to look at yourself in a new way. You may be involved with more than the usual number of Sagittarius or Pisces people now.

Moon/Saturn Conjunction

There will be problems that may relate to your home situation, your parents or other elderly relatives. You could feel depressed and rather lonely, even though you are surrounded by people. You will have extra responsibilities with very little time to rest and, apart from feeling downhearted, you might actually be ill, or just over-tired and run down. Life will feel restricted and rather boring at this time and your love life may also be depressing, it's possible that your loved one is living or working at some distance from you at the moment. Business matters will go slowly, but plans made now will work out well in the long run. Dealings with people in positions of responsibility or with older people may be awkward but should work out well after the progression has passed. There could be the need to make far-reaching decisions with regard to your parents. Money may be short, especially in the home but that will also improve soon. A good time to do some long-range thinking and to chat to knowledgeable and responsible people about your plans for the future. You may meet more than the usual number of Capricorn or Aquarius people now.

Moon/Uranus Conjunction

Sudden changes in mood characterise this progression. This is one of those times when you will suddenly realise that you can no longer bear the job you're in or the person you are living with. This is the kind of situation that brews up slowly, possibly for years beforehand, and then, apparently all of a sudden, changes for good. You may make an unexpected change of house or suddenly decide to tear down and rebuild some part of your home; there could be unexpected family problems or sudden changes with the home set-up. Friends will be more in evidence at this time. You could have some brilliant ideas or you may find answers to questions that have been bothering you for ages. Working life could bring unexpected changes and benefits, almost anything could happen and you will have to study the signs and the houses involved in order to work out all the possibilities. You might even take up astrology! You should have more than the usual number of dealings with Aquarian people at this time.

Moon/Neptune Conjunction

If you fall in love now you will see your loved one through rose-coloured glasses. There will be a strong element of fantasy in any love affair at this time, therefore you could do most of your loving at a distance or even confine it to the inside of your own head. Old half-buried memories will come back to haunt you, and you could find yourself dealing with ancient fears and phobias, possibly facing up to them at last. There will be an increase in your intuition and you could have some interesting psychic experiences. You will be re-examining your philosophical views and religious outlook and could even go so far as to change your religion. You may spend much time daydreaming or you may go in for some inspired forms of meditation. You will feel atmospheres acutely and could well develop clairvoyant and precognitive abilities.

Business matters could become confusing and you might find out that you have been dealing with dishonest people. You may have some great ideas but will have to wait until the progression has passed before putting them into practice. There may be travel to the sea or over it for you, and there should be renewed contact with family and friends overseas. You may rearrange the method of water supply in your home or you may become interested in or work with fluids, gasses, oil and photography. There could be increased contacts with mystical people, those born under the sign of Pisces or who have strongly Piscean birthcharts. Love affairs could be wonderful, inspired or they could really screw you up but you will definitely be awash with emotion and hardly able to think straight. You might be involved with hospitals especially in connection with family members. There may be work in a hospital or institution for you at this time. You may develop a taste for alcohol or develop strange allergic ailments.

Moon/Pluto Conjunction

This is a transforming progression that could change your whole life, and it will certainly change your outlook on life and your view of yourself. You will be emotionally wrought up, possibly because you are coping with some pretty monumental problems. There will be financial matters to sort out and these may stem from a previous divorce, a legacy or some kind of outstanding tax problem. There could be outstanding business finances to sort out and even liquidation is a possibility. You will want to alter a bad family situation and perhaps clear the air with a really terrific argument. You could even walk out for good. There may be dealings with the police, the courts or hospitals, and the matters that are involved could be quite serious. There may be births and deaths around you now, certainly there will be figurative ones. There is even the possibility that your life could be affected by geological upheavals or by war! There could be a connection with mines and miners or explosives. There may be some rather strange occult and psychic experiences. Any kind of subterranean rumblings of discontent that have been going on in your life could erupt explosively now.

Moon/Chiron Conjunction

When the progressed Moon conjuncts Chiron, a major healing process is set in motion. You probably instigate this by making decisions to change your life for the better, but things can happen of their own accord that also bring changes for the better.

This is not an easy time to live through though, because the run up to it is reminiscent of an increase of heat and pressure inside a volcano, and when the Moon meets Chiron, the volcano explodes. This may affect any area of life, but let's say that your adult child's behaviour has become increasingly destructive, and you now reach a point where you say enough is enough and refuse to bail them out any more.

Other scenarios might be the end of a bad marriage, leaving a rotten job, moving to a new area or even a move to a new country. You may dump a friendship that has always been based on you doing all the giving, or you may have a much-needed operation. You may even have a wakeup call that makes you change your own behaviour for the better.

Whatever the scenario, the problem comes to a head, and that brings it to a close. The doors of opportunity may open for you, causing you to consider whether you want to continue with you life as it is, or throw caution to the wind and go with the flow, even though it means leaving other people and places behind. The result will definitely be to your benefit.

Chiron rules wounds, and while these might be painful psychological wounds that have been left over from the past, this conjunction can also refer to actual wounds, such as those caused by an accident or an operation. Take very good care of your health at this time and get all the medical attention and advice that you need.

Moon/Ascendant Conjunction

This is a time of new beginnings as the Moon moves from the twelfth house to the first. You will want to come out of the shadows and be noticed. Your personal and domestic affairs will change for the better now although it might be uncomfortable while this progression is in operation. You will probably change your appearance and your attitudes soon.

Moon/Midheaven Conjunction

This is the culmination of a phase of your life. You should feel that you have reached as far as you can in your present job and now want to change direction. You could become more involved with the public or find that your status and public image is improving. You may achieve some long-cherished dream regarding your career. Domestic matters will go well, and if you move house, you will make money on the deal and will like your new home. Domestic matters will influence your professional life either indirectly, via changes in your home and family arrangements or directly, as a result of working in industries related to food and household goods. A woman may influence your thinking in regard to your objectives in life.

Moon/IC Conjunction

This could bring you closer to your family, especially your mother, and will bring you closer to your home. You may begin to work from home now. Any lingering emotional or relationship problem in the home can be sorted out for good now. You will be drawn to the past and you may meet up with people from your past, or sort out some issue that stems from the past.

Moon and the Nodes
When the Moon crosses the nodes, you may move, redecorate, have interesting visitors or go on holiday to a completely different place than the one you usually visit. You make take up some special project in the home or start working from home. You could re-appraise your direction in life now. You may have some kind of Karmic experience at this time.

Moon Phases

When you were born, the Moon may have been in the first, second, third or fourth quarter. Fortunately, if you have your birth chart to hand, this is very easy to work out - even for an absolute non-astrologer, as you will see in a minute. Start by photocopying or sketching the illustration below.

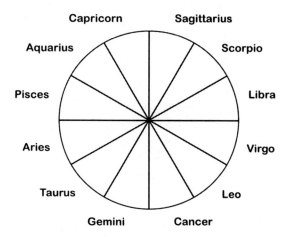

Now, write the Sun symbol in the segment for your Sun sign, and the Moon symbol in the segment that your Moon occupies.

The following example is for a person born with the Sun and Moon close together in Aries, in the first House. This is a birth at the time of a New Moon, and the aspect is called a Conjunction.

Remember that what we are looking at in this chapter is only the relationship between the Sun and Moon - not the Sign or House they occupy.

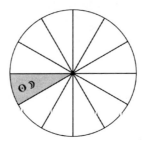

Here are the typical Sun and Moon symbols:

Sun: ☉

Moon: ☽

If the Moon is to the right of the Sun, but less than 90 degrees from it, it will be in the first quarter. At 90 degrees, it's in Square aspect.

1st Quarter

If it's between 90 degrees and 180 degrees, it's in the second quarter. At 180 degrees it's Full, and in Opposition:

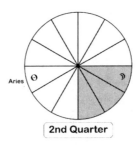

2nd Quarter

If between 180 degrees and 270 degrees, it's in its third quarter. At 270 degrees, the planets are again, in Square aspect:

3rd Quarter

If between 270 degrees and 360 degrees, it's in its fourth quarter. At 360 degrees, the Moon is again in Conjunction with the Sun, and it has become a new Moon:

4th Quarter

Moon Phases

First Quarter
Whatever sign you were born under, wherever your other planets are placed, you will have an underlying sense of youthful enthusiasm, a touch of Aries at the heart of your nature. You probably prefer to take the initiative, especially in romance and you will always be ready to look for new interests in life, new people and new ideas. Your lively outlook and optimistic approach to life is an attractive feature but you have to guard against selfishness. You can see how things can be made to work and how situations can be improved. You will spur others into action but then leave them to finish the project. You could be self-employed. You should get off to a good start and become quite successful when young, but other factors on the chart will indicate whether this early promise will be maintained throughout. No-one can make you do something if you really

don't want to, and this may stand in the way of successful relationships. You should try not to react too fast or to take others too much by surprise.

Second Quarter

You are ambitious and sociable with an underlying touch of Cancer and Leo in your nature, you are locked into your own goals and your strong need to create something which will be seen and remembered by other people. You need a place of your own where you can express your own personality and this may be your home or your workplace. Your rather charismatic personality will always draw others towards you. You try to be helpful to others but can't be called on to make sacrifices on their behalf for very long. You may use others for your own ends; this behaviour is instinctive rather than calculated. You need the status and outlet of a career but one where your face is out in front, possibly in sales or reception work. You draw attention to yourself and while you can achieve much, you may miss some of the needs of others. You should reach considerable heights of success while still young, other factors in your chart will determine whether you maintain that success. You are slow to anger but formidable when you do lose your temper. You hate to be hurried, and may be slightly suspicious of methods and ideas that are presented to you as a fait accompli. You don't mind hurrying other people, as you know that it puts them slightly off balance and tips the odds in your favour.

Third Quarter

You are sensitive to the needs of others and you want them to be equally sensitive to your needs. There is an underlying watchfulness with this quarter rather reminiscent of Scorpio. You need friendships, colleagues and relationships and you relate well to individuals within a group. You like an exciting life but want others to share the excitement. You are aware of what others think of you and may not be entirely sure of yourself unless acceptably reflected in the eyes of others. You are drawn to more active, more successful people and can help them to achieve their aims; this phase of the Moon suggests that you will be a supreme achiever in your own right but you would still need the help and encouragement of others. There is a nerviness about you, a kind of coiled-spring tension that can lend you originality and wit, but also a short attention span and a hungry search for new people and new experiences. In some peculiar way, sex could have a special importance to you and it may transform your life in some way. It's said that people who are born just after an eclipsed full Moon has passed the Mid-heaven on their birthchart will be rich and famous! Your most successful time of your life is in your middle years.

Fourth Quarter

Whatever else there may be on your chart, there is an underlying feeling of Capricorn or Pisces here. You finish the projects that others start, and you reorganise and sort out problems left by others. You may never start projects of your own. You have clairvoyant insight and may follow hunches rather than work things out logically. You are aware of all kinds of undercurrents and can become upset by the demands of others. You have to try to let their feelings flow past you and always trust your basic instincts. You can be too inclined to sit back and let things happen around you. You are probably at your best when helping a group to achieve something beneficial. You can blend in with a large group or work entirely alone. You are probably not too materialistic but you do need job satisfaction. You may be very slow to grow up, happy to sit back and allow things to change around you, however, you are likely to go through some kind of metamorphosis later in life and achieve success in something unusual and completely individual.

Romany Tradition and Moon Phases

~ Those born between the new Moon and the first quarter will have a long life.
~ Born in the first twenty-four hours of a new Moon brings luck.
~ Born on the second day, you will be exceptionally lucky.
~ Born on the third day, you will have important and influential friends.
~ Born on the fourth day, life will be up and down, with some luck and some reverses.
~ Fifth and sixth day, pride could be your downfall.
~ Seventh day, you have to hide the wishes that you want to come true from others.
~ Those born between the first quarter and the full Moon will do better in life than your parents did.
~ First day, prosperity.
~ Second day, easy life.
~ Third day, wealth through travel.
~ Fourth and fifth days, charm.

~ Sixth, easy success.

~ Seventh, many friends.

~ Those born between the full Moon and the last quarter will have difficulties but will overcome them by doggedness.

~ First day, you will succeed in another continent.

~ Second day, you will do well in business.

~ Third day, success as a result of (and probably foreseen by) intuition.

~ Fourth day, bravery.

~ Fifth day, care must be taken with money.

~ Sixth and seventh, great strength.

~ Those born between the last quarter and the new Moon will be affectionate and honest.

~ First and second days, you will be happy in your home.

~ Third day, you are dependable.

~ Fourth day, you are sensitive.

~ Fifth day, you will make ideal parents.

~ Sixth and seventh days, you will acquire money (or maybe non-material wealth) through loyalty.

Progressed Moon Phases

Use the same system as for natal Moon phases to work out the progressed phase. For instance, if the progressed Moon passes the natal Sun's position, it will be new. From the progressed Sun/Moon position you can easily work out whether the Moon is in the first, second, third or fourth quarter, and then you can read the natal information to get a feeling of what these quarters will bring. If you want more detailed information than this, there is some advanced professional astrology software that carries fine details of lunar progressions.

Transits

Check out the actual Moon in the actual sky from time to time. If you notice a New Moon and then check your ephemeris and discover that it's making an aspect to something on your chart, you will probably notice a small fresh start or adjustment to some part of your life. A full Moon often seems to work in a similar way, as it brings a small phase to an end and allows something or someone new to come in.

Eclipses and Occultations

This chapter is probably of more use to those who are already into astrology, but beginners can always consult an astrologer to find out when eclipses and occultations will occur. Professional quality astrology software gives dates of eclipses, but not always of occultations. Neil Michelsen's American Ephemeris of the 21st Century will show eclipses, but you will need Raphael's Ephemeris for the relevant year, to study the occultations.

```
❯ Phases & Eclipses
Dy Hr Mn
 5  9:55    ☾  12♊32
13  6:42    ●☌20♍10
 ☌ 6:55:18  P  0.788
21  9:00    ❯  28♐04
28  2:52    O☍ 4♈40
 ☍ 2:48     T  1.276

 4 21:07    ☾  11♋19
13  0:07    ●  19♎20
20 20:32    ❯  27♑08
27 12:06    O   3♉45
```

Eclipses in the Ephemeris
The illustration above shows the situation for September 2015.

Most of the letters and numbers will become familiar to you as you learn and use astrology, so the only ones I am going into in this book are the symbols relating to eclipses.

Look under the column marked Dy (Day) and find the number 13. Then, track along that line to the right, to the two symbols in the middle of the line. They show that a solar eclipse is exact at that time, on that day. The first symbol, the black circle, represents a New Moon. The next symbol, a smaller black circle with a small 'handle' means 'Conjunction'

The next line shows that the eclipse is at its greatest at 6:55:18, and that it is a partial eclipse (P), with 0.788 of the Sun being eclipsed.

Now, look down to the 28th, when there is a Lunar eclipse, exact at 2:52a.m. The eclipse is total (T) and greatest at 2:48a.m. with more than the entire lunar surface being covered (1.276).

Note that the exact aspect and greatest visual effect don't need to happen at the same time; in fact, the greatest coverage often happens before the eclipse is exact.

Solar Eclipse

If you were born on a solar eclipse, the Sun and Moon are in the same place, so your inner and outer natures interact well. Your emotional reactions will be fast, so you act instinctively. This would enable you to avoid or get out of sticky situations admirably but it might be hard for you to make plans and carry them out.

Lunar Eclipse

If you were born on a lunar eclipse, the Earth would be standing between the Moon and the Sun, so you would have a less integrated personality, with the inner and outer sides being less harmonious than they might otherwise be. This shows a slower and more careful type of personality because you stop think before you act.

Eclipses in General

The Romans feared eclipses because they brought bad events, and I think they were right, as eclipses do tend to bring unpleasant events, but in my experience, these don't come completely out of the blue. The eclipse effect seems to bring an existing problem out into the open or to bring it to a head.

I have a theory that those born under the signs of Cancer and Leo suffer more from eclipses than other signs, because the Moon rules Cancer and the Sun rules Leo, and by its very nature, an eclipse must temporarily block one or the other of these planets.

Raphael's Ephemeris

Regardless of how much software you buy, you still need to buy the Raphael's Ephemeris for each year, and the following example explains just one of the reasons. This illustration shows a couple of days to remember (for all the wrong reasons), as it reveals a solar eclipse and an occultation to Jupiter on the same day!

The section headed Lunar Aspects shows when there will be a solar eclipse, as shown by the solar eclipse symbol on the 26th in the column headed by the Sun (first column).

Lunar Aspects								
☉	☿	♀	♂	♃	♄	♅	♆	♇
⚹			⚹					⚹
	∠			∠	⚺	☌	⚺	
	⚹	⚺	□	⚹			∠	□
□		∠		□			⚺	△
		⚹				∠	⚹	
△	□		△		⚼			⚼
⚼			⚼	△	△	⚹	□	
	△	□		⚼				
⚼			△		□	□	△	☍
			△	☍			⚼	
☍		⚼		☍	⚹	△		
	☍				∠	⚼		⚼
			⚼		⚺		☍	△
⚼		☍	△	⚼				
△	⚼				☌	☍		
	△			△			⚼	□
			□			⚺	△	
□	□	⚼		□	∠	⚼		⚹
		△	⚹			△		∠
⚹	⚹				⚹		□	⚺
		∠		∠	⚹			
∠		□	⚺	∠	□	□	⚹	
⚺	⚺			⚺			∠	☌
					⚹			
	☌	⚹	⚫		△		⚺	⚺
⚫		∠		⚫	⚼	∠		∠
	⚺	⚺	⚺			⚺	☌	∠
	∠			⚺				⚹
⚺			∠	∠	☍	☌		
∠	⚹	☌	⚹				⚺	□
⚹				⚹			∠	

The same symbol in a column relating to a planet other than the Sun is called an occultation rather than an eclipse, but the idea is the same, because it shows that the Moon is obscuring or 'occluding' the light of the planet. In this example, Mars on the 25th and Jupiter on the 26th.

You only see the opposition symbol that refers to a lunar eclipse in the Sun's column, never in a planet's column.

Occultations

An occultation occurs when the Moon moves in front of a planet. If the planet is an inner one, such as Mercury, Venus or Mars, this may be repeated for no more than two months running, as the planet's orbit soon carries it away from the occlusion spot; however, when an outer planet is involved, it sits in a particular position for months on end, and the Moon can occlude the planet month after month for quite a long time. Occultations are never pleasant, but the most dramatic effect occurs when it hits an inner planet that also happens to connect with something on your own chart. The effect can be dramatic and very nasty. Here is a true story about a Moon/Venus occultation. (I've changed the names and circumstances of this story to protect the innocent.)

Marianne was enjoying spending time with her new boyfriend, Frazer. Frazer was extremely sympathetic when she started to be plagued by frightening 'heavy-breather' and 'funny-voice' phone calls. Mobile phones didn't exist at that time and Marianne used her phone for business, so she couldn't just change her number at the drop of a hat without damaging or even destroying her business. She was stuck with this unpleasant situation.

One day, Marianne and I were talking about her problem, when my psychic hackles went up. I had never met Frazer but I got the strangest feeling that the calls might have something to do with him. Marianne mentioned that there was an ex-girlfriend who might be at the back of it, but I had the feeling that it was Frazer himself who was making the calls. Marianne's first response was to say that I was being ridiculous, but when I asked Marianne if the calls ever came when Frazer was in the house or whether they only did so when he was at work. Marianne realised that they only ever came when he was at work. Frazer worked in the electronics field, so he could easily find ways of disguising his voice over the phone.

I checked the Raphael's ephemeris against Marianne's chart, and sure enough, there was a Venus occultation coming up that would occur right on the position of Marianne's natal Moon. I warned her that something would come to light when the occultation hit.

Marianne phoned me a week later and told me that when the next obscene call came, she answered it by saying, "I know it's you Frazer, and if this doesn't stop, I'm going to the police." Later that night, Frazer came to the house and picked a fight, but Marianne had warned the neighbours that this might happen and she threatened to scream so that they would phone the police for her. Frazer eventually went away, and that was the end of the affair.

Weighting and Aspects

Weighting

Weighting is what we do when working out how many items are of which gender, element or quality in order to assess the nature of the chart, and of the person.

When you have discovered the degree and sign of your Ascendant, place it on the left-hand side of the chart and arrange the other eleven signs round the chart in an anti-clockwise direction. Finally, put the Sun and the Moon in their respective positions.

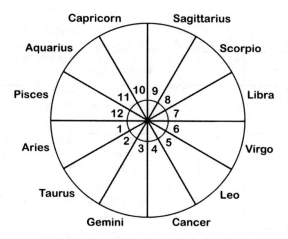

Now check the weighting of the Sun, Moon and Ascendant:

How many of these are in masculine or feminine signs,

How many are in fire, earth, air or water signs,

How many are in cardinal, fixed or mutable signs.

When the Sun and Moon are in compatible signs, the inner and outer personalities are in harmony, but if the two planets are in incompatible signs, the instinctive reactions are different from the outer manner. This is further complicated by the fact that most people actually project the Ascendant or a combination of Sun and Ascendant out to the world, while the lunar side hides away until the emotions come into play or if the subject is ill, drunk or under the influence of drugs. For instance, a modest Virgoan with nervous Gemini rising and the Moon in expansive Sagittarius will become loud and boastful when drunk. An example of someone who has all three features in the same place is Queen Victoria, who had the Sun, Moon and Asc. in conjunction in Gemini.

Aspects
Aspects are the angles that the planets make to each other in a chart, and these show how any two features fit with each other. Try this with any combination of Sun, Moon and Asc. The following table defines the main aspects, also showing the normal orbs for each. 'Orb' is the technical term for how many degrees variance from the exact separation is acceptable.

Aspect	Glyph	Degrees apart	Orb	Character
Conjunction		0	8	Usually the same sign and house, thus acting in a similar way.
Semi-sextile		30	2	The two signs have nothing in common, but they do share a cusp and that seems to help.
Sextile		60	6	These signs share a gender. The elements are also similar (fire & air or earth & water) so they get on fairly well together.
Square		90	6	Although often challenging, these two signs share a quality.
Trine		120	6	These share a gender and element, so they have an easy relationship.
Inconjunct		150	2	This is a truly awkward aspect, as the signs have nothing in common.
Opposition		180	8	These two share a gender and quality, so although challenging, this aspect is also stimulating.

The Nodes of the Moon

Here are the glyphs for:

The Moon's North Node: ☊   The Moon's South Node: ☋

We know that the Sun, Moon and planets lie along the ecliptic, but the Moon and planets move above and below the ecliptic as they orbit the Sun. The Moon spends two weeks above the ecliptic and then it crosses the ecliptic to spend the next two weeks below it. When the Moon crosses the ecliptic in an upward direction, this point is called the north node, and when the Moon crosses the ecliptic in downward direction, this point is called the south node. For the most part, the nodes move backwards through the zodiac, but this backwards motion is interrupted every now and again by short period of forward motion, so the actual motion is forwards and backwards, with the whole sequence gradually moving back over a period of time.

   Wherever the north node is, the south node is exactly opposite, so when the north node is in Aries, the south node is in Libra. They always share the same gender and quality, but they never share the same element.

NORTH NODE	SOUTH NODE
Aries	Libra
Taurus	Scorpio
Gemini	Sagittarius
Cancer	Capricorn
Leo	Aquarius
Virgo	Pisces
Libra	Aries
Scorpio	Taurus
Sagittarius	Gemini
Capricorn	Cancer
Aquarius	Leo
Pisces	Virgo

The Dates for the North Node Positions
The nodes spend about a year in each sign, and the following tables give
you the dates from 1930 to 2020.

DATE	SIGN
8 Jul 1930	Aries
29 Dec 1931	Pisces
25 Jun 1933	Aquarius
9 Mar 1935	Capricorn
15 Sept 1936	Sagittarius
3 Mar 1938	Scorpio
12 Sept 1939	Libra
25 May 1941	Virgo
22 Nov 1942	Leo
12 May 1944	Cancer
3 Dec 1945	Gemini
3 Aug 1947	Taurus
26 Jan 1949	Aries
27 Jul 1950	Pisces
29 Mar 1952	Aquarius
10 Oct 1953	Capricorn
3 Apr 1955	Sagittarius
5 Oct 1956	Scorpio
17 Jun 1958	Libra
16 Dec 1959	Virgo
11 Jun 1961	Leo
24 Dec 1962	Cancer
26 Aug 1964	Gemini
20 Feb 1966	Taurus
20 Aug 1967	Aries
20 Apr 1969	Pisces
3 Nov 1970	Aquarius
28 Apr 1972	Capricorn
28 Oct 1973	Sagittarius
11 Jul 1975	Scorpio
8 Jan 1977	Libra

DATE	SIGN
6 Jul 1978	Virgo
13 Jan 1980	Leo
21 Sept 1981	Cancer
17 Mar 1983	Gemini
12 Sept 1984	Taurus
7 Apr 1986	Aries
3 Dec 1987	Pisces
23 May 1989	Aquarius
19 Nov 1990	Capricorn
2 Aug 1992	Sagittarius
2 Feb 1994	Scorpio
1 Aug 1995	Libra
26 Jan 1997	Virgo
21 Oct 1998	Leo
10 Apr 2000	Cancer
14 Oct 2001	Gemini
15 Mar 2003	Taurus
27 Dec 2004	Aries
23 Jun 2006	Pisces
19 Dec 2007	Aquarius
22 Aug 2009	Capricorn
4 Mar 2011	Sagittarius
31 Aug 2010	Scorpio
19 Feb 2014	Libra
12 Nov 2015	Virgo
10 May 2017	Leo
7 Nov 2018	Cancer
6 May 2020	Gemini

The Hindu View

Hindu astrologers call the nodes of the Moon Rahu and Ketu, meaning the dragon's head and the dragon's tail. The idea is that the tail of the dragon is leaving a previous life, while the head is preparing for the next one. The astrological idea is that certain things come easily to us because we learned them in a past life, while the current incarnation is filled with lessons that help our souls to develop. The south node represents at least one past lifetime, while the north node represents the lessons and tasks for the current one. If you don't believe in karma or reincarnation, you could say that we find it natural to do the things that the south node represents, and difficult to achieve those that the north node stands for.

Politics, Society, Timing and Geography

Leaving aside the ideas of karma, there is a completely opposite view of the nodes, and this is the one that I find useful. The theory here is that the north node represents those areas where the current business, social or political atmosphere runs in your favour. For example, let us say that you wish to open a health-food shop. This would have been a great success at any time during the past twenty years and it would probably do well now. However, if you wanted to open a high street shop selling fur coats, you would need a time machine to take you back to the 1950s, or you would have to move to Russia. It's easier to get something off the ground when a planet transits the north node than when it sits on the south node. This isn't to say that you shouldn't try, but you will have to accept that things will take longer and be more difficult when the south node is being activated.

The Parents and the Past

Because these nodes are linked to the Moon, they can throw light on the experience of being nurtured or mothered - by whoever did the mothering. Sometimes, the nodes tell us something about our own experiences as parents. Oddly enough, the signs that denote a difficult childhood when they are on the Ascendant or as Moon sign are not necessarily so difficult for the nodes. For instance, Gemini is not an easy sign to have rising, but a Gemini node is not bad at all. When planets make aspects to the nodes by transit or progression, events concerning parents (especially the mother) tend to come into focus.

Premises and Property

The nodes seem to have a bearing on home premises and also those that we may rent or buy to run a farm or for any kind of a business or to let out for income. This is not hard to understand, because the home, premises, small businesses, family, heritage and the past are all assigned to the Moon, so these things are bound to have an influence on the nodes.

Sasha's Notes

Despite everything that has ever been written about the nodes saying that the north node is fortunate or easy and the south node difficult, I find the opposite to be true. When the north node is conjunct a particular planet or spot on my chart (and the south node is opposing it) things do not go well. I think this is a case of doing some research of your own to see how the transiting nodes affect you.

Connections

A fascinating area of astrology shows the way that charts connect, because one person's Sun sign is often another's Moon or a third's ascendant, and two Sun signs that are apparently incompatible can be eased by these links. For instance, Jan and I don't have 'compatible' Sun signs, but his Moon and several planets are in Gemini, while my Asc and several planets are also in Gemini.

The following is a real family group:

Mother:	Sun Cancer, Moon Taurus, Scorpio rising
Son:	Sun Scorpio, Moon Taurus, Cancer rising
Daughter:	Sun Leo, Moon Scorpio, Cancer rising

Clearly, the mother and son share three signs, while the daughter is only slightly different.

You may find yourself drawn to lovers or friends of a particular Sun sign, and this gets even more interesting when you start to look at Sun, Moon and Asc combinations. One friend of mine has had a variety of husbands and lovers, all of whom had Aries/Capricorn combinations.

People who work together or come together for a common cause often share signs, probably due to the nature of the job:

~ I once worked in a major psychic festival where everyone in our group had the Sun, Moon or both, in Pisces.

~ A bank in Brighton employed nine accountants, and eight of them had the Sun in Gemini.

~ Similarly, a publisher that I used to write for employed nine Sun in Capricorn people.

~ A friend once employed a number of carpenters, builders, electricians and whatnot to do some building at her place of work, and every single one of them had the Sun in Aquarius.
~ I worked on a committee whose members all had watery Moons, with seven lunar Pisceans and two lunar Cancerians.
~ Lastly, I remember reading a book by a cat burglar who remarked that he and eleven of his burglar friends were all Sun in Aquarius!

Sun/Moon Combinations

Sun Aries, Moon Aries
An extrovert and self-starter with an endless supply of enthusiasm, quick to think and act. You lack patience and may be too self-centred.

Sun Aries, Moon Taurus
Confident, enthusiastic and lovable, good builder, architect or gardener with an artistic eye. Could be dogmatic.

Sun Aries, Moon Gemini
Dextrous, good engineer or draftsman, full of bright ideas. Clever with words but sharp and sarcastic at times. You may leave tasks for others to finish off.

Sun Aries, Moon Cancer
Very determined, a good business head on your shoulders and a pleasant manner. Home life is very important to you. Sensitive but you hide it from others.

Sun Aries, Moon Leo
A real go-getter, you need the limelight. Enthusiastic and optimistic you may be bossy and domineering. Very creative, but blind to underlying influences at times.

Sun Aries, Moon Virgo
Probing, analytical and clever. Very efficient and clever worker, shy in personal matters. Good writer, harsh critic, may be too fond of nit-picking details.

Sun Aries, Moon Libra
Outwardly confident and ebullient, inwardly calmer. Sensitive to others; also loving and passionate. Good business sense but may be over-ambitious.

Sun Aries, Moon Scorpio
An excellent soldier or surgeon, good concentration level. Single-minded, intense and passionate about everything; you may be too much for anyone to handle for long. Try to relax and let others do the same.

Sun Aries, Moon Sagittarius
Restless and energetic, you are a born explorer on both the physical and mental level. You can fill others with a zest for life and idealism. Tactless and sarcastic.

Sun Aries, Moon Capricorn
Determined, unstoppable, must reach the top but this could be at the expense of your personal life. You seek to dominate others by force of your personality.

Sun Aries, Moon Aquarius
Humanitarian and enthusiastic, you would make a wonderful sports coach or teacher, but you must be careful not to hurt others by thoughtlessly sarcastic remarks.

Sun Aries, Moon Pisces
Outwardly enthusiastic, inwardly shy and lacking in confidence. Kind and well-meaning but could be apt to preach. You need to get away from others from time to time.

Sun Taurus, Moon Aries
Outwardly calm, inwardly ambitious and determined. Could be very creative in a practical way. You may be too fond of your own opinions. Good engineer and builder, artistic too.

Sun Taurus, Moon Taurus
Stubborn, fixed in your views and materialistic, but also creative and artistic with a love of music. You will make things that stand the test of time. Loyal in love.

Sun Taurus, Moon Gemini
Artistic and perceptive, a good media worker or marketing expert. Home-loving but occasional outbursts of restlessness. Affectionate, but not too sensual.

Sun Taurus, Moon Cancer
A real homemaker and family person. You can motivate others to achieve a great deal but you hold back from the limelight. Your imagination can be successfully harnessed.

Sun Taurus, Moon Leo
Very fixed opinions and a definite personality, you find it hard to adapt to change. You love children and are intensely loyal to others. You could be a good singer or dancer.

Sun Taurus, Moon Virgo
A careful worker who can combine detail and artistry. Good family person. Can learn and teach wordy or musical skills. Don't be too critical or pessimistic. A strong interest in nutrition.

Sun Taurus, Moon Libra
Very sensual and also artistic with a good business head. Maybe too lazy to achieve much but when motivated can reach the top. Lovable and kind, but selfish too.

Sun Taurus, Moon Scorpio
Artistic and sensual, you can achieve much. Your opinions are fixed and your nature stubborn. Very loyal and persistent, could be a good sales person, also strongly independent. Extreme stinginess may be a problem.

Sun Taurus, Moon Sagittarius
Outwardly steady, inwardly restless. Could be an armchair traveller. Traditional religion interests you; don't be too old-fashioned or quick to judge others.

Sun Taurus, Moon Capricorn
Determined and ambitious with a strong need for security. A shrewd and practical business head, but inwardly shy and nervous in personal situations. Very loyal and loving. Careful with money.

Sun Taurus, Moon Aquarius
Innovative and artistic you are good company and a hard worker. You need freedom but will insist on others toeing the line. Good concentration and high level of confidence.

Sun Taurus, Moon Pisces
Dreamy and patient, highly artistic you may have difficulty in getting projects off the ground. Your sympathy may land you with the care of lame ducks. Sensual and loving.

Sun Gemini, Moon Aries
Very sharp mind and a great deal of enthusiasm that can carry you away. Good media type, interesting friend but a touch too sarcastic for comfort.

Sun Gemini, Moon Taurus
You have good ideas and the patience to finish what you start. A good homemaker and parent. You need communication and comfort in a relationship and work in a mentally artistic field.

Sun Gemini, Moon Gemini
You have dozens of bright ideas but difficulty in completing anything. Very clever and dextrous but could be a bit unfeeling. Tension is your problem, try to relax and feel.

Sun Gemini, Moon Cancer
Friendly and chatty, usually on the phone. You love travel and novelty plus family life. Don't be put upon by stronger characters. You can make a happy home for others. Your memory is good.

Sun Gemini, Moon Leo
Lively, friendly and good looking you will always be popular. You need to express your ideas creatively. Good with children as you will never quite grow up yourself.

Sun Gemini, Moon Virgo
Inventive, versatile and full of ideas, but lacking in confidence. Your nerves sometimes get the better of you. Good researcher, writer, secretary.

Sun Gemini, Moon Libra
You are full of ideas that may not always get off the ground. Diplomatic and fun, you can be a bit too restless. Flirtatious and fun, but inclined to be long-winded.

Sun Gemini, Moon Scorpio
Brilliant and perceptive mind. Outwardly a cool-hearted loner, but burning with secret passions; also emotionally vulnerable. Very creative writer, musician, doctor or spy. Clever with words, sarcastic. Had awful childhood.

Sun Gemini, Moon Sagittarius
Restless, good sportsman or adventurous traveller. Good scholar and teacher. Might need to get in touch with your own feelings and those of others.

Sun Gemini, Moon Capricorn
Clever and ambitious, literate would succeed in the media. Relationships may bring suffering; you must try to be warmer to others. Capable and businesslike.

Sun Gemini, Moon Aquarius
Broad-minded, good scholar and teacher. Wide-ranging ideas, perceptive. May fear emotional display or even own feelings. Detachment sought, good journalist or traveller.

Sun Gemini, Moon Pisces
Hidden depths to personality, good with children, also sports and dancing. Imaginative writer, but too ready to explain all to others. Bubbly personality, but lacking in confidence; nervous and incapable if under severe stress.

Sun Cancer, Moon Aries
Capable and competitive type with a good business head and the ability to understand others. Would need a good home but easily bored if spending too much time on it. A strange mixture of caring and impatience.

Sun Cancer, Moon Taurus
Kind, caring and cuddly. You love your home and family, you also have a good head for business. Artistic, musical and rather lazy, inclined to brood.

Sun Cancer, Moon Gemini
Clever and businesslike, pleasant and successful. You appear slow but can be quick and cunning. Good politician, terrific traveller. Could have sporting abilities.

Sun Cancer, Moon Cancer
Strong emotions, strong attachment to family. You tend to be moody and to cut off from other people. Kind-hearted, aware of the needs of others. Attached to the past, good historian.

Sun Cancer, Moon Leo
Caring and compassionate, very loving towards your family and friends. Emotionally vulnerable. You have high standards and can cut off your nose to spite your face.

Sun Cancer, Moon Virgo
Good placement for a nurse or doctor, caring in a practical way. Good with details, excellent memory. Will cut off from others when hurt. Good business head, rather dogged, good salesperson. A worrier.

Sun Cancer, Moon Libra
Good business head on your shoulders. Ambitious for self and your family. Love of beauty and harmony, probably artistic. May have difficulty in putting ideas into practice.

Sun Cancer, Moon Scorpio
Strongly intuitive and probably very moody. You would be hard to ignore. Try to keep a positive outlook on life and avoid being too pessimistic.

Sun Cancer, Moon Sagittarius
This combination makes you a family person who needs emotional freedom. You are idealistic and lovable but you may ask more from life than you could reasonably expect to obtain.

Sun Cancer, Moon Capricorn
You have a very good head for business, and you are shrewd and intuitive. You can succeed as long as you don't try to cut corners or to save money in silly ways.

Sun Cancer, Moon Aquarius
A clever politician with a quirky mind that operates behind a placid facade. You can put your point of view across well. You keep your eye firmly fixed on the main chance.

Sun Cancer, Moon Pisces
Very sensitive and intuitive, you are so tuned in to others that you can forget your own needs. You may prefer to work in a field where you can care for less fortunate people (or animals).

Sun Leo, Moon Aries
You have courage, verve and enthusiasm but you must learn not to ride roughshod over others. If you can see beyond your own needs, you can go far.

Sun Leo, Moon Taurus
You are kind, reliable; dedicated to your family and highly practical but you may be too obstinate for your own good. Traditional outlook on life.

Sun Leo, Moon Gemini
You like to be busy and your mind works overtime. You are independent, creative and clever with good leadership qualities but your sarcasm might be a bit too much for some people.

Sun Leo, Moon Cancer
A real family person with strong need to mother people. Your emotions may overtake you at times. You like the past and tradition. Very caring and kind.

Sun Leo, Moon Leo
Dramatic and outgoing, you need to dazzle others. You are funny and entertaining but might be a bit too self-centred for comfort. Try to cope with details rather than ignore them.

Sun Leo, Moon Virgo

You could be an excellent employer as you can delegate and also work in a logical manner. Your sharp tongue might be a bit hard to live with. You are very honest and basically kind natured.

Sun Leo, Moon Libra

Very affectionate and probably very sexy, you have a great sense of style. You also have a good head for business but you may be too fond of having things your own way.

Sun Leo, Moon Scorpio

Very intense and strong personality, possibly too dramatic. You are very loyal and may be rather possessive but your colleagues will respect you for your honesty and your capacity for work.

Sun Leo, Moon Sagittarius

Very adventurous, you cannot be tied down. You are loyal, proud and kind-hearted. You have high personal standards but will have to curb your sarcasm and also think before committing yourself.

Sun Leo, Moon Capricorn

Very organised and ambitious, you are destined to succeed in some traditional field of work. Don't ride roughshod over others or cover up your softness too much.

Sun Leo, Moon Aquarius

You have strong opinions and can throw yourself into a cause. You are loyal, faithful and have a well-developed sense of fair play. Try to develop practicality and a flexible outlook.

Sun Leo, Moon Pisces

A dreamer and mystic who can bring dreams to life. It's hard for you to turn away from those who need your help and strength. Don't become downhearted if all your plans don't work out. Creative and kind-hearted.

Sun Virgo, Moon Aries

Your mind is sharp and so is your tongue. Being quick and clever you can succeed at many jobs. Self-expression in the form of writing is essential for you.

Sun Virgo, Moon Taurus
Interested in the growing and preparing of food, creative in a structured way and kind. You may lack the confidence to get things off the ground. Sensible, helpful and practical outlook.

Sun Virgo, Moon Gemini
You are very quick and clever, your mind and tongue are rarely still. You can gather and analyse information but your intellect may prevent you from getting in touch with your own and other people's feelings.

Sun Virgo, Moon Cancer
Very canny, interested in food and nutrition. Could be a good businessperson in a small way. You worry about your family and can be a bit too fussy and moody for comfort.

Sun Virgo, Moon Leo
Caring, conscientious and organised, you can be relied upon to get things done. You may work with children. Your personal standards are very high but you lack confidence.

Sun Virgo, Moon Virgo
Lack of confidence, partly due to an unhappy childhood. You may pay too much attention to details and worry too much about small matters. Honest and kind, you always try to help others and do your duty in every way.

Sun Virgo, Moon Libra
You are neat and tidy, and you enjoy organising. Could be a good mediator or co-operative worker. Good thinker but slow to make decisions. A good cook.

Sun Virgo, Moon Scorpio
Clever and critical, you would make a very good doctor or nurse. You need to get to the bottom of things but may be too cool for comfort towards others.

Sun Virgo, Moon Sagittarius
Humanitarian and thoughtful, you are interested in education. Warm and friendly and sometimes impulsive, you can also attend to details. Could make a good teacher but an even better travel agent.

Sun Virgo, Moon Capricorn
Good in business but possibly too self-disciplined and serious. You are capable, conscientious and clever but you need to cultivate a sense of fun and give some attention to the needs of others. Very reliable family member.

Sun Virgo, Moon Aquarius
You could be a wonderful teacher. Deep thinker, very helpful to those in need. Don't let your need for independence deprive you of family life or keep you separated from your feelings.

Sun Virgo, Moon Pisces
You live to serve the needs of others and then wonder why your own needs are not being met. Your mind is good when projected outwardly towards intellectual pursuits. Intuitive, interested in medicine and nutrition.

Sun Libra, Moon Aries
You are a good initiator, but might find it difficult to finish what you start. Others may help you to do this. You are clever and intuitive but can be selfish and impatient. Good in a crisis.

Sun Libra, Moon Taurus
You are attractive to look at and have excellent taste. You love music and art but may be too lazy to become skilled yourself. Good homemaker and family person with practical business mind.

Sun Libra, Moon Gemini
A theoriser with a good mind, you can be superficial. Dextrous and clever you have the ability to put techniques into practice as long as you have help from others. Keep in touch with your feelings and those of others.

Sun Libra, Moon Cancer
Kind and pleasant, you make a nice home and are a good caring family member. Good personnel manager or accountant. You need to close off from others from time to time to do your own thing.

Sun Libra, Moon Leo
You are in love with love half the time with a romantic and dramatic attitude to life. Clever and creative but could become easily bored. Very clever in business or politics.

Sun Libra, Moon Virgo
Pleasant, charming and sensible, you can do most things as long as they are not messy or dirty. Loyal to friends. Good at detailed work. Literate and musical.

Sun Libra, Moon Libra
You are very attractive both in looks and as a personality but you may be in a bit of a dream half the time. You may need to be more decisive and more energetic.

Sun Libra, Moon Scorpio
Strongly sexed and intense, you would be a handful for anyone who comes close to you. You are determined and businesslike but must watch a tendency to dominate others.

Sun Libra, Moon Sagittarius
You will probably travel quite a bit on business and should be great at dealing with and negotiating with foreigners. The legal profession would draw you as you have a good sense of judgement.

Sun Libra, Moon Capricorn
You are very purposeful and a harder worker, which is unusual for a Libran. You could be very successful as your judgement of people is pretty acute.

Sun Libra, Moon Aquarius
Very independent and also quite clever. You have good judgement and are able to lead others strongly but calmly. Your imagination is strong and could be used to make your living.

Sun Libra, Moon Pisces
Very artistic and musical, you can be a dreamy romantic. Both your appearance and your nature are attractive. You have a deep level of intuition but may be a bit slow to put things into action.

Sun Scorpio, Moon Aries
You have a strong character but might be too ready to fight everything and everyone. Your feelings are intense and your temper rather short but you have deep reserves of courage and can achieve a great deal.

Sun Scorpio, Moon Taurus
Sensual and musical you might have great talent for something attractive like horticulture. You may be too obstinate or too practical. A very reliable type.

Sun Scorpio, Moon Gemini
This combination shows a difficult childhood and an early sense of loss. Don't continue to view the world with too much suspicion. Very clever and intuitive about people.

Sun Scorpio, Moon Cancer
Attractive to look at and talk to, you are deeply intuitive but may be able to relate more easily to animals than to people. Your moodiness will be your weak point.

Sun Scorpio, Moon Leo
Very fixed opinions. It's hard for you to adapt. Loyal to your family especially your children. You can finish what you start. Guard against over-dramatising everything.

Sun Scorpio, Moon Virgo
This shows a difficult childhood with feelings of alienation. Try to develop trust in others. Clever and dutiful, you could be drawn to a career in the medical profession.

Sun Scorpio, Moon Libra
You are attractive and clever, this combination gives diplomacy and determination, and you would make a good politician. You may either

swamp your family with your personality or ignore them while pursuing your career.

Sun Scorpio, Moon Scorpio
You have a powerful personality and often feel passionate about everything. Try not to dominate others. You can achieve almost anything you set your mind to, but your resentment and moaning about others isn't very attractive.

Sun Scorpio, Moon Sagittarius
Clever and clairvoyant, you would make a good lawyer or businessman but also a good detective. Your sense of humour helps you to keep everything in perspective.

Sun Scorpio, Moon Capricorn
You could be a rather serious and determined person. You would reach the top in any field you set your heart on but could miss out on the personal side of life until your later years.

Sun Scorpio, Moon Aquarius
You are independent and clever with a strong intuitive streak. You are decisive and instinctive but might be something of an intolerant tough guy.

Sun Scorpio, Moon Pisces
Intuitive and artistic, probably musical. You have a strong drive to help others, probably in the field of health. You can withdraw into injured silence or spitefulness if you feel threatened.

Sun Sagittarius, Moon Aries
You are open and honest but may be too quick to jump into exciting new schemes. Your restlessness might take you around the world but also may make it difficult for you to hang on to relationships.

Sun Sagittarius, Moon Taurus
You are kind and good-hearted with great enthusiasm for the good things of life. You could be an inspired cook or artist and have the ability to combine practicality with imagination.

Sun Sagittarius, Moon Gemini
You are always busy and restless. You could be a very good sportsman or entertainer. Clever and articulate, you could make a good writer.

Sun Sagittarius, Moon Cancer
You are intuitive and creative and would make a good medium. There is a split between your need for home comforts and your need for freedom. Childish at times.

Sun Sagittarius, Moon Leo
Dramatic and outgoing, you would do well on the stage. Try to tune in a bit more to the needs of others. Youthful and active, you are great fun to be with.

Sun Sagittarius, Moon Virgo
You have the ability to think both deeply and in an organised manner. You would make a wonderful teacher. Don't lay the law down to others.

Sun Sagittarius, Moon Libra
You would make a fabulous barrister as you have a gift for all things legal. Don't be too hard on others who are not as bright or as successful as you.

Sun Sagittarius, Moon Scorpio
You could make a good detective as you have both investigative ability and a legal mind. Don't be too hard on those who either don't share your interests or are not as capable as you.

Sun Sagittarius, Moon Sagittarius
You would make a terrific explorer as you love travel and are too restless to sit still for long. Try to tune into ordinary people, as not everyone will understand the breadth of your mind.

Sun Sagittarius, Moon Capricorn
Clever and determined, honest and entertaining, you could go far in life. You should travel and be involved with business but you must have some patience with less capable people.

Sun Sagittarius, Moon Aquarius
Your mind is broad and you can teach others. You tend to live in a world of your own which is out of step with most of the rest of the world. Could be an eccentric genius.

Sun Sagittarius, Moon Pisces
You are intuitive, kind and spiritual and would make a good teacher. You are artistic and imaginative and have much to give others but you may be a bit vague and impractical at times.

Sun Capricorn, Moon Aries
You have a great deal of determination and may be very clever as well. Once you have set your mind on something, you will get there for sure but you may tread on a few toes while doing it.

Sun Capricorn, Moon Taurus
Practical and sensible, you can achieve much both in the artistic and the business world. Guard against stubbornness and try to see the other person's point of view.

Sun Capricorn, Moon Gemini
Clever but organised. Could make a good writer, salesman, and businessperson with the ability to put good ideas into practice and finish what you start.

Sun Capricorn, Moon Cancer
Home-loving family person, very loyal, decent, also extremely businesslike. Can have a tendency to withdraw into your shell. You worry about everything. A good teacher or counsellor.

Sun Capricorn, Moon Leo
Good in positions of authority. A caring boss. Decent, reliable, but also very determined, might be apt to ride over people who are weaker.

Sun Capricorn, Moon Virgo
Very stable, reliable, family person. Probably a very good cook. Very good head for business. Could be a bit too lacking in humour or too pedantic.

Sun Capricorn, Moon Libra
A good mixture of stability plus business ability. Can get on with people and also achieve a great deal, but may be a bit over enthusiastic when it comes to money-making ideas.

Sun Capricorn, Moon Scorpio
Great strength of character. Clear idea of where you are going and what you want out of life. Very dependable, loyal, kind, but you have no time for fools. You hate to show your feelings.

Sun Capricorn, Moon Sagittarius
Great stability and ability plus a broad, sweeping mind. Could work in the travel industry or teaching, legal or church work. Good in any sort of concentrated work where you deal with people in authority.

Sun Capricorn, Moon Capricorn
Very shy and withdrawn. Very hard worker, good with the elderly. Could find life very difficult until later on. A creative hobby or outlet would be very beneficial to you.

Sun Capricorn, Moon Aquarius
Good organiser. Able to do things on a big scale. Can be a bit hard on you and on other people, but very determined and capable.

Sun Capricorn, Moon Pisces
Deep, kindly, intuitive, very good in a caring profession, particularly dealing with the old, but could be a bit too shy and too easily hurt. Rather serious.

Sun Aquarius, Moon Aries
A very broad-ranging mind. Good teacher, engineer, very clever, but might be difficult to live with. Don't judge other people too harshly. Good sense of humour.

Sun Aquarius, Moon Taurus
You can cope with a lot and achieve a lot. You are very steady, determined and reliable, but could be too stubborn. You may be interested in music, art or beauty products.

Sun Aquarius, Moon Gemini
A natural student or teacher, very clever. A bit inclined to flip from one idea to another and also need to develop stability in relationships with other people.

Sun Aquarius, Moon Cancer
A good family person, good with small children and animals. Can teach, a good companion but can be a bit inclined to withdraw into a shell.

Sun Aquarius, Moon Leo
Very lively personality, and you are always busy doing a lot of things at once. Loyal, a bit stubborn, determined, but can be independent and awkward.

Sun Aquarius, Moon Virgo
Clever, studious, able to put ideas into practice in a very detailed way. Probably very good in research but could be a bit eccentric and nit picking, difficult to live with.

Sun Aquarius, Moon Libra
Great fun, easy-going, great friend to everybody, logical mind, but a bit unreliable in close relationships. Good in almost any field that doesn't require too much steady effort.

Sun Aquarius, Moon Scorpio
Full of self-confidence. The ability to be a leader. Can be too inclined to ride roughshod over other people. A very original thinker. Easily irritated with fools.

Sun Aquarius, Moon Sagittarius
Very independent, outspoken, a bit tactless, interested in any kind of novel idea. Intelligent, a good teacher. You have a tendency to rush into things without thinking.

Sun Aquarius, Moon Capricorn
A mixture of seriousness and spontaneity. Responsible, capable, a good family person, a good businessperson. Original ideas and a lot of determination.

Sun Aquarius, Moon Aquarius
Very eccentric, very freedom-loving, independent, great fun. Original ideas and an original lifestyle, but not really a family person. Don't judge others too harshly.

Sun Aquarius, Moon Pisces
Very imaginative, intuitive, with the ability to blend common sense and mysticism. Kindly, intelligent, a bit apt to wander off on you're own and go into flights of fancy.

Sun Pisces, Moon Aries
Intuitive, quick and clever, quite determined, great fun and good friend, but not a very reliable family person. You may fluctuate between selfishness and consideration for others.

Sun Pisces, Moon Taurus
Sociable and pleasant, artistic, kind and musical. It's difficult for you to start things but once started you will finish them. You are good looking and graceful. Inclined to be lazy.

Sun Pisces, Moon Gemini
Nervous, talkative, clever, a worrier. You need a stable partner. You're good fun, good looking and interesting, but you never really grow up. Your nerves let you down from time to time.

Sun Pisces, Moon Cancer
Sensitive, kind, thoughtful, very moody, but also kind and caring. You would make a good nurse, doctor or teacher. You may be interested in diets and cooking. Understanding but somewhat impractical.

Sun Pisces, Moon Leo
Generous, imaginative, creative and kindly. You need to be out and about. You like stimulation of new people but your confidence goes very quickly and you can be susceptible to flattery.

Sun Pisces, Moon Virgo
Nervous, thoughtful, deep, intuitive, could work very well on your own in a creative way. Can be too fussy, too worrying, would need a strong partner. Interested in food and diets.

Sun Pisces, Moon Libra
You will need to keep in touch with reality. Your ideas are good. You could achieve a lot if allied to somebody with strength and practicality. You need other people to encourage you.

Sun Pisces, Moon Scorpio
Perceptive, intuitive, deep, attracted to medicine, police and forensic work. Deep insight into people, can manipulate others. Moody, but also caring and kind. Can be self-absorbed and difficult to live with.

Sun Pisces, Moon Sagittarius
Great traveller with a deep and thoughtful mind. Could work in the religious field or as a conservationist. Unreliable as a family person as your mind is elsewhere most of the time.

Sun Pisces, Moon Capricorn
Creativity, intuition and practicality mixed together here, so you can make achievements on the work front and also be a good family person. The only problem is lack of confidence.

Sun Pisces, Moon Aquarius
Friendly, could start projects and then lose interest. Mystical, a good teacher and a caring person but you need a stable and practical partner, as you don't often have your feet on the ground.

Sun Pisces, Moon Pisces
Very active imagination. You see omens and meanings in things. You prefer to work from home by yourself: You find people tend to wear you out; you soak up other people's problems and do find family life hard sometimes.

Information and Suggestions

The following ephemeris table shows the dates on which the Moon changed signs during the years 1930 to 2020. The technical term is the Moon's *ingress* into each new sign.

Here are a couple of things you need to look out for:

If your birth date is shown, check the time at which the Moon changed sign. For instance, if you can see that the Moon changes from Taurus to Gemini at 22:35 and you were born *before* that time, your Moon sign would be Taurus; if you were born *after* that time, it would be Gemini.

If your actual birth date isn't shown, look for the nearest date that precedes yours, as the Moon still occupied that sign on your birth date.

Progressions

If you want to do a quick rule-of-thumb, day-for-a-year progression, you need to count forward by one day for each year of your life. For instance, if you were born on the 10th of October 1974 and you want to look at the situation when you reach the age of 35, your progressed date for that year is the 15th of November 1974. Now, all you need to do is look at the ephemeris for the 15th of November 1974.

Remember that April, June, September and November each have thirty days, while all the rest have thirty-one. February has twenty-eight, except when there is a leap year, when it has twenty-nine. A leap year occurs whenever you can evenly divide a year by four, and by 400 as well.

Transits

Look up the date that interests you, and check out the Moon sign. The Moon takes a mere two-and-a-half-days to transit a sign, so it's only useful if you have something 'time-specific' going on, such as a job interview, an important date, or looking into a new venture.

See whether the transiting Moon is making good, bad or indifferent aspects to your natal Sun and Moon. For instance, if your natal Sun is in Scorpio and your transiting Moon is in Aquarius, it may be making an unpleasant square aspect, signifying that the event will be stressful and tiresome. It might just work to your advantage if you push hard for what you want, but equally, it could turn out to be an upsetting waste of effort.

Review the chapter on phases of the Moon to judge whether your important date coincides with a new Moon (fresh start), a full Moon (other people involved, for good or ill), or an old Moon (nothing will come of it).

Check whether the Moon is 'Void of Course', as this also means that nothing useful will come of it.

And Finally...

Don't become neurotic about all the above. If you really do have some seriously important date to consider, it's worth checking the Moon and as much else on your chart as you can, before the event. However, in the normal run of things, it's usually better for your mental health just to live life and let things happen as they will. It's also interesting, if you've had a particularly good or bad day, to check the status of the Moon (and much else) after the event.

Appendix

The following table shows exact times and dates for the Moon's changes of sign, for the period from 1930 to 2019.

DATE	TIME	SIGN
1 Jan 1930	18:29	AQU
4 Jan 1930	07:04	PIS
6 Jan 1930	18:27	ARI
9 Jan 1930	02:57	TAU
11 Jan 1930	07:33	GEM
13 Jan 1930	08:34	CAN
15 Jan 1930	07:37	LEO
17 Jan 1930	06:56	VIR
19 Jan 1930	08:45	LIB
21 Jan 1930	14:26	SCO
23 Jan 1930	23:56	SAG
26 Jan 1930	11:53	CAP
29 Jan 1930	00:34	AQU
31 Jan 1930	12:58	PIS
3 Feb 1930	00:22	ARI
5 Feb 1930	09:47	TAU
7 Feb 1930	16:07	GEM
9 Feb 1930	18:54	CAN
11 Feb 1930	19:00	LEO
13 Feb 1930	18:14	VIR
15 Feb 1930	18:50	LIB
17 Feb 1930	22:46	SCO
20 Feb 1930	06:48	SAG
22 Feb 1930	18:12	CAP
25 Feb 1930	06:56	AQU
27 Feb 1930	19:12	PIS
2 Mar 1930	06:08	ARI
4 Mar 1930	15:18	TAU
6 Mar 1930	22:14	GEM
9 Mar 1930	02:33	CAN
11 Mar 1930	04:25	LEO
13 Mar 1930	04:53	VIR
15 Mar 1930	05:43	LIB
17 Mar 1930	08:47	SCO
19 Mar 1930	15:24	SAG
22 Mar 1930	01:40	CAP
24 Mar 1930	14:04	AQU
27 Mar 1930	02:23	PIS
29 Mar 1930	12:59	ARI
31 Mar 1930	21:22	TAU
3 Apr 1930	03:41	GEM
5 Apr 1930	08:10	CAN
7 Apr 1930	11:08	LEO
9 Apr 1930	13:10	VIR
11 Apr 1930	15:17	LIB
13 Apr 1930	18:44	SCO
16 Apr 1930	00:50	SAG
18 Apr 1930	10:07	CAP
20 Apr 1930	21:58	AQU
23 Apr 1930	10:22	PIS
25 Apr 1930	21:09	ARI
28 Apr 1930	05:07	TAU
30 Apr 1930	10:25	GEM
2 May 1930	13:53	CAN
4 May 1930	16:31	LEO
6 May 1930	19:10	VIR
8 May 1930	22:30	LIB
11 May 1930	03:06	SCO
13 May 1930	09:39	SAG
15 May 1930	18:39	CAP
18 May 1930	06:03	AQU
20 May 1930	18:33	PIS
23 May 1930	05:55	ARI
25 May 1930	14:14	TAU

DATE	TIME	SIGN
27 May 1930	19:06	GEM
29 May 1930	21:25	CAN
31 May 1930	22:45	LEO
3 Jun 1930	00:37	VIR
5 Jun 1930	04:04	LIB
7 Jun 1930	09:30	SCO
9 Jun 1930	16:56	SAG
12 Jun 1930	02:20	CAP
14 Jun 1930	13:39	AQU
17 Jun 1930	02:11	PIS
19 Jun 1930	14:14	ARI
21 Jun 1930	23:33	TAU
24 Jun 1930	04:59	GEM
26 Jun 1930	06:57	CAN
28 Jun 1930	07:06	LEO
30 Jun 1930	07:28	VIR
2 Jul 1930	09:48	LIB
4 Jul 1930	14:56	SCO
6 Jul 1930	22:49	SAG
9 Jul 1930	08:49	CAP
11 Jul 1930	20:22	AQU
14 Jul 1930	08:57	PIS
16 Jul 1930	21:25	ARI
19 Jul 1930	07:53	TAU
21 Jul 1930	14:37	GEM
23 Jul 1930	17:22	CAN
25 Jul 1930	17:18	LEO
27 Jul 1930	16:34	VIR
29 Jul 1930	17:18	LIB
31 Jul 1930	21:06	SCO
3 Aug 1930	04:24	SAG
5 Aug 1930	14:34	CAP
8 Aug 1930	02:26	AQU
10 Aug 1930	15:02	PIS
13 Aug 1930	03:31	ARI
15 Aug 1930	14:37	TAU
17 Aug 1930	22:44	GEM
20 Aug 1930	03:00	CAN
22 Aug 1930	03:57	LEO
24 Aug 1930	03:13	VIR
26 Aug 1930	02:58	LIB
28 Aug 1930	05:10	SCO
30 Aug 1930	11:05	SAG
1 Sep 1930	20:35	CAP
4 Sep 1930	08:27	AQU
6 Sep 1930	21:06	PIS
9 Sep 1930	09:20	ARI
11 Sep 1930	20:17	TAU
14 Sep 1930	05:00	GEM
16 Sep 1930	10:41	CAN
18 Sep 1930	13:17	LEO
20 Sep 1930	13:45	VIR
22 Sep 1930	13:44	LIB
24 Sep 1930	15:08	SCO
26 Sep 1930	19:34	SAG
29 Sep 1930	03:48	CAP
1 Oct 1930	15:09	AQU
4 Oct 1930	03:47	PIS
6 Oct 1930	15:51	ARI
9 Oct 1930	02:13	TAU
11 Oct 1930	10:28	GEM
13 Oct 1930	16:28	CAN
15 Oct 1930	20:18	LEO
17 Oct 1930	22:25	VIR

DATE	TIME	SIGN
19 Oct 1930	23:43	LIB
22 Oct 1930	01:33	SCO
24 Oct 1930	05:23	SAG
26 Oct 1930	12:27	CAP
28 Oct 1930	22:54	AQU
31 Oct 1930	11:22	PIS
2 Nov 1930	23:33	ARI
5 Nov 1930	09:36	TAU
7 Nov 1930	16:58	GEM
9 Nov 1930	22:04	CAN
12 Nov 1930	01:44	LEO
14 Nov 1930	04:41	VIR
16 Nov 1930	07:27	LIB
18 Nov 1930	10:36	SCO
20 Nov 1930	15:00	SAG
22 Nov 1930	21:42	CAP
25 Nov 1930	07:22	AQU
27 Nov 1930	19:32	PIS
30 Nov 1930	08:06	ARI
2 Dec 1930	18:31	TAU
5 Dec 1930	01:30	GEM
7 Dec 1930	05:31	CAN
9 Dec 1930	07:52	LEO
11 Dec 1930	10:04	VIR
13 Dec 1930	13:05	LIB
15 Dec 1930	17:19	SCO
17 Dec 1930	22:54	SAG
20 Dec 1930	06:11	CAP
22 Dec 1930	15:43	AQU
25 Dec 1930	03:35	PIS
27 Dec 1930	16:29	ARI
30 Dec 1930	03:50	TAU
1 Jan 1931	11:32	GEM
3 Jan 1931	15:20	CAN
5 Jan 1931	16:31	LEO
7 Jan 1931	17:06	VIR
9 Jan 1931	18:48	LIB
11 Jan 1931	22:41	SCO
14 Jan 1931	04:50	SAG
16 Jan 1931	13:02	CAP
18 Jan 1931	23:04	AQU
21 Jan 1931	10:55	PIS
23 Jan 1931	23:54	ARI
26 Jan 1931	12:08	TAU
28 Jan 1931	21:16	GEM
31 Jan 1931	02:07	CAN
2 Feb 1931	03:23	LEO
4 Feb 1931	02:56	VIR
6 Feb 1931	02:55	LIB
8 Feb 1931	05:04	SCO
10 Feb 1931	10:22	SAG
12 Feb 1931	18:39	CAP
15 Feb 1931	05:14	AQU
17 Feb 1931	17:23	PIS
20 Feb 1931	06:20	ARI
22 Feb 1931	18:53	TAU
25 Feb 1931	05:12	GEM
27 Feb 1931	11:45	CAN
1 Mar 1931	14:24	LEO
3 Mar 1931	14:20	VIR
5 Mar 1931	13:32	LIB
7 Mar 1931	14:03	SCO
9 Mar 1931	17:30	SAG
12 Mar 1931	00:39	CAP

DATE	TIME	SIGN	DATE	TIME	SIGN	DATE	TIME	SIGN
14 Mar 1931	11:03	AQU	10 Sep 1931	23:03	VIR	8 Mar 1932	10:35	ARI
16 Mar 1931	23:26	PIS	12 Sep 1931	22:43	LIB	10 Mar 1932	23:19	TAU
19 Mar 1931	12:23	ARI	14 Sep 1931	22:41	SCO	13 Mar 1932	12:02	GEM
22 Mar 1931	00:43	TAU	17 Sep 1931	00:40	SAG	15 Mar 1932	22:44	CAN
24 Mar 1931	11:18	GEM	19 Sep 1931	05:47	CAP	18 Mar 1932	05:55	LEO
26 Mar 1931	19:04	CAN	21 Sep 1931	14:18	AQU	20 Mar 1932	09:17	VIR
28 Mar 1931	23:27	LEO	24 Sep 1931	01:28	PIS	22 Mar 1932	09:56	LIB
31 Mar 1931	00:56	VIR	26 Sep 1931	14:09	ARI	24 Mar 1932	09:35	SCO
2 Apr 1931	00:49	LIB	29 Sep 1931	03:06	TAU	26 Mar 1932	10:07	SAG
4 Apr 1931	00:51	SCO	1 Oct 1931	15:02	GEM	28 Mar 1932	13:08	CAP
6 Apr 1931	02:53	SAG	4 Oct 1931	00:36	CAN	30 Mar 1932	19:30	AQU
8 Apr 1931	08:21	CAP	6 Oct 1931	06:48	LEO	2 Apr 1932	05:04	PIS
10 Apr 1931	17:40	AQU	8 Oct 1931	09:33	VIR	4 Apr 1932	16:53	ARI
13 Apr 1931	05:48	PIS	10 Oct 1931	09:49	LIB	7 Apr 1932	05:43	TAU
15 Apr 1931	18:47	ARI	12 Oct 1931	09:17	SCO	9 Apr 1932	18:26	GEM
18 Apr 1931	06:50	TAU	14 Oct 1931	09:52	SAG	12 Apr 1932	05:46	CAN
20 Apr 1931	16:55	GEM	16 Oct 1931	13:19	CAP	14 Apr 1932	14:20	LEO
23 Apr 1931	00:41	CAN	18 Oct 1931	20:39	AQU	16 Apr 1932	19:20	VIR
25 Apr 1931	06:03	LEO	21 Oct 1931	07:32	PIS	18 Apr 1932	20:59	LIB
27 Apr 1931	09:09	VIR	23 Oct 1931	20:20	ARI	20 Apr 1932	20:33	SCO
29 Apr 1931	10:34	LIB	26 Oct 1931	09:11	TAU	22 Apr 1932	19:57	SAG
1 May 1931	11:26	SCO	28 Oct 1931	20:47	GEM	24 Apr 1932	21:15	CAP
3 May 1931	13:14	SAG	31 Oct 1931	06:26	CAN	27 Apr 1932	02:05	AQU
5 May 1931	17:35	CAP	2 Nov 1931	13:38	LEO	29 Apr 1932	10:56	PIS
8 May 1931	01:37	AQU	4 Nov 1931	18:07	VIR	1 May 1932	22:46	ARI
10 May 1931	13:02	PIS	6 Nov 1931	20:02	LIB	4 May 1932	11:45	TAU
13 May 1931	01:56	ARI	8 Nov 1931	20:20	SCO	7 May 1932	00:19	GEM
15 May 1931	13:53	TAU	10 Nov 1931	20:39	SAG	9 May 1932	11:33	CAN
17 May 1931	23:25	GEM	12 Nov 1931	22:53	CAP	11 May 1932	20:45	LEO
20 May 1931	06:25	CAN	15 Nov 1931	04:40	AQU	14 May 1932	03:12	VIR
22 May 1931	11:26	LEO	17 Nov 1931	14:33	PIS	16 May 1932	06:32	LIB
24 May 1931	15:06	VIR	20 Nov 1931	03:08	ARI	18 May 1932	07:14	SCO
26 May 1931	17:50	LIB	22 Nov 1931	15:59	TAU	20 May 1932	06:47	SAG
28 May 1931	20:07	SCO	25 Nov 1931	03:11	GEM	22 May 1932	07:12	CAP
30 May 1931	22:48	SAG	27 Nov 1931	12:08	CAN	24 May 1932	10:32	AQU
2 Jun 1931	03:08	CAP	29 Nov 1931	19:05	LEO	26 May 1932	17:57	PIS
4 Jun 1931	10:24	AQU	2 Dec 1931	00:15	VIR	29 May 1932	05:08	ARI
6 Jun 1931	21:01	PIS	4 Dec 1931	03:43	LIB	31 May 1932	18:04	TAU
9 Jun 1931	09:43	ARI	6 Dec 1931	05:43	SCO	3 Jun 1932	06:32	GEM
11 Jun 1931	21:53	TAU	8 Dec 1931	07:04	SAG	5 Jun 1932	17:20	CAN
14 Jun 1931	07:21	GEM	10 Dec 1931	09:18	CAP	8 Jun 1932	02:13	LEO
16 Jun 1931	13:37	CAN	12 Dec 1931	14:10	AQU	10 Jun 1932	09:05	VIR
18 Jun 1931	17:36	LEO	14 Dec 1931	22:51	PIS	12 Jun 1932	13:40	LIB
20 Jun 1931	20:32	VIR	17 Dec 1931	10:49	ARI	14 Jun 1932	15:59	SCO
22 Jun 1931	23:22	LIB	19 Dec 1931	23:44	TAU	16 Jun 1932	16:45	SAG
25 Jun 1931	02:34	SCO	22 Dec 1931	10:58	GEM	18 Jun 1932	17:31	CAP
27 Jun 1931	06:26	SAG	24 Dec 1931	19:21	CAN	20 Jun 1932	20:12	AQU
29 Jun 1931	11:35	CAP	27 Dec 1931	01:15	LEO	23 Jun 1932	02:26	PIS
1 Jul 1931	18:56	AQU	29 Dec 1931	05:40	VIR	25 Jun 1932	12:34	ARI
4 Jul 1931	05:09	PIS	31 Dec 1931	09:17	LIB	28 Jun 1932	01:07	TAU
6 Jul 1931	17:39	ARI	2 Jan 1932	12:23	SCO	30 Jun 1932	13:34	GEM
9 Jul 1931	06:13	TAU	4 Jan 1932	15:15	SAG	3 Jul 1932	00:05	CAN
11 Jul 1931	16:13	GEM	6 Jan 1932	18:37	CAP	5 Jul 1932	08:17	LEO
13 Jul 1931	22:29	CAN	8 Jan 1932	23:44	AQU	7 Jul 1932	14:32	VIR
16 Jul 1931	01:40	LEO	11 Jan 1932	07:49	PIS	9 Jul 1932	19:12	LIB
18 Jul 1931	03:21	VIR	13 Jan 1932	19:07	ARI	11 Jul 1932	22:27	SCO
20 Jul 1931	05:06	LIB	16 Jan 1932	08:02	TAU	14 Jul 1932	00:37	SAG
22 Jul 1931	07:56	SCO	18 Jan 1932	19:46	GEM	16 Jul 1932	02:35	CAP
24 Jul 1931	12:19	SAG	21 Jan 1932	04:21	CAN	18 Jul 1932	05:44	AQU
26 Jul 1931	18:22	CAP	23 Jan 1932	09:38	LEO	20 Jul 1932	11:35	PIS
29 Jul 1931	02:24	AQU	25 Jan 1932	12:46	VIR	22 Jul 1932	20:52	ARI
31 Jul 1931	12:46	PIS	27 Jan 1932	15:07	LIB	25 Jul 1932	08:54	TAU
3 Aug 1931	01:10	ARI	29 Jan 1932	17:43	SCO	27 Jul 1932	21:25	GEM
5 Aug 1931	14:04	TAU	31 Jan 1932	21:07	SAG	30 Jul 1932	08:06	CAN
8 Aug 1931	00:59	GEM	3 Feb 1932	01:39	CAP	1 Aug 1932	15:56	LEO
10 Aug 1931	08:09	CAN	5 Feb 1932	07:48	AQU	3 Aug 1932	21:14	VIR
12 Aug 1931	11:29	LEO	7 Feb 1932	16:15	PIS	6 Aug 1932	00:55	LIB
14 Aug 1931	12:24	VIR	10 Feb 1932	03:17	ARI	8 Aug 1932	03:49	SCO
16 Aug 1931	12:45	LIB	12 Feb 1932	16:04	TAU	10 Aug 1932	06:31	SAG
18 Aug 1931	14:11	SCO	15 Feb 1932	04:27	GEM	12 Aug 1932	09:38	CAP
20 Aug 1931	17:46	SAG	17 Feb 1932	14:01	CAN	14 Aug 1932	13:54	AQU
22 Aug 1931	23:59	CAP	19 Feb 1932	19:48	LEO	16 Aug 1932	20:13	PIS
25 Aug 1931	08:38	AQU	21 Feb 1932	22:24	VIR	19 Aug 1932	05:18	ARI
27 Aug 1931	19:27	PIS	23 Feb 1932	23:21	LIB	21 Aug 1932	16:55	TAU
30 Aug 1931	07:56	ARI	26 Feb 1932	00:20	SCO	24 Aug 1932	05:33	GEM
1 Sep 1931	20:58	TAU	28 Feb 1932	02:39	SAG	26 Aug 1932	16:49	CAN
4 Sep 1931	08:42	GEM	1 Mar 1932	07:06	CAP	29 Aug 1932	01:01	LEO
6 Sep 1931	17:14	CAN	3 Mar 1932	14:00	AQU	31 Aug 1932	05:58	VIR
8 Sep 1931	21:46	LEO	5 Mar 1932	23:15	PIS	2 Sep 1932	08:31	LIB

DATE	TIME	SIGN	DATE	TIME	SIGN	DATE	TIME	SIGN
4 Sep 1932	10:06	SCO	3 Mar 1933	07:17	GEM	30 Aug 1933	04:51	CAP
6 Sep 1932	12:00	SAG	5 Mar 1933	19:42	CAN	1 Sep 1933	06:59	AQU
8 Sep 1932	15:11	CAP	8 Mar 1933	06:17	LEO	3 Sep 1933	09:44	PIS
10 Sep 1932	20:16	AQU	10 Mar 1933	13:40	VIR	5 Sep 1933	14:15	ARI
13 Sep 1932	03:31	PIS	12 Mar 1933	18:02	LIB	7 Sep 1933	21:35	TAU
15 Sep 1932	13:01	ARI	14 Mar 1933	20:27	SCO	10 Sep 1933	08:00	GEM
18 Sep 1932	00:33	TAU	16 Mar 1933	22:18	SAG	12 Sep 1933	20:24	CAN
20 Sep 1932	13:13	GEM	19 Mar 1933	00:47	CAP	15 Sep 1933	08:29	LEO
23 Sep 1932	01:12	CAN	21 Mar 1933	04:39	AQU	17 Sep 1933	18:13	VIR
25 Sep 1932	10:30	LEO	23 Mar 1933	10:16	PIS	20 Sep 1933	00:50	LIB
27 Sep 1932	16:05	VIR	25 Mar 1933	17:49	ARI	22 Sep 1933	04:59	SCO
29 Sep 1932	18:21	LIB	28 Mar 1933	03:32	TAU	24 Sep 1933	07:48	SAG
1 Oct 1932	18:43	SCO	30 Mar 1933	15:13	GEM	26 Sep 1933	10:23	CAP
3 Oct 1932	19:02	SAG	2 Apr 1933	03:49	CAN	28 Sep 1933	13:26	AQU
5 Oct 1932	21:00	CAP	4 Apr 1933	15:15	LEO	30 Sep 1933	17:26	PIS
8 Oct 1932	01:44	AQU	6 Apr 1933	23:31	VIR	2 Oct 1933	22:51	ARI
10 Oct 1932	09:26	PIS	9 Apr 1933	03:59	LIB	5 Oct 1933	06:17	TAU
12 Oct 1932	19:35	ARI	11 Apr 1933	05:31	SCO	7 Oct 1933	16:18	GEM
15 Oct 1932	07:23	TAU	13 Apr 1933	05:51	SAG	10 Oct 1933	04:29	CAN
17 Oct 1932	20:02	GEM	15 Apr 1933	06:53	CAP	12 Oct 1933	17:01	LEO
20 Oct 1932	08:25	CAN	17 Apr 1933	10:03	AQU	15 Oct 1933	03:23	VIR
22 Oct 1932	18:56	LEO	19 Apr 1933	15:54	PIS	17 Oct 1933	10:06	LIB
25 Oct 1932	02:01	VIR	22 Apr 1933	00:14	ARI	19 Oct 1933	13:26	SCO
27 Oct 1932	05:15	LIB	24 Apr 1933	10:31	TAU	21 Oct 1933	14:53	SAG
29 Oct 1932	05:30	SCO	26 Apr 1933	22:18	GEM	23 Oct 1933	16:13	CAP
31 Oct 1932	04:40	SAG	29 Apr 1933	10:57	CAN	25 Oct 1933	18:48	AQU
2 Nov 1932	04:54	CAP	1 May 1933	23:05	LEO	27 Oct 1933	23:17	PIS
4 Nov 1932	08:06	AQU	4 May 1933	08:39	VIR	30 Oct 1933	05:40	ARI
6 Nov 1932	15:07	PIS	6 May 1933	14:15	LIB	1 Nov 1933	13:53	TAU
9 Nov 1932	01:25	ARI	8 May 1933	16:06	SCO	4 Nov 1933	00:02	GEM
11 Nov 1932	13:33	TAU	10 May 1933	15:42	SAG	6 Nov 1933	12:05	CAN
14 Nov 1932	02:13	GEM	12 May 1933	15:15	CAP	9 Nov 1933	00:57	LEO
16 Nov 1932	14:31	CAN	14 May 1933	16:46	AQU	11 Nov 1933	12:22	VIR
19 Nov 1932	01:34	LEO	16 May 1933	21:34	PIS	13 Nov 1933	20:11	LIB
21 Nov 1932	10:07	VIR	19 May 1933	05:45	ARI	15 Nov 1933	23:50	SCO
23 Nov 1932	15:06	LIB	21 May 1933	16:26	TAU	18 Nov 1933	00:34	SAG
25 Nov 1932	16:37	SCO	24 May 1933	04:31	GEM	20 Nov 1933	00:24	CAP
27 Nov 1932	15:58	SAG	26 May 1933	17:11	CAN	22 Nov 1933	01:21	AQU
29 Nov 1932	15:16	CAP	29 May 1933	05:33	LEO	24 Nov 1933	04:50	PIS
1 Dec 1932	16:46	AQU	31 May 1933	16:05	VIR	26 Nov 1933	11:13	ARI
3 Dec 1932	22:09	PIS	2 Jun 1933	23:13	LIB	28 Nov 1933	20:03	TAU
6 Dec 1932	07:35	ARI	5 Jun 1933	02:23	SCO	1 Dec 1933	06:44	GEM
8 Dec 1932	19:41	TAU	7 Jun 1933	02:31	SAG	3 Dec 1933	18:52	CAN
11 Dec 1932	08:25	GEM	9 Jun 1933	01:33	CAP	6 Dec 1933	07:48	LEO
13 Dec 1932	20:27	CAN	11 Jun 1933	01:42	AQU	8 Dec 1933	19:59	VIR
16 Dec 1932	07:12	LEO	13 Jun 1933	04:50	PIS	11 Dec 1933	05:18	LIB
18 Dec 1932	16:08	VIR	15 Jun 1933	11:51	ARI	13 Dec 1933	10:25	SCO
20 Dec 1932	22:30	LIB	17 Jun 1933	22:12	TAU	15 Dec 1933	11:47	SAG
23 Dec 1932	01:51	SCO	20 Jun 1933	10:25	GEM	17 Dec 1933	11:08	CAP
25 Dec 1932	02:41	SAG	22 Jun 1933	23:06	CAN	19 Dec 1933	10:38	AQU
27 Dec 1932	02:31	CAP	25 Jun 1933	11:16	LEO	21 Dec 1933	12:16	PIS
29 Dec 1932	03:23	AQU	27 Jun 1933	22:00	VIR	23 Dec 1933	17:15	ARI
31 Dec 1932	07:16	PIS	30 Jun 1933	06:10	LIB	26 Dec 1933	01:43	TAU
2 Jan 1933	15:14	ARI	2 Jul 1933	10:55	SCO	28 Dec 1933	12:43	GEM
5 Jan 1933	02:36	TAU	4 Jul 1933	12:30	SAG	31 Dec 1933	01:06	CAN
7 Jan 1933	15:19	GEM	6 Jul 1933	12:15	CAP	2 Jan 1934	13:55	LEO
10 Jan 1933	03:15	CAN	8 Jul 1933	12:05	AQU	5 Jan 1934	02:08	VIR
12 Jan 1933	13:25	LEO	10 Jul 1933	14:02	PIS	7 Jan 1934	12:19	LIB
14 Jan 1933	21:41	VIR	12 Jul 1933	19:31	ARI	9 Jan 1934	19:10	SCO
17 Jan 1933	04:02	LIB	15 Jul 1933	04:49	TAU	11 Jan 1934	22:16	SAG
19 Jan 1933	08:23	SCO	17 Jul 1933	16:44	GEM	13 Jan 1934	22:36	CAP
21 Jan 1933	10:54	SAG	20 Jul 1933	05:24	CAN	15 Jan 1934	21:56	AQU
23 Jan 1933	12:17	CAP	22 Jul 1933	17:18	LEO	17 Jan 1934	22:18	PIS
25 Jan 1933	13:57	AQU	25 Jul 1933	03:35	VIR	20 Jan 1934	01:29	ARI
27 Jan 1933	17:31	PIS	27 Jul 1933	11:43	LIB	22 Jan 1934	08:26	TAU
30 Jan 1933	00:22	ARI	29 Jul 1933	17:21	SCO	24 Jan 1934	18:54	GEM
1 Feb 1933	10:40	TAU	31 Jul 1933	20:26	SAG	27 Jan 1934	07:23	CAN
3 Feb 1933	23:04	GEM	2 Aug 1933	21:40	CAP	29 Jan 1934	20:11	LEO
6 Feb 1933	11:12	CAN	4 Aug 1933	22:22	AQU	1 Feb 1934	07:59	VIR
8 Feb 1933	21:15	LEO	7 Aug 1933	00:11	PIS	3 Feb 1934	17:59	LIB
11 Feb 1933	04:42	VIR	9 Aug 1933	04:41	ARI	6 Feb 1934	01:30	SCO
13 Feb 1933	09:58	LIB	11 Aug 1933	12:45	TAU	8 Feb 1934	06:14	SAG
15 Feb 1933	13:45	SCO	13 Aug 1933	23:57	GEM	10 Feb 1934	08:22	CAP
17 Feb 1933	16:42	SAG	16 Aug 1933	12:32	CAN	12 Feb 1934	08:57	AQU
19 Feb 1933	19:22	CAP	19 Aug 1933	00:21	LEO	14 Feb 1934	09:27	PIS
21 Feb 1933	22:29	AQU	21 Aug 1933	10:06	VIR	16 Feb 1934	11:40	ARI
24 Feb 1933	02:56	PIS	23 Aug 1933	17:29	LIB	18 Feb 1934	17:03	TAU
26 Feb 1933	09:42	ARI	25 Aug 1933	22:43	SCO	21 Feb 1934	02:17	GEM
28 Feb 1933	19:20	TAU	28 Aug 1933	02:20	SAG	23 Feb 1934	14:22	CAN

DATE	TIME	SIGN	DATE	TIME	SIGN	DATE	TIME	SIGN
26 Feb 1934	03:13	LEO	24 Aug 1934	18:07	PIS	21 Feb 1935	02:02	LIB
28 Feb 1934	14:45	VIR	26 Aug 1934	18:43	ARI	23 Feb 1935	13:03	SCO
3 Mar 1934	00:01	LIB	28 Aug 1934	21:55	TAU	25 Feb 1935	21:39	SAG
5 Mar 1934	06:58	SCO	31 Aug 1934	04:55	GEM	28 Feb 1935	03:03	CAP
7 Mar 1934	11:57	SAG	2 Sep 1934	15:40	CAN	2 Mar 1935	05:15	AQU
9 Mar 1934	15:21	CAP	5 Sep 1934	04:31	LEO	4 Mar 1935	05:13	PIS
11 Mar 1934	17:35	AQU	7 Sep 1934	17:16	VIR	6 Mar 1935	04:40	ARI
13 Mar 1934	19:25	PIS	10 Sep 1934	04:22	LIB	8 Mar 1935	05:43	TAU
15 Mar 1934	22:00	ARI	12 Sep 1934	13:18	SCO	10 Mar 1935	10:12	GEM
18 Mar 1934	02:46	TAU	14 Sep 1934	20:02	SAG	12 Mar 1935	18:51	CAN
20 Mar 1934	10:52	GEM	17 Sep 1934	00:34	CAP	15 Mar 1935	06:47	LEO
22 Mar 1934	22:13	CAN	19 Sep 1934	03:05	AQU	17 Mar 1935	19:51	VIR
25 Mar 1934	11:02	LEO	21 Sep 1934	04:13	PIS	20 Mar 1935	08:07	LIB
27 Mar 1934	22:43	VIR	23 Sep 1934	05:13	ARI	22 Mar 1935	18:44	SCO
30 Mar 1934	07:36	LIB	25 Sep 1934	07:47	TAU	25 Mar 1935	03:23	SAG
1 Apr 1934	13:34	SCO	27 Sep 1934	13:34	GEM	27 Mar 1935	09:47	CAP
3 Apr 1934	17:36	SAG	29 Sep 1934	23:15	CAN	29 Mar 1935	13:40	AQU
5 Apr 1934	20:45	CAP	2 Oct 1934	11:44	LEO	31 Mar 1935	15:14	PIS
7 Apr 1934	23:42	AQU	5 Oct 1934	00:30	VIR	2 Apr 1935	15:31	ARI
10 Apr 1934	02:52	PIS	7 Oct 1934	11:19	LIB	4 Apr 1935	16:18	TAU
12 Apr 1934	06:40	ARI	9 Oct 1934	19:31	SCO	6 Apr 1935	19:35	GEM
14 Apr 1934	11:56	TAU	12 Oct 1934	01:31	SAG	9 Apr 1935	02:49	CAN
16 Apr 1934	19:41	GEM	14 Oct 1934	06:03	CAP	11 Apr 1935	13:52	LEO
19 Apr 1934	06:26	CAN	16 Oct 1934	09:31	AQU	14 Apr 1935	02:46	VIR
21 Apr 1934	19:09	LEO	18 Oct 1934	12:09	PIS	16 Apr 1935	15:00	LIB
24 Apr 1934	07:19	VIR	20 Oct 1934	14:28	ARI	19 Apr 1935	01:08	SCO
26 Apr 1934	16:31	LIB	22 Oct 1934	17:34	TAU	21 Apr 1935	09:05	SAG
28 Apr 1934	22:05	SCO	24 Oct 1934	22:58	GEM	23 Apr 1935	15:12	CAP
1 May 1934	01:01	SAG	27 Oct 1934	07:46	CAN	25 Apr 1935	19:43	AQU
3 May 1934	02:53	CAP	29 Oct 1934	19:42	LEO	27 Apr 1935	22:39	PIS
5 May 1934	05:06	AQU	1 Nov 1934	08:35	VIR	30 Apr 1935	00:26	ARI
7 May 1934	08:26	PIS	3 Nov 1934	19:40	LIB	2 May 1935	02:09	TAU
9 May 1934	13:09	ARI	6 Nov 1934	03:31	SCO	4 May 1935	05:26	GEM
11 May 1934	19:23	TAU	8 Nov 1934	08:32	SAG	6 May 1935	11:51	CAN
14 May 1934	03:38	GEM	10 Nov 1934	11:56	CAP	8 May 1935	21:55	LEO
16 May 1934	14:17	CAN	12 Nov 1934	14:51	AQU	11 May 1935	10:25	VIR
19 May 1934	02:54	LEO	14 Nov 1934	17:56	PIS	13 May 1935	22:47	LIB
21 May 1934	15:34	VIR	16 Nov 1934	21:26	ARI	16 May 1935	08:53	SCO
24 May 1934	01:41	LIB	19 Nov 1934	01:47	TAU	18 May 1935	16:12	SAG
26 May 1934	07:51	SCO	21 Nov 1934	07:47	GEM	20 May 1935	21:19	CAP
28 May 1934	10:27	SAG	23 Nov 1934	16:25	CAN	23 May 1935	01:08	AQU
30 May 1934	11:11	CAP	26 Nov 1934	03:54	LEO	25 May 1935	04:13	PIS
1 Jun 1934	11:55	AQU	28 Nov 1934	16:51	VIR	27 May 1935	06:58	ARI
3 Jun 1934	14:07	PIS	1 Dec 1934	04:38	LIB	29 May 1935	09:59	TAU
5 Jun 1934	18:31	ARI	3 Dec 1934	13:04	SCO	31 May 1935	14:11	GEM
8 Jun 1934	01:17	TAU	5 Dec 1934	17:52	SAG	2 Jun 1935	20:44	CAN
10 Jun 1934	10:14	GEM	7 Dec 1934	20:08	CAP	5 Jun 1935	06:19	LEO
12 Jun 1934	21:14	CAN	9 Dec 1934	21:33	AQU	7 Jun 1935	18:25	VIR
15 Jun 1934	09:52	LEO	11 Dec 1934	23:31	PIS	10 Jun 1935	06:59	LIB
17 Jun 1934	22:50	VIR	14 Dec 1934	02:51	ARI	12 Jun 1935	17:35	SCO
20 Jun 1934	09:57	LIB	16 Dec 1934	07:56	TAU	15 Jun 1935	00:55	SAG
22 Jun 1934	17:24	SCO	18 Dec 1934	14:58	GEM	17 Jun 1935	05:20	CAP
24 Jun 1934	20:48	SAG	21 Dec 1934	00:11	CAN	19 Jun 1935	07:55	AQU
26 Jun 1934	21:23	CAP	23 Dec 1934	11:37	LEO	21 Jun 1935	09:55	PIS
28 Jun 1934	21:02	AQU	26 Dec 1934	00:31	VIR	23 Jun 1935	12:21	ARI
30 Jun 1934	21:38	PIS	28 Dec 1934	12:58	LIB	25 Jun 1935	15:54	TAU
3 Jul 1934	00:39	ARI	30 Dec 1934	22:39	SCO	27 Jun 1935	21:06	GEM
5 Jul 1934	06:47	TAU	2 Jan 1935	05:43	SAG	30 Jun 1935	04:26	CAN
7 Jul 1934	15:55	GEM	4 Jan 1935	06:43	CAP	2 Jul 1935	14:13	LEO
10 Jul 1934	03:20	CAN	6 Jan 1935	07:03	AQU	5 Jul 1935	02:08	VIR
12 Jul 1934	16:07	LEO	8 Jan 1935	07:17	PIS	7 Jul 1935	14:52	LIB
15 Jul 1934	05:06	VIR	10 Jan 1935	09:03	ARI	10 Jul 1935	02:14	SCO
17 Jul 1934	16:46	LIB	12 Jan 1935	13:25	TAU	12 Jul 1935	10:26	SAG
20 Jul 1934	01:29	SCO	14 Jan 1935	20:43	GEM	14 Jul 1935	15:01	CAP
22 Jul 1934	06:27	SAG	17 Jan 1935	06:37	CAN	16 Jul 1935	16:53	AQU
24 Jul 1934	08:02	CAP	19 Jan 1935	18:26	LEO	18 Jul 1935	17:30	PIS
26 Jul 1934	07:43	AQU	22 Jan 1935	07:19	VIR	20 Jul 1935	18:32	ARI
28 Jul 1934	07:20	PIS	24 Jan 1935	19:58	LIB	22 Jul 1935	21:21	TAU
30 Jul 1934	08:46	ARI	27 Jan 1935	06:45	SCO	25 Jul 1935	02:42	GEM
1 Aug 1934	13:26	TAU	29 Jan 1935	14:09	SAG	27 Jul 1935	10:43	CAN
3 Aug 1934	21:49	GEM	31 Jan 1935	17:47	CAP	29 Jul 1935	21:04	LEO
6 Aug 1934	09:13	CAN	2 Feb 1935	18:25	AQU	1 Aug 1935	09:06	VIR
8 Aug 1934	22:07	LEO	4 Feb 1935	17:46	PIS	3 Aug 1935	21:54	LIB
11 Aug 1934	10:58	VIR	6 Feb 1935	17:48	ARI	6 Aug 1935	09:56	SCO
13 Aug 1934	22:32	LIB	8 Feb 1935	20:23	TAU	8 Aug 1935	19:24	SAG
16 Aug 1934	07:50	SCO	11 Feb 1935	02:36	GEM	11 Aug 1935	01:08	CAP
18 Aug 1934	14:10	SAG	13 Feb 1935	12:24	CAN	13 Aug 1935	03:20	AQU
20 Aug 1934	17:26	CAP	16 Feb 1935	00:35	LEO	15 Aug 1935	03:18	PIS
22 Aug 1934	18:18	AQU	18 Feb 1935	13:32	VIR	17 Aug 1935	02:55	ARI

DATE	TIME	SIGN	DATE	TIME	SIGN	DATE	TIME	SIGN
19 Aug 1935	04:08	TAU	15 Feb 1936	23:55	SAG	12 Aug 1936	23:52	CAN
21 Aug 1935	08:26	GEM	18 Feb 1936	08:20	CAP	15 Aug 1936	06:20	LEO
23 Aug 1935	16:17	CAN	20 Feb 1936	12:45	AQU	17 Aug 1936	14:45	VIR
26 Aug 1935	03:00	LEO	22 Feb 1936	13:54	PIS	20 Aug 1936	01:17	LIB
28 Aug 1935	15:20	VIR	24 Feb 1936	13:34	ARI	22 Aug 1936	13:36	SCO
31 Aug 1935	04:07	LIB	26 Feb 1936	13:51	TAU	25 Aug 1936	02:08	SAG
2 Sep 1935	16:21	SCO	28 Feb 1936	16:30	GEM	27 Aug 1936	12:33	CAP
5 Sep 1935	02:47	SAG	1 Mar 1936	22:26	CAN	29 Aug 1936	19:11	AQU
7 Sep 1935	10:06	CAP	4 Mar 1936	07:20	LEO	31 Aug 1936	22:04	PIS
9 Sep 1935	13:42	AQU	6 Mar 1936	18:17	VIR	2 Sep 1936	22:42	ARI
11 Sep 1935	14:14	PIS	9 Mar 1936	06:25	LIB	4 Sep 1936	23:04	TAU
13 Sep 1935	13:20	ARI	11 Mar 1936	19:03	SCO	7 Sep 1936	00:55	GEM
15 Sep 1935	13:11	TAU	14 Mar 1936	07:05	SAG	9 Sep 1936	05:15	CAN
17 Sep 1935	15:48	GEM	16 Mar 1936	16:51	CAP	11 Sep 1936	12:13	LEO
19 Sep 1935	22:28	CAN	18 Mar 1936	22:50	AQU	13 Sep 1936	21:20	VIR
22 Sep 1935	08:50	LEO	21 Mar 1936	00:57	PIS	16 Sep 1936	08:12	LIB
24 Sep 1935	21:18	VIR	23 Mar 1936	00:31	ARI	18 Sep 1936	20:32	SCO
27 Sep 1935	10:05	LIB	24 Mar 1936	23:38	TAU	21 Sep 1936	09:23	SAG
29 Sep 1935	22:05	SCO	27 Mar 1936	00:32	GEM	23 Sep 1936	20:52	CAP
2 Oct 1935	08:40	SAG	29 Mar 1936	04:52	CAN	26 Sep 1936	04:52	AQU
4 Oct 1935	17:02	CAP	31 Mar 1936	13:04	LEO	28 Sep 1936	08:38	PIS
6 Oct 1935	22:19	AQU	3 Apr 1936	00:07	VIR	30 Sep 1936	09:09	ARI
9 Oct 1935	00:25	PIS	5 Apr 1936	12:30	LIB	2 Oct 1936	08:25	TAU
11 Oct 1935	00:19	ARI	8 Apr 1936	01:04	SCO	4 Oct 1936	08:37	GEM
12 Oct 1935	23:54	TAU	10 Apr 1936	13:02	SAG	6 Oct 1936	11:29	CAN
15 Oct 1935	01:18	GEM	12 Apr 1936	23:21	CAP	8 Oct 1936	17:44	LEO
17 Oct 1935	06:20	CAN	15 Apr 1936	06:48	AQU	11 Oct 1936	03:01	VIR
19 Oct 1935	15:35	LEO	17 Apr 1936	10:36	PIS	13 Oct 1936	14:19	LIB
22 Oct 1935	03:44	VIR	19 Apr 1936	11:19	ARI	16 Oct 1936	02:46	SCO
24 Oct 1935	16:31	LIB	21 Apr 1936	10:37	TAU	18 Oct 1936	15:37	SAG
27 Oct 1935	04:14	SCO	23 Apr 1936	10:38	GEM	21 Oct 1936	03:36	CAP
29 Oct 1935	14:16	SAG	25 Apr 1936	13:23	CAN	23 Oct 1936	12:58	AQU
31 Oct 1935	22:30	CAP	27 Apr 1936	20:03	LEO	25 Oct 1936	18:27	PIS
3 Nov 1935	04:37	AQU	30 Apr 1936	06:22	VIR	27 Oct 1936	20:08	ARI
5 Nov 1935	08:19	PIS	2 May 1936	18:42	LIB	29 Oct 1936	19:34	TAU
7 Nov 1935	09:53	ARI	5 May 1936	07:16	SCO	31 Oct 1936	18:49	GEM
9 Nov 1935	10:29	TAU	7 May 1936	18:53	SAG	2 Nov 1936	20:00	CAN
11 Nov 1935	11:53	GEM	10 May 1936	04:56	CAP	5 Nov 1936	00:38	LEO
13 Nov 1935	15:57	CAN	12 May 1936	12:46	AQU	7 Nov 1936	09:00	VIR
15 Nov 1935	23:51	LEO	14 May 1936	17:52	PIS	9 Nov 1936	20:14	LIB
18 Nov 1935	11:10	VIR	16 May 1936	20:13	ARI	12 Nov 1936	08:51	SCO
20 Nov 1935	23:51	LIB	18 May 1936	20:47	TAU	14 Nov 1936	21:33	SAG
23 Nov 1935	11:35	SCO	20 May 1936	21:12	GEM	17 Nov 1936	09:19	CAP
25 Nov 1935	21:07	SAG	22 May 1936	23:20	CAN	19 Nov 1936	19:10	AQU
28 Nov 1935	04:27	CAP	25 May 1936	04:41	LEO	22 Nov 1936	02:02	PIS
30 Nov 1935	09:59	AQU	27 May 1936	13:48	VIR	24 Nov 1936	05:36	ARI
2 Dec 1935	14:02	PIS	30 May 1936	01:38	LIB	26 Nov 1936	06:28	TAU
4 Dec 1935	16:52	ARI	1 Jun 1936	14:10	SCO	28 Nov 1936	06:11	GEM
6 Dec 1935	19:03	TAU	4 Jun 1936	01:36	SAG	30 Nov 1936	06:40	CAN
8 Dec 1935	21:37	GEM	6 Jun 1936	11:01	CAP	2 Dec 1936	09:44	LEO
11 Dec 1935	01:54	CAN	8 Jun 1936	18:17	AQU	4 Dec 1936	16:31	VIR
13 Dec 1935	09:07	LEO	10 Jun 1936	23:26	PIS	7 Dec 1936	02:55	LIB
15 Dec 1935	19:32	VIR	13 Jun 1936	02:46	ARI	9 Dec 1936	15:27	SCO
18 Dec 1935	07:58	LIB	15 Jun 1936	04:48	TAU	12 Dec 1936	04:06	SAG
20 Dec 1935	20:02	SCO	17 Jun 1936	06:29	GEM	14 Dec 1936	15:24	CAP
23 Dec 1935	05:44	SAG	19 Jun 1936	09:09	CAN	17 Dec 1936	00:41	AQU
25 Dec 1935	12:26	CAP	21 Jun 1936	14:06	LEO	19 Dec 1936	07:43	PIS
27 Dec 1935	16:45	AQU	23 Jun 1936	22:16	VIR	21 Dec 1936	12:25	ARI
29 Dec 1935	19:41	PIS	26 Jun 1936	09:23	LIB	23 Dec 1936	15:05	TAU
31 Dec 1935	22:15	ARI	28 Jun 1936	21:52	SCO	25 Dec 1936	16:24	GEM
3 Jan 1936	01:11	TAU	1 Jul 1936	09:26	SAG	27 Dec 1936	17:36	CAN
5 Jan 1936	05:04	GEM	3 Jul 1936	18:33	CAP	29 Dec 1936	20:14	LEO
7 Jan 1936	10:29	CAN	6 Jul 1936	00:55	AQU	1 Jan 1937	01:46	VIR
9 Jan 1936	18:01	LEO	8 Jul 1936	05:10	PIS	3 Jan 1937	10:55	LIB
12 Jan 1936	04:05	VIR	10 Jul 1936	08:09	ARI	5 Jan 1937	22:58	SCO
14 Jan 1936	16:10	LIB	12 Jul 1936	10:45	TAU	8 Jan 1937	11:42	SAG
17 Jan 1936	04:38	SCO	14 Jul 1936	13:38	GEM	10 Jan 1937	22:52	CAP
19 Jan 1936	15:10	SAG	16 Jul 1936	17:27	CAN	13 Jan 1937	07:24	AQU
21 Jan 1936	22:17	CAP	18 Jul 1936	22:58	LEO	15 Jan 1937	13:27	PIS
24 Jan 1936	02:01	AQU	21 Jul 1936	06:53	VIR	17 Jan 1937	17:48	ARI
26 Jan 1936	03:34	PIS	23 Jul 1936	17:30	LIB	19 Jan 1937	21:06	TAU
28 Jan 1936	04:35	ARI	26 Jul 1936	05:53	SCO	21 Jan 1937	23:53	GEM
30 Jan 1936	06:37	TAU	28 Jul 1936	17:55	SAG	24 Jan 1937	02:38	CAN
1 Feb 1936	10:39	GEM	31 Jul 1936	03:23	CAP	26 Jan 1937	06:07	LEO
3 Feb 1936	16:58	CAN	2 Aug 1936	09:24	AQU	28 Jan 1937	11:31	VIR
6 Feb 1936	01:26	LEO	4 Aug 1936	12:35	PIS	30 Jan 1937	19:49	LIB
8 Feb 1936	11:48	VIR	6 Aug 1936	14:21	ARI	2 Feb 1937	07:10	SCO
10 Feb 1936	23:45	LIB	8 Aug 1936	16:11	TAU	4 Feb 1937	19:58	SAG
13 Feb 1936	12:23	SCO	10 Aug 1936	19:11	GEM	7 Feb 1937	07:33	CAP

DATE	TIME	SIGN
9 Feb 1937	15:59	AQU
11 Feb 1937	21:09	PIS
14 Feb 1937	00:11	ARI
16 Feb 1937	02:34	TAU
18 Feb 1937	05:22	GEM
20 Feb 1937	09:04	CAN
22 Feb 1937	13:51	LEO
24 Feb 1937	20:04	VIR
27 Feb 1937	04:26	LIB
1 Mar 1937	15:23	SCO
4 Mar 1937	04:07	SAG
6 Mar 1937	16:22	CAP
9 Mar 1937	01:34	AQU
11 Mar 1937	06:49	PIS
13 Mar 1937	08:59	ARI
15 Mar 1937	09:53	TAU
17 Mar 1937	11:19	GEM
19 Mar 1937	14:25	CAN
21 Mar 1937	10:35	LEO
24 Mar 1937	02:44	VIR
26 Mar 1937	11:47	LIB
28 Mar 1937	22:51	SCO
31 Mar 1937	11:32	SAG
3 Apr 1937	00:15	CAP
5 Apr 1937	10:37	AQU
7 Apr 1937	16:58	PIS
9 Apr 1937	19:27	ARI
11 Apr 1937	19:39	TAU
13 Apr 1937	19:34	GEM
15 Apr 1937	21:03	CAN
18 Apr 1937	01:12	LEO
20 Apr 1937	08:16	VIR
22 Apr 1937	17:50	LIB
25 Apr 1937	05:20	SCO
27 Apr 1937	18:04	SAG
30 Apr 1937	06:56	CAP
2 May 1937	18:08	AQU
5 May 1937	01:55	PIS
7 May 1937	05:47	ARI
9 May 1937	06:31	TAU
11 May 1937	05:56	GEM
13 May 1937	06:00	CAN
15 May 1937	08:27	LEO
17 May 1937	14:19	VIR
19 May 1937	23:35	LIB
22 May 1937	11:18	SCO
25 May 1937	00:09	SAG
27 May 1937	12:52	CAP
30 May 1937	00:12	AQU
1 Jun 1937	08:56	PIS
3 Jun 1937	14:20	ARI
5 Jun 1937	16:35	TAU
7 Jun 1937	16:45	GEM
9 Jun 1937	16:31	CAN
11 Jun 1937	17:44	LEO
13 Jun 1937	22:02	VIR
16 Jun 1937	06:08	LIB
18 Jun 1937	17:30	SCO
21 Jun 1937	06:25	SAG
23 Jun 1937	18:57	CAP
26 Jun 1937	05:53	AQU
28 Jun 1937	14:35	PIS
30 Jun 1937	20:49	ARI
3 Jul 1937	00:33	TAU
5 Jul 1937	02:14	GEM
7 Jul 1937	02:53	CAN
9 Jul 1937	03:59	LEO
11 Jul 1937	07:15	VIR
13 Jul 1937	14:05	LIB
16 Jul 1937	00:36	SCO
18 Jul 1937	13:20	SAG
21 Jul 1937	01:49	CAP
23 Jul 1937	12:18	AQU
25 Jul 1937	20:20	PIS
28 Jul 1937	02:14	ARI
30 Jul 1937	06:31	TAU
1 Aug 1937	09:28	GEM
3 Aug 1937	11:33	CAN
5 Aug 1937	13:35	LEO

DATE	TIME	SIGN
7 Aug 1937	16:54	VIR
9 Aug 1937	22:59	LIB
12 Aug 1937	08:37	SCO
14 Aug 1937	20:58	SAG
17 Aug 1937	09:36	CAP
19 Aug 1937	20:04	AQU
22 Aug 1937	03:27	PIS
24 Aug 1937	08:22	ARI
26 Aug 1937	11:56	TAU
28 Aug 1937	15:01	GEM
30 Aug 1937	18:03	CAN
1 Sep 1937	21:21	LEO
4 Sep 1937	01:35	VIR
6 Sep 1937	07:48	LIB
8 Sep 1937	16:59	SCO
11 Sep 1937	04:58	SAG
13 Sep 1937	17:51	CAP
16 Sep 1937	04:50	AQU
18 Sep 1937	12:17	PIS
20 Sep 1937	16:00	ARI
22 Sep 1937	18:49	TAU
24 Sep 1937	20:46	GEM
26 Sep 1937	23:24	CAN
29 Sep 1937	03:14	LEO
1 Oct 1937	08:29	VIR
3 Oct 1937	15:31	LIB
6 Oct 1937	00:55	SCO
8 Oct 1937	12:44	SAG
11 Oct 1937	01:46	CAP
13 Oct 1937	13:36	AQU
15 Oct 1937	22:01	PIS
18 Oct 1937	02:31	ARI
20 Oct 1937	04:09	TAU
22 Oct 1937	04:39	GEM
24 Oct 1937	05:46	CAN
26 Oct 1937	08:43	LEO
28 Oct 1937	14:02	VIR
30 Oct 1937	21:47	LIB
2 Nov 1937	07:48	SCO
4 Nov 1937	19:46	SAG
7 Nov 1937	08:49	CAP
9 Nov 1937	21:18	AQU
12 Nov 1937	07:06	PIS
14 Nov 1937	12:58	ARI
16 Nov 1937	15:10	TAU
18 Nov 1937	15:09	GEM
20 Nov 1937	14:47	CAN
22 Nov 1937	15:55	LEO
24 Nov 1937	19:56	VIR
27 Nov 1937	03:22	LIB
29 Nov 1937	13:46	SCO
2 Dec 1937	02:05	SAG
4 Dec 1937	15:07	CAP
7 Dec 1937	03:39	AQU
9 Dec 1937	14:20	PIS
11 Dec 1937	21:53	ARI
14 Dec 1937	01:48	TAU
16 Dec 1937	02:41	GEM
18 Dec 1937	02:02	CAN
20 Dec 1937	01:49	LEO
22 Dec 1937	03:57	VIR
24 Dec 1937	09:54	LIB
26 Dec 1937	19:44	SCO
29 Dec 1937	08:11	SAG
31 Dec 1937	21:16	CAP
3 Jan 1938	09:30	AQU
5 Jan 1938	20:06	PIS
8 Jan 1938	04:28	ARI
10 Jan 1938	10:04	TAU
12 Jan 1938	12:49	GEM
14 Jan 1938	13:21	CAN
16 Jan 1938	13:09	LEO
18 Jan 1938	14:13	VIR
20 Jan 1938	18:27	LIB
23 Jan 1938	02:55	SCO
25 Jan 1938	14:51	SAG
28 Jan 1938	03:57	CAP
30 Jan 1938	15:59	AQU
2 Feb 1938	01:57	PIS

DATE	TIME	SIGN
4 Feb 1938	09:53	ARI
6 Feb 1938	15:57	TAU
8 Feb 1938	20:07	GEM
10 Feb 1938	22:25	CAN
12 Feb 1938	23:33	LEO
15 Feb 1938	00:57	VIR
17 Feb 1938	04:28	LIB
19 Feb 1938	11:38	SCO
21 Feb 1938	22:34	SAG
24 Feb 1938	11:27	CAP
26 Feb 1938	23:34	AQU
1 Mar 1938	09:12	PIS
3 Mar 1938	16:15	ARI
5 Mar 1938	21:28	TAU
8 Mar 1938	01:32	GEM
10 Mar 1938	04:45	CAN
12 Mar 1938	07:22	LEO
14 Mar 1938	10:05	VIR
16 Mar 1938	14:08	LIB
18 Mar 1938	20:54	SCO
21 Mar 1938	07:01	SAG
23 Mar 1938	19:31	CAP
26 Mar 1938	07:55	AQU
28 Mar 1938	17:51	PIS
31 Mar 1938	00:32	ARI
2 Apr 1938	04:42	TAU
4 Apr 1938	07:33	GEM
6 Apr 1938	10:07	CAN
8 Apr 1938	13:04	LEO
10 Apr 1938	16:51	VIR
12 Apr 1938	22:02	LIB
15 Apr 1938	05:21	SCO
17 Apr 1938	15:19	SAG
20 Apr 1938	03:31	CAP
22 Apr 1938	16:10	AQU
25 Apr 1938	02:52	PIS
27 Apr 1938	10:07	ARI
29 Apr 1938	14:00	TAU
1 May 1938	15:44	GEM
3 May 1938	16:50	CAN
5 May 1938	18:41	LEO
7 May 1938	22:17	VIR
10 May 1938	04:05	LIB
12 May 1938	12:16	SCO
14 May 1938	22:41	SAG
17 May 1938	10:51	CAP
19 May 1938	23:37	AQU
22 May 1938	11:07	PIS
24 May 1938	19:34	ARI
27 May 1938	00:15	TAU
29 May 1938	01:51	GEM
31 May 1938	01:52	CAN
2 Jun 1938	02:09	LEO
4 Jun 1938	04:21	VIR
6 Jun 1938	09:36	LIB
8 Jun 1938	18:01	SCO
11 Jun 1938	04:57	SAG
13 Jun 1938	17:20	CAP
16 Jun 1938	06:07	AQU
18 Jun 1938	18:02	PIS
21 Jun 1938	03:38	ARI
23 Jun 1938	09:48	TAU
25 Jun 1938	12:23	GEM
27 Jun 1938	12:26	CAN
29 Jun 1938	11:45	LEO
1 Jul 1938	12:24	VIR
3 Jul 1938	16:09	LIB
5 Jul 1938	23:49	SCO
8 Jul 1938	10:45	SAG
10 Jul 1938	23:21	CAP
13 Jul 1938	12:05	AQU
15 Jul 1938	23:54	PIS
18 Jul 1938	10:01	ARI
20 Jul 1938	17:30	TAU
22 Jul 1938	21:41	GEM
24 Jul 1938	22:53	CAN
26 Jul 1938	22:25	LEO
28 Jul 1938	22:17	VIR
31 Jul 1938	00:36	LIB

DATE	TIME	SIGN	DATE	TIME	SIGN	DATE	TIME	SIGN
2 Aug 1938	06:49	SCO	30 Jan 1939	06:49	GEM	28 Jul 1939	04:50	CAP
4 Aug 1938	17:01	SAG	1 Feb 1939	09:20	CAN	30 Jul 1939	16:14	AQU
7 Aug 1938	05:33	CAP	3 Feb 1939	09:05	LEO	2 Aug 1939	04:41	PIS
9 Aug 1938	18:14	AQU	5 Feb 1939	08:02	VIR	4 Aug 1939	17:22	ARI
12 Aug 1938	05:44	PIS	7 Feb 1939	08:30	LIB	7 Aug 1939	04:46	TAU
14 Aug 1938	15:33	ARI	9 Feb 1939	12:23	SCO	9 Aug 1939	13:04	GEM
16 Aug 1938	23:24	TAU	11 Feb 1939	20:24	SAG	11 Aug 1939	17:20	CAN
19 Aug 1938	04:50	GEM	14 Feb 1939	07:41	CAP	13 Aug 1939	18:09	LEO
21 Aug 1938	07:39	CAN	16 Feb 1939	20:21	AQU	15 Aug 1939	17:19	VIR
23 Aug 1938	08:26	LEO	19 Feb 1939	08:51	PIS	17 Aug 1939	17:03	LIB
25 Aug 1938	08:43	VIR	21 Feb 1939	20:22	ARI	19 Aug 1939	19:20	SCO
27 Aug 1938	10:27	LIB	24 Feb 1939	06:18	TAU	22 Aug 1939	01:14	SAG
29 Aug 1938	15:26	SCO	26 Feb 1939	13:46	GEM	24 Aug 1939	10:34	CAP
1 Sep 1938	00:28	SAG	28 Feb 1939	18:06	CAN	26 Aug 1939	22:09	AQU
3 Sep 1938	12:30	CAP	2 Mar 1939	19:29	LEO	29 Aug 1939	10:42	PIS
6 Sep 1938	01:09	AQU	4 Mar 1939	19:16	VIR	31 Aug 1939	23:14	ARI
8 Sep 1938	12:27	PIS	6 Mar 1939	19:25	LIB	3 Sep 1939	10:46	TAU
10 Sep 1938	21:39	ARI	8 Mar 1939	22:00	SCO	5 Sep 1939	20:01	GEM
13 Sep 1938	04:53	TAU	11 Mar 1939	04:23	SAG	8 Sep 1939	01:50	CAN
15 Sep 1938	10:22	GEM	13 Mar 1939	14:35	CAP	10 Sep 1939	04:10	LEO
17 Sep 1938	14:08	CAN	16 Mar 1939	03:01	AQU	12 Sep 1939	04:08	VIR
19 Sep 1938	16:25	LEO	18 Mar 1939	15:31	PIS	14 Sep 1939	03:38	LIB
21 Sep 1938	18:00	VIR	21 Mar 1939	02:40	ARI	16 Sep 1939	04:43	SCO
23 Sep 1938	20:19	LIB	23 Mar 1939	11:57	TAU	18 Sep 1939	09:02	SAG
26 Sep 1938	00:57	SCO	25 Mar 1939	19:14	GEM	20 Sep 1939	17:10	CAP
28 Sep 1938	09:02	SAG	28 Mar 1939	00:18	CAN	23 Sep 1939	04:24	AQU
30 Sep 1938	20:20	CAP	30 Mar 1939	03:14	LEO	25 Sep 1939	16:59	PIS
3 Oct 1938	08:57	AQU	1 Apr 1939	04:38	VIR	28 Sep 1939	05:21	ARI
5 Oct 1938	20:26	PIS	3 Apr 1939	05:48	LIB	30 Sep 1939	16:28	TAU
8 Oct 1938	05:22	ARI	5 Apr 1939	08:22	SCO	3 Oct 1939	01:37	GEM
10 Oct 1938	11:41	TAU	7 Apr 1939	13:48	SAG	5 Oct 1939	08:15	CAN
12 Oct 1938	16:09	GEM	9 Apr 1939	22:47	CAP	7 Oct 1939	12:08	LEO
14 Oct 1938	19:30	CAN	12 Apr 1939	10:33	AQU	9 Oct 1939	13:45	VIR
16 Oct 1938	22:19	LEO	14 Apr 1939	23:04	PIS	11 Oct 1939	14:15	LIB
19 Oct 1938	01:09	VIR	17 Apr 1939	10:12	ARI	13 Oct 1939	15:18	SCO
21 Oct 1938	04:43	LIB	19 Apr 1939	18:56	TAU	15 Oct 1939	18:36	SAG
23 Oct 1938	10:00	SCO	22 Apr 1939	01:15	GEM	18 Oct 1939	01:22	CAP
25 Oct 1938	17:54	SAG	24 Apr 1939	05:43	CAN	20 Oct 1939	11:40	AQU
28 Oct 1938	04:38	CAP	26 Apr 1939	08:54	LEO	23 Oct 1939	00:05	PIS
30 Oct 1938	17:08	AQU	28 Apr 1939	11:26	VIR	25 Oct 1939	12:27	ARI
2 Nov 1938	05:08	PIS	30 Apr 1939	14:02	LIB	27 Oct 1939	23:08	TAU
4 Nov 1938	14:33	ARI	2 May 1939	17:36	SCO	30 Oct 1939	07:30	GEM
6 Nov 1938	20:39	TAU	4 May 1939	23:11	SAG	1 Nov 1939	13:40	CAN
9 Nov 1938	00:02	GEM	7 May 1939	07:34	CAP	3 Nov 1939	18:01	LEO
11 Nov 1938	01:59	CAN	9 May 1939	18:41	AQU	5 Nov 1939	20:56	VIR
13 Nov 1938	03:49	LEO	12 May 1939	07:09	PIS	7 Nov 1939	23:03	LIB
15 Nov 1938	06:37	VIR	14 May 1939	18:40	ARI	10 Nov 1939	01:14	SCO
17 Nov 1938	11:03	LIB	17 May 1939	03:27	TAU	12 Nov 1939	04:41	SAG
19 Nov 1938	17:25	SCO	19 May 1939	09:05	GEM	14 Nov 1939	10:43	CAP
22 Nov 1938	01:57	SAG	21 May 1939	12:22	CAN	16 Nov 1939	20:00	AQU
24 Nov 1938	12:38	CAP	23 May 1939	14:33	LEO	19 Nov 1939	08:00	PIS
27 Nov 1938	00:58	AQU	25 May 1939	16:50	VIR	21 Nov 1939	20:35	ARI
29 Nov 1938	13:29	PIS	27 May 1939	20:06	LIB	24 Nov 1939	07:22	TAU
2 Dec 1938	00:01	ARI	30 May 1939	00:47	SCO	26 Nov 1939	15:08	GEM
4 Dec 1938	07:00	TAU	1 Jun 1939	07:15	SAG	28 Nov 1939	20:11	CAN
6 Dec 1938	10:17	GEM	3 Jun 1939	15:50	CAP	30 Nov 1939	23:33	LEO
8 Dec 1938	11:07	CAN	6 Jun 1939	02:40	AQU	3 Dec 1939	02:22	VIR
10 Dec 1938	11:17	LEO	8 Jun 1939	15:04	PIS	5 Dec 1939	05:22	LIB
12 Dec 1938	12:38	VIR	11 Jun 1939	03:09	ARI	7 Dec 1939	08:57	SCO
14 Dec 1938	16:27	LIB	13 Jun 1939	12:41	TAU	9 Dec 1939	13:32	SAG
16 Dec 1938	23:13	SCO	15 Jun 1939	18:31	GEM	11 Dec 1939	19:51	CAP
19 Dec 1938	08:31	SAG	17 Jun 1939	21:05	CAN	14 Dec 1939	04:42	AQU
21 Dec 1938	19:38	CAP	19 Jun 1939	21:57	LEO	16 Dec 1939	16:14	PIS
24 Dec 1938	07:58	AQU	21 Jun 1939	22:56	VIR	19 Dec 1939	05:02	ARI
26 Dec 1938	20:40	PIS	24 Jun 1939	01:31	LIB	21 Dec 1939	16:31	TAU
29 Dec 1938	08:13	ARI	26 Jun 1939	06:25	SCO	24 Dec 1939	00:35	GEM
31 Dec 1938	16:46	TAU	28 Jun 1939	13:39	SAG	26 Dec 1939	05:02	CAN
2 Jan 1939	21:18	GEM	30 Jun 1939	22:53	CAP	28 Dec 1939	07:04	LEO
4 Jan 1939	22:19	CAN	3 Jul 1939	09:54	AQU	30 Dec 1939	08:28	VIR
6 Jan 1939	21:32	LEO	5 Jul 1939	22:17	PIS	1 Jan 1940	10:44	LIB
8 Jan 1939	21:08	VIR	8 Jul 1939	10:49	ARI	3 Jan 1940	14:36	SCO
10 Jan 1939	23:12	LIB	10 Jul 1939	21:25	TAU	5 Jan 1940	20:12	SAG
13 Jan 1939	04:54	SCO	13 Jul 1939	04:19	GEM	8 Jan 1940	03:30	CAP
15 Jan 1939	14:10	SAG	15 Jul 1939	07:15	CAN	10 Jan 1940	12:42	AQU
18 Jan 1939	01:43	CAP	17 Jul 1939	07:30	LEO	13 Jan 1940	00:03	PIS
20 Jan 1939	14:14	AQU	19 Jul 1939	07:07	VIR	15 Jan 1940	12:55	ARI
23 Jan 1939	02:50	PIS	21 Jul 1939	08:10	LIB	18 Jan 1940	01:14	TAU
25 Jan 1939	14:41	ARI	23 Jul 1939	12:05	SCO	20 Jan 1940	10:30	GEM
28 Jan 1939	00:27	TAU	25 Jul 1939	19:09	SAG	22 Jan 1940	15:33	CAN

DATE	TIME	SIGN	DATE	TIME	SIGN	DATE	TIME	SIGN
24 Jan 1940	17:10	LEO	22 Jul 1940	01:58	PIS	18 Jan 1941	06:59	LIB
26 Jan 1940	17:11	VIR	24 Jul 1940	14:01	ARI	20 Jan 1941	10:03	SCO
28 Jan 1940	17:42	LIB	27 Jul 1940	02:55	TAU	22 Jan 1941	13:16	SAG
30 Jan 1940	20:18	SCO	29 Jul 1940	14:02	GEM	24 Jan 1941	17:01	CAP
2 Feb 1940	01:36	SAG	31 Jul 1940	21:30	CAN	26 Jan 1941	22:06	AQU
4 Feb 1940	09:27	CAP	3 Aug 1940	01:19	LEO	29 Jan 1941	05:34	PIS
6 Feb 1940	19:21	AQU	5 Aug 1940	02:50	VIR	31 Jan 1941	16:02	ARI
9 Feb 1940	06:58	PIS	7 Aug 1940	03:49	LIB	3 Feb 1941	04:40	TAU
11 Feb 1940	19:49	ARI	9 Aug 1940	05:45	SCO	5 Feb 1941	17:09	GEM
14 Feb 1940	08:35	TAU	11 Aug 1940	09:29	SAG	8 Feb 1941	02:56	CAN
16 Feb 1940	19:09	GEM	13 Aug 1940	15:15	CAP	10 Feb 1941	09:06	LEO
19 Feb 1940	01:44	CAN	15 Aug 1940	23:07	AQU	12 Feb 1941	12:20	VIR
21 Feb 1940	04:18	LEO	18 Aug 1940	09:10	PIS	14 Feb 1941	14:07	LIB
23 Feb 1940	04:11	VIR	20 Aug 1940	21:14	ARI	16 Feb 1941	15:52	SCO
25 Feb 1940	03:29	LIB	23 Aug 1940	10:16	TAU	18 Feb 1941	18:36	SAG
27 Feb 1940	04:14	SCO	25 Aug 1940	22:11	GEM	20 Feb 1941	22:54	CAP
29 Feb 1940	07:55	SAG	28 Aug 1940	06:53	CAN	23 Feb 1941	05:01	AQU
2 Mar 1940	15:03	CAP	30 Aug 1940	11:29	LEO	25 Feb 1941	13:18	PIS
5 Mar 1940	01:07	AQU	1 Sep 1940	12:55	VIR	27 Feb 1941	23:54	ARI
7 Mar 1940	13:07	PIS	3 Sep 1940	12:54	LIB	2 Mar 1941	12:23	TAU
10 Mar 1940	02:00	ARI	5 Sep 1940	13:17	SCO	5 Mar 1941	01:11	GEM
12 Mar 1940	14:43	TAU	7 Sep 1940	15:36	SAG	7 Mar 1941	12:02	CAN
15 Mar 1940	01:51	GEM	9 Sep 1940	20:46	CAP	9 Mar 1941	19:18	LEO
17 Mar 1940	09:55	CAN	12 Sep 1940	04:51	AQU	11 Mar 1941	22:50	VIR
19 Mar 1940	14:13	LEO	14 Sep 1940	15:25	PIS	13 Mar 1941	23:50	LIB
21 Mar 1940	15:19	VIR	17 Sep 1940	03:43	ARI	16 Mar 1941	00:03	SCO
23 Mar 1940	14:47	LIB	19 Sep 1940	16:45	TAU	18 Mar 1941	01:08	SAG
25 Mar 1940	14:33	SCO	22 Sep 1940	05:05	GEM	20 Mar 1941	04:25	CAP
27 Mar 1940	16:31	SAG	24 Sep 1940	14:56	CAN	22 Mar 1941	10:34	AQU
29 Mar 1940	22:00	CAP	26 Sep 1940	21:07	LEO	24 Mar 1941	19:30	PIS
1 Apr 1940	07:13	AQU	28 Sep 1940	23:40	VIR	27 Mar 1941	06:39	ARI
3 Apr 1940	19:10	PIS	30 Sep 1940	23:46	LIB	29 Mar 1941	19:13	TAU
6 Apr 1940	08:09	ARI	2 Oct 1940	23:12	SCO	1 Apr 1941	08:06	GEM
8 Apr 1940	20:38	TAU	4 Oct 1940	23:55	SAG	3 Apr 1941	19:43	CAN
11 Apr 1940	07:31	GEM	7 Oct 1940	03:29	CAP	6 Apr 1941	04:25	LEO
13 Apr 1940	16:03	CAN	9 Oct 1940	10:44	AQU	8 Apr 1941	09:19	VIR
15 Apr 1940	21:42	LEO	11 Oct 1940	21:18	PIS	10 Apr 1941	10:53	LIB
18 Apr 1940	00:33	VIR	14 Oct 1940	09:50	ARI	12 Apr 1941	10:31	SCO
20 Apr 1940	01:22	LIB	16 Oct 1940	22:48	TAU	14 Apr 1941	10:08	SAG
22 Apr 1940	01:33	SCO	19 Oct 1940	10:58	GEM	16 Apr 1941	11:39	CAP
24 Apr 1940	02:49	SAG	21 Oct 1940	21:17	CAN	18 Apr 1941	16:31	AQU
26 Apr 1940	06:49	CAP	24 Oct 1940	04:50	LEO	21 Apr 1941	01:07	PIS
28 Apr 1940	14:39	AQU	26 Oct 1940	09:08	VIR	23 Apr 1941	12:34	ARI
1 May 1940	01:56	PIS	28 Oct 1940	10:35	LIB	26 Apr 1941	01:22	TAU
3 May 1940	14:51	ARI	30 Oct 1940	10:24	SCO	28 Apr 1941	14:10	GEM
6 May 1940	03:11	TAU	1 Nov 1940	10:21	SAG	1 May 1941	01:55	CAN
8 May 1940	13:32	GEM	3 Nov 1940	12:23	CAP	3 May 1941	11:32	LEO
10 May 1940	21:32	CAN	5 Nov 1940	18:03	AQU	5 May 1941	18:05	VIR
13 May 1940	03:21	LEO	8 Nov 1940	03:46	PIS	7 May 1941	21:10	LIB
15 May 1940	07:17	VIR	10 Nov 1940	16:13	ARI	9 May 1941	21:33	SCO
17 May 1940	09:40	LIB	13 Nov 1940	05:12	TAU	11 May 1941	20:49	SAG
19 May 1940	11:11	SCO	15 Nov 1940	17:00	GEM	13 May 1941	21:04	CAP
21 May 1940	13:00	SAG	18 Nov 1940	02:51	CAN	16 May 1941	00:16	AQU
23 May 1940	16:35	CAP	20 Nov 1940	10:37	LEO	18 May 1941	07:33	PIS
25 May 1940	23:20	AQU	22 Nov 1940	16:10	VIR	20 May 1941	18:34	ARI
28 May 1940	09:39	PIS	24 Nov 1940	19:24	LIB	23 May 1941	07:26	TAU
30 May 1940	22:18	ARI	26 Nov 1940	20:44	SCO	25 May 1941	20:09	GEM
2 Jun 1940	10:42	TAU	28 Nov 1940	21:18	SAG	28 May 1941	07:36	CAN
4 Jun 1940	20:48	GEM	30 Nov 1940	22:51	CAP	30 May 1941	17:14	LEO
7 Jun 1940	04:01	CAN	3 Dec 1940	03:13	AQU	2 Jun 1941	00:37	VIR
9 Jun 1940	09:00	LEO	5 Dec 1940	11:36	PIS	4 Jun 1941	05:16	LIB
11 Jun 1940	12:40	VIR	7 Dec 1940	23:26	ARI	6 Jun 1941	07:13	SCO
13 Jun 1940	15:43	LIB	10 Dec 1940	12:26	TAU	8 Jun 1941	07:23	SAG
15 Jun 1940	18:31	SCO	13 Dec 1940	00:06	GEM	10 Jun 1941	07:31	CAP
17 Jun 1940	21:34	SAG	15 Dec 1940	09:19	CAN	12 Jun 1941	09:42	AQU
20 Jun 1940	01:45	CAP	17 Dec 1940	16:15	LEO	14 Jun 1941	15:34	PIS
22 Jun 1940	08:15	AQU	19 Dec 1940	21:34	VIR	17 Jun 1941	01:30	ARI
24 Jun 1940	17:55	PIS	22 Dec 1940	01:36	LIB	19 Jun 1941	14:02	TAU
27 Jun 1940	06:12	ARI	24 Dec 1940	04:29	SCO	22 Jun 1941	02:43	GEM
29 Jun 1940	18:52	TAU	26 Dec 1940	06:36	SAG	24 Jun 1941	13:50	CAN
2 Jul 1940	05:14	GEM	28 Dec 1940	08:58	CAP	26 Jun 1941	22:54	LEO
4 Jul 1940	12:09	CAN	30 Dec 1940	13:09	AQU	29 Jun 1941	06:02	VIR
6 Jul 1940	16:11	LEO	1 Jan 1941	20:35	PIS	1 Jul 1941	11:16	LIB
8 Jul 1940	18:44	VIR	4 Jan 1941	07:34	ARI	3 Jul 1941	14:32	SCO
10 Jul 1940	21:06	LIB	6 Jan 1941	20:28	TAU	5 Jul 1941	16:13	SAG
13 Jul 1940	00:07	SCO	9 Jan 1941	08:26	GEM	7 Jul 1941	17:20	CAP
15 Jul 1940	04:04	SAG	11 Jan 1941	17:33	CAN	9 Jul 1941	19:36	AQU
17 Jul 1940	09:18	CAP	13 Jan 1941	23:38	LEO	12 Jul 1941	00:43	PIS
19 Jul 1940	16:22	AQU	16 Jan 1941	03:45	VIR	14 Jul 1941	09:35	ARI

DATE	TIME	SIGN
16 Jul 1941	21:29	TAU
19 Jul 1941	10:09	GEM
21 Jul 1941	21:14	CAN
24 Jul 1941	05:47	LEO
26 Jul 1941	12:02	VIR
28 Jul 1941	16:40	LIB
30 Jul 1941	20:08	SCO
1 Aug 1941	22:49	SAG
4 Aug 1941	01:17	CAP
6 Aug 1941	04:32	AQU
8 Aug 1941	09:51	PIS
10 Aug 1941	18:12	ARI
13 Aug 1941	05:32	TAU
15 Aug 1941	18:09	GEM
18 Aug 1941	05:37	CAN
20 Aug 1941	14:14	LEO
22 Aug 1941	19:52	VIR
24 Aug 1941	23:20	LIB
27 Aug 1941	01:48	SCO
29 Aug 1941	04:12	SAG
31 Aug 1941	07:17	CAP
2 Sep 1941	11:39	AQU
4 Sep 1941	17:51	PIS
7 Sep 1941	02:29	ARI
9 Sep 1941	13:32	TAU
12 Sep 1941	02:05	GEM
14 Sep 1941	14:08	CAN
16 Sep 1941	23:34	LEO
19 Sep 1941	05:28	VIR
21 Sep 1941	08:16	LIB
23 Sep 1941	09:23	SCO
25 Sep 1941	10:24	SAG
27 Sep 1941	12:45	CAP
29 Sep 1941	17:16	AQU
2 Oct 1941	00:18	PIS
4 Oct 1941	09:37	ARI
6 Oct 1941	20:51	TAU
9 Oct 1941	09:22	GEM
11 Oct 1941	21:52	CAN
14 Oct 1941	08:28	LEO
16 Oct 1941	15:35	VIR
18 Oct 1941	18:53	LIB
20 Oct 1941	19:25	SCO
22 Oct 1941	19:00	SAG
24 Oct 1941	19:40	CAP
26 Oct 1941	23:03	AQU
29 Oct 1941	05:50	PIS
31 Oct 1941	15:38	ARI
3 Nov 1941	03:19	TAU
5 Nov 1941	15:52	GEM
8 Nov 1941	04:25	CAN
10 Nov 1941	15:48	LEO
13 Nov 1941	00:27	VIR
15 Nov 1941	05:21	LIB
17 Nov 1941	06:39	SCO
19 Nov 1941	05:53	SAG
21 Nov 1941	05:11	CAP
23 Nov 1941	06:46	AQU
25 Nov 1941	12:10	PIS
27 Nov 1941	21:26	ARI
30 Nov 1941	09:18	TAU
2 Dec 1941	21:59	GEM
5 Dec 1941	10:21	CAN
7 Dec 1941	21:42	LEO
10 Dec 1941	07:11	VIR
12 Dec 1941	13:44	LIB
14 Dec 1941	16:51	SCO
16 Dec 1941	17:09	SAG
18 Dec 1941	16:26	CAP
20 Dec 1941	16:53	AQU
22 Dec 1941	20:33	PIS
25 Dec 1941	04:24	ARI
27 Dec 1941	15:43	TAU
30 Dec 1941	04:27	GEM
1 Jan 1942	16:41	CAN
4 Jan 1942	03:32	LEO
6 Jan 1942	12:41	VIR
8 Jan 1942	19:47	LIB
11 Jan 1942	00:23	SCO

DATE	TIME	SIGN
13 Jan 1942	02:30	SAG
15 Jan 1942	03:06	CAP
17 Jan 1942	03:52	AQU
19 Jan 1942	06:43	PIS
21 Jan 1942	13:09	ARI
23 Jan 1942	23:19	TAU
26 Jan 1942	11:43	GEM
29 Jan 1942	00:02	CAN
31 Jan 1942	10:36	LEO
2 Feb 1942	18:57	VIR
5 Feb 1942	01:17	LIB
7 Feb 1942	05:55	SCO
9 Feb 1942	09:06	SAG
11 Feb 1942	11:18	CAP
13 Feb 1942	13:27	AQU
15 Feb 1942	16:50	PIS
17 Feb 1942	22:47	ARI
20 Feb 1942	07:57	TAU
22 Feb 1942	19:47	GEM
25 Feb 1942	08:15	CAN
27 Feb 1942	19:05	LEO
2 Mar 1942	03:05	VIR
4 Mar 1942	08:22	LIB
6 Mar 1942	11:49	SCO
8 Mar 1942	14:28	SAG
10 Mar 1942	17:08	CAP
12 Mar 1942	20:30	AQU
15 Mar 1942	01:09	PIS
17 Mar 1942	07:41	ARI
19 Mar 1942	16:38	TAU
22 Mar 1942	04:00	GEM
24 Mar 1942	16:32	CAN
27 Mar 1942	04:03	LEO
29 Mar 1942	12:35	VIR
31 Mar 1942	17:36	LIB
2 Apr 1942	19:54	SCO
4 Apr 1942	21:04	SAG
6 Apr 1942	22:42	CAP
9 Apr 1942	01:57	AQU
11 Apr 1942	07:19	PIS
13 Apr 1942	14:49	ARI
16 Apr 1942	00:18	TAU
18 Apr 1942	11:36	GEM
21 Apr 1942	00:09	CAN
23 Apr 1942	12:20	LEO
25 Apr 1942	22:01	VIR
28 Apr 1942	03:49	LIB
30 Apr 1942	05:59	SCO
2 May 1942	06:02	SAG
4 May 1942	06:04	CAP
6 May 1942	07:56	AQU
8 May 1942	12:44	PIS
10 May 1942	20:31	ARI
13 May 1942	06:36	TAU
15 May 1942	18:14	GEM
18 May 1942	06:49	CAN
20 May 1942	19:20	LEO
23 May 1942	06:07	VIR
25 May 1942	13:20	LIB
27 May 1942	16:31	SCO
29 May 1942	16:38	SAG
31 May 1942	15:43	CAP
2 Jun 1942	15:59	AQU
4 Jun 1942	19:14	PIS
7 Jun 1942	02:11	ARI
9 Jun 1942	12:16	TAU
12 Jun 1942	00:11	GEM
14 Jun 1942	12:49	CAN
17 Jun 1942	01:18	LEO
19 Jun 1942	12:32	VIR
21 Jun 1942	21:03	LIB
24 Jun 1942	01:49	SCO
26 Jun 1942	03:08	SAG
28 Jun 1942	02:29	CAP
30 Jun 1942	02:01	AQU
2 Jul 1942	03:46	PIS
4 Jul 1942	09:11	ARI
6 Jul 1942	18:22	TAU
9 Jul 1942	06:10	GEM

DATE	TIME	SIGN
11 Jul 1942	18:51	CAN
14 Jul 1942	07:07	LEO
16 Jul 1942	18:08	VIR
19 Jul 1942	03:01	LIB
21 Jul 1942	09:01	SCO
23 Jul 1942	11:57	SAG
25 Jul 1942	12:37	CAP
27 Jul 1942	12:37	AQU
29 Jul 1942	13:49	PIS
31 Jul 1942	17:55	ARI
3 Aug 1942	01:48	TAU
5 Aug 1942	12:54	GEM
8 Aug 1942	01:30	CAN
10 Aug 1942	13:38	LEO
13 Aug 1942	00:08	VIR
15 Aug 1942	08:30	LIB
17 Aug 1942	14:37	SCO
19 Aug 1942	18:34	SAG
21 Aug 1942	20:46	CAP
23 Aug 1942	22:07	AQU
25 Aug 1942	23:55	PIS
28 Aug 1942	03:39	ARI
30 Aug 1942	10:30	TAU
1 Sep 1942	20:40	GEM
4 Sep 1942	09:00	CAN
6 Sep 1942	21:14	LEO
9 Sep 1942	07:30	VIR
11 Sep 1942	15:04	LIB
13 Sep 1942	20:18	SCO
15 Sep 1942	23:57	SAG
18 Sep 1942	02:47	CAP
20 Sep 1942	05:27	AQU
22 Sep 1942	08:33	PIS
24 Sep 1942	12:57	ARI
26 Sep 1942	19:34	TAU
29 Sep 1942	05:05	GEM
1 Oct 1942	17:03	CAN
4 Oct 1942	05:35	LEO
6 Oct 1942	16:12	VIR
8 Oct 1942	23:31	LIB
11 Oct 1942	03:45	SCO
13 Oct 1942	06:10	SAG
15 Oct 1942	08:13	CAP
17 Oct 1942	11:01	AQU
19 Oct 1942	15:05	PIS
21 Oct 1942	20:36	ARI
24 Oct 1942	03:52	TAU
26 Oct 1942	13:19	GEM
29 Oct 1942	01:00	CAN
31 Oct 1942	13:47	LEO
3 Nov 1942	01:17	VIR
5 Nov 1942	09:20	LIB
7 Nov 1942	13:25	SCO
9 Nov 1942	14:46	SAG
11 Nov 1942	15:17	CAP
13 Nov 1942	16:48	AQU
15 Nov 1942	20:28	PIS
18 Nov 1942	02:30	ARI
20 Nov 1942	10:38	TAU
22 Nov 1942	20:34	GEM
25 Nov 1942	08:16	CAN
27 Nov 1942	21:09	LEO
30 Nov 1942	09:28	VIR
2 Dec 1942	18:54	LIB
5 Dec 1942	00:04	SCO
7 Dec 1942	01:32	SAG
9 Dec 1942	01:06	CAP
11 Dec 1942	00:57	AQU
13 Dec 1942	02:56	PIS
15 Dec 1942	08:04	ARI
17 Dec 1942	16:16	TAU
20 Dec 1942	02:46	GEM
22 Dec 1942	14:45	CAN
25 Dec 1942	03:35	LEO
27 Dec 1942	16:09	VIR
30 Dec 1942	02:43	LIB
1 Jan 1943	09:38	SCO
3 Jan 1943	12:32	SAG
5 Jan 1943	12:34	CAP

DATE	TIME	SIGN	DATE	TIME	SIGN	DATE	TIME	SIGN
7 Jan 1943	11:42	AQU	6 Jul 1943	18:44	VIR	2 Jan 1944	00:34	ARI
9 Jan 1943	12:04	PIS	9 Jul 1943	06:43	LIB	4 Jan 1944	04:58	TAU
11 Jan 1943	15:21	ARI	11 Jul 1943	15:39	SCO	6 Jan 1944	11:44	GEM
13 Jan 1943	22:22	TAU	13 Jul 1943	20:35	SAG	8 Jan 1944	20:48	CAN
16 Jan 1943	08:39	GEM	15 Jul 1943	22:05	CAP	11 Jan 1944	07:57	LEO
18 Jan 1943	20:53	CAN	17 Jul 1943	21:45	AQU	13 Jan 1944	20:38	VIR
21 Jan 1943	09:43	LEO	19 Jul 1943	21:31	PIS	16 Jan 1944	09:28	LIB
23 Jan 1943	22:02	VIR	21 Jul 1943	23:09	ARI	18 Jan 1944	20:26	SCO
26 Jan 1943	08:46	LIB	24 Jul 1943	03:53	TAU	21 Jan 1944	03:52	SAG
28 Jan 1943	16:50	SCO	26 Jul 1943	12:04	GEM	23 Jan 1944	07:26	CAP
30 Jan 1943	21:32	SAG	28 Jul 1943	23:04	CAN	25 Jan 1944	08:09	AQU
1 Feb 1943	23:14	CAP	31 Jul 1943	11:43	LEO	27 Jan 1944	07:47	PIS
3 Feb 1943	23:10	AQU	3 Aug 1943	00:44	VIR	29 Jan 1944	08:15	ARI
5 Feb 1943	23:08	PIS	5 Aug 1943	12:50	LIB	31 Jan 1944	11:07	TAU
8 Feb 1943	01:01	ARI	7 Aug 1943	22:38	SCO	2 Feb 1944	17:17	GEM
10 Feb 1943	06:17	TAU	10 Aug 1943	05:07	SAG	5 Feb 1944	02:40	CAN
12 Feb 1943	15:25	GEM	12 Aug 1943	08:08	CAP	7 Feb 1944	14:20	LEO
15 Feb 1943	03:24	CAN	14 Aug 1943	08:36	AQU	10 Feb 1944	03:07	VIR
17 Feb 1943	16:18	LEO	16 Aug 1943	08:06	PIS	12 Feb 1944	15:54	LIB
20 Feb 1943	04:19	VIR	18 Aug 1943	08:32	ARI	15 Feb 1944	03:23	SCO
22 Feb 1943	14:29	LIB	20 Aug 1943	11:40	TAU	17 Feb 1944	12:13	SAG
24 Feb 1943	22:24	SCO	22 Aug 1943	18:34	GEM	19 Feb 1944	17:32	CAP
27 Feb 1943	03:58	SAG	25 Aug 1943	05:06	CAN	21 Feb 1944	19:26	AQU
1 Mar 1943	07:18	CAP	27 Aug 1943	17:49	LEO	23 Feb 1944	19:08	PIS
3 Mar 1943	08:55	AQU	30 Aug 1943	06:46	VIR	25 Feb 1944	18:30	ARI
5 Mar 1943	09:54	PIS	1 Sep 1943	18:33	LIB	27 Feb 1944	19:36	TAU
7 Mar 1943	11:42	ARI	4 Sep 1943	04:19	SCO	1 Mar 1944	00:07	GEM
9 Mar 1943	15:53	TAU	6 Sep 1943	11:37	SAG	3 Mar 1944	08:38	CAN
11 Mar 1943	23:40	GEM	8 Sep 1943	16:12	CAP	5 Mar 1944	20:19	LEO
14 Mar 1943	10:51	CAN	10 Sep 1943	18:18	AQU	8 Mar 1944	09:18	VIR
16 Mar 1943	23:40	LEO	12 Sep 1943	18:46	PIS	10 Mar 1944	21:54	LIB
19 Mar 1943	11:42	VIR	14 Sep 1943	19:08	ARI	13 Mar 1944	09:11	SCO
21 Mar 1943	21:20	LIB	16 Sep 1943	21:15	TAU	15 Mar 1944	18:30	SAG
24 Mar 1943	04:22	SCO	19 Sep 1943	02:43	GEM	18 Mar 1944	01:12	CAP
26 Mar 1943	09:22	SAG	21 Sep 1943	12:11	CAN	20 Mar 1944	04:54	AQU
28 Mar 1943	13:04	CAP	24 Sep 1943	00:33	LEO	22 Mar 1944	05:58	PIS
30 Mar 1943	15:56	AQU	26 Sep 1943	13:29	VIR	24 Mar 1944	05:41	ARI
1 Apr 1943	18:26	PIS	29 Sep 1943	00:55	LIB	26 Mar 1944	06:00	TAU
3 Apr 1943	21:17	ARI	1 Oct 1943	10:03	SCO	28 Mar 1944	08:59	GEM
6 Apr 1943	01:38	TAU	3 Oct 1943	17:02	SAG	30 Mar 1944	15:59	CAN
8 Apr 1943	08:42	GEM	5 Oct 1943	22:10	CAP	2 Apr 1944	02:54	LEO
10 Apr 1943	19:03	CAN	8 Oct 1943	01:38	AQU	4 Apr 1944	15:48	VIR
13 Apr 1943	07:39	LEO	10 Oct 1943	03:44	PIS	7 Apr 1944	04:21	LIB
15 Apr 1943	19:58	VIR	12 Oct 1943	05:11	ARI	9 Apr 1944	15:11	SCO
18 Apr 1943	05:40	LIB	14 Oct 1943	07:26	TAU	12 Apr 1944	00:01	SAG
20 Apr 1943	12:02	SCO	16 Oct 1943	12:08	GEM	14 Apr 1944	06:55	CAP
22 Apr 1943	15:55	SAG	18 Oct 1943	20:28	CAN	16 Apr 1944	11:44	AQU
24 Apr 1943	18:39	CAP	21 Oct 1943	08:12	LEO	18 Apr 1944	14:27	PIS
26 Apr 1943	21:21	AQU	23 Oct 1943	21:09	VIR	20 Apr 1944	15:35	ARI
29 Apr 1943	00:35	PIS	26 Oct 1943	08:37	LIB	22 Apr 1944	16:28	TAU
1 May 1943	04:39	ARI	28 Oct 1943	17:14	SCO	24 Apr 1944	18:58	GEM
3 May 1943	09:57	TAU	30 Oct 1943	23:13	SAG	27 Apr 1944	00:49	CAN
5 May 1943	17:15	GEM	2 Nov 1943	03:36	CAP	29 Apr 1944	10:36	LEO
8 May 1943	03:17	CAN	4 Nov 1943	07:09	AQU	1 May 1944	23:04	VIR
10 May 1943	15:38	LEO	6 Nov 1943	10:15	PIS	4 May 1944	11:38	LIB
13 May 1943	04:21	VIR	8 Nov 1943	13:10	ARI	6 May 1944	22:17	SCO
15 May 1943	14:43	LIB	10 Nov 1943	16:32	TAU	9 May 1944	06:26	SAG
17 May 1943	21:18	SCO	12 Nov 1943	21:32	GEM	11 May 1944	12:32	CAP
20 May 1943	00:32	SAG	15 Nov 1943	05:22	CAN	13 May 1944	17:09	AQU
22 May 1943	01:59	CAP	17 Nov 1943	16:27	LEO	15 May 1944	20:34	PIS
24 May 1943	03:23	AQU	20 Nov 1943	05:21	VIR	17 May 1944	23:03	ARI
26 May 1943	05:57	PIS	22 Nov 1943	17:18	LIB	20 May 1944	01:15	TAU
28 May 1943	10:16	ARI	25 Nov 1943	02:07	SCO	22 May 1944	04:26	GEM
30 May 1943	16:25	TAU	27 Nov 1943	07:34	SAG	24 May 1944	10:04	CAN
2 Jun 1943	00:30	GEM	29 Nov 1943	10:42	CAP	26 May 1944	19:04	LEO
4 Jun 1943	10:45	CAN	1 Dec 1943	13:01	AQU	29 May 1944	06:58	VIR
6 Jun 1943	23:03	LEO	3 Dec 1943	15:35	PIS	31 May 1944	19:37	LIB
9 Jun 1943	12:02	VIR	5 Dec 1943	18:59	ARI	3 Jun 1944	06:31	SCO
11 Jun 1943	23:20	LIB	7 Dec 1943	23:30	TAU	5 Jun 1944	14:26	SAG
14 Jun 1943	06:58	SCO	10 Dec 1943	05:32	GEM	7 Jun 1944	19:40	CAP
16 Jun 1943	10:34	SAG	12 Dec 1943	13:47	CAN	9 Jun 1944	23:11	AQU
18 Jun 1943	11:29	CAP	15 Dec 1943	00:37	LEO	12 Jun 1944	01:58	PIS
20 Jun 1943	11:33	AQU	17 Dec 1943	13:22	VIR	14 Jun 1944	04:40	ARI
22 Jun 1943	12:37	PIS	20 Dec 1943	01:54	LIB	16 Jun 1944	07:51	TAU
24 Jun 1943	15:53	ARI	22 Dec 1943	11:44	SCO	18 Jun 1944	12:11	GEM
26 Jun 1943	21:52	TAU	24 Dec 1943	17:43	SAG	20 Jun 1944	18:28	CAN
29 Jun 1943	06:26	GEM	26 Dec 1943	20:23	CAP	23 Jun 1944	03:26	LEO
1 Jul 1943	17:13	CAN	28 Dec 1943	21:20	AQU	25 Jun 1944	14:58	VIR
4 Jul 1943	05:39	LEO	30 Dec 1943	22:17	PIS	28 Jun 1944	03:39	LIB

DATE	TIME	SIGN
30 Jun 1944	15:09	SCO
2 Jul 1944	23:36	SAG
5 Jul 1944	04:41	CAP
7 Jul 1944	07:13	AQU
9 Jul 1944	08:38	PIS
11 Jul 1944	10:18	ARI
13 Jul 1944	13:16	TAU
15 Jul 1944	18:11	GEM
18 Jul 1944	01:22	CAN
20 Jul 1944	10:51	LEO
22 Jul 1944	22:24	VIR
25 Jul 1944	11:07	LIB
27 Jul 1944	23:15	SCO
30 Jul 1944	08:49	SAG
1 Aug 1944	14:41	CAP
3 Aug 1944	17:09	AQU
5 Aug 1944	17:34	PIS
7 Aug 1944	17:43	ARI
9 Aug 1944	19:19	TAU
11 Aug 1944	23:39	GEM
14 Aug 1944	07:03	CAN
16 Aug 1944	17:08	LEO
19 Aug 1944	05:00	VIR
21 Aug 1944	17:45	LIB
24 Aug 1944	06:12	SCO
26 Aug 1944	16:51	SAG
29 Aug 1944	00:10	CAP
31 Aug 1944	03:43	AQU
2 Sep 1944	04:14	PIS
4 Sep 1944	03:27	ARI
6 Sep 1944	03:29	TAU
8 Sep 1944	06:13	GEM
10 Sep 1944	12:47	CAN
12 Sep 1944	22:50	LEO
15 Sep 1944	11:00	VIR
17 Sep 1944	23:47	LIB
20 Sep 1944	12:10	SCO
22 Sep 1944	23:15	SAG
25 Sep 1944	07:54	CAP
27 Sep 1944	13:08	AQU
29 Sep 1944	14:56	PIS
1 Oct 1944	14:29	ARI
3 Oct 1944	13:46	TAU
5 Oct 1944	15:00	GEM
7 Oct 1944	19:56	CAN
10 Oct 1944	05:03	LEO
12 Oct 1944	17:04	VIR
15 Oct 1944	05:55	LIB
17 Oct 1944	18:03	SCO
20 Oct 1944	04:49	SAG
22 Oct 1944	13:47	CAP
24 Oct 1944	20:18	AQU
26 Oct 1944	23:51	PIS
29 Oct 1944	00:53	ARI
31 Oct 1944	00:45	TAU
2 Nov 1944	01:29	GEM
4 Nov 1944	05:04	CAN
6 Nov 1944	12:45	LEO
8 Nov 1944	23:59	VIR
11 Nov 1944	12:44	LIB
14 Nov 1944	00:47	SCO
16 Nov 1944	11:01	SAG
18 Nov 1944	19:19	CAP
21 Nov 1944	01:46	AQU
23 Nov 1944	06:18	PIS
25 Nov 1944	08:56	ARI
27 Nov 1944	10:22	TAU
29 Nov 1944	11:55	GEM
1 Dec 1944	15:17	CAN
3 Dec 1944	21:53	LEO
6 Dec 1944	08:04	VIR
8 Dec 1944	20:28	LIB
11 Dec 1944	08:41	SCO
13 Dec 1944	18:49	SAG
16 Dec 1944	02:20	CAP
18 Dec 1944	07:43	AQU
20 Dec 1944	11:38	PIS
22 Dec 1944	14:42	ARI
24 Dec 1944	17:24	TAU

DATE	TIME	SIGN
26 Dec 1944	20:26	GEM
29 Dec 1944	00:44	CAN
31 Dec 1944	07:19	LEO
2 Jan 1945	16:49	VIR
5 Jan 1945	04:43	LIB
7 Jan 1945	17:12	SCO
10 Jan 1945	03:54	SAG
12 Jan 1945	11:26	CAP
14 Jan 1945	15:56	AQU
16 Jan 1945	18:27	PIS
18 Jan 1945	20:20	ARI
20 Jan 1945	22:48	TAU
23 Jan 1945	02:35	GEM
25 Jan 1945	08:05	CAN
27 Jan 1945	15:33	LEO
30 Jan 1945	01:09	VIR
1 Feb 1945	12:45	LIB
4 Feb 1945	01:21	SCO
6 Feb 1945	12:56	SAG
8 Feb 1945	21:28	CAP
11 Feb 1945	02:10	AQU
13 Feb 1945	03:52	PIS
15 Feb 1945	04:12	ARI
17 Feb 1945	05:05	TAU
19 Feb 1945	08:01	GEM
21 Feb 1945	13:43	CAN
23 Feb 1945	21:58	LEO
26 Feb 1945	08:13	VIR
28 Feb 1945	19:56	LIB
3 Mar 1945	08:32	SCO
5 Mar 1945	20:44	SAG
8 Mar 1945	06:37	CAP
10 Mar 1945	12:38	AQU
12 Mar 1945	14:48	PIS
14 Mar 1945	14:31	ARI
16 Mar 1945	13:54	TAU
18 Mar 1945	15:05	GEM
20 Mar 1945	19:31	CAN
23 Mar 1945	03:32	LEO
25 Mar 1945	14:11	VIR
28 Mar 1945	02:15	LIB
30 Mar 1945	14:49	SCO
2 Apr 1945	03:07	SAG
4 Apr 1945	13:50	CAP
6 Apr 1945	21:26	AQU
9 Apr 1945	01:08	PIS
11 Apr 1945	01:37	ARI
13 Apr 1945	00:39	TAU
15 Apr 1945	00:32	GEM
17 Apr 1945	03:14	CAN
19 Apr 1945	09:53	LEO
21 Apr 1945	20:03	VIR
24 Apr 1945	08:14	LIB
26 Apr 1945	20:52	SCO
29 Apr 1945	08:55	SAG
1 May 1945	19:39	CAP
4 May 1945	04:05	AQU
6 May 1945	09:19	PIS
8 May 1945	11:23	ARI
10 May 1945	11:24	TAU
12 May 1945	11:12	GEM
14 May 1945	12:52	CAN
16 May 1945	17:56	LEO
19 May 1945	02:56	VIR
21 May 1945	14:43	LIB
24 May 1945	03:20	SCO
26 May 1945	15:10	SAG
29 May 1945	01:23	CAP
31 May 1945	09:34	AQU
2 Jun 1945	15:24	PIS
4 Jun 1945	18:50	ARI
6 Jun 1945	20:22	TAU
8 Jun 1945	21:14	GEM
10 Jun 1945	23:02	CAN
13 Jun 1945	03:20	LEO
15 Jun 1945	11:08	VIR
17 Jun 1945	22:06	LIB
20 Jun 1945	10:35	SCO
22 Jun 1945	22:26	SAG

DATE	TIME	SIGN
25 Jun 1945	08:13	CAP
27 Jun 1945	15:35	AQU
29 Jun 1945	20:50	PIS
2 Jul 1945	00:28	ARI
4 Jul 1945	03:04	TAU
6 Jul 1945	05:19	GEM
8 Jul 1945	08:10	CAN
10 Jul 1945	12:44	LEO
12 Jul 1945	19:58	VIR
15 Jul 1945	06:12	LIB
17 Jul 1945	18:28	SCO
20 Jul 1945	06:35	SAG
22 Jul 1945	16:28	CAP
24 Jul 1945	23:15	AQU
27 Jul 1945	03:26	PIS
29 Jul 1945	06:07	ARI
31 Jul 1945	08:28	TAU
2 Aug 1945	11:23	GEM
4 Aug 1945	15:22	CAN
6 Aug 1945	20:53	LEO
9 Aug 1945	04:24	VIR
11 Aug 1945	14:21	LIB
14 Aug 1945	02:24	SCO
16 Aug 1945	14:55	SAG
19 Aug 1945	01:29	CAP
21 Aug 1945	08:31	AQU
23 Aug 1945	12:04	PIS
25 Aug 1945	13:29	ARI
27 Aug 1945	14:33	TAU
29 Aug 1945	16:47	GEM
31 Aug 1945	21:00	CAN
3 Sep 1945	03:19	LEO
5 Sep 1945	11:37	VIR
7 Sep 1945	21:48	LIB
10 Sep 1945	09:47	SCO
12 Sep 1945	22:37	SAG
15 Sep 1945	10:10	CAP
17 Sep 1945	18:19	AQU
19 Sep 1945	22:17	PIS
21 Sep 1945	23:10	ARI
23 Sep 1945	22:53	TAU
25 Sep 1945	23:32	GEM
28 Sep 1945	02:39	CAN
30 Sep 1945	08:47	LEO
2 Oct 1945	17:33	VIR
5 Oct 1945	04:16	LIB
7 Oct 1945	16:23	SCO
10 Oct 1945	05:17	SAG
12 Oct 1945	17:32	CAP
15 Oct 1945	03:05	AQU
17 Oct 1945	08:32	PIS
19 Oct 1945	10:08	ARI
21 Oct 1945	09:30	TAU
23 Oct 1945	08:50	GEM
25 Oct 1945	10:12	CAN
27 Oct 1945	14:56	LEO
29 Oct 1945	23:12	VIR
1 Nov 1945	10:08	LIB
3 Nov 1945	22:29	SCO
6 Nov 1945	11:17	SAG
8 Nov 1945	23:34	CAP
11 Nov 1945	09:57	AQU
13 Nov 1945	17:04	PIS
15 Nov 1945	20:23	ARI
17 Nov 1945	20:47	TAU
19 Nov 1945	20:02	GEM
21 Nov 1945	20:14	CAN
23 Nov 1945	23:13	LEO
26 Nov 1945	05:59	VIR
28 Nov 1945	16:18	LIB
1 Dec 1945	04:43	SCO
3 Dec 1945	17:29	SAG
6 Dec 1945	05:23	CAP
8 Dec 1945	15:33	AQU
10 Dec 1945	23:19	PIS
13 Dec 1945	04:14	ARI
15 Dec 1945	06:29	TAU
17 Dec 1945	07:02	GEM
19 Dec 1945	07:27	CAN

DATE	TIME	SIGN	DATE	TIME	SIGN	DATE	TIME	SIGN
21 Dec 1945	09:31	LEO	20 Jun 1946	05:42	PIS	16 Dec 1946	00:08	LIB
23 Dec 1945	14:44	VIR	22 Jun 1946	12:18	ARI	18 Dec 1946	09:43	SCO
25 Dec 1945	23:45	LIB	24 Jun 1946	15:55	TAU	20 Dec 1946	21:48	SAG
28 Dec 1945	11:43	SCO	26 Jun 1946	17:07	GEM	23 Dec 1946	10:50	CAP
31 Dec 1945	00:31	SAG	28 Jun 1946	17:10	CAN	25 Dec 1946	23:29	AQU
2 Jan 1946	12:10	CAP	30 Jun 1946	17:47	LEO	28 Dec 1946	10:42	PIS
4 Jan 1946	21:37	AQU	2 Jul 1946	20:45	VIR	30 Dec 1946	19:30	ARI
7 Jan 1946	04:46	PIS	5 Jul 1946	03:21	LIB	2 Jan 1947	01:04	TAU
9 Jan 1946	09:55	ARI	7 Jul 1946	13:42	SCO	4 Jan 1947	03:25	GEM
11 Jan 1946	13:24	TAU	10 Jul 1946	02:20	SAG	6 Jan 1947	03:27	CAN
13 Jan 1946	15:42	GEM	12 Jul 1946	15:05	CAP	8 Jan 1947	02:53	LEO
15 Jan 1946	17:32	CAN	15 Jul 1946	02:16	AQU	10 Jan 1947	03:45	VIR
17 Jan 1946	20:03	LEO	17 Jul 1946	11:14	PIS	12 Jan 1947	07:54	LIB
20 Jan 1946	00:41	VIR	19 Jul 1946	17:58	ARI	14 Jan 1947	16:15	SCO
22 Jan 1946	08:32	LIB	21 Jul 1946	22:34	TAU	17 Jan 1947	04:03	SAG
24 Jan 1946	19:40	SCO	24 Jul 1946	01:17	GEM	19 Jan 1947	17:10	CAP
27 Jan 1946	08:26	SAG	26 Jul 1946	02:43	CAN	22 Jan 1947	05:36	AQU
29 Jan 1946	20:17	CAP	28 Jul 1946	03:57	LEO	24 Jan 1947	16:22	PIS
1 Feb 1946	05:23	AQU	30 Jul 1946	06:32	VIR	27 Jan 1947	01:09	ARI
3 Feb 1946	11:31	PIS	1 Aug 1946	12:05	LIB	29 Jan 1947	07:44	TAU
5 Feb 1946	15:37	ARI	3 Aug 1946	21:23	SCO	31 Jan 1947	11:50	GEM
7 Feb 1946	18:46	TAU	6 Aug 1946	09:36	SAG	2 Feb 1947	13:37	CAN
9 Feb 1946	21:45	GEM	8 Aug 1946	22:22	CAP	4 Feb 1947	14:01	LEO
12 Feb 1946	00:58	CAN	11 Aug 1946	09:22	AQU	6 Feb 1947	14:42	VIR
14 Feb 1946	04:50	LEO	13 Aug 1946	17:40	PIS	8 Feb 1947	17:39	LIB
16 Feb 1946	10:03	VIR	15 Aug 1946	23:36	ARI	11 Feb 1947	00:29	SCO
18 Feb 1946	17:36	LIB	18 Aug 1946	03:58	TAU	13 Feb 1947	11:16	SAG
21 Feb 1946	04:05	SCO	20 Aug 1946	07:22	GEM	16 Feb 1947	00:11	CAP
23 Feb 1946	16:40	SAG	22 Aug 1946	10:06	CAN	18 Feb 1947	12:37	AQU
26 Feb 1946	05:01	CAP	24 Aug 1946	12:38	LEO	20 Feb 1947	22:56	PIS
28 Feb 1946	14:33	AQU	26 Aug 1946	15:54	VIR	23 Feb 1947	06:57	ARI
2 Mar 1946	20:24	PIS	28 Aug 1946	21:15	LIB	25 Feb 1947	13:07	TAU
4 Mar 1946	23:22	ARI	31 Aug 1946	05:49	SCO	27 Feb 1947	17:46	GEM
7 Mar 1946	01:08	TAU	2 Sep 1946	17:31	SAG	1 Mar 1947	20:58	CAN
9 Mar 1946	03:12	GEM	5 Sep 1946	06:23	CAP	3 Mar 1947	22:59	LEO
11 Mar 1946	06:28	CAN	7 Sep 1946	17:41	AQU	6 Mar 1947	00:46	VIR
13 Mar 1946	11:14	LEO	10 Sep 1946	01:47	PIS	8 Mar 1947	03:51	LIB
15 Mar 1946	17:32	VIR	12 Sep 1946	06:48	ARI	10 Mar 1947	09:51	SCO
18 Mar 1946	01:40	LIB	14 Sep 1946	10:03	TAU	12 Mar 1947	19:34	SAG
20 Mar 1946	12:05	SCO	16 Sep 1946	12:45	GEM	15 Mar 1947	08:00	CAP
23 Mar 1946	00:30	SAG	18 Sep 1946	15:41	CAN	17 Mar 1947	20:34	AQU
25 Mar 1946	13:16	CAP	20 Sep 1946	19:12	LEO	20 Mar 1947	06:57	PIS
27 Mar 1946	23:49	AQU	22 Sep 1946	23:38	VIR	22 Mar 1947	14:22	ARI
30 Mar 1946	06:25	PIS	25 Sep 1946	05:40	LIB	24 Mar 1947	19:28	TAU
1 Apr 1946	09:15	ARI	27 Sep 1946	14:12	SCO	26 Mar 1947	23:15	GEM
3 Apr 1946	09:56	TAU	30 Sep 1946	01:32	SAG	29 Mar 1947	02:25	CAN
5 Apr 1946	10:25	GEM	2 Oct 1946	14:28	CAP	31 Mar 1947	05:22	LEO
7 Apr 1946	12:21	CAN	5 Oct 1946	02:26	AQU	2 Apr 1947	08:30	VIR
9 Apr 1946	16:37	LEO	7 Oct 1946	11:07	PIS	4 Apr 1947	12:40	LIB
11 Apr 1946	23:20	VIR	9 Oct 1946	16:04	ARI	6 Apr 1947	18:56	SCO
14 Apr 1946	08:13	LIB	11 Oct 1946	18:20	TAU	9 Apr 1947	04:12	SAG
16 Apr 1946	19:03	SCO	13 Oct 1946	19:36	GEM	11 Apr 1947	16:08	CAP
19 Apr 1946	07:29	SAG	15 Oct 1946	21:23	CAN	14 Apr 1947	04:50	AQU
21 Apr 1946	20:27	CAP	18 Oct 1946	00:35	LEO	16 Apr 1947	15:46	PIS
24 Apr 1946	07:55	AQU	20 Oct 1946	05:35	VIR	18 Apr 1947	23:24	ARI
26 Apr 1946	15:53	PIS	22 Oct 1946	12:33	LIB	21 Apr 1947	03:55	TAU
28 Apr 1946	19:44	ARI	24 Oct 1946	21:41	SCO	23 Apr 1947	06:27	GEM
30 Apr 1946	20:30	TAU	27 Oct 1946	09:03	SAG	25 Apr 1947	08:22	CAN
2 May 1946	20:03	GEM	29 Oct 1946	21:59	CAP	27 Apr 1947	10:44	LEO
4 May 1946	20:23	CAN	1 Nov 1946	10:35	AQU	29 Apr 1947	14:15	VIR
6 May 1946	23:05	LEO	3 Nov 1946	20:30	PIS	1 May 1947	19:23	LIB
9 May 1946	04:57	VIR	6 Nov 1946	02:26	ARI	4 May 1947	02:35	SCO
11 May 1946	13:54	LIB	8 Nov 1946	04:48	TAU	6 May 1947	12:09	SAG
14 May 1946	01:08	SCO	10 Nov 1946	05:07	GEM	8 May 1947	23:55	CAP
16 May 1946	13:46	SAG	12 Nov 1946	05:15	CAN	11 May 1947	12:40	AQU
19 May 1946	02:41	CAP	14 Nov 1946	06:52	LEO	14 May 1947	00:19	PIS
21 May 1946	14:30	AQU	16 Nov 1946	11:05	VIR	16 May 1947	08:55	ARI
23 May 1946	23:37	PIS	18 Nov 1946	18:12	LIB	18 May 1947	13:50	TAU
26 May 1946	05:04	ARI	21 Nov 1946	03:58	SCO	20 May 1947	15:50	GEM
28 May 1946	07:03	TAU	23 Nov 1946	15:43	SAG	22 May 1947	16:26	CAN
30 May 1946	06:54	GEM	26 Nov 1946	04:39	CAP	24 May 1947	17:18	LEO
1 Jun 1946	06:28	CAN	28 Nov 1946	17:29	AQU	26 May 1947	19:50	VIR
3 Jun 1946	07:39	LEO	1 Dec 1946	04:29	PIS	29 May 1947	00:54	LIB
5 Jun 1946	11:58	VIR	3 Dec 1946	12:03	ARI	31 May 1947	08:42	SCO
7 Jun 1946	19:57	LIB	5 Dec 1946	15:47	TAU	2 Jun 1947	18:54	SAG
10 Jun 1946	07:04	SCO	7 Dec 1946	16:29	GEM	5 Jun 1947	06:51	CAP
12 Jun 1946	19:50	SAG	9 Dec 1946	15:49	CAN	7 Jun 1947	19:37	AQU
15 Jun 1946	08:39	CAP	11 Dec 1946	15:46	LEO	10 Jun 1947	07:46	PIS
17 Jun 1946	20:15	AQU	13 Dec 1946	18:08	VIR	12 Jun 1947	17:33	ARI

DATE	TIME	SIGN	DATE	TIME	SIGN	DATE	TIME	SIGN
14 Jun 1947	23:43	TAU	10 Dec 1947	22:49	SAG	8 Jun 1948	11:27	CAN
17 Jun 1947	02:20	GEM	13 Dec 1947	09:14	CAP	10 Jun 1948	13:11	LEO
19 Jun 1947	02:31	CAN	15 Dec 1947	21:15	AQU	12 Jun 1948	14:48	VIR
21 Jun 1947	02:06	LEO	18 Dec 1947	09:58	PIS	14 Jun 1948	17:33	LIB
23 Jun 1947	03:01	VIR	20 Dec 1947	21:35	ARI	16 Jun 1948	22:03	SCO
25 Jun 1947	06:51	LIB	23 Dec 1947	06:11	TAU	19 Jun 1948	04:28	SAG
27 Jun 1947	14:17	SCO	25 Dec 1947	10:45	GEM	21 Jun 1948	12:51	CAP
30 Jun 1947	00:46	SAG	27 Dec 1947	12:02	CAN	23 Jun 1948	23:15	AQU
2 Jul 1947	13:02	CAP	29 Dec 1947	11:41	LEO	26 Jun 1948	11:23	PIS
5 Jul 1947	01:49	AQU	31 Dec 1947	11:47	VIR	28 Jun 1948	23:55	ARI
7 Jul 1947	14:02	PIS	2 Jan 1948	14:11	LIB	1 Jul 1948	10:38	TAU
10 Jul 1947	00:33	ARI	4 Jan 1948	19:51	SCO	3 Jul 1948	17:47	GEM
12 Jul 1947	08:11	TAU	7 Jan 1948	04:40	SAG	5 Jul 1948	21:05	CAN
14 Jul 1947	12:15	GEM	9 Jan 1948	15:41	CAP	7 Jul 1948	21:52	LEO
16 Jul 1947	13:13	CAN	12 Jan 1948	03:54	AQU	9 Jul 1948	22:04	VIR
18 Jul 1947	12:34	LEO	14 Jan 1948	16:35	PIS	11 Jul 1948	23:31	LIB
20 Jul 1947	12:20	VIR	17 Jan 1948	04:43	ARI	14 Jul 1948	03:28	SCO
22 Jul 1947	14:34	LIB	19 Jan 1948	14:41	TAU	16 Jul 1948	10:11	SAG
24 Jul 1947	20:41	SCO	21 Jan 1948	21:00	GEM	18 Jul 1948	19:13	CAP
27 Jul 1947	06:40	SAG	23 Jan 1948	23:21	CAN	21 Jul 1948	06:02	AQU
29 Jul 1947	19:01	CAP	25 Jan 1948	22:59	LEO	23 Jul 1948	18:12	PIS
1 Aug 1947	07:49	AQU	27 Jan 1948	21:56	VIR	26 Jul 1948	06:57	ARI
3 Aug 1947	19:48	PIS	29 Jan 1948	22:30	LIB	28 Jul 1948	18:33	TAU
6 Aug 1947	06:19	ARI	1 Feb 1948	02:28	SCO	31 Jul 1948	03:00	GEM
8 Aug 1947	14:42	TAU	3 Feb 1948	10:26	SAG	2 Aug 1948	07:19	CAN
10 Aug 1947	20:16	GEM	5 Feb 1948	21:29	CAP	4 Aug 1948	08:12	LEO
12 Aug 1947	22:48	CAN	8 Feb 1948	09:59	AQU	6 Aug 1948	07:32	VIR
14 Aug 1947	23:05	LEO	10 Feb 1948	22:36	PIS	8 Aug 1948	07:30	LIB
16 Aug 1947	22:49	VIR	13 Feb 1948	10:36	ARI	10 Aug 1948	09:57	SCO
19 Aug 1947	00:05	LIB	15 Feb 1948	21:07	TAU	12 Aug 1948	15:49	SAG
21 Aug 1947	04:44	SCO	18 Feb 1948	04:55	GEM	15 Aug 1948	00:52	CAP
23 Aug 1947	13:35	SAG	20 Feb 1948	09:07	CAN	17 Aug 1948	12:02	AQU
26 Aug 1947	01:30	CAP	22 Feb 1948	10:06	LEO	20 Aug 1948	00:23	PIS
28 Aug 1947	14:17	AQU	24 Feb 1948	09:22	VIR	22 Aug 1948	13:05	ARI
31 Aug 1947	02:02	PIS	26 Feb 1948	09:05	LIB	25 Aug 1948	01:02	TAU
2 Sep 1947	12:01	ARI	28 Feb 1948	11:25	SCO	27 Aug 1948	10:38	GEM
4 Sep 1947	20:09	TAU	1 Mar 1948	17:41	SAG	29 Aug 1948	16:33	CAN
7 Sep 1947	02:17	GEM	4 Mar 1948	03:50	CAP	31 Aug 1948	18:40	LEO
9 Sep 1947	06:12	CAN	6 Mar 1948	16:14	AQU	2 Sep 1948	18:20	VIR
11 Sep 1947	08:02	LEO	9 Mar 1948	04:52	PIS	4 Sep 1948	17:35	LIB
13 Sep 1947	08:50	VIR	11 Mar 1948	16:32	ARI	6 Sep 1948	18:34	SCO
15 Sep 1947	10:16	LIB	14 Mar 1948	02:39	TAU	8 Sep 1948	22:52	SAG
17 Sep 1947	14:11	SCO	16 Mar 1948	10:44	GEM	11 Sep 1948	06:56	CAP
19 Sep 1947	21:50	SAG	18 Mar 1948	16:13	CAN	13 Sep 1948	17:58	AQU
22 Sep 1947	08:57	CAP	20 Mar 1948	18:57	LEO	16 Sep 1948	06:26	PIS
24 Sep 1947	21:37	AQU	22 Mar 1948	19:42	VIR	18 Sep 1948	19:01	ARI
27 Sep 1947	09:23	PIS	24 Mar 1948	20:01	LIB	21 Sep 1948	06:45	TAU
29 Sep 1947	18:57	ARI	26 Mar 1948	21:50	SCO	23 Sep 1948	16:39	GEM
2 Oct 1947	02:14	TAU	29 Mar 1948	02:47	SAG	25 Sep 1948	23:44	CAN
4 Oct 1947	07:43	GEM	31 Mar 1948	11:34	CAP	28 Sep 1948	03:34	LEO
6 Oct 1947	11:46	CAN	2 Apr 1948	23:18	AQU	30 Sep 1948	04:40	VIR
8 Oct 1947	14:41	LEO	5 Apr 1948	11:55	PIS	2 Oct 1948	04:30	LIB
10 Oct 1947	16:56	VIR	7 Apr 1948	23:27	ARI	4 Oct 1948	04:58	SCO
12 Oct 1947	19:31	LIB	10 Apr 1948	08:57	TAU	6 Oct 1948	07:55	SAG
14 Oct 1947	23:46	SCO	12 Apr 1948	16:19	GEM	8 Oct 1948	14:31	CAP
17 Oct 1947	06:52	SAG	14 Apr 1948	21:40	CAN	11 Oct 1948	00:42	AQU
19 Oct 1947	17:14	CAP	17 Apr 1948	01:15	LEO	13 Oct 1948	13:03	PIS
22 Oct 1947	05:38	AQU	19 Apr 1948	03:30	VIR	16 Oct 1948	01:35	ARI
24 Oct 1947	17:45	PIS	21 Apr 1948	05:16	LIB	18 Oct 1948	12:53	TAU
27 Oct 1947	03:30	ARI	23 Apr 1948	07:49	SCO	20 Oct 1948	22:13	GEM
29 Oct 1947	10:15	TAU	25 Apr 1948	12:32	SAG	23 Oct 1948	05:21	CAN
31 Oct 1947	14:35	GEM	27 Apr 1948	20:22	CAP	25 Oct 1948	10:08	LEO
2 Nov 1947	17:31	CAN	30 Apr 1948	07:16	AQU	27 Oct 1948	12:52	VIR
4 Nov 1947	20:03	LEO	2 May 1948	19:43	PIS	29 Oct 1948	14:15	LIB
6 Nov 1947	22:55	VIR	5 May 1948	07:27	ARI	31 Oct 1948	15:31	SCO
9 Nov 1947	02:42	LIB	7 May 1948	16:47	TAU	2 Nov 1948	18:10	SAG
11 Nov 1947	08:02	SCO	9 May 1948	23:18	GEM	4 Nov 1948	23:40	CAP
13 Nov 1947	15:33	SAG	12 May 1948	03:37	CAN	7 Nov 1948	08:41	AQU
16 Nov 1947	01:37	CAP	14 May 1948	06:38	LEO	9 Nov 1948	20:33	PIS
18 Nov 1947	13:45	AQU	16 May 1948	09:14	VIR	12 Nov 1948	09:11	ARI
21 Nov 1947	02:15	PIS	18 May 1948	12:07	LIB	14 Nov 1948	20:23	TAU
23 Nov 1947	12:51	ARI	20 May 1948	15:55	SCO	17 Nov 1948	05:01	GEM
25 Nov 1947	20:05	TAU	22 May 1948	21:22	SAG	19 Nov 1948	11:10	CAN
27 Nov 1947	23:54	GEM	25 May 1948	05:07	CAP	21 Nov 1948	15:31	LEO
30 Nov 1947	01:30	CAN	27 May 1948	15:31	AQU	23 Nov 1948	18:48	VIR
2 Dec 1947	02:30	LEO	30 May 1948	03:45	PIS	25 Nov 1948	21:32	LIB
4 Dec 1947	04:23	VIR	1 Jun 1948	15:54	ARI	28 Nov 1948	00:18	SCO
6 Dec 1947	08:14	LIB	4 Jun 1948	01:42	TAU	30 Nov 1948	03:52	SAG
8 Dec 1947	14:24	SCO	6 Jun 1948	08:05	GEM	2 Dec 1948	09:17	CAP

DATE	TIME	SIGN	DATE	TIME	SIGN	DATE	TIME	SIGN
4 Dec 1948	17:31	AQU	3 Jun 1949	04:53	VIR	29 Nov 1949	12:18	ARI
7 Dec 1948	04:45	PIS	5 Jun 1949	07:57	LIB	2 Dec 1949	01:21	TAU
9 Dec 1948	17:29	ARI	7 Jun 1949	10:13	SCO	4 Dec 1949	13:27	GEM
12 Dec 1948	05:08	TAU	9 Jun 1949	12:23	SAG	6 Dec 1949	23:30	CAN
14 Dec 1948	13:42	GEM	11 Jun 1949	15:40	CAP	9 Dec 1949	07:27	LEO
16 Dec 1948	19:00	CAN	13 Jun 1949	21:27	AQU	11 Dec 1949	13:30	VIR
18 Dec 1948	22:02	LEO	16 Jun 1949	06:38	PIS	13 Dec 1949	17:44	LIB
21 Dec 1948	00:19	VIR	18 Jun 1949	18:44	ARI	15 Dec 1949	20:13	SCO
23 Dec 1948	02:59	LIB	21 Jun 1949	07:29	TAU	17 Dec 1949	21:31	SAG
25 Dec 1948	06:38	SCO	23 Jun 1949	18:19	GEM	19 Dec 1949	23:00	CAP
27 Dec 1948	11:29	SAG	26 Jun 1949	02:00	CAN	22 Dec 1949	02:25	AQU
29 Dec 1948	17:46	CAP	28 Jun 1949	07:00	LEO	24 Dec 1949	09:20	PIS
1 Jan 1949	02:08	AQU	30 Jun 1949	10:26	VIR	26 Dec 1949	20:04	ARI
3 Jan 1949	12:58	PIS	2 Jul 1949	13:21	LIB	29 Dec 1949	08:57	TAU
6 Jan 1949	01:40	ARI	4 Jul 1949	16:21	SCO	31 Dec 1949	21:12	GEM
8 Jan 1949	14:02	TAU	6 Jul 1949	19:45	SAG	3 Jan 1950	06:55	CAN
10 Jan 1949	23:29	GEM	9 Jul 1949	00:02	CAP	5 Jan 1950	13:57	LEO
13 Jan 1949	04:56	CAN	11 Jul 1949	06:08	AQU	7 Jan 1950	19:05	VIR
15 Jan 1949	07:07	LEO	13 Jul 1949	15:02	PIS	9 Jan 1950	23:07	LIB
17 Jan 1949	07:52	VIR	16 Jul 1949	02:43	ARI	12 Jan 1950	02:27	SCO
19 Jan 1949	09:03	LIB	18 Jul 1949	15:35	TAU	14 Jan 1950	05:16	SAG
21 Jan 1949	12:00	SCO	21 Jul 1949	02:56	GEM	16 Jan 1950	08:06	CAP
23 Jan 1949	17:09	SAG	23 Jul 1949	10:50	CAN	18 Jan 1950	12:07	AQU
26 Jan 1949	00:22	CAP	25 Jul 1949	15:18	LEO	20 Jan 1950	18:41	PIS
28 Jan 1949	09:26	AQU	27 Jul 1949	17:35	VIR	23 Jan 1950	04:37	ARI
30 Jan 1949	20:26	PIS	29 Jul 1949	19:19	LIB	25 Jan 1950	17:07	TAU
2 Feb 1949	09:04	ARI	31 Jul 1949	21:44	SCO	28 Jan 1950	05:42	GEM
4 Feb 1949	21:56	TAU	3 Aug 1949	01:25	SAG	30 Jan 1950	15:49	CAN
7 Feb 1949	08:39	GEM	5 Aug 1949	06:36	CAP	1 Feb 1950	22:32	LEO
9 Feb 1949	15:21	CAN	7 Aug 1949	13:34	AQU	4 Feb 1950	02:36	VIR
11 Feb 1949	18:00	LEO	9 Aug 1949	22:46	PIS	6 Feb 1950	05:18	LIB
13 Feb 1949	18:05	VIR	12 Aug 1949	10:20	ARI	8 Feb 1950	07:50	SCO
15 Feb 1949	17:43	LIB	14 Aug 1949	23:17	TAU	10 Feb 1950	10:51	SAG
17 Feb 1949	18:53	SCO	17 Aug 1949	11:21	GEM	12 Feb 1950	14:44	CAP
19 Feb 1949	22:50	SAG	19 Aug 1949	20:13	CAN	14 Feb 1950	19:57	AQU
22 Feb 1949	05:50	CAP	22 Aug 1949	01:06	LEO	17 Feb 1950	03:11	PIS
24 Feb 1949	15:26	AQU	24 Aug 1949	02:55	VIR	19 Feb 1950	13:01	ARI
27 Feb 1949	02:54	PIS	26 Aug 1949	03:24	LIB	22 Feb 1950	01:11	TAU
1 Mar 1949	15:35	ARI	28 Aug 1949	04:19	SCO	24 Feb 1950	14:02	GEM
4 Mar 1949	04:32	TAU	30 Aug 1949	07:00	SAG	27 Feb 1950	01:01	CAN
6 Mar 1949	16:04	GEM	1 Sep 1949	12:05	CAP	1 Mar 1950	08:29	LEO
9 Mar 1949	00:19	CAN	3 Sep 1949	19:37	AQU	3 Mar 1950	12:23	VIR
11 Mar 1949	04:32	LEO	6 Sep 1949	05:26	PIS	5 Mar 1950	13:59	LIB
13 Mar 1949	05:23	VIR	8 Sep 1949	17:13	ARI	7 Mar 1950	14:55	SCO
15 Mar 1949	04:39	LIB	11 Sep 1949	06:12	TAU	9 Mar 1950	16:37	SAG
17 Mar 1949	04:25	SCO	13 Sep 1949	18:46	GEM	11 Mar 1950	20:07	CAP
19 Mar 1949	06:30	SAG	16 Sep 1949	04:51	CAN	14 Mar 1950	01:52	AQU
21 Mar 1949	12:05	CAP	18 Sep 1949	11:03	LEO	16 Mar 1950	09:59	PIS
23 Mar 1949	21:10	AQU	20 Sep 1949	13:32	VIR	18 Mar 1950	20:21	ARI
26 Mar 1949	08:50	PIS	22 Sep 1949	13:41	LIB	21 Mar 1950	08:32	TAU
28 Mar 1949	21:41	ARI	24 Sep 1949	13:21	SCO	23 Mar 1950	21:27	GEM
31 Mar 1949	10:28	TAU	26 Sep 1949	14:21	SAG	26 Mar 1950	09:16	CAN
2 Apr 1949	22:01	GEM	28 Sep 1949	18:06	CAP	28 Mar 1950	18:04	LEO
5 Apr 1949	07:09	CAN	1 Oct 1949	01:14	AQU	30 Mar 1950	22:59	VIR
7 Apr 1949	12:57	LEO	3 Oct 1949	11:20	PIS	2 Apr 1950	00:39	LIB
9 Apr 1949	15:30	VIR	5 Oct 1949	23:27	ARI	4 Apr 1950	00:35	SCO
11 Apr 1949	15:47	LIB	8 Oct 1949	12:26	TAU	6 Apr 1950	00:37	SAG
13 Apr 1949	15:27	SCO	11 Oct 1949	01:01	GEM	8 Apr 1950	02:30	CAP
15 Apr 1949	16:23	SAG	13 Oct 1949	11:49	CAN	10 Apr 1950	07:24	AQU
17 Apr 1949	20:16	CAP	15 Oct 1949	19:34	LEO	12 Apr 1950	15:38	PIS
20 Apr 1949	03:59	AQU	17 Oct 1949	23:41	VIR	15 Apr 1950	02:31	ARI
22 Apr 1949	15:08	PIS	20 Oct 1949	00:46	LIB	17 Apr 1950	14:59	TAU
25 Apr 1949	04:00	ARI	22 Oct 1949	00:18	SCO	20 Apr 1950	03:53	GEM
27 Apr 1949	16:40	TAU	24 Oct 1949	00:08	SAG	22 Apr 1950	16:01	CAN
30 Apr 1949	03:47	GEM	26 Oct 1949	02:11	CAP	25 Apr 1950	01:56	LEO
2 May 1949	12:42	CAN	28 Oct 1949	07:50	AQU	27 Apr 1950	08:28	VIR
4 May 1949	19:10	LEO	30 Oct 1949	17:21	PIS	29 Apr 1950	11:23	LIB
6 May 1949	23:10	VIR	2 Nov 1949	05:34	ARI	1 May 1950	11:36	SCO
9 May 1949	01:06	LIB	4 Nov 1949	18:36	TAU	3 May 1950	10:50	SAG
11 May 1949	01:53	SCO	7 Nov 1949	06:54	GEM	5 May 1950	11:09	CAP
13 May 1949	02:57	SAG	9 Nov 1949	17:34	CAN	7 May 1950	14:23	AQU
15 May 1949	05:56	CAP	12 Nov 1949	01:59	LEO	9 May 1950	21:34	PIS
17 May 1949	12:20	AQU	14 Nov 1949	07:41	VIR	12 May 1950	08:18	ARI
19 May 1949	22:26	PIS	16 Nov 1949	10:34	LIB	14 May 1950	20:58	TAU
22 May 1949	11:01	ARI	18 Nov 1949	11:18	SCO	17 May 1950	09:52	GEM
24 May 1949	23:40	TAU	20 Nov 1949	11:15	SAG	19 May 1950	21:50	CAN
27 May 1949	10:26	GEM	22 Nov 1949	12:20	CAP	22 May 1950	08:05	LEO
29 May 1949	18:38	CAN	24 Nov 1949	16:24	AQU	24 May 1950	15:49	VIR
1 Jun 1949	00:35	LEO	27 Nov 1949	00:36	PIS	26 May 1950	20:25	LIB

DATE	TIME	SIGN	DATE	TIME	SIGN	DATE	TIME	SIGN
28 May 1950	22:00	SCO	24 Nov 1950	11:38	GEM	23 May 1951	06:06	CAP
30 May 1950	21:43	SAG	27 Nov 1950	00:12	CAN	25 May 1951	06:41	AQU
1 Jun 1950	21:27	CAP	29 Nov 1950	12:01	LEO	27 May 1951	10:06	PIS
3 Jun 1950	23:19	AQU	1 Dec 1950	21:52	VIR	29 May 1951	16:53	ARI
6 Jun 1950	04:57	PIS	4 Dec 1950	04:28	LIB	1 Jun 1951	02:33	TAU
8 Jun 1950	14:44	ARI	6 Dec 1950	07:18	SCO	3 Jun 1951	14:02	GEM
11 Jun 1950	03:12	TAU	8 Dec 1950	07:16	SAG	6 Jun 1951	02:31	CAN
13 Jun 1950	16:04	GEM	10 Dec 1950	06:16	CAP	8 Jun 1951	15:11	LEO
16 Jun 1950	03:44	CAN	12 Dec 1950	06:34	AQU	11 Jun 1951	02:45	VIR
18 Jun 1950	13:36	LEO	14 Dec 1950	10:11	PIS	13 Jun 1951	11:29	LIB
20 Jun 1950	21:30	VIR	16 Dec 1950	17:58	ARI	15 Jun 1951	16:16	SCO
23 Jun 1950	03:08	LIB	19 Dec 1950	05:09	TAU	17 Jun 1951	17:25	SAG
25 Jun 1950	06:18	SCO	21 Dec 1950	17:49	GEM	19 Jun 1951	16:37	CAP
27 Jun 1950	07:25	SAG	24 Dec 1950	06:17	CAN	21 Jun 1951	16:04	AQU
29 Jun 1950	07:48	CAP	26 Dec 1950	17:45	LEO	23 Jun 1951	17:49	PIS
1 Jul 1950	09:20	AQU	29 Dec 1950	03:40	VIR	25 Jun 1951	23:14	ARI
3 Jul 1950	13:52	PIS	31 Dec 1950	11:18	LIB	28 Jun 1951	08:17	TAU
5 Jul 1950	22:25	ARI	2 Jan 1951	15:57	SCO	30 Jun 1951	19:51	GEM
8 Jul 1950	10:13	TAU	4 Jan 1951	17:38	SAG	3 Jul 1951	08:27	CAN
10 Jul 1950	23:01	GEM	6 Jan 1951	17:31	CAP	5 Jul 1951	21:00	LEO
13 Jul 1950	10:32	CAN	8 Jan 1951	17:35	AQU	8 Jul 1951	08:35	VIR
15 Jul 1950	19:51	LEO	10 Jan 1951	19:56	PIS	10 Jul 1951	18:04	LIB
18 Jul 1950	03:04	VIR	13 Jan 1951	02:06	ARI	13 Jul 1951	00:17	SCO
20 Jul 1950	08:33	LIB	15 Jan 1951	12:11	TAU	15 Jul 1951	03:02	SAG
22 Jul 1950	12:26	SCO	18 Jan 1951	00:35	GEM	17 Jul 1951	03:13	CAP
24 Jul 1950	14:54	SAG	20 Jan 1951	13:05	CAN	19 Jul 1951	02:41	AQU
26 Jul 1950	16:39	CAP	23 Jan 1951	00:10	LEO	21 Jul 1951	03:29	PIS
28 Jul 1950	18:55	AQU	25 Jan 1951	09:25	VIR	23 Jul 1951	07:21	ARI
30 Jul 1950	23:19	PIS	27 Jan 1951	16:45	LIB	25 Jul 1951	15:07	TAU
2 Aug 1950	07:02	ARI	29 Jan 1951	22:02	SCO	28 Jul 1951	02:07	GEM
4 Aug 1950	18:05	TAU	1 Feb 1951	01:15	SAG	30 Jul 1951	14:42	CAN
7 Aug 1950	06:43	GEM	3 Feb 1951	02:52	CAP	2 Aug 1951	03:07	LEO
9 Aug 1950	18:26	CAN	5 Feb 1951	04:03	AQU	4 Aug 1951	14:17	VIR
12 Aug 1950	03:35	LEO	7 Feb 1951	06:28	PIS	6 Aug 1951	23:33	LIB
14 Aug 1950	10:02	VIR	9 Feb 1951	11:43	ARI	9 Aug 1951	06:23	SCO
16 Aug 1950	14:30	LIB	11 Feb 1951	20:33	TAU	11 Aug 1951	10:29	SAG
18 Aug 1950	17:48	SCO	14 Feb 1951	08:18	GEM	13 Aug 1951	12:17	CAP
20 Aug 1950	20:35	SAG	16 Feb 1951	20:50	CAN	15 Aug 1951	12:53	AQU
22 Aug 1950	23:23	CAP	19 Feb 1951	08:00	LEO	17 Aug 1951	13:53	PIS
25 Aug 1950	02:53	AQU	21 Feb 1951	16:42	VIR	19 Aug 1951	16:58	ARI
27 Aug 1950	08:02	PIS	23 Feb 1951	23:00	LIB	21 Aug 1951	23:27	TAU
29 Aug 1950	15:45	ARI	26 Feb 1951	03:30	SCO	24 Aug 1951	09:27	GEM
1 Sep 1950	02:19	TAU	28 Feb 1951	06:49	SAG	26 Aug 1951	21:44	CAN
3 Sep 1950	14:45	GEM	2 Mar 1951	09:29	CAP	29 Aug 1951	10:09	LEO
6 Sep 1950	02:52	CAN	4 Mar 1951	12:10	AQU	31 Aug 1951	20:59	VIR
8 Sep 1950	12:32	LEO	6 Mar 1951	15:45	PIS	3 Sep 1951	05:31	LIB
10 Sep 1950	18:54	VIR	8 Mar 1951	21:16	ARI	5 Sep 1951	11:47	SCO
12 Sep 1950	22:27	LIB	11 Mar 1951	05:32	TAU	7 Sep 1951	16:10	SAG
15 Sep 1950	00:26	SCO	13 Mar 1951	16:36	GEM	9 Sep 1951	19:05	CAP
17 Sep 1950	02:12	SAG	16 Mar 1951	05:05	CAN	11 Sep 1951	21:11	AQU
19 Sep 1950	04:48	CAP	18 Mar 1951	16:44	LEO	13 Sep 1951	23:22	PIS
21 Sep 1950	09:00	AQU	21 Mar 1951	01:37	VIR	16 Sep 1951	02:47	ARI
23 Sep 1950	15:09	PIS	23 Mar 1951	07:20	LIB	18 Sep 1951	08:41	TAU
25 Sep 1950	23:32	ARI	25 Mar 1951	10:35	SCO	20 Sep 1951	17:46	GEM
28 Sep 1950	10:08	TAU	27 Mar 1951	12:40	SAG	23 Sep 1951	05:34	CAN
30 Sep 1950	22:26	GEM	29 Mar 1951	14:51	CAP	25 Sep 1951	18:07	LEO
3 Oct 1950	10:58	CAN	31 Mar 1951	18:02	AQU	28 Sep 1951	05:05	VIR
5 Oct 1950	21:38	LEO	2 Apr 1951	22:45	PIS	30 Sep 1951	13:07	LIB
8 Oct 1950	04:53	VIR	5 Apr 1951	05:15	ARI	2 Oct 1951	18:23	SCO
10 Oct 1950	08:28	LIB	7 Apr 1951	13:52	TAU	4 Oct 1951	21:47	SAG
12 Oct 1950	09:30	SCO	10 Apr 1951	00:41	GEM	7 Oct 1951	00:29	CAP
14 Oct 1950	09:44	SAG	12 Apr 1951	13:04	CAN	9 Oct 1951	03:19	AQU
16 Oct 1950	10:55	CAP	15 Apr 1951	01:17	LEO	11 Oct 1951	06:46	PIS
18 Oct 1950	14:27	AQU	17 Apr 1951	11:05	VIR	13 Oct 1951	11:20	ARI
20 Oct 1950	20:53	PIS	19 Apr 1951	17:13	LIB	15 Oct 1951	17:37	TAU
23 Oct 1950	05:58	ARI	21 Apr 1951	19:54	SCO	18 Oct 1951	02:22	GEM
25 Oct 1950	17:02	TAU	23 Apr 1951	20:39	SAG	20 Oct 1951	13:42	CAN
28 Oct 1950	05:22	GEM	25 Apr 1951	21:20	CAP	23 Oct 1951	02:24	LEO
30 Oct 1950	18:03	CAN	27 Apr 1951	23:33	AQU	25 Oct 1951	14:00	VIR
2 Nov 1950	05:37	LEO	30 Apr 1951	04:13	PIS	27 Oct 1951	22:23	LIB
4 Nov 1950	14:19	VIR	2 May 1951	11:26	ARI	30 Oct 1951	03:08	SCO
6 Nov 1950	19:09	LIB	4 May 1951	20:46	TAU	1 Nov 1951	05:19	SAG
8 Nov 1950	20:28	SCO	7 May 1951	07:50	GEM	3 Nov 1951	06:39	CAP
10 Nov 1950	19:51	SAG	9 May 1951	20:12	CAN	5 Nov 1951	08:43	AQU
12 Nov 1950	19:25	CAP	12 May 1951	08:48	LEO	7 Nov 1951	12:23	PIS
14 Nov 1950	21:15	AQU	14 May 1951	19:43	VIR	9 Nov 1951	17:52	ARI
17 Nov 1950	02:39	PIS	17 May 1951	03:03	LIB	12 Nov 1951	01:07	TAU
19 Nov 1950	11:40	ARI	19 May 1951	06:22	SCO	14 Nov 1951	10:15	GEM
21 Nov 1950	23:07	TAU	21 May 1951	06:43	SAG	16 Nov 1951	21:27	CAN

DATE	TIME	SIGN
19 Nov 1951	10:11	LEO
21 Nov 1951	22:34	VIR
24 Nov 1951	08:07	LIB
26 Nov 1951	13:30	SCO
28 Nov 1951	15:19	SAG
30 Nov 1951	15:22	CAP
2 Dec 1951	15:45	AQU
4 Dec 1951	18:07	PIS
6 Dec 1951	23:18	ARI
9 Dec 1951	07:04	TAU
11 Dec 1951	16:54	GEM
14 Dec 1951	04:22	CAN
16 Dec 1951	17:04	LEO
19 Dec 1951	05:52	VIR
21 Dec 1951	16:40	LIB
23 Dec 1951	23:36	SCO
26 Dec 1951	02:25	SAG
28 Dec 1951	02:23	CAP
30 Dec 1951	01:26	AQU
1 Jan 1952	02:11	PIS
3 Jan 1952	05:41	ARI
5 Jan 1952	12:44	TAU
7 Jan 1952	22:42	GEM
10 Jan 1952	10:34	CAN
12 Jan 1952	23:19	LEO
15 Jan 1952	11:59	VIR
17 Jan 1952	23:18	LIB
20 Jan 1952	07:43	SCO
22 Jan 1952	12:20	SAG
24 Jan 1952	13:38	CAP
26 Jan 1952	13:06	AQU
28 Jan 1952	12:46	PIS
30 Jan 1952	14:33	ARI
1 Feb 1952	19:51	TAU
4 Feb 1952	04:55	GEM
6 Feb 1952	16:44	CAN
9 Feb 1952	05:35	LEO
11 Feb 1952	18:01	VIR
14 Feb 1952	04:59	LIB
16 Feb 1952	13:43	SCO
18 Feb 1952	19:41	SAG
20 Feb 1952	22:48	CAP
22 Feb 1952	23:47	AQU
25 Feb 1952	00:01	PIS
27 Feb 1952	01:12	ARI
29 Feb 1952	05:01	TAU
2 Mar 1952	12:37	GEM
4 Mar 1952	23:40	CAN
7 Mar 1952	12:29	LEO
10 Mar 1952	00:50	VIR
12 Mar 1952	11:15	LIB
14 Mar 1952	19:20	SCO
17 Mar 1952	01:14	SAG
19 Mar 1952	05:19	CAP
21 Mar 1952	07:54	AQU
23 Mar 1952	09:38	PIS
25 Mar 1952	11:34	ARI
27 Mar 1952	15:06	TAU
29 Mar 1952	21:36	GEM
1 Apr 1952	07:39	CAN
3 Apr 1952	20:09	LEO
6 Apr 1952	08:39	VIR
8 Apr 1952	18:55	LIB
11 Apr 1952	02:12	SCO
13 Apr 1952	07:07	SAG
15 Apr 1952	10:41	CAP
17 Apr 1952	13:43	AQU
19 Apr 1952	16:40	PIS
21 Apr 1952	19:56	ARI
24 Apr 1952	00:15	TAU
26 Apr 1952	06:40	GEM
28 Apr 1952	16:06	CAN
1 May 1952	04:12	LEO
3 May 1952	16:57	VIR
6 May 1952	03:38	LIB
8 May 1952	11:50	SCO
10 May 1952	14:49	SAG
12 May 1952	17:08	CAP
14 May 1952	19:14	AQU
16 May 1952	22:05	PIS
19 May 1952	02:07	ARI
21 May 1952	07:29	TAU
23 May 1952	14:37	GEM
26 May 1952	00:06	CAN
28 May 1952	11:59	LEO
31 May 1952	00:56	VIR
2 Jun 1952	12:24	LIB
4 Jun 1952	20:18	SCO
7 Jun 1952	00:19	SAG
9 Jun 1952	01:45	CAP
11 Jun 1952	02:26	AQU
13 Jun 1952	04:00	PIS
15 Jun 1952	07:29	ARI
17 Jun 1952	13:11	TAU
19 Jun 1952	21:03	GEM
22 Jun 1952	07:04	CAN
24 Jun 1952	19:02	LEO
27 Jun 1952	08:05	VIR
29 Jun 1952	20:17	LIB
2 Jul 1952	05:24	SCO
4 Jul 1952	10:25	SAG
6 Jul 1952	12:01	CAP
8 Jul 1952	11:54	AQU
10 Jul 1952	11:59	PIS
12 Jul 1952	13:57	ARI
14 Jul 1952	18:45	TAU
17 Jul 1952	02:38	GEM
19 Jul 1952	13:05	CAN
22 Jul 1952	01:20	LEO
24 Jul 1952	14:24	VIR
27 Jul 1952	02:53	LIB
29 Jul 1952	13:02	SCO
31 Jul 1952	19:36	SAG
2 Aug 1952	22:26	CAP
4 Aug 1952	22:40	AQU
6 Aug 1952	22:05	PIS
8 Aug 1952	22:34	ARI
11 Aug 1952	01:46	TAU
13 Aug 1952	08:37	GEM
15 Aug 1952	18:52	CAN
18 Aug 1952	07:18	LEO
20 Aug 1952	20:22	VIR
23 Aug 1952	08:41	LIB
25 Aug 1952	19:09	SCO
28 Aug 1952	02:52	SAG
30 Aug 1952	07:23	CAP
1 Sep 1952	09:02	AQU
3 Sep 1952	08:59	PIS
5 Sep 1952	08:57	ARI
7 Sep 1952	10:49	TAU
9 Sep 1952	16:06	GEM
12 Sep 1952	01:24	CAN
14 Sep 1952	13:38	LEO
17 Sep 1952	02:41	VIR
19 Sep 1952	14:40	LIB
22 Sep 1952	00:42	SCO
24 Sep 1952	08:32	SAG
26 Sep 1952	14:05	CAP
28 Sep 1952	17:24	AQU
30 Sep 1952	18:52	PIS
2 Oct 1952	19:33	ARI
4 Oct 1952	21:06	TAU
7 Oct 1952	01:16	GEM
9 Oct 1952	09:16	CAN
11 Oct 1952	20:50	LEO
14 Oct 1952	09:50	VIR
16 Oct 1952	21:43	LIB
19 Oct 1952	07:09	SCO
21 Oct 1952	14:11	SAG
23 Oct 1952	19:28	CAP
25 Oct 1952	23:27	AQU
28 Oct 1952	02:22	PIS
30 Oct 1952	04:34	ARI
1 Nov 1952	06:58	TAU
3 Nov 1952	11:03	GEM
5 Nov 1952	18:12	CAN
8 Nov 1952	04:56	LEO
10 Nov 1952	17:46	VIR
13 Nov 1952	05:57	LIB
15 Nov 1952	15:17	SCO
17 Nov 1952	21:32	SAG
20 Nov 1952	01:39	CAP
22 Nov 1952	04:51	AQU
24 Nov 1952	07:54	PIS
26 Nov 1952	11:09	ARI
28 Nov 1952	14:54	TAU
30 Nov 1952	19:53	GEM
3 Dec 1952	03:09	CAN
5 Dec 1952	13:23	LEO
8 Dec 1952	01:57	VIR
10 Dec 1952	14:34	LIB
13 Dec 1952	00:37	SCO
15 Dec 1952	06:59	SAG
17 Dec 1952	10:16	CAP
19 Dec 1952	12:02	AQU
21 Dec 1952	13:45	PIS
23 Dec 1952	16:30	ARI
25 Dec 1952	20:46	TAU
28 Dec 1952	02:48	GEM
30 Dec 1952	10:53	CAN
1 Jan 1953	21:17	LEO
4 Jan 1953	09:40	VIR
6 Jan 1953	22:35	LIB
9 Jan 1953	09:42	SCO
11 Jan 1953	17:13	SAG
13 Jan 1953	20:54	CAP
15 Jan 1953	21:56	AQU
17 Jan 1953	22:07	PIS
19 Jan 1953	23:09	ARI
22 Jan 1953	02:21	TAU
24 Jan 1953	08:21	GEM
26 Jan 1953	17:06	CAN
29 Jan 1953	04:06	LEO
31 Jan 1953	16:35	VIR
3 Feb 1953	05:31	LIB
5 Feb 1953	17:20	SCO
8 Feb 1953	02:18	SAG
10 Feb 1953	07:31	CAP
12 Feb 1953	09:15	AQU
14 Feb 1953	08:57	PIS
16 Feb 1953	08:31	ARI
18 Feb 1953	09:51	TAU
20 Feb 1953	14:28	GEM
22 Feb 1953	22:48	CAN
25 Feb 1953	10:05	LEO
27 Feb 1953	22:50	VIR
2 Mar 1953	11:40	LIB
4 Mar 1953	23:30	SCO
7 Mar 1953	09:19	SAG
9 Mar 1953	16:09	CAP
11 Mar 1953	19:36	AQU
13 Mar 1953	20:16	PIS
15 Mar 1953	19:38	ARI
17 Mar 1953	19:44	TAU
19 Mar 1953	22:36	GEM
22 Mar 1953	05:29	CAN
24 Mar 1953	16:14	LEO
27 Mar 1953	05:03	VIR
29 Mar 1953	17:51	LIB
1 Apr 1953	05:19	SCO
3 Apr 1953	14:57	SAG
5 Apr 1953	22:28	CAP
8 Apr 1953	03:26	AQU
10 Apr 1953	05:49	PIS
12 Apr 1953	06:18	ARI
14 Apr 1953	06:31	TAU
16 Apr 1953	08:27	GEM
18 Apr 1953	13:54	CAN
20 Apr 1953	23:27	LEO
23 Apr 1953	11:52	VIR
26 Apr 1953	00:39	LIB
28 Apr 1953	11:51	SCO
30 Apr 1953	20:51	SAG
3 May 1953	03:54	CAP
5 May 1953	09:11	AQU
7 May 1953	12:45	PIS
9 May 1953	14:48	ARI

DATE	TIME	SIGN
11 May 1953	16:12	TAU
13 May 1953	18:26	GEM
15 May 1953	23:17	CAN
18 May 1953	07:47	LEO
20 May 1953	19:30	VIR
23 May 1953	08:15	LIB
25 May 1953	19:31	SCO
28 May 1953	04:07	SAG
30 May 1953	10:16	CAP
1 Jun 1953	14:44	AQU
3 Jun 1953	18:11	PIS
5 Jun 1953	21:01	ARI
7 Jun 1953	23:41	TAU
10 Jun 1953	03:03	GEM
12 Jun 1953	08:17	CAN
14 Jun 1953	16:27	LEO
17 Jun 1953	03:36	VIR
19 Jun 1953	16:16	LIB
22 Jun 1953	03:56	SCO
24 Jun 1953	12:46	SAG
26 Jun 1953	18:28	CAP
28 Jun 1953	21:50	AQU
1 Jul 1953	00:08	PIS
3 Jul 1953	02:23	ARI
5 Jul 1953	05:23	TAU
7 Jul 1953	09:42	GEM
9 Jul 1953	15:54	CAN
12 Jul 1953	00:28	LEO
14 Jul 1953	11:28	VIR
17 Jul 1953	00:03	LIB
19 Jul 1953	12:15	SCO
21 Jul 1953	21:57	SAG
24 Jul 1953	04:05	CAP
26 Jul 1953	07:02	AQU
28 Jul 1953	08:06	PIS
30 Jul 1953	08:55	ARI
1 Aug 1953	10:57	TAU
3 Aug 1953	15:11	GEM
5 Aug 1953	22:00	CAN
8 Aug 1953	07:16	LEO
10 Aug 1953	18:33	VIR
13 Aug 1953	07:08	LIB
15 Aug 1953	19:43	SCO
18 Aug 1953	06:29	SAG
20 Aug 1953	13:51	CAP
22 Aug 1953	17:28	AQU
24 Aug 1953	18:11	PIS
26 Aug 1953	17:45	ARI
28 Aug 1953	18:09	TAU
30 Aug 1953	21:07	GEM
2 Sep 1953	03:30	CAN
4 Sep 1953	13:05	LEO
7 Sep 1953	00:47	VIR
9 Sep 1953	13:27	LIB
12 Sep 1953	02:05	SCO
14 Sep 1953	13:30	SAG
16 Sep 1953	22:19	CAP
19 Sep 1953	03:28	AQU
21 Sep 1953	05:06	PIS
23 Sep 1953	04:30	ARI
25 Sep 1953	03:45	TAU
27 Sep 1953	05:01	GEM
29 Sep 1953	09:57	CAN
1 Oct 1953	18:53	LEO
4 Oct 1953	06:40	VIR
6 Oct 1953	19:27	LIB
9 Oct 1953	07:55	SCO
11 Oct 1953	19:18	SAG
14 Oct 1953	04:51	CAP
16 Oct 1953	11:32	AQU
18 Oct 1953	14:54	PIS
20 Oct 1953	15:26	ARI
22 Oct 1953	14:46	TAU
24 Oct 1953	15:04	GEM
26 Oct 1953	18:23	CAN
29 Oct 1953	01:55	LEO
31 Oct 1953	13:04	VIR
3 Nov 1953	01:50	LIB
5 Nov 1953	14:11	SCO
8 Nov 1953	01:05	SAG
10 Nov 1953	10:17	CAP
12 Nov 1953	17:30	AQU
14 Nov 1953	22:16	PIS
17 Nov 1953	00:34	ARI
19 Nov 1953	01:14	TAU
21 Nov 1953	01:55	GEM
23 Nov 1953	04:32	CAN
25 Nov 1953	10:41	LEO
27 Nov 1953	20:41	VIR
30 Nov 1953	09:05	LIB
2 Dec 1953	21:29	SCO
5 Dec 1953	08:08	SAG
7 Dec 1953	16:32	CAP
9 Dec 1953	22:58	AQU
12 Dec 1953	03:45	PIS
14 Dec 1953	07:05	ARI
16 Dec 1953	09:22	TAU
18 Dec 1953	11:27	GEM
20 Dec 1953	14:40	CAN
22 Dec 1953	20:23	LEO
25 Dec 1953	05:24	VIR
27 Dec 1953	17:10	LIB
30 Dec 1953	05:42	SCO
1 Jan 1954	16:39	SAG
4 Jan 1954	00:44	CAP
6 Jan 1954	06:08	AQU
8 Jan 1954	09:42	PIS
10 Jan 1954	12:26	ARI
12 Jan 1954	15:09	TAU
14 Jan 1954	18:29	GEM
16 Jan 1954	23:01	CAN
19 Jan 1954	05:24	LEO
21 Jan 1954	14:14	VIR
24 Jan 1954	01:30	LIB
26 Jan 1954	14:03	SCO
29 Jan 1954	01:41	SAG
31 Jan 1954	10:25	CAP
2 Feb 1954	15:37	AQU
4 Feb 1954	18:03	PIS
6 Feb 1954	19:14	ARI
8 Feb 1954	20:47	TAU
10 Feb 1954	23:54	GEM
13 Feb 1954	05:10	CAN
15 Feb 1954	12:35	LEO
17 Feb 1954	22:00	VIR
20 Feb 1954	09:14	LIB
22 Feb 1954	21:43	SCO
25 Feb 1954	09:59	SAG
27 Feb 1954	19:56	CAP
2 Mar 1954	02:05	AQU
4 Mar 1954	04:31	PIS
6 Mar 1954	04:39	ARI
8 Mar 1954	04:32	TAU
10 Mar 1954	06:06	GEM
12 Mar 1954	10:38	CAN
14 Mar 1954	18:16	LEO
17 Mar 1954	04:21	VIR
19 Mar 1954	15:57	LIB
22 Mar 1954	04:26	SCO
24 Mar 1954	16:55	SAG
27 Mar 1954	03:54	CAP
29 Mar 1954	11:35	AQU
31 Mar 1954	15:15	PIS
2 Apr 1954	15:39	ARI
4 Apr 1954	14:42	TAU
6 Apr 1954	14:40	GEM
8 Apr 1954	17:28	CAN
11 Apr 1954	00:06	LEO
13 Apr 1954	10:03	VIR
15 Apr 1954	21:57	LIB
18 Apr 1954	10:32	SCO
20 Apr 1954	22:54	SAG
23 Apr 1954	10:10	CAP
25 Apr 1954	19:01	AQU
28 Apr 1954	00:19	PIS
30 Apr 1954	02:07	ARI
2 May 1954	01:42	TAU
4 May 1954	01:07	GEM
6 May 1954	02:31	CAN
8 May 1954	07:29	LEO
10 May 1954	16:22	VIR
13 May 1954	04:03	LIB
15 May 1954	16:41	SCO
18 May 1954	04:53	SAG
20 May 1954	15:48	CAP
23 May 1954	00:47	AQU
25 May 1954	07:07	PIS
27 May 1954	10:30	ARI
29 May 1954	11:32	TAU
31 May 1954	11:40	GEM
2 Jun 1954	12:46	CAN
4 Jun 1954	16:34	LEO
7 Jun 1954	00:07	VIR
9 Jun 1954	10:59	LIB
11 Jun 1954	23:29	SCO
14 Jun 1954	11:36	SAG
16 Jun 1954	22:04	CAP
19 Jun 1954	06:25	AQU
21 Jun 1954	12:35	PIS
23 Jun 1954	16:43	ARI
25 Jun 1954	19:08	TAU
27 Jun 1954	20:41	GEM
29 Jun 1954	22:36	CAN
2 Jul 1954	02:17	LEO
4 Jul 1954	08:56	VIR
6 Jul 1954	18:53	LIB
9 Jul 1954	07:03	SCO
11 Jul 1954	19:18	SAG
14 Jul 1954	05:39	CAP
16 Jul 1954	13:18	AQU
18 Jul 1954	18:32	PIS
20 Jul 1954	22:06	ARI
23 Jul 1954	00:52	TAU
25 Jul 1954	03:30	GEM
27 Jul 1954	06:41	CAN
29 Jul 1954	11:11	LEO
31 Jul 1954	17:49	VIR
3 Aug 1954	03:14	LIB
5 Aug 1954	15:02	SCO
8 Aug 1954	03:31	SAG
10 Aug 1954	14:19	CAP
12 Aug 1954	21:53	AQU
15 Aug 1954	02:16	PIS
17 Aug 1954	04:37	ARI
19 Aug 1954	06:25	TAU
21 Aug 1954	08:56	GEM
23 Aug 1954	12:50	CAN
25 Aug 1954	18:22	LEO
28 Aug 1954	01:44	VIR
30 Aug 1954	11:12	LIB
1 Sep 1954	22:48	SCO
4 Sep 1954	11:31	SAG
6 Sep 1954	23:08	CAP
9 Sep 1954	07:30	AQU
11 Sep 1954	11:53	PIS
13 Sep 1954	13:21	ARI
15 Sep 1954	13:44	TAU
17 Sep 1954	14:55	GEM
19 Sep 1954	18:12	CAN
22 Sep 1954	00:04	LEO
24 Sep 1954	08:10	VIR
26 Sep 1954	18:10	LIB
29 Sep 1954	05:51	SCO
1 Oct 1954	18:41	SAG
4 Oct 1954	07:03	CAP
6 Oct 1954	16:44	AQU
8 Oct 1954	22:15	PIS
10 Oct 1954	23:57	ARI
12 Oct 1954	23:31	TAU
14 Oct 1954	23:10	GEM
17 Oct 1954	00:51	CAN
19 Oct 1954	05:41	LEO
21 Oct 1954	13:45	VIR
24 Oct 1954	00:12	LIB
26 Oct 1954	12:10	SCO
29 Oct 1954	00:58	SAG
31 Oct 1954	13:35	CAP

DATE	TIME	SIGN	DATE	TIME	SIGN	DATE	TIME	SIGN
3 Nov 1954	00:20	AQU	30 Apr 1955	19:58	VIR	28 Oct 1955	15:45	ARI
5 Nov 1954	07:33	PIS	3 May 1955	04:26	LIB	30 Oct 1955	18:29	TAU
7 Nov 1954	10:41	ARI	5 May 1955	15:04	SCO	1 Nov 1955	19:22	GEM
9 Nov 1954	10:47	TAU	8 May 1955	03:18	SAG	3 Nov 1955	20:11	CAN
11 Nov 1954	09:50	GEM	10 May 1955	16:18	CAP	5 Nov 1955	22:20	LEO
13 Nov 1954	10:00	CAN	13 May 1955	04:28	AQU	8 Nov 1955	02:37	VIR
15 Nov 1954	13:04	LEO	15 May 1955	13:51	PIS	10 Nov 1955	09:15	LIB
17 Nov 1954	19:52	VIR	17 May 1955	19:20	ARI	12 Nov 1955	18:12	SCO
20 Nov 1954	06:02	LIB	19 May 1955	21:10	TAU	15 Nov 1955	05:17	SAG
22 Nov 1954	18:12	SCO	21 May 1955	20:56	GEM	17 Nov 1955	17:58	CAP
25 Nov 1954	07:01	SAG	23 May 1955	20:33	CAN	20 Nov 1955	06:58	AQU
27 Nov 1954	19:23	CAP	25 May 1955	21:53	LEO	22 Nov 1955	18:10	PIS
30 Nov 1954	06:18	AQU	28 May 1955	02:16	VIR	25 Nov 1955	01:45	ARI
2 Dec 1954	14:37	PIS	30 May 1955	10:08	LIB	27 Nov 1955	05:26	TAU
4 Dec 1954	19:34	ARI	1 Jun 1955	20:54	SCO	29 Nov 1955	06:10	GEM
6 Dec 1954	21:21	TAU	4 Jun 1955	09:23	SAG	1 Dec 1955	05:46	CAN
8 Dec 1954	21:16	GEM	6 Jun 1955	22:20	CAP	3 Dec 1955	06:07	LEO
10 Dec 1954	21:06	CAN	9 Jun 1955	10:29	AQU	5 Dec 1955	08:50	VIR
12 Dec 1954	22:49	LEO	11 Jun 1955	20:31	PIS	7 Dec 1955	14:48	LIB
15 Dec 1954	03:54	VIR	14 Jun 1955	03:22	ARI	10 Dec 1955	00:00	SCO
17 Dec 1954	12:52	LIB	16 Jun 1955	06:49	TAU	12 Dec 1955	11:33	SAG
20 Dec 1954	00:43	SCO	18 Jun 1955	07:36	GEM	15 Dec 1955	00:23	CAP
22 Dec 1954	13:34	SAG	20 Jun 1955	07:15	CAN	17 Dec 1955	13:18	AQU
25 Dec 1954	01:39	CAP	22 Jun 1955	07:36	LEO	20 Dec 1955	01:01	PIS
27 Dec 1954	11:59	AQU	24 Jun 1955	10:27	VIR	22 Dec 1955	10:04	ARI
29 Dec 1954	20:08	PIS	26 Jun 1955	16:55	LIB	24 Dec 1955	15:32	TAU
1 Jan 1955	01:55	ARI	29 Jun 1955	03:04	SCO	26 Dec 1955	17:32	GEM
3 Jan 1955	05:23	TAU	1 Jul 1955	15:34	SAG	28 Dec 1955	17:17	CAN
5 Jan 1955	07:04	GEM	4 Jul 1955	04:29	CAP	30 Dec 1955	16:36	LEO
7 Jan 1955	08:00	CAN	6 Jul 1955	16:17	AQU	1 Jan 1956	17:30	VIR
9 Jan 1955	09:41	LEO	9 Jul 1955	02:07	PIS	3 Jan 1956	21:45	LIB
11 Jan 1955	13:43	VIR	11 Jul 1955	09:32	ARI	6 Jan 1956	05:59	SCO
13 Jan 1955	21:15	LIB	13 Jul 1955	14:19	TAU	8 Jan 1956	17:32	SAG
16 Jan 1955	08:14	SCO	15 Jul 1955	16:42	GEM	11 Jan 1956	06:33	CAP
18 Jan 1955	21:01	SAG	17 Jul 1955	17:29	CAN	13 Jan 1956	19:19	AQU
21 Jan 1955	09:08	CAP	19 Jul 1955	18:03	LEO	16 Jan 1956	06:47	PIS
23 Jan 1955	18:58	AQU	21 Jul 1955	20:06	VIR	18 Jan 1956	16:16	ARI
26 Jan 1955	02:10	PIS	24 Jul 1955	01:17	LIB	20 Jan 1956	23:09	TAU
28 Jan 1955	07:19	ARI	26 Jul 1955	10:19	SCO	23 Jan 1956	03:04	GEM
30 Jan 1955	11:05	TAU	28 Jul 1955	22:24	SAG	25 Jan 1956	04:19	CAN
1 Feb 1955	14:02	GEM	31 Jul 1955	11:18	CAP	27 Jan 1956	04:06	LEO
3 Feb 1955	16:36	CAN	2 Aug 1955	22:50	AQU	29 Jan 1956	04:17	VIR
5 Feb 1955	19:28	LEO	5 Aug 1955	08:03	PIS	31 Jan 1956	06:56	LIB
7 Feb 1955	23:43	VIR	7 Aug 1955	14:59	ARI	2 Feb 1956	13:34	SCO
10 Feb 1955	06:33	LIB	9 Aug 1955	20:02	TAU	5 Feb 1956	00:13	SAG
12 Feb 1955	16:38	SCO	11 Aug 1955	23:32	GEM	7 Feb 1956	13:08	CAP
15 Feb 1955	05:07	SAG	14 Aug 1955	01:50	CAN	10 Feb 1956	01:51	AQU
17 Feb 1955	17:34	CAP	16 Aug 1955	03:34	LEO	12 Feb 1956	12:51	PIS
20 Feb 1955	03:32	AQU	18 Aug 1955	05:57	VIR	14 Feb 1956	21:47	ARI
22 Feb 1955	10:08	PIS	20 Aug 1955	10:34	LIB	17 Feb 1956	04:48	TAU
24 Feb 1955	14:05	ARI	22 Aug 1955	18:37	SCO	19 Feb 1956	09:49	GEM
26 Feb 1955	16:46	TAU	25 Aug 1955	06:03	SAG	21 Feb 1956	12:48	CAN
28 Feb 1955	19:23	GEM	27 Aug 1955	18:56	CAP	23 Feb 1956	14:10	LEO
2 Mar 1955	22:39	CAN	30 Aug 1955	06:34	AQU	25 Feb 1956	15:05	VIR
5 Mar 1955	02:48	LEO	1 Sep 1955	15:22	PIS	27 Feb 1956	17:20	LIB
7 Mar 1955	08:09	VIR	3 Sep 1955	21:23	ARI	29 Feb 1956	22:46	SCO
9 Mar 1955	15:20	LIB	6 Sep 1955	01:36	TAU	3 Mar 1956	08:09	SAG
12 Mar 1955	01:04	SCO	8 Sep 1955	04:58	GEM	5 Mar 1956	20:32	CAP
14 Mar 1955	13:13	SAG	10 Sep 1955	08:00	CAN	8 Mar 1956	09:18	AQU
17 Mar 1955	02:00	CAP	12 Sep 1955	11:02	LEO	10 Mar 1956	20:10	PIS
19 Mar 1955	12:45	AQU	14 Sep 1955	14:33	VIR	13 Mar 1956	04:25	ARI
21 Mar 1955	19:44	PIS	16 Sep 1955	19:35	LIB	15 Mar 1956	10:31	TAU
23 Mar 1955	23:08	ARI	19 Sep 1955	03:19	SCO	17 Mar 1956	15:11	GEM
26 Mar 1955	00:31	TAU	21 Sep 1955	14:11	SAG	19 Mar 1956	18:47	CAN
28 Mar 1955	01:42	GEM	24 Sep 1955	03:00	CAP	21 Mar 1956	21:30	LEO
30 Mar 1955	04:05	CAN	26 Sep 1955	15:06	AQU	23 Mar 1956	23:53	VIR
1 Apr 1955	08:20	LEO	29 Sep 1955	00:11	PIS	26 Mar 1956	03:00	LIB
3 Apr 1955	14:31	VIR	1 Oct 1955	05:46	ARI	28 Mar 1956	08:19	SCO
5 Apr 1955	22:34	LIB	3 Oct 1955	08:51	TAU	30 Mar 1956	16:55	SAG
8 Apr 1955	08:38	SCO	5 Oct 1955	10:59	GEM	2 Apr 1956	04:37	CAP
10 Apr 1955	20:41	SAG	7 Oct 1955	13:22	CAN	4 Apr 1956	17:24	AQU
13 Apr 1955	09:40	CAP	9 Oct 1955	16:41	LEO	7 Apr 1956	04:36	PIS
15 Apr 1955	21:18	AQU	11 Oct 1955	21:11	VIR	9 Apr 1956	12:45	ARI
18 Apr 1955	05:27	PIS	14 Oct 1955	03:13	LIB	11 Apr 1956	18:03	TAU
20 Apr 1955	09:28	ARI	16 Oct 1955	11:24	SCO	13 Apr 1956	21:30	GEM
22 Apr 1955	10:28	TAU	18 Oct 1955	22:08	SAG	16 Apr 1956	00:14	CAN
24 Apr 1955	10:24	GEM	21 Oct 1955	10:51	CAP	18 Apr 1956	03:00	LEO
26 Apr 1955	11:09	CAN	23 Oct 1955	23:31	AQU	20 Apr 1956	06:16	VIR
28 Apr 1955	14:09	LEO	26 Oct 1955	09:35	PIS	22 Apr 1956	10:36	LIB

DATE	TIME	SIGN
24 Apr 1956	16:44	SCO
27 Apr 1956	01:26	SAG
29 Apr 1956	12:44	CAP
2 May 1956	01:27	AQU
4 May 1956	13:14	PIS
6 May 1956	22:04	ARI
9 May 1956	03:23	TAU
11 May 1956	06:00	GEM
13 May 1956	07:20	CAN
15 May 1956	08:52	LEO
17 May 1956	11:40	VIR
19 May 1956	16:25	LIB
21 May 1956	23:27	SCO
24 May 1956	08:46	SAG
26 May 1956	20:11	CAP
29 May 1956	08:51	AQU
31 May 1956	21:08	PIS
3 Jun 1956	07:04	ARI
5 Jun 1956	13:20	TAU
7 Jun 1956	16:08	GEM
9 Jun 1956	16:41	CAN
11 Jun 1956	16:44	LEO
13 Jun 1956	18:03	VIR
15 Jun 1956	21:59	LIB
18 Jun 1956	05:02	SCO
20 Jun 1956	14:55	SAG
23 Jun 1956	02:43	CAP
25 Jun 1956	15:25	AQU
28 Jun 1956	03:54	PIS
30 Jun 1956	14:41	ARI
2 Jul 1956	22:24	TAU
5 Jul 1956	02:24	GEM
7 Jul 1956	03:19	CAN
9 Jul 1956	02:42	LEO
11 Jul 1956	02:35	VIR
13 Jul 1956	04:54	LIB
15 Jul 1956	10:57	SCO
17 Jul 1956	20:38	SAG
20 Jul 1956	08:40	CAP
22 Jul 1956	21:28	AQU
25 Jul 1956	09:49	PIS
27 Jul 1956	20:53	ARI
30 Jul 1956	05:39	TAU
1 Aug 1956	11:14	GEM
3 Aug 1956	13:31	CAN
5 Aug 1956	13:26	LEO
7 Aug 1956	12:50	VIR
9 Aug 1956	13:51	LIB
11 Aug 1956	18:20	SCO
14 Aug 1956	03:00	SAG
16 Aug 1956	14:47	CAP
19 Aug 1956	03:37	AQU
21 Aug 1956	15:46	PIS
24 Aug 1956	02:29	ARI
26 Aug 1956	11:22	TAU
28 Aug 1956	17:59	GEM
30 Aug 1956	21:50	CAN
1 Sep 1956	23:13	LEO
3 Sep 1956	23:20	VIR
6 Sep 1956	00:05	LIB
8 Sep 1956	03:27	SCO
10 Sep 1956	10:47	SAG
12 Sep 1956	21:46	CAP
15 Sep 1956	10:27	AQU
17 Sep 1956	22:32	PIS
20 Sep 1956	08:46	ARI
22 Sep 1956	17:00	TAU
24 Sep 1956	23:24	GEM
27 Sep 1956	03:59	CAN
29 Sep 1956	06:48	LEO
1 Oct 1956	08:24	VIR
3 Oct 1956	10:01	LIB
5 Oct 1956	13:20	SCO
7 Oct 1956	19:46	SAG
10 Oct 1956	05:47	CAP
12 Oct 1956	18:09	AQU
15 Oct 1956	06:24	PIS
17 Oct 1956	16:34	ARI
20 Oct 1956	00:06	TAU

DATE	TIME	SIGN
22 Oct 1956	05:28	GEM
24 Oct 1956	09:22	CAN
26 Oct 1956	12:26	LEO
28 Oct 1956	15:09	VIR
30 Oct 1956	18:09	LIB
1 Nov 1956	22:25	SCO
4 Nov 1956	04:56	SAG
6 Nov 1956	14:24	CAP
9 Nov 1956	02:19	AQU
11 Nov 1956	14:50	PIS
14 Nov 1956	01:35	ARI
16 Nov 1956	09:11	TAU
18 Nov 1956	13:44	GEM
20 Nov 1956	16:17	CAN
22 Nov 1956	18:09	LEO
24 Nov 1956	20:32	VIR
27 Nov 1956	00:11	LIB
29 Nov 1956	05:34	SCO
1 Dec 1956	12:59	SAG
3 Dec 1956	22:36	CAP
6 Dec 1956	10:16	AQU
8 Dec 1956	22:56	PIS
11 Dec 1956	10:35	ARI
13 Dec 1956	19:14	TAU
16 Dec 1956	00:04	GEM
18 Dec 1956	01:51	CAN
20 Dec 1956	02:11	LEO
22 Dec 1956	02:56	VIR
24 Dec 1956	05:38	LIB
26 Dec 1956	11:09	SCO
28 Dec 1956	19:20	SAG
31 Dec 1956	05:36	CAP
2 Jan 1957	17:24	AQU
5 Jan 1957	06:04	PIS
7 Jan 1957	18:22	ARI
10 Jan 1957	04:25	TAU
12 Jan 1957	10:42	GEM
14 Jan 1957	13:04	CAN
16 Jan 1957	12:50	LEO
18 Jan 1957	12:04	VIR
20 Jan 1957	12:56	LIB
22 Jan 1957	17:02	SCO
25 Jan 1957	00:52	SAG
27 Jan 1957	11:32	CAP
29 Jan 1957	23:41	AQU
1 Feb 1957	12:20	PIS
4 Feb 1957	00:41	ARI
6 Feb 1957	11:36	TAU
8 Feb 1957	19:33	GEM
10 Feb 1957	23:37	CAN
13 Feb 1957	00:17	LEO
14 Feb 1957	23:17	VIR
16 Feb 1957	22:50	LIB
19 Feb 1957	01:07	SCO
21 Feb 1957	07:23	SAG
23 Feb 1957	17:26	CAP
26 Feb 1957	05:42	AQU
28 Feb 1957	18:24	PIS
3 Mar 1957	06:30	ARI
5 Mar 1957	17:20	TAU
8 Mar 1957	02:02	GEM
10 Mar 1957	07:44	CAN
12 Mar 1957	10:10	LEO
14 Mar 1957	10:19	VIR
16 Mar 1957	09:59	LIB
18 Mar 1957	11:15	SCO
20 Mar 1957	15:54	SAG
23 Mar 1957	00:35	CAP
25 Mar 1957	12:17	AQU
28 Mar 1957	00:59	PIS
30 Mar 1957	12:54	ARI
1 Apr 1957	23:10	TAU
4 Apr 1957	07:29	GEM
6 Apr 1957	13:36	CAN
8 Apr 1957	17:23	LEO
10 Apr 1957	19:12	VIR
12 Apr 1957	20:08	LIB
14 Apr 1957	21:46	SCO
17 Apr 1957	01:43	SAG

DATE	TIME	SIGN
19 Apr 1957	09:08	CAP
21 Apr 1957	19:53	AQU
24 Apr 1957	08:22	PIS
26 Apr 1957	20:21	ARI
29 Apr 1957	06:17	TAU
1 May 1957	13:45	GEM
3 May 1957	19:07	CAN
5 May 1957	22:53	LEO
8 May 1957	01:36	VIR
10 May 1957	03:57	LIB
12 May 1957	06:48	SCO
14 May 1957	11:14	SAG
16 May 1957	18:13	CAP
19 May 1957	04:12	AQU
21 May 1957	16:20	PIS
24 May 1957	04:33	ARI
26 May 1957	14:42	TAU
28 May 1957	21:45	GEM
31 May 1957	02:04	CAN
2 Jun 1957	04:44	LEO
4 Jun 1957	06:59	VIR
6 Jun 1957	09:45	LIB
8 Jun 1957	13:41	SCO
10 Jun 1957	19:09	SAG
13 Jun 1957	02:36	CAP
15 Jun 1957	12:23	AQU
18 Jun 1957	00:14	PIS
20 Jun 1957	12:45	ARI
22 Jun 1957	23:36	TAU
25 Jun 1957	07:06	GEM
27 Jun 1957	10:59	CAN
29 Jun 1957	12:30	LEO
1 Jul 1957	13:23	VIR
3 Jul 1957	15:16	LIB
5 Jul 1957	19:10	SCO
8 Jul 1957	01:20	SAG
10 Jul 1957	09:35	CAP
12 Jul 1957	19:43	AQU
15 Jul 1957	07:32	PIS
17 Jul 1957	20:14	ARI
20 Jul 1957	07:57	TAU
22 Jul 1957	16:33	GEM
24 Jul 1957	21:03	CAN
26 Jul 1957	22:15	LEO
28 Jul 1957	21:59	VIR
30 Jul 1957	22:20	LIB
2 Aug 1957	01:01	SCO
4 Aug 1957	06:47	SAG
6 Aug 1957	15:23	CAP
9 Aug 1957	02:01	AQU
11 Aug 1957	14:02	PIS
14 Aug 1957	02:45	ARI
16 Aug 1957	14:59	TAU
19 Aug 1957	00:49	GEM
21 Aug 1957	06:48	CAN
23 Aug 1957	08:50	LEO
25 Aug 1957	08:25	VIR
27 Aug 1957	07:41	LIB
29 Aug 1957	08:46	SCO
31 Aug 1957	13:08	SAG
2 Sep 1957	21:05	CAP
5 Sep 1957	07:50	AQU
7 Sep 1957	20:03	PIS
10 Sep 1957	08:44	ARI
12 Sep 1957	20:56	TAU
15 Sep 1957	07:25	GEM
17 Sep 1957	14:48	CAN
19 Sep 1957	18:30	LEO
21 Sep 1957	19:10	VIR
23 Sep 1957	18:32	LIB
25 Sep 1957	18:40	SCO
27 Sep 1957	21:28	SAG
30 Sep 1957	03:59	CAP
2 Oct 1957	14:04	AQU
5 Oct 1957	02:17	PIS
7 Oct 1957	14:56	ARI
10 Oct 1957	02:47	TAU
12 Oct 1957	12:59	GEM
14 Oct 1957	20:53	CAN

DATE	TIME	SIGN	DATE	TIME	SIGN	DATE	TIME	SIGN
17 Oct 1957	01:58	LEO	14 Apr 1958	04:38	PIS	11 Oct 1958	14:43	LIB
19 Oct 1957	04:23	VIR	16 Apr 1958	17:22	ARI	13 Oct 1958	14:11	SCO
21 Oct 1957	05:02	LIB	19 Apr 1958	06:16	TAU	15 Oct 1958	14:09	SAG
23 Oct 1957	05:30	SCO	21 Apr 1958	18:02	GEM	17 Oct 1958	16:23	CAP
25 Oct 1957	07:33	SAG	24 Apr 1958	03:45	CAN	19 Oct 1958	22:05	AQU
27 Oct 1957	12:42	CAP	26 Apr 1958	10:42	LEO	22 Oct 1958	07:19	PIS
29 Oct 1957	21:32	AQU	28 Apr 1958	14:39	VIR	24 Oct 1958	19:10	ARI
1 Nov 1957	09:18	PIS	30 Apr 1958	16:06	LIB	27 Oct 1958	08:07	TAU
3 Nov 1957	21:59	ARI	2 May 1958	16:14	SCO	29 Oct 1958	20:49	GEM
6 Nov 1957	09:37	TAU	4 May 1958	16:43	SAG	1 Nov 1958	08:08	CAN
8 Nov 1957	19:08	GEM	6 May 1958	19:21	CAP	3 Nov 1958	17:02	LEO
11 Nov 1957	02:22	CAN	9 May 1958	01:30	AQU	5 Nov 1958	22:44	VIR
13 Nov 1957	07:35	LEO	11 May 1958	11:27	PIS	8 Nov 1958	01:15	LIB
15 Nov 1957	11:06	VIR	13 May 1958	23:57	ARI	10 Nov 1958	01:29	SCO
17 Nov 1957	13:24	LIB	16 May 1958	12:49	TAU	12 Nov 1958	01:03	SAG
19 Nov 1957	15:17	SCO	19 May 1958	00:12	GEM	14 Nov 1958	01:55	CAP
21 Nov 1957	17:51	SAG	21 May 1958	09:22	CAN	16 Nov 1958	05:52	AQU
23 Nov 1957	22:30	CAP	23 May 1958	16:14	LEO	18 Nov 1958	13:57	PIS
26 Nov 1957	06:16	AQU	25 May 1958	20:59	VIR	21 Nov 1958	01:28	ARI
28 Nov 1957	17:15	PIS	27 May 1958	23:54	LIB	23 Nov 1958	14:30	TAU
1 Dec 1957	05:56	ARI	30 May 1958	01:33	SCO	26 Nov 1958	02:59	GEM
3 Dec 1957	17:47	TAU	1 Jun 1958	02:53	SAG	28 Nov 1958	13:50	CAN
6 Dec 1957	02:59	GEM	3 Jun 1958	05:22	CAP	30 Nov 1958	22:39	LEO
8 Dec 1957	09:15	CAN	5 Jun 1958	10:34	AQU	3 Dec 1958	05:17	VIR
10 Dec 1957	13:22	LEO	7 Jun 1958	19:24	PIS	5 Dec 1958	09:29	LIB
12 Dec 1957	16:28	VIR	10 Jun 1958	07:20	ARI	7 Dec 1958	11:27	SCO
14 Dec 1957	19:22	LIB	12 Jun 1958	20:12	TAU	9 Dec 1958	12:01	SAG
16 Dec 1957	22:35	SCO	15 Jun 1958	07:30	GEM	11 Dec 1958	12:47	CAP
19 Dec 1957	02:30	SAG	17 Jun 1958	16:03	CAN	13 Dec 1958	15:38	AQU
21 Dec 1957	07:47	CAP	19 Jun 1958	22:03	LEO	15 Dec 1958	22:13	PIS
23 Dec 1957	15:19	AQU	22 Jun 1958	02:21	VIR	18 Dec 1958	08:45	ARI
26 Dec 1957	01:41	PIS	24 Jun 1958	05:42	LIB	20 Dec 1958	21:37	TAU
28 Dec 1957	14:12	ARI	26 Jun 1958	08:30	SCO	23 Dec 1958	10:08	GEM
31 Dec 1957	02:36	TAU	28 Jun 1958	11:11	SAG	25 Dec 1958	20:32	CAN
2 Jan 1958	12:19	GEM	30 Jun 1958	14:32	CAP	28 Dec 1958	04:32	LEO
4 Jan 1958	18:21	CAN	2 Jul 1958	19:44	AQU	30 Dec 1958	10:40	VIR
6 Jan 1958	21:20	LEO	5 Jul 1958	03:57	PIS	1 Jan 1959	15:20	LIB
8 Jan 1958	22:58	VIR	7 Jul 1958	15:18	ARI	3 Jan 1959	18:41	SCO
11 Jan 1958	00:52	LIB	10 Jul 1958	04:08	TAU	5 Jan 1959	20:55	SAG
13 Jan 1958	04:02	SCO	12 Jul 1958	15:45	GEM	7 Jan 1959	22:50	CAP
15 Jan 1958	08:49	SAG	15 Jul 1958	00:14	CAN	10 Jan 1959	01:52	AQU
17 Jan 1958	15:13	CAP	17 Jul 1958	05:30	LEO	12 Jan 1959	07:40	PIS
19 Jan 1958	23:22	AQU	19 Jul 1958	08:41	VIR	14 Jan 1959	17:09	ARI
22 Jan 1958	09:42	PIS	21 Jul 1958	11:11	LIB	17 Jan 1959	05:32	TAU
24 Jan 1958	22:03	ARI	23 Jul 1958	13:57	SCO	19 Jan 1959	18:15	GEM
27 Jan 1958	10:55	TAU	25 Jul 1958	17:25	SAG	22 Jan 1959	04:46	CAN
29 Jan 1958	21:45	GEM	27 Jul 1958	21:53	CAP	24 Jan 1959	12:12	LEO
1 Feb 1958	04:39	CAN	30 Jul 1958	03:52	AQU	26 Jan 1959	17:13	VIR
3 Feb 1958	07:37	LEO	1 Aug 1958	12:12	PIS	28 Jan 1959	20:53	LIB
5 Feb 1958	08:10	VIR	3 Aug 1958	23:14	ARI	31 Jan 1959	00:05	SCO
7 Feb 1958	08:23	LIB	6 Aug 1958	12:03	TAU	2 Feb 1959	03:10	SAG
9 Feb 1958	10:03	SCO	9 Aug 1958	00:15	GEM	4 Feb 1959	06:28	CAP
11 Feb 1958	14:12	SAG	11 Aug 1958	09:23	CAN	6 Feb 1959	10:40	AQU
13 Feb 1958	20:55	CAP	13 Aug 1958	14:42	LEO	8 Feb 1959	16:50	PIS
16 Feb 1958	05:51	AQU	15 Aug 1958	17:06	VIR	11 Feb 1959	01:55	ARI
18 Feb 1958	16:39	PIS	17 Aug 1958	18:16	LIB	13 Feb 1959	13:47	TAU
21 Feb 1958	05:01	ARI	19 Aug 1958	19:49	SCO	16 Feb 1959	02:38	GEM
23 Feb 1958	18:04	TAU	21 Aug 1958	22:48	SAG	18 Feb 1959	13:49	CAN
26 Feb 1958	05:52	GEM	24 Aug 1958	03:38	CAP	20 Feb 1959	21:36	LEO
28 Feb 1958	14:15	CAN	26 Aug 1958	10:28	AQU	23 Feb 1959	02:04	VIR
2 Mar 1958	18:26	LEO	28 Aug 1958	19:25	PIS	25 Feb 1959	04:28	LIB
4 Mar 1958	19:14	VIR	31 Aug 1958	06:35	ARI	27 Feb 1959	06:14	SCO
6 Mar 1958	18:35	LIB	2 Sep 1958	19:23	TAU	1 Mar 1959	08:33	SAG
8 Mar 1958	18:34	SCO	5 Sep 1958	08:06	GEM	3 Mar 1959	12:06	CAP
10 Mar 1958	20:57	SAG	7 Sep 1958	18:21	CAN	5 Mar 1959	17:16	AQU
13 Mar 1958	02:37	CAP	10 Sep 1958	00:40	LEO	8 Mar 1959	00:26	PIS
15 Mar 1958	11:28	AQU	12 Sep 1958	03:18	VIR	10 Mar 1959	09:54	ARI
17 Mar 1958	22:41	PIS	14 Sep 1958	03:44	LIB	12 Mar 1959	21:36	TAU
20 Mar 1958	11:17	ARI	16 Sep 1958	03:49	SCO	15 Mar 1959	10:30	GEM
23 Mar 1958	00:15	TAU	18 Sep 1958	05:16	SAG	17 Mar 1959	22:26	CAN
25 Mar 1958	12:18	GEM	20 Sep 1958	09:13	CAP	20 Mar 1959	07:21	LEO
27 Mar 1958	21:51	CAN	22 Sep 1958	16:03	AQU	22 Mar 1959	12:26	VIR
30 Mar 1958	03:44	LEO	25 Sep 1958	01:33	PIS	24 Mar 1959	14:26	LIB
1 Apr 1958	06:00	VIR	27 Sep 1958	13:07	ARI	26 Mar 1959	14:53	SCO
3 Apr 1958	05:53	LIB	30 Sep 1958	01:57	TAU	28 Mar 1959	15:31	SAG
5 Apr 1958	05:16	SCO	2 Oct 1958	14:49	GEM	30 Mar 1959	17:48	CAP
7 Apr 1958	06:06	SAG	5 Oct 1958	01:59	CAN	1 Apr 1959	22:42	AQU
9 Apr 1958	10:01	CAP	7 Oct 1958	09:49	LEO	4 Apr 1959	06:23	PIS
11 Apr 1958	17:41	AQU	9 Oct 1958	13:48	VIR	6 Apr 1959	16:32	ARI

DATE	TIME	SIGN	DATE	TIME	SIGN	DATE	TIME	SIGN
9 Apr 1959	04:31	TAU	6 Oct 1959	00:54	SAG	3 Apr 1960	01:45	CAN
11 Apr 1959	17:24	GEM	8 Oct 1959	02:38	CAP	5 Apr 1960	14:00	LEO
14 Apr 1959	05:47	CAN	10 Oct 1959	06:12	AQU	8 Apr 1960	00:00	VIR
16 Apr 1959	15:54	LEO	12 Oct 1959	12:06	PIS	10 Apr 1960	06:35	LIB
18 Apr 1959	22:26	VIR	14 Oct 1959	20:20	ARI	12 Apr 1960	10:00	SCO
21 Apr 1959	01:17	LIB	17 Oct 1959	06:39	TAU	14 Apr 1960	11:37	SAG
23 Apr 1959	01:33	SCO	19 Oct 1959	18:39	GEM	16 Apr 1960	13:01	CAP
25 Apr 1959	00:59	SAG	22 Oct 1959	07:22	CAN	18 Apr 1960	15:32	AQU
27 Apr 1959	01:33	CAP	24 Oct 1959	19:02	LEO	20 Apr 1960	19:55	PIS
29 Apr 1959	04:55	AQU	27 Oct 1959	03:47	VIR	23 Apr 1960	02:23	ARI
1 May 1959	11:59	PIS	29 Oct 1959	08:40	LIB	25 Apr 1960	10:51	TAU
3 May 1959	22:19	ARI	31 Oct 1959	10:13	SCO	27 Apr 1960	21:16	GEM
6 May 1959	10:38	TAU	2 Nov 1959	10:01	SAG	30 Apr 1960	09:22	CAN
8 May 1959	23:34	GEM	4 Nov 1959	10:05	CAP	2 May 1960	21:58	LEO
11 May 1959	11:56	CAN	6 Nov 1959	12:15	AQU	5 May 1960	08:57	VIR
13 May 1959	22:39	LEO	8 Nov 1959	17:35	PIS	7 May 1960	16:29	LIB
16 May 1959	06:37	VIR	11 Nov 1959	02:10	ARI	9 May 1960	20:05	SCO
18 May 1959	11:05	LIB	13 Nov 1959	13:04	TAU	11 May 1960	20:54	SAG
20 May 1959	12:23	SCO	16 Nov 1959	01:16	GEM	13 May 1960	20:50	CAP
22 May 1959	11:50	SAG	18 Nov 1959	13:56	CAN	15 May 1960	21:51	AQU
24 May 1959	11:24	CAP	21 Nov 1959	02:03	LEO	18 May 1960	01:24	PIS
26 May 1959	13:10	AQU	23 Nov 1959	12:06	VIR	20 May 1960	07:55	ARI
28 May 1959	18:42	PIS	25 Nov 1959	18:40	LIB	22 May 1960	17:00	TAU
31 May 1959	04:18	ARI	27 Nov 1959	21:20	SCO	25 May 1960	03:54	GEM
2 Jun 1959	16:36	TAU	29 Nov 1959	21:11	SAG	27 May 1960	16:06	CAN
5 Jun 1959	05:35	GEM	1 Dec 1959	20:11	CAP	30 May 1960	04:50	LEO
7 Jun 1959	17:43	CAN	3 Dec 1959	20:35	AQU	1 Jun 1960	16:37	VIR
10 Jun 1959	04:18	LEO	6 Dec 1959	00:17	PIS	4 Jun 1960	01:29	LIB
12 Jun 1959	12:49	VIR	8 Dec 1959	07:59	ARI	6 Jun 1960	06:19	SCO
14 Jun 1959	18:41	LIB	10 Dec 1959	18:55	TAU	8 Jun 1960	07:30	SAG
16 Jun 1959	21:37	SCO	13 Dec 1959	07:24	GEM	10 Jun 1960	06:47	CAP
18 Jun 1959	22:14	SAG	15 Dec 1959	20:00	CAN	12 Jun 1960	06:22	AQU
20 Jun 1959	22:01	CAP	18 Dec 1959	07:57	LEO	14 Jun 1960	08:18	PIS
22 Jun 1959	23:01	AQU	20 Dec 1959	18:29	VIR	16 Jun 1960	13:43	ARI
25 Jun 1959	03:10	PIS	23 Dec 1959	02:27	LIB	18 Jun 1960	22:33	TAU
27 Jun 1959	11:28	ARI	25 Dec 1959	07:00	SCO	21 Jun 1960	09:46	GEM
29 Jun 1959	23:11	TAU	27 Dec 1959	08:15	SAG	23 Jun 1960	22:09	CAN
2 Jul 1959	12:05	GEM	29 Dec 1959	07:37	CAP	26 Jun 1960	10:51	LEO
5 Jul 1959	00:02	CAN	31 Dec 1959	07:15	AQU	28 Jun 1960	22:52	VIR
7 Jul 1959	10:07	LEO	2 Jan 1960	09:20	PIS	1 Jul 1960	08:45	LIB
9 Jul 1959	18:15	VIR	4 Jan 1960	15:22	ARI	3 Jul 1960	15:07	SCO
12 Jul 1959	00:25	LIB	7 Jan 1960	01:23	TAU	5 Jul 1960	17:42	SAG
14 Jul 1959	04:32	SCO	9 Jan 1960	13:45	GEM	7 Jul 1960	17:34	CAP
16 Jul 1959	06:41	SAG	12 Jan 1960	02:23	CAN	9 Jul 1960	16:43	AQU
18 Jul 1959	07:41	CAP	14 Jan 1960	13:58	LEO	11 Jul 1960	17:19	PIS
20 Jul 1959	09:05	AQU	17 Jan 1960	00:02	VIR	13 Jul 1960	21:08	ARI
22 Jul 1959	12:42	PIS	19 Jan 1960	08:13	LIB	16 Jul 1960	04:48	TAU
24 Jul 1959	19:53	ARI	21 Jan 1960	13:58	SCO	18 Jul 1960	15:40	GEM
27 Jul 1959	06:43	TAU	23 Jan 1960	17:02	SAG	21 Jul 1960	04:08	CAN
29 Jul 1959	19:23	GEM	25 Jan 1960	17:59	CAP	23 Jul 1960	16:45	LEO
1 Aug 1959	07:23	CAN	27 Jan 1960	18:18	AQU	26 Jul 1960	04:31	VIR
3 Aug 1959	17:08	LEO	29 Jan 1960	19:57	PIS	28 Jul 1960	14:32	LIB
6 Aug 1959	00:28	VIR	1 Feb 1960	00:40	ARI	30 Jul 1960	21:53	SCO
8 Aug 1959	05:56	LIB	3 Feb 1960	09:16	TAU	2 Aug 1960	02:02	SAG
10 Aug 1959	09:59	SCO	5 Feb 1960	20:58	GEM	4 Aug 1960	03:25	CAP
12 Aug 1959	12:57	SAG	8 Feb 1960	09:36	CAN	6 Aug 1960	03:20	AQU
14 Aug 1959	15:18	CAP	10 Feb 1960	21:07	LEO	8 Aug 1960	03:42	PIS
16 Aug 1959	17:53	AQU	13 Feb 1960	06:34	VIR	10 Aug 1960	06:21	ARI
18 Aug 1959	22:00	PIS	15 Feb 1960	13:54	LIB	12 Aug 1960	12:36	TAU
21 Aug 1959	04:51	ARI	17 Feb 1960	19:23	SCO	14 Aug 1960	22:29	GEM
23 Aug 1959	14:58	TAU	19 Feb 1960	23:11	SAG	17 Aug 1960	10:42	CAN
26 Aug 1959	03:18	GEM	22 Feb 1960	01:39	CAP	19 Aug 1960	23:17	LEO
28 Aug 1959	15:32	CAN	24 Feb 1960	03:32	AQU	22 Aug 1960	10:40	VIR
31 Aug 1959	01:32	LEO	26 Feb 1960	06:03	PIS	24 Aug 1960	20:08	LIB
2 Sep 1959	08:30	VIR	28 Feb 1960	10:38	ARI	27 Aug 1960	03:22	SCO
4 Sep 1959	12:55	LIB	1 Mar 1960	18:18	TAU	29 Aug 1960	08:18	SAG
6 Sep 1959	15:52	SCO	4 Mar 1960	05:07	GEM	31 Aug 1960	11:08	CAP
8 Sep 1959	18:20	SAG	6 Mar 1960	17:36	CAN	2 Sep 1960	12:34	AQU
10 Sep 1959	21:04	CAP	9 Mar 1960	05:24	LEO	4 Sep 1960	13:51	PIS
13 Sep 1959	00:43	AQU	11 Mar 1960	14:46	VIR	6 Sep 1960	16:26	ARI
15 Sep 1959	05:53	PIS	13 Mar 1960	21:18	LIB	8 Sep 1960	21:45	TAU
17 Sep 1959	13:16	ARI	16 Mar 1960	01:36	SCO	11 Sep 1960	06:31	GEM
19 Sep 1959	23:12	TAU	18 Mar 1960	04:37	SAG	13 Sep 1960	18:10	CAN
22 Sep 1959	11:16	GEM	20 Mar 1960	07:14	CAP	16 Sep 1960	06:46	LEO
24 Sep 1959	23:48	CAN	22 Mar 1960	10:10	AQU	18 Sep 1960	18:06	VIR
27 Sep 1959	10:35	LEO	24 Mar 1960	14:02	PIS	21 Sep 1960	02:57	LIB
29 Sep 1959	18:03	VIR	26 Mar 1960	19:29	ARI	23 Sep 1960	09:17	SCO
1 Oct 1959	22:07	LIB	29 Mar 1960	03:13	TAU	25 Sep 1960	13:41	SAG
3 Oct 1959	23:53	SCO	31 Mar 1960	13:32	GEM	27 Sep 1960	16:53	CAP

DATE	TIME	SIGN	DATE	TIME	SIGN	DATE	TIME	SIGN
29 Sep 1960	19:32	AQU	28 Mar 1961	21:29	VIR	24 Sep 1961	09:40	ARI
1 Oct 1960	22:14	PIS	31 Mar 1961	08:20	LIB	26 Sep 1961	10:42	TAU
4 Oct 1960	01:46	ARI	2 Apr 1961	16:36	SCO	28 Sep 1961	14:32	GEM
6 Oct 1960	07:09	TAU	4 Apr 1961	22:33	SAG	30 Sep 1961	22:20	CAN
8 Oct 1960	15:17	GEM	7 Apr 1961	02:51	CAP	3 Oct 1961	09:43	LEO
11 Oct 1960	02:18	CAN	9 Apr 1961	06:02	AQU	5 Oct 1961	22:45	VIR
13 Oct 1960	14:54	LEO	11 Apr 1961	08:31	PIS	8 Oct 1961	11:03	LIB
16 Oct 1960	02:39	VIR	13 Apr 1961	10:55	ARI	10 Oct 1961	21:18	SCO
18 Oct 1960	11:31	LIB	15 Apr 1961	14:17	TAU	13 Oct 1961	05:20	SAG
20 Oct 1960	17:05	SCO	17 Apr 1961	19:55	GEM	15 Oct 1961	11:22	CAP
22 Oct 1960	20:15	SAG	20 Apr 1961	04:50	CAN	17 Oct 1961	15:36	AQU
24 Oct 1960	22:28	CAP	22 Apr 1961	16:43	LEO	19 Oct 1961	18:09	PIS
27 Oct 1960	00:57	AQU	25 Apr 1961	05:30	VIR	21 Oct 1961	19:35	ARI
29 Oct 1960	04:26	PIS	27 Apr 1961	16:33	LIB	23 Oct 1961	21:07	TAU
31 Oct 1960	09:11	ARI	30 Apr 1961	00:25	SCO	26 Oct 1961	00:25	GEM
2 Nov 1960	15:27	TAU	2 May 1961	05:24	SAG	28 Oct 1961	07:03	CAN
4 Nov 1960	23:45	GEM	4 May 1961	08:39	CAP	30 Oct 1961	17:29	LEO
7 Nov 1960	10:26	CAN	6 May 1961	11:23	AQU	2 Nov 1961	06:17	VIR
9 Nov 1960	22:59	LEO	8 May 1961	14:22	PIS	4 Nov 1961	18:42	LIB
12 Nov 1960	11:23	VIR	10 May 1961	17:55	ARI	7 Nov 1961	04:39	SCO
14 Nov 1960	21:06	LIB	12 May 1961	22:25	TAU	9 Nov 1961	11:49	SAG
17 Nov 1960	02:52	SCO	15 May 1961	04:34	GEM	11 Nov 1961	16:59	CAP
19 Nov 1960	05:16	SAG	17 May 1961	13:17	CAN	13 Nov 1961	20:58	AQU
21 Nov 1960	06:01	CAP	20 May 1961	00:45	LEO	16 Nov 1961	00:18	PIS
23 Nov 1960	07:04	AQU	22 May 1961	13:37	VIR	18 Nov 1961	03:10	ARI
25 Nov 1960	09:50	PIS	25 May 1961	01:16	LIB	20 Nov 1961	06:02	TAU
27 Nov 1960	14:51	ARI	27 May 1961	09:33	SCO	22 Nov 1961	09:59	GEM
29 Nov 1960	22:00	TAU	29 May 1961	14:09	SAG	24 Nov 1961	16:20	CAN
2 Dec 1960	07:00	GEM	31 May 1961	16:19	CAP	27 Nov 1961	02:01	LEO
4 Dec 1960	17:52	CAN	2 Jun 1961	17:44	AQU	29 Nov 1961	14:25	VIR
7 Dec 1960	06:20	LEO	4 Jun 1961	19:50	PIS	2 Dec 1961	03:07	LIB
9 Dec 1960	19:12	VIR	6 Jun 1961	23:24	ARI	4 Dec 1961	13:28	SCO
12 Dec 1960	06:10	LIB	9 Jun 1961	04:37	TAU	6 Dec 1961	20:23	SAG
14 Dec 1960	13:11	SCO	11 Jun 1961	11:40	GEM	9 Dec 1961	00:29	CAP
16 Dec 1960	16:06	SAG	13 Jun 1961	20:50	CAN	11 Dec 1961	03:11	AQU
18 Dec 1960	16:15	CAP	16 Jun 1961	08:15	LEO	13 Dec 1961	05:41	PIS
20 Dec 1960	15:48	AQU	18 Jun 1961	21:11	VIR	15 Dec 1961	08:44	ARI
22 Dec 1960	16:47	PIS	21 Jun 1961	09:30	LIB	17 Dec 1961	12:39	TAU
24 Dec 1960	20:35	ARI	23 Jun 1961	18:50	SCO	19 Dec 1961	17:47	GEM
27 Dec 1960	03:30	TAU	26 Jun 1961	00:04	SAG	22 Dec 1961	00:50	CAN
29 Dec 1960	13:01	GEM	28 Jun 1961	01:58	CAP	24 Dec 1961	10:26	LEO
1 Jan 1961	00:21	CAN	30 Jun 1961	02:17	AQU	26 Dec 1961	22:29	VIR
3 Jan 1961	12:53	LEO	2 Jul 1961	02:53	PIS	29 Dec 1961	11:25	LIB
6 Jan 1961	01:47	VIR	4 Jul 1961	05:12	ARI	31 Dec 1961	22:40	SCO
8 Jan 1961	13:30	LIB	6 Jul 1961	10:02	TAU	3 Jan 1962	06:22	SAG
10 Jan 1961	22:07	SCO	8 Jul 1961	17:27	GEM	5 Jan 1962	10:22	CAP
13 Jan 1961	02:39	SAG	11 Jul 1961	03:13	CAN	7 Jan 1962	11:59	AQU
15 Jan 1961	03:40	CAP	13 Jul 1961	14:56	LEO	9 Jan 1962	12:53	PIS
17 Jan 1961	02:55	AQU	16 Jul 1961	03:54	VIR	11 Jan 1962	14:34	ARI
19 Jan 1961	02:32	PIS	18 Jul 1961	16:38	LIB	13 Jan 1962	18:01	TAU
21 Jan 1961	04:27	ARI	21 Jul 1961	03:03	SCO	15 Jan 1962	23:42	GEM
23 Jan 1961	09:52	TAU	23 Jul 1961	09:40	SAG	18 Jan 1962	07:39	CAN
25 Jan 1961	18:50	GEM	25 Jul 1961	12:27	CAP	20 Jan 1962	17:49	LEO
28 Jan 1961	06:21	CAN	27 Jul 1961	12:40	AQU	23 Jan 1962	05:53	VIR
30 Jan 1961	19:04	LEO	29 Jul 1961	12:13	PIS	25 Jan 1962	18:51	LIB
2 Feb 1961	07:48	VIR	31 Jul 1961	12:56	ARI	28 Jan 1962	06:53	SCO
4 Feb 1961	19:26	LIB	2 Aug 1961	16:19	TAU	30 Jan 1962	15:58	SAG
7 Feb 1961	04:50	SCO	4 Aug 1961	23:04	GEM	1 Feb 1962	21:08	CAP
9 Feb 1961	10:59	SAG	7 Aug 1961	08:56	CAN	3 Feb 1962	22:55	AQU
11 Feb 1961	13:49	CAP	9 Aug 1961	20:59	LEO	5 Feb 1962	22:52	PIS
13 Feb 1961	14:14	AQU	12 Aug 1961	10:00	VIR	7 Feb 1962	22:51	ARI
15 Feb 1961	13:53	PIS	14 Aug 1961	22:43	LIB	10 Feb 1962	00:35	TAU
17 Feb 1961	14:41	ARI	17 Aug 1961	09:43	SCO	12 Feb 1962	05:18	GEM
19 Feb 1961	18:21	TAU	19 Aug 1961	17:43	SAG	14 Feb 1962	13:20	CAN
22 Feb 1961	01:52	GEM	21 Aug 1961	22:05	CAP	17 Feb 1962	00:04	LEO
24 Feb 1961	12:49	CAN	23 Aug 1961	23:24	AQU	19 Feb 1962	12:26	VIR
27 Feb 1961	01:34	LEO	25 Aug 1961	23:02	PIS	22 Feb 1962	01:21	LIB
1 Mar 1961	14:11	VIR	27 Aug 1961	22:49	ARI	24 Feb 1962	13:35	SCO
4 Mar 1961	01:20	LIB	30 Aug 1961	00:38	TAU	26 Feb 1962	23:45	SAG
6 Mar 1961	10:22	SCO	1 Sep 1961	05:52	GEM	1 Mar 1962	06:37	CAP
8 Mar 1961	17:03	SAG	3 Sep 1961	15:00	CAN	3 Mar 1962	09:50	AQU
10 Mar 1961	21:18	CAP	6 Sep 1961	03:00	LEO	5 Mar 1962	10:15	PIS
12 Mar 1961	23:28	AQU	8 Sep 1961	16:04	VIR	7 Mar 1962	09:32	ARI
15 Mar 1961	00:26	PIS	11 Sep 1961	04:33	LIB	9 Mar 1962	09:40	TAU
17 Mar 1961	01:32	ARI	13 Sep 1961	15:22	SCO	11 Mar 1962	12:36	GEM
19 Mar 1961	04:25	TAU	15 Sep 1961	23:53	SAG	13 Mar 1962	19:25	CAN
21 Mar 1961	10:33	GEM	18 Sep 1961	05:41	CAP	16 Mar 1962	05:55	LEO
23 Mar 1961	20:22	CAN	20 Sep 1961	08:42	AQU	18 Mar 1962	18:32	VIR
26 Mar 1961	08:48	LEO	22 Sep 1961	09:35	PIS	21 Mar 1962	07:28	LIB

DATE	TIME	SIGN	DATE	TIME	SIGN	DATE	TIME	SIGN
23 Mar 1962	19:28	SCO	18 Sep 1962	19:29	GEM	18 Mar 1963	17:34	CAP
26 Mar 1962	05:48	SAG	21 Sep 1962	00:26	CAN	21 Mar 1963	01:19	AQU
28 Mar 1962	13:44	CAP	23 Sep 1962	09:07	LEO	23 Mar 1963	05:03	PIS
30 Mar 1962	18:42	AQU	25 Sep 1962	20:30	VIR	25 Mar 1963	05:37	ARI
1 Apr 1962	20:41	PIS	28 Sep 1962	09:07	LIB	27 Mar 1963	04:56	TAU
3 Apr 1962	20:40	ARI	30 Sep 1962	21:48	SCO	29 Mar 1963	05:13	GEM
5 Apr 1962	20:25	TAU	3 Oct 1962	09:39	SAG	31 Mar 1963	08:14	CAN
7 Apr 1962	22:00	GEM	5 Oct 1962	19:34	CAP	2 Apr 1963	14:46	LEO
10 Apr 1962	03:13	CAN	8 Oct 1962	02:20	AQU	5 Apr 1963	00:20	VIR
12 Apr 1962	12:36	LEO	10 Oct 1962	05:28	PIS	7 Apr 1963	11:49	LIB
15 Apr 1962	00:56	VIR	12 Oct 1962	05:40	ARI	10 Apr 1963	00:13	SCO
17 Apr 1962	13:53	LIB	14 Oct 1962	04:43	TAU	12 Apr 1963	12:47	SAG
20 Apr 1962	01:36	SCO	16 Oct 1962	04:50	GEM	15 Apr 1963	00:26	CAP
22 Apr 1962	11:26	SAG	18 Oct 1962	08:05	CAN	17 Apr 1963	09:32	AQU
24 Apr 1962	19:19	CAP	20 Oct 1962	15:30	LEO	19 Apr 1963	14:52	PIS
27 Apr 1962	01:06	AQU	23 Oct 1962	02:31	VIR	21 Apr 1963	16:29	ARI
29 Apr 1962	04:39	PIS	25 Oct 1962	15:13	LIB	23 Apr 1963	15:50	TAU
1 May 1962	06:11	ARI	28 Oct 1962	03:48	SCO	25 Apr 1963	15:06	GEM
3 May 1962	06:49	TAU	30 Oct 1962	15:19	SAG	27 Apr 1963	16:27	CAN
5 May 1962	08:16	GEM	2 Nov 1962	01:16	CAP	29 Apr 1963	21:26	LEO
7 May 1962	12:29	CAN	4 Nov 1962	09:01	AQU	2 May 1963	06:12	VIR
9 May 1962	20:36	LEO	6 Nov 1962	13:51	PIS	4 May 1963	17:42	LIB
12 May 1962	08:11	VIR	8 Nov 1962	15:44	ARI	7 May 1963	06:15	SCO
14 May 1962	21:02	LIB	10 Nov 1962	15:44	TAU	9 May 1963	18:42	SAG
17 May 1962	08:42	SCO	12 Nov 1962	15:43	GEM	12 May 1963	06:13	CAP
19 May 1962	18:02	SAG	14 Nov 1962	17:48	CAN	14 May 1963	15:50	AQU
22 May 1962	01:07	CAP	16 Nov 1962	23:41	LEO	16 May 1963	22:30	PIS
24 May 1962	06:30	AQU	19 Nov 1962	09:33	VIR	19 May 1963	01:46	ARI
26 May 1962	10:28	PIS	21 Nov 1962	21:57	LIB	21 May 1963	02:20	TAU
28 May 1962	13:14	ARI	24 Nov 1962	10:32	SCO	23 May 1963	01:53	GEM
30 May 1962	15:16	TAU	26 Nov 1962	21:42	SAG	25 May 1963	02:29	CAN
1 Jun 1962	17:40	GEM	29 Nov 1962	07:00	CAP	27 May 1963	05:58	LEO
3 Jun 1962	21:57	CAN	1 Dec 1962	14:25	AQU	29 May 1963	13:22	VIR
6 Jun 1962	05:23	LEO	3 Dec 1962	19:52	PIS	1 Jun 1963	00:09	LIB
8 Jun 1962	16:12	VIR	5 Dec 1962	23:16	ARI	3 Jun 1963	12:38	SCO
11 Jun 1962	04:50	LIB	8 Dec 1962	00:58	TAU	6 Jun 1963	01:00	SAG
13 Jun 1962	16:44	SCO	10 Dec 1962	02:07	GEM	8 Jun 1963	12:06	CAP
16 Jun 1962	02:02	SAG	12 Dec 1962	04:21	CAN	10 Jun 1963	21:21	AQU
18 Jun 1962	08:29	CAP	14 Dec 1962	09:21	LEO	13 Jun 1963	04:20	PIS
20 Jun 1962	12:48	AQU	16 Dec 1962	17:59	VIR	15 Jun 1963	08:45	ARI
22 Jun 1962	15:58	PIS	19 Dec 1962	05:41	LIB	17 Jun 1963	10:53	TAU
24 Jun 1962	18:42	ARI	21 Dec 1962	18:17	SCO	19 Jun 1963	11:43	GEM
26 Jun 1962	21:34	TAU	24 Dec 1962	05:32	SAG	21 Jun 1963	12:47	CAN
29 Jun 1962	01:09	GEM	26 Dec 1962	14:17	CAP	23 Jun 1963	15:44	LEO
1 Jul 1962	06:18	CAN	28 Dec 1962	20:41	AQU	25 Jun 1963	21:57	VIR
3 Jul 1962	13:56	LEO	31 Dec 1962	01:19	PIS	28 Jun 1963	07:40	LIB
6 Jul 1962	00:22	VIR	2 Jan 1963	04:47	ARI	30 Jun 1963	19:47	SCO
8 Jul 1962	12:47	LIB	4 Jan 1963	07:33	TAU	3 Jul 1963	08:10	SAG
11 Jul 1962	01:04	SCO	6 Jan 1963	10:14	GEM	5 Jul 1963	19:02	CAP
13 Jul 1962	10:59	SAG	8 Jan 1963	13:41	CAN	8 Jul 1963	03:35	AQU
15 Jul 1962	17:31	CAP	10 Jan 1963	19:01	LEO	10 Jul 1963	09:52	PIS
17 Jul 1962	21:06	AQU	13 Jan 1963	03:07	VIR	12 Jul 1963	14:15	ARI
19 Jul 1962	22:59	PIS	15 Jan 1963	14:04	LIB	14 Jul 1963	17:14	TAU
22 Jul 1962	00:33	ARI	18 Jan 1963	02:35	SCO	16 Jul 1963	19:27	GEM
24 Jul 1962	02:57	TAU	20 Jan 1963	14:19	SAG	18 Jul 1963	21:45	CAN
26 Jul 1962	06:56	GEM	22 Jan 1963	23:22	CAP	21 Jul 1963	01:15	LEO
28 Jul 1962	13:00	CAN	25 Jan 1963	05:13	AQU	23 Jul 1963	07:06	VIR
30 Jul 1962	21:21	LEO	27 Jan 1963	08:34	PIS	25 Jul 1963	16:02	LIB
2 Aug 1962	07:57	VIR	29 Jan 1963	10:43	ARI	28 Jul 1963	03:38	SCO
4 Aug 1962	20:17	LIB	31 Jan 1963	12:55	TAU	30 Jul 1963	16:07	SAG
7 Aug 1962	08:55	SCO	2 Feb 1963	16:03	GEM	2 Aug 1963	03:11	CAP
9 Aug 1962	19:47	SAG	4 Feb 1963	20:40	CAN	4 Aug 1963	11:24	AQU
12 Aug 1962	03:16	CAP	7 Feb 1963	03:06	LEO	6 Aug 1963	16:45	PIS
14 Aug 1962	07:06	AQU	9 Feb 1963	11:36	VIR	8 Aug 1963	20:06	ARI
16 Aug 1962	08:16	PIS	11 Feb 1963	22:18	LIB	10 Aug 1963	22:37	TAU
18 Aug 1962	08:25	ARI	14 Feb 1963	10:38	SCO	13 Aug 1963	01:15	GEM
20 Aug 1962	09:20	TAU	16 Feb 1963	22:56	SAG	15 Aug 1963	04:39	CAN
22 Aug 1962	12:28	GEM	19 Feb 1963	08:59	CAP	17 Aug 1963	09:17	LEO
24 Aug 1962	18:33	CAN	21 Feb 1963	15:22	AQU	19 Aug 1963	15:40	VIR
27 Aug 1962	03:30	LEO	23 Feb 1963	18:17	PIS	22 Aug 1963	00:26	LIB
29 Aug 1962	14:35	VIR	25 Feb 1963	19:04	ARI	24 Aug 1963	11:39	SCO
1 Sep 1962	03:00	LIB	27 Feb 1963	19:38	TAU	27 Aug 1963	00:14	SAG
3 Sep 1962	15:46	SCO	1 Mar 1963	21:39	GEM	29 Aug 1963	11:56	CAP
6 Sep 1962	03:25	SAG	4 Mar 1963	02:08	CAN	31 Aug 1963	20:36	AQU
8 Sep 1962	12:18	CAP	6 Mar 1963	09:15	LEO	3 Sep 1963	01:35	PIS
10 Sep 1962	17:25	AQU	8 Mar 1963	18:33	VIR	5 Sep 1963	03:51	ARI
12 Sep 1962	19:01	PIS	11 Mar 1963	05:34	LIB	7 Sep 1963	05:02	TAU
14 Sep 1962	18:32	ARI	13 Mar 1963	17:51	SCO	9 Sep 1963	06:45	GEM
16 Sep 1962	18:00	TAU	16 Mar 1963	06:26	SAG	11 Sep 1963	10:08	CAN

DATE	TIME	SIGN	DATE	TIME	SIGN	DATE	TIME	SIGN
13 Sep 1963	15:30	LEO	12 Mar 1964	09:04	PIS	7 Sep 1964	09:19	LIB
15 Sep 1963	22:47	VIR	14 Mar 1964	13:14	ARI	9 Sep 1964	16:20	SCO
18 Sep 1963	07:59	LIB	16 Mar 1964	15:29	TAU	12 Sep 1964	02:47	SAG
20 Sep 1963	19:10	SCO	18 Mar 1964	17:25	GEM	14 Sep 1964	15:30	CAP
23 Sep 1963	07:49	SAG	20 Mar 1964	20:11	CAN	17 Sep 1964	03:46	AQU
25 Sep 1963	20:14	CAP	23 Mar 1964	00:15	LEO	19 Sep 1964	13:21	PIS
28 Sep 1963	06:03	AQU	25 Mar 1964	05:41	VIR	21 Sep 1964	19:43	ARI
30 Sep 1963	11:44	PIS	27 Mar 1964	12:48	LIB	23 Sep 1964	23:45	TAU
2 Oct 1963	13:47	ARI	29 Mar 1964	22:04	SCO	26 Sep 1964	02:45	GEM
4 Oct 1963	13:49	TAU	1 Apr 1964	09:40	SAG	28 Sep 1964	05:39	CAN
6 Oct 1963	13:58	GEM	3 Apr 1964	22:35	CAP	30 Sep 1964	08:52	LEO
8 Oct 1963	16:01	CAN	6 Apr 1964	10:23	AQU	2 Oct 1964	12:42	VIR
10 Oct 1963	20:54	LEO	8 Apr 1964	18:46	PIS	4 Oct 1964	17:44	LIB
13 Oct 1963	04:34	VIR	10 Apr 1964	23:07	ARI	7 Oct 1964	00:57	SCO
15 Oct 1963	14:24	LIB	13 Apr 1964	00:36	TAU	9 Oct 1964	11:02	SAG
18 Oct 1963	01:52	SCO	15 Apr 1964	01:06	GEM	11 Oct 1964	23:31	CAP
20 Oct 1963	14:32	SAG	17 Apr 1964	02:24	CAN	14 Oct 1964	12:14	AQU
23 Oct 1963	03:20	CAP	19 Apr 1964	05:39	LEO	16 Oct 1964	22:31	PIS
25 Oct 1963	14:18	AQU	21 Apr 1964	11:18	VIR	19 Oct 1964	05:04	ARI
27 Oct 1963	21:34	PIS	23 Apr 1964	19:08	LIB	21 Oct 1964	08:23	TAU
30 Oct 1963	00:38	ARI	26 Apr 1964	05:00	SCO	23 Oct 1964	10:03	GEM
1 Nov 1963	00:41	TAU	28 Apr 1964	16:45	SAG	25 Oct 1964	11:37	CAN
2 Nov 1963	23:48	GEM	1 May 1964	05:42	CAP	27 Oct 1964	14:14	LEO
5 Nov 1963	00:09	CAN	3 May 1964	18:06	AQU	29 Oct 1964	18:25	VIR
7 Nov 1963	03:24	LEO	6 May 1964	03:42	PIS	1 Nov 1964	00:24	LIB
9 Nov 1963	10:14	VIR	8 May 1964	09:14	ARI	3 Nov 1964	08:25	SCO
11 Nov 1963	20:07	LIB	10 May 1964	11:08	TAU	5 Nov 1964	18:43	SAG
14 Nov 1963	07:56	SCO	12 May 1964	11:01	GEM	8 Nov 1964	07:05	CAP
16 Nov 1963	20:39	SAG	14 May 1964	10:54	CAN	10 Nov 1964	20:07	AQU
19 Nov 1963	09:22	CAP	16 May 1964	12:32	LEO	13 Nov 1964	07:27	PIS
21 Nov 1963	20:50	AQU	18 May 1964	17:02	VIR	15 Nov 1964	15:09	ARI
24 Nov 1963	05:32	PIS	21 May 1964	00:42	LIB	17 Nov 1964	18:56	TAU
26 Nov 1963	10:23	ARI	23 May 1964	10:58	SCO	19 Nov 1964	19:58	GEM
28 Nov 1963	11:48	TAU	25 May 1964	23:03	SAG	21 Nov 1964	20:03	CAN
30 Nov 1963	11:14	GEM	28 May 1964	11:59	CAP	23 Nov 1964	20:59	LEO
2 Dec 1963	10:45	CAN	31 May 1964	00:31	AQU	26 Nov 1964	00:03	VIR
4 Dec 1963	12:21	LEO	2 Jun 1964	11:00	PIS	28 Nov 1964	05:54	LIB
6 Dec 1963	17:26	VIR	4 Jun 1964	18:02	ARI	30 Nov 1964	14:31	SCO
9 Dec 1963	02:22	LIB	6 Jun 1964	21:18	TAU	3 Dec 1964	01:24	SAG
11 Dec 1963	14:04	SCO	8 Jun 1964	21:49	GEM	5 Dec 1964	13:53	CAP
14 Dec 1963	02:53	SAG	10 Jun 1964	21:16	CAN	8 Dec 1964	02:57	AQU
16 Dec 1963	15:20	CAP	12 Jun 1964	21:35	LEO	10 Dec 1964	14:59	PIS
19 Dec 1963	02:28	AQU	15 Jun 1964	00:28	VIR	13 Dec 1964	00:10	ARI
21 Dec 1963	11:27	PIS	17 Jun 1964	06:54	LIB	15 Dec 1964	05:32	TAU
23 Dec 1963	17:40	ARI	19 Jun 1964	16:49	SCO	17 Dec 1964	07:20	GEM
25 Dec 1963	20:56	TAU	22 Jun 1964	05:03	SAG	19 Dec 1964	07:02	CAN
27 Dec 1963	21:57	GEM	24 Jun 1964	18:01	CAP	21 Dec 1964	06:30	LEO
29 Dec 1963	22:07	CAN	27 Jun 1964	06:21	AQU	23 Dec 1964	07:42	VIR
31 Dec 1963	23:10	LEO	29 Jun 1964	16:55	PIS	25 Dec 1964	12:05	LIB
3 Jan 1964	02:48	VIR	2 Jul 1964	00:51	ARI	27 Dec 1964	20:11	SCO
5 Jan 1964	10:10	LIB	4 Jul 1964	05:42	TAU	30 Dec 1964	07:20	SAG
7 Jan 1964	21:04	SCO	6 Jul 1964	07:42	GEM	1 Jan 1965	20:06	CAP
10 Jan 1964	09:48	SAG	8 Jul 1964	07:56	CAN	4 Jan 1965	09:03	AQU
12 Jan 1964	22:13	CAP	10 Jul 1964	08:01	LEO	6 Jan 1965	21:05	PIS
15 Jan 1964	08:47	AQU	12 Jul 1964	09:45	VIR	9 Jan 1965	07:07	ARI
17 Jan 1964	17:03	PIS	14 Jul 1964	14:42	LIB	11 Jan 1965	14:09	TAU
19 Jan 1964	23:09	ARI	16 Jul 1964	23:33	SCO	13 Jan 1965	17:48	GEM
22 Jan 1964	03:22	TAU	19 Jul 1964	11:28	SAG	15 Jan 1965	18:34	CAN
24 Jan 1964	06:04	GEM	22 Jul 1964	00:26	CAP	17 Jan 1965	17:57	LEO
26 Jan 1964	07:51	CAN	24 Jul 1964	12:29	AQU	19 Jan 1965	17:54	VIR
28 Jan 1964	09:45	LEO	26 Jul 1964	22:34	PIS	21 Jan 1965	20:28	LIB
30 Jan 1964	13:09	VIR	29 Jul 1964	06:25	ARI	24 Jan 1965	03:01	SCO
1 Feb 1964	19:25	LIB	31 Jul 1964	11:59	TAU	26 Jan 1965	13:32	SAG
4 Feb 1964	05:12	SCO	2 Aug 1964	15:27	GEM	29 Jan 1965	02:21	CAP
6 Feb 1964	17:35	SAG	4 Aug 1964	17:12	CAN	31 Jan 1965	15:17	AQU
9 Feb 1964	06:10	CAP	6 Aug 1964	18:10	LEO	3 Feb 1965	02:55	PIS
11 Feb 1964	16:38	AQU	8 Aug 1964	19:50	VIR	5 Feb 1965	12:42	ARI
14 Feb 1964	00:07	PIS	10 Aug 1964	23:52	LIB	7 Feb 1965	20:23	TAU
16 Feb 1964	05:09	ARI	13 Aug 1964	07:31	SCO	10 Feb 1965	01:35	GEM
18 Feb 1964	08:44	TAU	15 Aug 1964	18:44	SAG	12 Feb 1965	04:13	CAN
20 Feb 1964	11:47	GEM	18 Aug 1964	07:37	CAP	14 Feb 1965	04:54	LEO
22 Feb 1964	14:49	CAN	20 Aug 1964	19:38	AQU	16 Feb 1965	05:05	VIR
24 Feb 1964	18:10	LEO	23 Aug 1964	05:13	PIS	18 Feb 1965	06:45	LIB
26 Feb 1964	22:30	VIR	25 Aug 1964	12:14	ARI	20 Feb 1965	11:46	SCO
29 Feb 1964	04:46	LIB	27 Aug 1964	17:23	TAU	22 Feb 1965	20:57	SAG
2 Mar 1964	13:54	SCO	29 Aug 1964	21:15	GEM	25 Feb 1965	09:17	CAP
5 Mar 1964	01:46	SAG	1 Sep 1964	00:12	CAN	27 Feb 1965	22:13	AQU
7 Mar 1964	14:34	CAP	3 Sep 1964	02:36	LEO	2 Mar 1965	09:37	PIS
10 Mar 1964	01:34	AQU	5 Sep 1964	05:12	VIR	4 Mar 1965	18:44	ARI

DATE	TIME	SIGN
7 Mar 1965	01:48	TAU
9 Mar 1965	07:13	GEM
11 Mar 1965	11:02	CAN
13 Mar 1965	13:22	LEO
15 Mar 1965	14:55	VIR
17 Mar 1965	17:04	LIB
19 Mar 1965	21:33	SCO
22 Mar 1965	05:36	SAG
24 Mar 1965	17:06	CAP
27 Mar 1965	05:58	AQU
29 Mar 1965	17:31	PIS
1 Apr 1965	02:17	ARI
3 Apr 1965	08:28	TAU
5 Apr 1965	12:54	GEM
7 Apr 1965	16:24	CAN
9 Apr 1965	19:23	LEO
11 Apr 1965	22:14	VIR
14 Apr 1965	01:38	LIB
16 Apr 1965	06:42	SCO
18 Apr 1965	14:32	SAG
21 Apr 1965	01:24	CAP
23 Apr 1965	14:03	AQU
26 Apr 1965	02:01	PIS
28 Apr 1965	11:10	ARI
30 Apr 1965	17:03	TAU
2 May 1965	20:26	GEM
4 May 1965	22:38	CAN
7 May 1965	00:49	LEO
9 May 1965	03:47	VIR
11 May 1965	08:04	LIB
13 May 1965	14:10	SCO
15 May 1965	22:32	SAG
18 May 1965	09:20	CAP
20 May 1965	21:50	AQU
23 May 1965	10:13	PIS
25 May 1965	20:17	ARI
28 May 1965	02:47	TAU
30 May 1965	05:58	GEM
1 Jun 1965	07:05	CAN
3 Jun 1965	07:46	LEO
5 Jun 1965	09:33	VIR
7 Jun 1965	13:30	LIB
9 Jun 1965	20:04	SCO
12 Jun 1965	05:09	SAG
14 Jun 1965	16:20	CAP
17 Jun 1965	04:51	AQU
19 Jun 1965	17:28	PIS
22 Jun 1965	04:28	ARI
24 Jun 1965	12:14	TAU
26 Jun 1965	16:17	GEM
28 Jun 1965	17:19	CAN
30 Jun 1965	16:58	LEO
2 Jul 1965	17:11	VIR
4 Jul 1965	19:43	LIB
7 Jul 1965	01:38	SCO
9 Jul 1965	10:54	SAG
11 Jul 1965	22:29	CAP
14 Jul 1965	11:07	AQU
16 Jul 1965	23:44	PIS
19 Jul 1965	11:11	ARI
21 Jul 1965	20:13	TAU
24 Jul 1965	01:46	GEM
26 Jul 1965	03:52	CAN
28 Jul 1965	03:36	LEO
30 Jul 1965	02:55	VIR
1 Aug 1965	03:54	LIB
3 Aug 1965	08:21	SCO
5 Aug 1965	16:49	SAG
8 Aug 1965	04:22	CAP
10 Aug 1965	17:09	AQU
13 Aug 1965	05:37	PIS
15 Aug 1965	16:56	ARI
18 Aug 1965	02:26	TAU
20 Aug 1965	09:19	GEM
22 Aug 1965	13:03	CAN
24 Aug 1965	14:00	LEO
26 Aug 1965	13:36	VIR
28 Aug 1965	13:53	LIB
30 Aug 1965	16:54	SCO

DATE	TIME	SIGN
2 Sep 1965	00:00	SAG
4 Sep 1965	10:51	CAP
6 Sep 1965	23:33	AQU
9 Sep 1965	11:56	PIS
11 Sep 1965	22:49	ARI
14 Sep 1965	07:55	TAU
16 Sep 1965	15:05	GEM
18 Sep 1965	20:00	CAN
20 Sep 1965	22:34	LEO
22 Sep 1965	23:29	VIR
25 Sep 1965	00:16	LIB
27 Sep 1965	02:47	SCO
29 Sep 1965	08:42	SAG
1 Oct 1965	18:28	CAP
4 Oct 1965	06:48	AQU
6 Oct 1965	19:13	PIS
9 Oct 1965	05:53	ARI
11 Oct 1965	14:15	TAU
13 Oct 1965	20:39	GEM
16 Oct 1965	01:26	CAN
18 Oct 1965	04:50	LEO
20 Oct 1965	07:13	VIR
22 Oct 1965	09:21	LIB
24 Oct 1965	12:32	SCO
26 Oct 1965	18:08	SAG
29 Oct 1965	03:05	CAP
31 Oct 1965	14:49	AQU
3 Nov 1965	03:22	PIS
5 Nov 1965	14:20	ARI
7 Nov 1965	22:28	TAU
10 Nov 1965	03:53	GEM
12 Nov 1965	07:29	CAN
14 Nov 1965	10:13	LEO
16 Nov 1965	12:54	VIR
18 Nov 1965	16:10	LIB
20 Nov 1965	20:37	SCO
23 Nov 1965	02:57	SAG
25 Nov 1965	11:46	CAP
27 Nov 1965	23:03	AQU
30 Nov 1965	11:39	PIS
2 Dec 1965	23:21	ARI
5 Dec 1965	08:10	TAU
7 Dec 1965	13:26	GEM
9 Dec 1965	15:56	CAN
11 Dec 1965	17:07	LEO
13 Dec 1965	18:35	VIR
15 Dec 1965	21:34	LIB
18 Dec 1965	02:40	SCO
20 Dec 1965	10:01	SAG
22 Dec 1965	19:26	CAP
25 Dec 1965	06:44	AQU
27 Dec 1965	19:17	PIS
30 Dec 1965	07:39	ARI
1 Jan 1966	17:45	TAU
4 Jan 1966	00:04	GEM
6 Jan 1966	02:39	CAN
8 Jan 1966	02:49	LEO
10 Jan 1966	02:34	VIR
12 Jan 1966	03:53	LIB
14 Jan 1966	08:09	SCO
16 Jan 1966	15:40	SAG
19 Jan 1966	01:45	CAP
21 Jan 1966	13:26	AQU
24 Jan 1966	01:58	PIS
26 Jan 1966	14:32	ARI
29 Jan 1966	01:41	TAU
31 Jan 1966	09:42	GEM
2 Feb 1966	13:39	CAN
4 Feb 1966	14:13	LEO
6 Feb 1966	13:11	VIR
8 Feb 1966	12:51	LIB
10 Feb 1966	15:15	SCO
12 Feb 1966	21:33	SAG
15 Feb 1966	07:25	CAP
17 Feb 1966	19:25	AQU
20 Feb 1966	08:04	PIS
22 Feb 1966	20:29	ARI
25 Feb 1966	07:52	TAU
27 Feb 1966	17:02	GEM

DATE	TIME	SIGN
1 Mar 1966	22:46	CAN
4 Mar 1966	00:55	LEO
6 Mar 1966	00:36	VIR
7 Mar 1966	23:49	LIB
10 Mar 1966	00:48	SCO
12 Mar 1966	05:18	SAG
14 Mar 1966	13:56	CAP
17 Mar 1966	01:34	AQU
19 Mar 1966	14:18	PIS
22 Mar 1966	02:32	ARI
24 Mar 1966	13:31	TAU
26 Mar 1966	22:40	GEM
29 Mar 1966	05:23	CAN
31 Mar 1966	09:11	LEO
2 Apr 1966	10:30	VIR
4 Apr 1966	10:39	LIB
6 Apr 1966	11:30	SCO
8 Apr 1966	14:54	SAG
10 Apr 1966	22:02	CAP
13 Apr 1966	08:42	AQU
15 Apr 1966	21:13	PIS
18 Apr 1966	09:26	ARI
20 Apr 1966	19:59	TAU
23 Apr 1966	04:26	GEM
25 Apr 1966	10:46	CAN
27 Apr 1966	15:08	LEO
29 Apr 1966	17:49	VIR
1 May 1966	19:30	LIB
3 May 1966	21:23	SCO
6 May 1966	00:53	SAG
8 May 1966	07:12	CAP
10 May 1966	16:51	AQU
13 May 1966	04:54	PIS
15 May 1966	17:15	ARI
18 May 1966	03:48	TAU
20 May 1966	11:38	GEM
22 May 1966	16:59	CAN
24 May 1966	20:36	LEO
26 May 1966	23:21	VIR
29 May 1966	02:00	LIB
31 May 1966	05:11	SCO
2 Jun 1966	09:39	SAG
4 Jun 1966	16:10	CAP
7 Jun 1966	01:21	AQU
9 Jun 1966	12:57	PIS
12 Jun 1966	01:25	ARI
14 Jun 1966	12:28	TAU
16 Jun 1966	20:25	GEM
19 Jun 1966	01:04	CAN
21 Jun 1966	03:28	LEO
23 Jun 1966	05:07	VIR
25 Jun 1966	07:22	LIB
27 Jun 1966	11:04	SCO
29 Jun 1966	16:31	SAG
1 Jul 1966	23:51	CAP
4 Jul 1966	09:14	AQU
6 Jul 1966	20:39	PIS
9 Jul 1966	09:15	ARI
11 Jul 1966	21:02	TAU
14 Jul 1966	05:51	GEM
16 Jul 1966	10:43	CAN
18 Jul 1966	12:26	LEO
20 Jul 1966	12:46	VIR
22 Jul 1966	13:38	LIB
24 Jul 1966	16:32	SCO
26 Jul 1966	22:05	SAG
29 Jul 1966	06:04	CAP
31 Jul 1966	16:01	AQU
3 Aug 1966	03:35	PIS
5 Aug 1966	16:14	ARI
8 Aug 1966	04:37	TAU
10 Aug 1966	14:37	GEM
12 Aug 1966	20:40	CAN
14 Aug 1966	22:48	LEO
16 Aug 1966	22:34	VIR
18 Aug 1966	22:05	LIB
20 Aug 1966	23:25	SCO
23 Aug 1966	03:51	SAG
25 Aug 1966	11:37	CAP

DATE	TIME	SIGN	DATE	TIME	SIGN	DATE	TIME	SIGN
27 Aug 1966	21:56	AQU	24 Feb 1967	09:03	VIR	22 Aug 1967	19:47	ARI
30 Aug 1966	09:48	PIS	26 Feb 1967	08:44	LIB	25 Aug 1967	08:21	TAU
1 Sep 1966	22:27	ARI	28 Feb 1967	09:10	SCO	27 Aug 1967	21:07	GEM
4 Sep 1966	10:58	TAU	2 Mar 1967	11:53	SAG	30 Aug 1967	07:33	CAN
6 Sep 1966	21:51	GEM	4 Mar 1967	17:35	CAP	1 Sep 1967	14:06	LEO
9 Sep 1966	05:26	CAN	7 Mar 1967	02:04	AQU	3 Sep 1967	17:07	VIR
11 Sep 1966	08:59	LEO	9 Mar 1967	12:41	PIS	5 Sep 1967	18:02	LIB
13 Sep 1966	09:25	VIR	12 Mar 1967	00:53	ARI	7 Sep 1967	18:44	SCO
15 Sep 1966	08:33	LIB	14 Mar 1967	13:53	TAU	9 Sep 1967	20:40	SAG
17 Sep 1966	08:34	SCO	17 Mar 1967	02:18	GEM	12 Sep 1967	00:43	CAP
19 Sep 1966	11:22	SAG	19 Mar 1967	12:08	CAN	14 Sep 1967	07:08	AQU
21 Sep 1966	17:52	CAP	21 Mar 1967	18:03	LEO	16 Sep 1967	15:53	PIS
24 Sep 1966	03:48	AQU	23 Mar 1967	20:07	VIR	19 Sep 1967	02:46	ARI
26 Sep 1966	15:48	PIS	25 Mar 1967	19:49	LIB	21 Sep 1967	15:20	TAU
29 Sep 1966	04:29	ARI	27 Mar 1967	19:10	SCO	24 Sep 1967	04:20	GEM
1 Oct 1966	16:46	TAU	29 Mar 1967	20:08	SAG	26 Sep 1967	15:44	CAN
4 Oct 1966	03:42	GEM	1 Apr 1967	00:11	CAP	28 Sep 1967	23:39	LEO
6 Oct 1966	12:11	CAN	3 Apr 1967	07:49	AQU	1 Oct 1967	03:37	VIR
8 Oct 1966	17:01	LEO	5 Apr 1967	18:28	PIS	3 Oct 1967	04:33	LIB
10 Oct 1966	19:26	VIR	8 Apr 1967	00:55	ARI	5 Oct 1967	04:14	SCO
12 Oct 1966	19:29	LIB	10 Apr 1967	19:55	TAU	7 Oct 1967	04:32	SAG
14 Oct 1966	19:21	SCO	13 Apr 1967	08:14	GEM	9 Oct 1967	07:03	CAP
16 Oct 1966	21:00	SAG	15 Apr 1967	18:36	CAN	11 Oct 1967	12:46	AQU
19 Oct 1966	01:56	CAP	18 Apr 1967	01:52	LEO	13 Oct 1967	21:38	PIS
21 Oct 1966	10:41	AQU	20 Apr 1967	05:42	VIR	16 Oct 1967	08:57	ARI
23 Oct 1966	22:20	PIS	22 Apr 1967	06:41	LIB	18 Oct 1967	21:41	TAU
26 Oct 1966	11:02	ARI	24 Apr 1967	06:18	SCO	21 Oct 1967	10:37	GEM
28 Oct 1966	23:04	TAU	26 Apr 1967	06:26	SAG	23 Oct 1967	22:26	CAN
31 Oct 1966	09:27	GEM	28 Apr 1967	08:54	CAP	26 Oct 1967	07:39	LEO
2 Nov 1966	17:42	CAN	30 Apr 1967	14:58	AQU	28 Oct 1967	13:17	VIR
4 Nov 1966	23:35	LEO	3 May 1967	00:47	PIS	30 Oct 1967	15:30	LIB
7 Nov 1966	03:09	VIR	5 May 1967	13:09	ARI	1 Nov 1967	15:25	SCO
9 Nov 1966	04:53	LIB	8 May 1967	02:09	TAU	3 Nov 1967	14:51	SAG
11 Nov 1966	05:53	SCO	10 May 1967	14:07	GEM	5 Nov 1967	15:44	CAP
13 Nov 1966	07:36	SAG	13 May 1967	00:09	CAN	7 Nov 1967	19:46	AQU
15 Nov 1966	11:37	CAP	15 May 1967	07:48	LEO	10 Nov 1967	03:43	PIS
17 Nov 1966	19:03	AQU	17 May 1967	12:50	VIR	12 Nov 1967	14:58	ARI
20 Nov 1966	05:52	PIS	19 May 1967	15:30	LIB	15 Nov 1967	03:52	TAU
22 Nov 1966	18:30	ARI	21 May 1967	16:29	SCO	17 Nov 1967	16:39	GEM
25 Nov 1966	06:36	TAU	23 May 1967	17:05	SAG	20 Nov 1967	04:12	CAN
27 Nov 1966	16:30	GEM	25 May 1967	18:58	CAP	22 Nov 1967	13:46	LEO
29 Nov 1966	23:48	CAN	27 May 1967	23:45	AQU	24 Nov 1967	20:44	VIR
2 Dec 1966	05:01	LEO	30 May 1967	08:18	PIS	27 Nov 1967	00:46	LIB
4 Dec 1966	08:47	VIR	1 Jun 1967	20:06	ARI	29 Nov 1967	02:12	SCO
6 Dec 1966	11:42	LIB	4 Jun 1967	09:03	TAU	1 Dec 1967	02:10	SAG
8 Dec 1966	14:17	SCO	6 Jun 1967	20:51	GEM	3 Dec 1967	02:25	CAP
10 Dec 1966	17:13	SAG	9 Jun 1967	06:17	CAN	5 Dec 1967	04:57	AQU
12 Dec 1966	21:31	CAP	11 Jun 1967	13:18	LEO	7 Dec 1967	11:20	PIS
15 Dec 1966	04:19	AQU	13 Jun 1967	18:23	VIR	9 Dec 1967	21:43	ARI
17 Dec 1966	14:17	PIS	15 Jun 1967	21:57	LIB	12 Dec 1967	10:31	TAU
20 Dec 1966	02:39	ARI	18 Jun 1967	00:24	SCO	14 Dec 1967	23:17	GEM
22 Dec 1966	15:06	TAU	20 Jun 1967	02:19	SAG	17 Dec 1967	10:22	CAN
25 Dec 1966	01:12	GEM	22 Jun 1967	04:46	CAP	19 Dec 1967	19:20	LEO
27 Dec 1966	07:57	CAN	24 Jun 1967	09:11	AQU	22 Dec 1967	02:20	VIR
29 Dec 1966	11:56	LEO	26 Jun 1967	16:49	PIS	24 Dec 1967	07:26	LIB
31 Dec 1966	14:32	VIR	29 Jun 1967	03:52	ARI	26 Dec 1967	10:35	SCO
2 Jan 1967	17:03	LIB	1 Jul 1967	16:42	TAU	28 Dec 1967	12:08	SAG
4 Jan 1967	20:16	SCO	4 Jul 1967	04:38	GEM	30 Dec 1967	13:11	CAP
7 Jan 1967	00:28	SAG	6 Jul 1967	13:46	CAN	1 Jan 1968	15:24	AQU
9 Jan 1967	05:53	CAP	8 Jul 1967	19:58	LEO	3 Jan 1968	20:36	PIS
11 Jan 1967	13:06	AQU	11 Jul 1967	00:07	VIR	6 Jan 1968	05:45	ARI
13 Jan 1967	22:45	PIS	13 Jul 1967	03:19	LIB	8 Jan 1968	18:02	TAU
16 Jan 1967	10:48	ARI	15 Jul 1967	06:17	SCO	11 Jan 1968	06:54	GEM
18 Jan 1967	23:38	TAU	17 Jul 1967	09:22	SAG	13 Jan 1968	17:53	CAN
21 Jan 1967	10:36	GEM	19 Jul 1967	12:59	CAP	16 Jan 1968	02:08	LEO
23 Jan 1967	17:50	CAN	21 Jul 1967	17:59	AQU	18 Jan 1968	08:10	VIR
25 Jan 1967	21:19	LEO	24 Jul 1967	01:28	PIS	20 Jan 1968	12:46	LIB
27 Jan 1967	22:35	VIR	26 Jul 1967	12:00	ARI	22 Jan 1968	16:27	SCO
29 Jan 1967	23:33	LIB	29 Jul 1967	00:40	TAU	24 Jan 1968	19:23	SAG
1 Feb 1967	01:44	SCO	31 Jul 1967	12:59	GEM	26 Jan 1968	21:57	CAP
3 Feb 1967	05:55	SAG	2 Aug 1967	22:30	CAN	29 Jan 1968	01:06	AQU
5 Feb 1967	12:10	CAP	5 Aug 1967	04:25	LEO	31 Jan 1968	06:15	PIS
7 Feb 1967	20:17	AQU	7 Aug 1967	07:35	VIR	2 Feb 1968	14:40	ARI
10 Feb 1967	06:18	PIS	9 Aug 1967	09:34	LIB	5 Feb 1968	02:15	TAU
12 Feb 1967	18:16	ARI	11 Aug 1967	11:44	SCO	7 Feb 1968	15:08	GEM
15 Feb 1967	07:18	TAU	13 Aug 1967	14:52	SAG	10 Feb 1968	02:33	CAN
17 Feb 1967	19:15	GEM	15 Aug 1967	19:18	CAP	12 Feb 1968	10:48	LEO
20 Feb 1967	03:46	CAN	18 Aug 1967	01:17	AQU	14 Feb 1968	16:02	VIR
22 Feb 1967	08:03	LEO	20 Aug 1967	09:18	PIS	16 Feb 1968	19:21	LIB

DATE	TIME	SIGN	DATE	TIME	SIGN	DATE	TIME	SIGN
18 Feb 1968	21:59	SCO	16 Aug 1968	15:51	GEM	12 Feb 1969	17:28	CAP
21 Feb 1968	00:47	SAG	19 Aug 1968	04:14	CAN	14 Feb 1969	18:30	AQU
23 Feb 1968	04:12	CAP	21 Aug 1968	14:38	LEO	16 Feb 1969	20:03	PIS
25 Feb 1968	08:37	AQU	23 Aug 1968	22:20	VIR	18 Feb 1969	23:49	ARI
27 Feb 1968	14:42	PIS	26 Aug 1968	03:44	LIB	21 Feb 1969	07:01	TAU
29 Feb 1968	23:15	ARI	28 Aug 1968	07:38	SCO	23 Feb 1969	17:41	GEM
3 Mar 1968	10:27	TAU	30 Aug 1968	10:40	SAG	26 Feb 1969	06:11	CAN
5 Mar 1968	23:16	GEM	1 Sep 1968	13:21	CAP	28 Feb 1969	18:11	LEO
8 Mar 1968	11:20	CAN	3 Sep 1968	16:19	AQU	3 Mar 1969	04:06	VIR
10 Mar 1968	20:26	LEO	5 Sep 1968	20:27	PIS	5 Mar 1969	11:33	LIB
13 Mar 1968	01:50	VIR	8 Sep 1968	02:49	ARI	7 Mar 1969	16:56	SCO
15 Mar 1968	04:22	LIB	10 Sep 1968	12:06	TAU	9 Mar 1969	20:47	SAG
17 Mar 1968	05:33	SCO	12 Sep 1968	23:54	GEM	11 Mar 1969	23:39	CAP
19 Mar 1968	06:53	SAG	15 Sep 1968	12:27	CAN	14 Mar 1969	02:09	AQU
21 Mar 1968	09:35	CAP	17 Sep 1968	23:24	LEO	16 Mar 1969	05:03	PIS
23 Mar 1968	14:17	AQU	20 Sep 1968	07:15	VIR	18 Mar 1969	09:27	ARI
25 Mar 1968	21:15	PIS	22 Sep 1968	11:58	LIB	20 Mar 1969	16:20	TAU
28 Mar 1968	06:31	ARI	24 Sep 1968	14:38	SCO	23 Mar 1969	02:13	GEM
30 Mar 1968	17:54	TAU	26 Sep 1968	16:30	SAG	25 Mar 1969	14:18	CAN
2 Apr 1968	06:40	GEM	28 Sep 1968	18:44	CAP	28 Mar 1969	02:36	LEO
4 Apr 1968	19:12	CAN	30 Sep 1968	22:11	AQU	30 Mar 1969	12:52	VIR
7 Apr 1968	05:28	LEO	3 Oct 1968	03:21	PIS	1 Apr 1969	20:02	LIB
9 Apr 1968	12:02	VIR	5 Oct 1968	10:35	ARI	4 Apr 1969	00:21	SCO
11 Apr 1968	14:59	LIB	7 Oct 1968	20:06	TAU	6 Apr 1969	02:57	SAG
13 Apr 1968	15:31	SCO	10 Oct 1968	07:43	GEM	8 Apr 1969	05:04	CAP
15 Apr 1968	15:23	SAG	12 Oct 1968	20:23	CAN	10 Apr 1969	07:46	AQU
17 Apr 1968	16:23	CAP	15 Oct 1968	08:07	LEO	12 Apr 1969	11:41	PIS
19 Apr 1968	19:57	AQU	17 Oct 1968	16:58	VIR	14 Apr 1969	17:13	ARI
22 Apr 1968	02:46	PIS	19 Oct 1968	22:03	LIB	17 Apr 1969	00:43	TAU
24 Apr 1968	12:32	ARI	22 Oct 1968	00:04	SCO	19 Apr 1969	10:28	GEM
27 Apr 1968	00:22	TAU	24 Oct 1968	00:32	SAG	21 Apr 1969	22:17	CAN
29 Apr 1968	13:10	GEM	26 Oct 1968	01:14	CAP	24 Apr 1969	10:50	LEO
2 May 1968	01:49	CAN	28 Oct 1968	03:43	AQU	26 Apr 1969	21:55	VIR
4 May 1968	12:52	LEO	30 Oct 1968	08:54	PIS	29 Apr 1969	05:43	LIB
6 May 1968	20:57	VIR	1 Nov 1968	16:50	ARI	1 May 1969	09:48	SCO
9 May 1968	01:19	LIB	4 Nov 1968	03:01	TAU	3 May 1969	11:18	SAG
11 May 1968	02:28	SCO	6 Nov 1968	14:47	GEM	5 May 1969	11:57	CAP
13 May 1968	01:53	SAG	9 Nov 1968	03:26	CAN	7 May 1969	13:28	AQU
15 May 1968	01:31	CAP	11 Nov 1968	15:44	LEO	9 May 1969	17:04	PIS
17 May 1968	03:22	AQU	14 Nov 1968	01:53	VIR	11 May 1969	23:09	ARI
19 May 1968	08:53	PIS	16 Nov 1968	08:25	LIB	14 May 1969	07:28	TAU
21 May 1968	18:14	ARI	18 Nov 1968	11:04	SCO	16 May 1969	17:41	GEM
24 May 1968	06:15	TAU	20 Nov 1968	11:03	SAG	19 May 1969	05:30	CAN
26 May 1968	19:11	GEM	22 Nov 1968	10:20	CAP	21 May 1969	18:12	LEO
29 May 1968	07:42	CAN	24 Nov 1968	11:03	AQU	24 May 1969	06:06	VIR
31 May 1968	18:53	LEO	26 Nov 1968	14:53	PIS	26 May 1969	15:06	LIB
3 Jun 1968	03:51	VIR	28 Nov 1968	22:26	ARI	28 May 1969	20:04	SCO
5 Jun 1968	09:48	LIB	1 Dec 1968	08:57	TAU	30 May 1969	21:29	SAG
7 Jun 1968	12:29	SCO	3 Dec 1968	21:05	GEM	1 Jun 1969	21:06	CAP
9 Jun 1968	12:41	SAG	6 Dec 1968	09:43	CAN	3 Jun 1969	21:04	AQU
11 Jun 1968	12:05	CAP	8 Dec 1968	22:02	LEO	5 Jun 1969	23:14	PIS
13 Jun 1968	12:47	AQU	11 Dec 1968	08:58	VIR	8 Jun 1969	04:36	ARI
15 Jun 1968	16:42	PIS	13 Dec 1968	17:08	LIB	10 Jun 1969	13:06	TAU
18 Jun 1968	00:50	ARI	15 Dec 1968	21:30	SCO	12 Jun 1969	23:48	GEM
20 Jun 1968	12:25	TAU	17 Dec 1968	22:26	SAG	15 Jun 1969	11:52	CAN
23 Jun 1968	01:21	GEM	19 Dec 1968	21:32	CAP	18 Jun 1969	00:35	LEO
25 Jun 1968	13:42	CAN	21 Dec 1968	21:00	AQU	20 Jun 1969	12:52	VIR
28 Jun 1968	00:29	LEO	23 Dec 1968	23:02	PIS	22 Jun 1969	23:02	LIB
30 Jun 1968	09:25	VIR	26 Dec 1968	05:02	ARI	25 Jun 1969	05:30	SCO
2 Jul 1968	16:09	LIB	28 Dec 1968	14:57	TAU	27 Jun 1969	07:59	SAG
4 Jul 1968	20:19	SCO	31 Dec 1968	03:10	GEM	29 Jun 1969	07:44	CAP
6 Jul 1968	22:03	SAG	2 Jan 1969	15:52	CAN	1 Jul 1969	06:49	AQU
8 Jul 1968	22:23	CAP	5 Jan 1969	03:54	LEO	3 Jul 1969	07:26	PIS
10 Jul 1968	23:04	AQU	7 Jan 1969	14:41	VIR	5 Jul 1969	11:17	ARI
13 Jul 1968	02:04	PIS	9 Jan 1969	23:31	LIB	7 Jul 1969	18:53	TAU
15 Jul 1968	08:52	ARI	12 Jan 1969	05:31	SCO	10 Jul 1969	05:31	GEM
17 Jul 1968	19:30	TAU	14 Jan 1969	08:18	SAG	12 Jul 1969	17:47	CAN
20 Jul 1968	08:12	GEM	16 Jan 1969	08:38	CAP	15 Jul 1969	06:28	LEO
22 Jul 1968	20:30	CAN	18 Jan 1969	08:17	AQU	17 Jul 1969	18:41	VIR
25 Jul 1968	06:54	LEO	20 Jan 1969	09:21	PIS	20 Jul 1969	05:19	LIB
27 Jul 1968	15:09	VIR	22 Jan 1969	13:44	ARI	22 Jul 1969	13:02	SCO
29 Jul 1968	21:31	LIB	24 Jan 1969	22:13	TAU	24 Jul 1969	17:10	SAG
1 Aug 1968	02:10	SCO	27 Jan 1969	09:53	GEM	26 Jul 1969	18:09	CAP
3 Aug 1968	05:10	SAG	29 Jan 1969	22:35	CAN	28 Jul 1969	17:34	AQU
5 Aug 1968	06:57	CAP	1 Feb 1969	10:28	LEO	30 Jul 1969	17:30	PIS
7 Aug 1968	08:37	AQU	3 Feb 1969	20:40	VIR	1 Aug 1969	19:55	ARI
9 Aug 1968	11:46	PIS	6 Feb 1969	04:59	LIB	4 Aug 1969	02:02	TAU
11 Aug 1968	17:52	ARI	8 Feb 1969	11:17	SCO	6 Aug 1969	11:50	GEM
14 Aug 1968	03:36	TAU	10 Feb 1969	15:22	SAG	8 Aug 1969	23:57	CAN

DATE	TIME	SIGN	DATE	TIME	SIGN	DATE	TIME	SIGN
11 Aug 1969	12:37	LEO	7 Feb 1970	03:37	PIS	6 Aug 1970	12:32	LIB
14 Aug 1969	00:31	VIR	9 Feb 1970	04:17	ARI	8 Aug 1970	23:55	SCO
16 Aug 1969	10:50	LIB	11 Feb 1970	07:59	TAU	11 Aug 1970	08:06	SAG
18 Aug 1969	18:53	SCO	13 Feb 1970	15:29	GEM	13 Aug 1970	12:23	CAP
21 Aug 1969	00:10	SAG	16 Feb 1970	02:17	CAN	15 Aug 1970	13:30	AQU
23 Aug 1969	02:48	CAP	18 Feb 1970	14:53	LEO	17 Aug 1970	13:01	PIS
25 Aug 1969	03:35	AQU	21 Feb 1970	03:41	VIR	19 Aug 1970	12:50	ARI
27 Aug 1969	04:03	PIS	23 Feb 1970	15:29	LIB	21 Aug 1970	14:46	TAU
29 Aug 1969	05:57	ARI	26 Feb 1970	01:22	SCO	23 Aug 1970	20:04	GEM
31 Aug 1969	10:51	TAU	28 Feb 1970	08:37	SAG	26 Aug 1970	04:58	CAN
2 Sep 1969	19:23	GEM	2 Mar 1970	12:52	CAP	28 Aug 1970	16:38	LEO
5 Sep 1969	06:56	CAN	4 Mar 1970	14:33	AQU	31 Aug 1970	05:35	VIR
7 Sep 1969	19:35	LEO	6 Mar 1970	14:48	PIS	2 Sep 1970	18:25	LIB
10 Sep 1969	07:20	VIR	8 Mar 1970	15:16	ARI	5 Sep 1970	05:54	SCO
12 Sep 1969	17:01	LIB	10 Mar 1970	17:43	TAU	7 Sep 1970	14:57	SAG
15 Sep 1969	00:24	SCO	12 Mar 1970	23:37	GEM	9 Sep 1970	20:50	CAP
17 Sep 1969	05:41	SAG	15 Mar 1970	09:19	CAN	11 Sep 1970	23:32	AQU
19 Sep 1969	09:13	CAP	17 Mar 1970	21:39	LEO	13 Sep 1970	23:56	PIS
21 Sep 1969	11:30	AQU	20 Mar 1970	10:29	VIR	15 Sep 1970	23:35	ARI
23 Sep 1969	13:22	PIS	22 Mar 1970	21:55	LIB	18 Sep 1970	00:22	TAU
25 Sep 1969	15:55	ARI	25 Mar 1970	07:09	SCO	20 Sep 1970	04:02	GEM
27 Sep 1969	20:29	TAU	27 Mar 1970	14:05	SAG	22 Sep 1970	11:41	CAN
30 Sep 1969	04:05	GEM	29 Mar 1970	18:59	CAP	24 Sep 1970	22:54	LEO
2 Oct 1969	14:52	CAN	31 Mar 1970	22:07	AQU	27 Sep 1970	11:53	VIR
5 Oct 1969	03:24	LEO	3 Apr 1970	00:00	PIS	30 Sep 1970	00:32	LIB
7 Oct 1969	15:20	VIR	5 Apr 1970	01:31	ARI	2 Oct 1970	11:34	SCO
10 Oct 1969	00:47	LIB	7 Apr 1970	04:02	TAU	4 Oct 1970	20:30	SAG
12 Oct 1969	07:18	SCO	9 Apr 1970	09:02	GEM	7 Oct 1970	03:09	CAP
14 Oct 1969	11:32	SAG	11 Apr 1970	17:33	CAN	9 Oct 1970	07:25	AQU
16 Oct 1969	14:35	CAP	14 Apr 1970	05:15	LEO	11 Oct 1970	09:29	PIS
18 Oct 1969	17:20	AQU	16 Apr 1970	18:06	VIR	13 Oct 1970	10:11	ARI
20 Oct 1969	20:25	PIS	19 Apr 1970	05:34	LIB	15 Oct 1970	11:00	TAU
23 Oct 1969	00:17	ARI	21 Apr 1970	14:14	SCO	17 Oct 1970	13:44	GEM
25 Oct 1969	05:32	TAU	23 Apr 1970	20:14	SAG	19 Oct 1970	19:59	CAN
27 Oct 1969	13:01	GEM	26 Apr 1970	00:25	CAP	22 Oct 1970	06:12	LEO
29 Oct 1969	23:13	CAN	28 Apr 1970	03:42	AQU	24 Oct 1970	18:56	VIR
1 Nov 1969	11:34	LEO	30 Apr 1970	06:37	PIS	27 Oct 1970	07:36	LIB
3 Nov 1969	23:59	VIR	2 May 1970	09:32	ARI	29 Oct 1970	18:14	SCO
6 Nov 1969	09:57	LIB	4 May 1970	13:05	TAU	1 Nov 1970	02:23	SAG
8 Nov 1969	16:17	SCO	6 May 1970	18:17	GEM	3 Nov 1970	08:31	CAP
10 Nov 1969	19:29	SAG	9 May 1970	02:17	CAN	5 Nov 1970	13:10	AQU
12 Nov 1969	21:08	CAP	11 May 1970	13:22	LEO	7 Nov 1970	16:32	PIS
14 Nov 1969	22:53	AQU	14 May 1970	02:10	VIR	9 Nov 1970	18:51	ARI
17 Nov 1969	01:52	PIS	16 May 1970	14:01	LIB	11 Nov 1970	20:50	TAU
19 Nov 1969	06:31	ARI	18 May 1970	22:48	SCO	13 Nov 1970	23:49	GEM
21 Nov 1969	12:52	TAU	21 May 1970	04:10	SAG	16 Nov 1970	05:23	CAN
23 Nov 1969	20:59	GEM	23 May 1970	07:12	CAP	18 Nov 1970	14:36	LEO
26 Nov 1969	07:10	CAN	25 May 1970	09:25	AQU	21 Nov 1970	02:49	VIR
28 Nov 1969	19:21	LEO	27 May 1970	11:58	PIS	23 Nov 1970	15:38	LIB
1 Dec 1969	08:13	VIR	29 May 1970	15:26	ARI	26 Nov 1970	02:23	SCO
3 Dec 1969	19:16	LIB	31 May 1970	20:03	TAU	28 Nov 1970	10:01	SAG
6 Dec 1969	02:28	SCO	3 Jun 1970	02:10	GEM	30 Nov 1970	15:05	CAP
8 Dec 1969	05:42	SAG	5 Jun 1970	10:26	CAN	2 Dec 1970	18:44	AQU
10 Dec 1969	06:20	CAP	7 Jun 1970	21:17	LEO	4 Dec 1970	21:55	PIS
12 Dec 1969	06:27	AQU	10 Jun 1970	10:01	VIR	7 Dec 1970	01:03	ARI
14 Dec 1969	07:56	PIS	12 Jun 1970	22:26	LIB	9 Dec 1970	04:24	TAU
16 Dec 1969	11:56	ARI	15 Jun 1970	08:00	SCO	11 Dec 1970	08:33	GEM
18 Dec 1969	18:35	TAU	17 Jun 1970	13:37	SAG	13 Dec 1970	14:32	CAN
21 Dec 1969	03:28	GEM	19 Jun 1970	16:04	CAP	15 Dec 1970	23:22	LEO
23 Dec 1969	14:08	CAN	21 Jun 1970	17:00	AQU	18 Dec 1970	11:04	VIR
26 Dec 1969	02:21	LEO	23 Jun 1970	18:11	PIS	21 Dec 1970	00:00	LIB
28 Dec 1969	15:19	VIR	25 Jun 1970	20:52	ARI	23 Dec 1970	11:25	SCO
31 Dec 1969	03:17	LIB	28 Jun 1970	01:35	TAU	25 Dec 1970	19:26	SAG
2 Jan 1970	12:01	SCO	30 Jun 1970	08:24	GEM	28 Dec 1970	00:00	CAP
4 Jan 1970	16:32	SAG	2 Jul 1970	17:20	CAN	30 Dec 1970	02:23	AQU
6 Jan 1970	17:29	CAP	5 Jul 1970	04:26	LEO	1 Jan 1971	04:07	PIS
8 Jan 1970	16:47	AQU	7 Jul 1970	17:10	VIR	3 Jan 1971	06:26	ARI
10 Jan 1970	16:36	PIS	10 Jul 1970	06:02	LIB	5 Jan 1971	10:00	TAU
12 Jan 1970	18:48	ARI	12 Jul 1970	16:40	SCO	7 Jan 1971	15:08	GEM
15 Jan 1970	00:21	TAU	14 Jul 1970	23:24	SAG	9 Jan 1971	22:09	CAN
17 Jan 1970	09:07	GEM	17 Jul 1970	02:18	CAP	12 Jan 1971	07:24	LEO
19 Jan 1970	20:13	CAN	19 Jul 1970	02:44	AQU	14 Jan 1971	18:57	VIR
22 Jan 1970	08:40	LEO	21 Jul 1970	02:36	PIS	17 Jan 1971	07:52	LIB
24 Jan 1970	21:32	VIR	23 Jul 1970	03:43	ARI	19 Jan 1971	20:03	SCO
27 Jan 1970	09:41	LIB	25 Jul 1970	07:18	TAU	22 Jan 1971	05:15	SAG
29 Jan 1970	19:33	SCO	27 Jul 1970	13:53	GEM	24 Jan 1971	10:31	CAP
1 Feb 1970	01:48	SAG	29 Jul 1970	23:14	CAN	26 Jan 1971	12:35	AQU
3 Feb 1970	04:20	CAP	1 Aug 1970	10:44	LEO	28 Jan 1971	13:01	PIS
5 Feb 1970	04:19	AQU	3 Aug 1970	23:34	VIR	30 Jan 1971	13:36	ARI

DATE	TIME	SIGN
1 Feb 1971	15:49	TAU
3 Feb 1971	20:35	GEM
6 Feb 1971	04:07	CAN
8 Feb 1971	14:06	LEO
11 Feb 1971	01:57	VIR
13 Feb 1971	14:49	LIB
16 Feb 1971	03:21	SCO
18 Feb 1971	13:44	SAG
20 Feb 1971	20:35	CAP
22 Feb 1971	23:41	AQU
25 Feb 1971	00:04	PIS
26 Feb 1971	23:30	ARI
28 Feb 1971	23:55	TAU
3 Mar 1971	03:02	GEM
5 Mar 1971	09:48	CAN
7 Mar 1971	19:55	LEO
10 Mar 1971	08:10	VIR
12 Mar 1971	21:05	LIB
15 Mar 1971	09:30	SCO
17 Mar 1971	20:22	SAG
20 Mar 1971	04:36	CAP
22 Mar 1971	09:27	AQU
24 Mar 1971	11:06	PIS
26 Mar 1971	10:45	ARI
28 Mar 1971	10:16	TAU
30 Mar 1971	11:44	GEM
1 Apr 1971	16:51	CAN
4 Apr 1971	02:06	LEO
6 Apr 1971	14:16	VIR
9 Apr 1971	03:16	LIB
11 Apr 1971	15:27	SCO
14 Apr 1971	02:02	SAG
16 Apr 1971	10:37	CAP
18 Apr 1971	16:45	AQU
20 Apr 1971	20:06	PIS
22 Apr 1971	21:07	ARI
24 Apr 1971	21:06	TAU
26 Apr 1971	21:59	GEM
29 Apr 1971	01:44	CAN
1 May 1971	09:35	LEO
3 May 1971	21:03	VIR
6 May 1971	09:58	LIB
8 May 1971	22:02	SCO
11 May 1971	08:07	SAG
13 May 1971	16:08	CAP
15 May 1971	22:18	AQU
18 May 1971	02:38	PIS
20 May 1971	05:10	ARI
22 May 1971	06:31	TAU
24 May 1971	08:01	GEM
26 May 1971	11:27	CAN
28 May 1971	18:16	LEO
31 May 1971	04:48	VIR
2 Jun 1971	17:26	LIB
5 Jun 1971	05:35	SCO
7 Jun 1971	15:27	SAG
9 Jun 1971	22:44	CAP
12 Jun 1971	04:02	AQU
14 Jun 1971	08:01	PIS
16 Jun 1971	11:05	ARI
18 Jun 1971	13:38	TAU
20 Jun 1971	16:23	GEM
22 Jun 1971	20:30	CAN
25 Jun 1971	03:12	LEO
27 Jun 1971	13:06	VIR
30 Jun 1971	01:22	LIB
2 Jul 1971	13:45	SCO
4 Jul 1971	23:57	SAG
7 Jul 1971	07:02	CAP
9 Jul 1971	11:25	AQU
11 Jul 1971	14:14	PIS
13 Jul 1971	16:32	ARI
15 Jul 1971	19:10	TAU
17 Jul 1971	22:47	GEM
20 Jul 1971	03:56	CAN
22 Jul 1971	11:17	LEO
24 Jul 1971	21:09	VIR
27 Jul 1971	09:11	LIB
29 Jul 1971	21:49	SCO

DATE	TIME	SIGN
1 Aug 1971	08:48	SAG
3 Aug 1971	16:31	CAP
5 Aug 1971	20:45	AQU
7 Aug 1971	22:33	PIS
9 Aug 1971	23:26	ARI
12 Aug 1971	00:56	TAU
14 Aug 1971	04:10	GEM
16 Aug 1971	09:50	CAN
18 Aug 1971	17:57	LEO
21 Aug 1971	04:18	VIR
23 Aug 1971	16:22	LIB
26 Aug 1971	05:08	SCO
28 Aug 1971	16:56	SAG
31 Aug 1971	01:53	CAP
2 Sep 1971	07:03	AQU
4 Sep 1971	08:50	PIS
6 Sep 1971	08:43	ARI
8 Sep 1971	08:37	TAU
10 Sep 1971	10:25	GEM
12 Sep 1971	15:21	CAN
14 Sep 1971	23:38	LEO
17 Sep 1971	10:29	VIR
19 Sep 1971	22:47	LIB
22 Sep 1971	11:32	SCO
24 Sep 1971	23:42	SAG
27 Sep 1971	09:51	CAP
29 Sep 1971	16:38	AQU
1 Oct 1971	19:35	PIS
3 Oct 1971	19:40	ARI
5 Oct 1971	18:41	TAU
7 Oct 1971	18:53	GEM
9 Oct 1971	22:11	CAN
12 Oct 1971	05:30	LEO
14 Oct 1971	16:16	VIR
17 Oct 1971	04:47	LIB
19 Oct 1971	17:30	SCO
22 Oct 1971	05:31	SAG
24 Oct 1971	16:04	CAP
27 Oct 1971	00:09	AQU
29 Oct 1971	04:56	PIS
31 Oct 1971	06:25	ARI
2 Nov 1971	05:55	TAU
4 Nov 1971	05:27	GEM
6 Nov 1971	07:15	CAN
8 Nov 1971	12:57	LEO
10 Nov 1971	22:44	VIR
13 Nov 1971	11:05	LIB
15 Nov 1971	23:49	SCO
18 Nov 1971	11:29	SAG
20 Nov 1971	21:35	CAP
23 Nov 1971	05:52	AQU
25 Nov 1971	11:46	PIS
27 Nov 1971	15:02	ARI
29 Nov 1971	16:07	TAU
1 Dec 1971	16:25	GEM
3 Dec 1971	17:50	CAN
5 Dec 1971	22:18	LEO
8 Dec 1971	06:40	VIR
10 Dec 1971	18:19	LIB
13 Dec 1971	07:01	SCO
15 Dec 1971	18:37	SAG
18 Dec 1971	04:06	CAP
20 Dec 1971	11:31	AQU
22 Dec 1971	17:09	PIS
24 Dec 1971	21:08	ARI
26 Dec 1971	23:44	TAU
29 Dec 1971	01:38	GEM
31 Dec 1971	04:01	CAN
2 Jan 1972	08:22	LEO
4 Jan 1972	15:50	VIR
7 Jan 1972	02:33	LIB
9 Jan 1972	15:03	SCO
12 Jan 1972	02:56	SAG
14 Jan 1972	12:24	CAP
16 Jan 1972	19:03	AQU
18 Jan 1972	23:27	PIS
21 Jan 1972	02:34	ARI
23 Jan 1972	05:17	TAU
25 Jan 1972	08:13	GEM

DATE	TIME	SIGN
27 Jan 1972	12:02	CAN
29 Jan 1972	17:21	LEO
1 Feb 1972	00:56	VIR
3 Feb 1972	11:07	LIB
5 Feb 1972	23:17	SCO
8 Feb 1972	11:37	SAG
10 Feb 1972	21:48	CAP
13 Feb 1972	04:35	AQU
15 Feb 1972	08:10	PIS
17 Feb 1972	09:50	ARI
19 Feb 1972	11:11	TAU
21 Feb 1972	13:36	GEM
23 Feb 1972	17:52	CAN
26 Feb 1972	00:15	LEO
28 Feb 1972	08:39	VIR
1 Mar 1972	19:00	LIB
4 Mar 1972	07:00	SCO
6 Mar 1972	19:36	SAG
9 Mar 1972	06:49	CAP
11 Mar 1972	14:41	AQU
13 Mar 1972	18:39	PIS
15 Mar 1972	19:36	ARI
17 Mar 1972	19:27	TAU
19 Mar 1972	20:13	GEM
21 Mar 1972	23:27	CAN
24 Mar 1972	05:45	LEO
26 Mar 1972	14:48	VIR
29 Mar 1972	01:42	LIB
31 Mar 1972	13:48	SCO
3 Apr 1972	02:26	SAG
5 Apr 1972	14:19	CAP
7 Apr 1972	23:35	AQU
10 Apr 1972	04:57	PIS
12 Apr 1972	06:32	ARI
14 Apr 1972	05:54	TAU
16 Apr 1972	05:16	GEM
18 Apr 1972	06:46	CAN
20 Apr 1972	11:47	LEO
22 Apr 1972	20:24	VIR
25 Apr 1972	07:34	LIB
27 Apr 1972	19:55	SCO
30 Apr 1972	08:30	SAG
2 May 1972	20:28	CAP
5 May 1972	06:34	AQU
7 May 1972	13:26	PIS
9 May 1972	16:34	ARI
11 May 1972	16:47	TAU
13 May 1972	15:57	GEM
15 May 1972	16:16	CAN
17 May 1972	19:38	LEO
20 May 1972	02:56	VIR
22 May 1972	13:36	LIB
25 May 1972	02:00	SCO
27 May 1972	14:32	SAG
30 May 1972	02:12	CAP
1 Jun 1972	12:14	AQU
3 Jun 1972	19:51	PIS
6 Jun 1972	00:26	ARI
8 Jun 1972	02:13	TAU
10 Jun 1972	02:24	GEM
12 Jun 1972	02:45	CAN
14 Jun 1972	05:09	LEO
16 Jun 1972	11:04	VIR
18 Jun 1972	20:39	LIB
21 Jun 1972	08:42	SCO
23 Jun 1972	21:13	SAG
26 Jun 1972	08:35	CAP
28 Jun 1972	18:02	AQU
1 Jul 1972	01:17	PIS
3 Jul 1972	06:21	ARI
5 Jul 1972	09:24	TAU
7 Jul 1972	11:04	GEM
9 Jul 1972	12:29	CAN
11 Jul 1972	15:05	LEO
13 Jul 1972	20:16	VIR
16 Jul 1972	04:49	LIB
18 Jul 1972	16:15	SCO
21 Jul 1972	04:46	SAG
23 Jul 1972	16:09	CAP

DATE	TIME	SIGN	DATE	TIME	SIGN	DATE	TIME	SIGN
26 Jul 1972	01:06	AQU	21 Jan 1973	02:24	VIR	20 Jul 1973	21:42	ARI
28 Jul 1972	07:28	PIS	23 Jan 1973	08:16	LIB	23 Jul 1973	03:40	TAU
30 Jul 1972	11:49	ARI	25 Jan 1973	17:51	SCO	25 Jul 1973	06:57	GEM
1 Aug 1972	14:57	TAU	28 Jan 1973	06:10	SAG	27 Jul 1973	08:09	CAN
3 Aug 1972	17:33	GEM	30 Jan 1973	18:53	CAP	29 Jul 1973	08:29	LEO
5 Aug 1972	20:17	CAN	2 Feb 1973	05:55	AQU	31 Jul 1973	09:35	VIR
7 Aug 1972	23:56	LEO	4 Feb 1973	14:21	PIS	2 Aug 1973	13:13	LIB
10 Aug 1972	05:22	VIR	6 Feb 1973	20:28	ARI	4 Aug 1973	20:36	SCO
12 Aug 1972	13:28	LIB	9 Feb 1973	00:53	TAU	7 Aug 1973	07:36	SAG
15 Aug 1972	00:19	SCO	11 Feb 1973	04:09	GEM	9 Aug 1973	20:29	CAP
17 Aug 1972	12:48	SAG	13 Feb 1973	06:44	CAN	12 Aug 1973	08:51	AQU
20 Aug 1972	00:36	CAP	15 Feb 1973	09:12	LEO	14 Aug 1973	19:13	PIS
22 Aug 1972	09:41	AQU	17 Feb 1973	12:31	VIR	17 Aug 1973	03:15	ARI
24 Aug 1972	15:27	PIS	19 Feb 1973	17:58	LIB	19 Aug 1973	09:13	TAU
26 Aug 1972	18:40	ARI	22 Feb 1973	02:35	SCO	21 Aug 1973	13:25	GEM
28 Aug 1972	20:42	TAU	24 Feb 1973	14:14	SAG	23 Aug 1973	16:07	CAN
30 Aug 1972	22:55	GEM	27 Feb 1973	03:03	CAP	25 Aug 1973	17:48	LEO
2 Sep 1972	02:11	CAN	1 Mar 1973	14:21	AQU	27 Aug 1973	19:33	VIR
4 Sep 1972	00:53	LEO	3 Mar 1973	22:29	PIS	29 Aug 1973	22:53	LIB
6 Sep 1972	13:15	VIR	6 Mar 1973	03:36	ARI	1 Sep 1973	05:17	SCO
8 Sep 1972	21:37	LIB	8 Mar 1973	09:50	TAU	3 Sep 1973	15:24	SAG
11 Sep 1972	08:15	SCO	10 Mar 1973	09:30	GEM	6 Sep 1973	04:00	CAP
13 Sep 1972	20:42	SAG	12 Mar 1973	12:29	CAN	8 Sep 1973	16:30	AQU
16 Sep 1972	09:06	CAP	14 Mar 1973	16:07	LEO	11 Sep 1973	02:39	PIS
18 Sep 1972	19:04	AQU	16 Mar 1973	20:42	VIR	13 Sep 1973	09:55	ARI
21 Sep 1972	01:07	PIS	19 Mar 1973	02:48	LIB	15 Sep 1973	14:58	TAU
23 Sep 1972	03:43	ARI	21 Mar 1973	11:16	SCO	17 Sep 1973	18:47	GEM
25 Sep 1972	04:27	TAU	23 Mar 1973	22:26	SAG	19 Sep 1973	22:00	CAN
27 Sep 1972	05:14	GEM	26 Mar 1973	11:15	CAP	22 Sep 1973	00:56	LEO
29 Sep 1972	07:38	CAN	28 Mar 1973	23:11	AQU	24 Sep 1973	03:58	VIR
1 Oct 1972	12:26	LEO	31 Mar 1973	07:54	PIS	26 Sep 1973	08:00	LIB
3 Oct 1972	19:30	VIR	2 Apr 1973	12:46	ARI	28 Sep 1973	14:18	SCO
6 Oct 1972	04:34	LIB	4 Apr 1973	14:57	TAU	30 Sep 1973	23:48	SAG
8 Oct 1972	15:27	SCO	6 Apr 1973	16:11	GEM	3 Oct 1973	12:02	CAP
11 Oct 1972	03:52	SAG	8 Apr 1973	18:04	CAN	6 Oct 1973	00:47	AQU
13 Oct 1972	16:43	CAP	10 Apr 1973	21:31	LEO	8 Oct 1973	11:22	PIS
16 Oct 1972	03:50	AQU	13 Apr 1973	02:47	VIR	10 Oct 1973	18:28	ARI
18 Oct 1972	11:10	PIS	15 Apr 1973	09:50	LIB	12 Oct 1973	22:35	TAU
20 Oct 1972	14:21	ARI	17 Apr 1973	18:51	SCO	15 Oct 1973	01:08	GEM
22 Oct 1972	14:36	TAU	20 Apr 1973	06:01	SAG	17 Oct 1973	03:28	CAN
24 Oct 1972	14:02	GEM	22 Apr 1973	18:48	CAP	19 Oct 1973	06:24	LEO
26 Oct 1972	14:45	CAN	25 Apr 1973	07:20	AQU	21 Oct 1973	10:19	VIR
28 Oct 1972	18:14	LEO	27 Apr 1973	17:09	PIS	23 Oct 1973	15:28	LIB
31 Oct 1972	00:59	VIR	29 Apr 1973	22:51	ARI	25 Oct 1973	22:28	SCO
2 Nov 1972	10:27	LIB	2 May 1973	01:00	TAU	28 Oct 1973	07:57	SAG
4 Nov 1972	21:46	SCO	4 May 1973	01:15	GEM	30 Oct 1973	19:57	CAP
7 Nov 1972	10:16	SAG	6 May 1973	01:35	CAN	2 Nov 1973	08:57	AQU
9 Nov 1972	23:10	CAP	8 May 1973	03:36	LEO	4 Nov 1973	20:25	PIS
12 Nov 1972	11:01	AQU	10 May 1973	08:13	VIR	7 Nov 1973	04:18	ARI
14 Nov 1972	19:55	PIS	12 May 1973	15:31	LIB	9 Nov 1973	08:24	TAU
17 Nov 1972	00:42	ARI	15 May 1973	01:09	SCO	11 Nov 1973	09:59	GEM
19 Nov 1972	01:51	TAU	17 May 1973	12:41	SAG	13 Nov 1973	10:46	CAN
21 Nov 1972	01:04	GEM	20 May 1973	01:29	CAP	15 Nov 1973	12:20	LEO
23 Nov 1972	00:31	CAN	22 May 1973	14:16	AQU	17 Nov 1973	15:41	VIR
25 Nov 1972	02:12	LEO	25 May 1973	01:03	PIS	19 Nov 1973	21:16	LIB
27 Nov 1972	07:24	VIR	27 May 1973	08:13	ARI	22 Nov 1973	05:06	SCO
29 Nov 1972	16:15	LIB	29 May 1973	11:26	TAU	24 Nov 1973	15:11	SAG
2 Dec 1972	03:42	SCO	31 May 1973	11:52	GEM	27 Nov 1973	03:12	CAP
4 Dec 1972	16:22	SAG	2 Jun 1973	11:21	CAN	29 Nov 1973	16:17	AQU
7 Dec 1972	05:06	CAP	4 Jun 1973	11:50	LEO	2 Dec 1973	04:31	PIS
9 Dec 1972	16:53	AQU	6 Jun 1973	14:52	VIR	4 Dec 1973	13:48	ARI
12 Dec 1972	02:31	PIS	8 Jun 1973	21:16	LIB	6 Dec 1973	19:07	TAU
14 Dec 1972	08:58	ARI	11 Jun 1973	06:51	SCO	8 Dec 1973	20:57	GEM
16 Dec 1972	11:57	TAU	13 Jun 1973	18:42	SAG	10 Dec 1973	20:51	CAN
18 Dec 1972	12:23	GEM	16 Jun 1973	07:36	CAP	12 Dec 1973	20:44	LEO
20 Dec 1972	11:57	CAN	18 Jun 1973	20:18	AQU	14 Dec 1973	22:21	VIR
22 Dec 1972	12:35	LEO	21 Jun 1973	07:28	PIS	17 Dec 1973	02:54	LIB
24 Dec 1972	16:03	VIR	23 Jun 1973	15:47	ARI	19 Dec 1973	10:44	SCO
26 Dec 1972	23:22	LIB	25 Jun 1973	20:36	TAU	21 Dec 1973	21:20	SAG
29 Dec 1972	10:10	SCO	27 Jun 1973	22:16	GEM	24 Dec 1973	09:41	CAP
31 Dec 1972	22:51	SAG	29 Jun 1973	22:08	CAN	26 Dec 1973	22:42	AQU
3 Jan 1973	11:29	CAP	1 Jul 1973	21:56	LEO	29 Dec 1973	11:09	PIS
5 Jan 1973	22:46	AQU	3 Jul 1973	23:32	VIR	31 Dec 1973	21:32	ARI
8 Jan 1973	08:02	PIS	6 Jul 1973	04:24	LIB	3 Jan 1974	04:37	TAU
10 Jan 1973	14:56	ARI	8 Jul 1973	13:06	SCO	5 Jan 1974	07:59	GEM
12 Jan 1973	19:24	TAU	11 Jul 1973	00:47	SAG	7 Jan 1974	08:27	CAN
14 Jan 1973	21:40	GEM	13 Jul 1973	13:45	CAP	9 Jan 1974	07:42	LEO
16 Jan 1973	22:38	CAN	16 Jul 1973	02:14	AQU	11 Jan 1974	07:41	VIR
18 Jan 1973	23:40	LEO	18 Jul 1973	13:06	PIS	13 Jan 1974	10:22	LIB

DATE	TIME	SIGN	DATE	TIME	SIGN	DATE	TIME	SIGN
15 Jan 1974	16:54	SCO	15 Jul 1974	15:53	GEM	10 Jan 1975	15:58	CAP
18 Jan 1974	03:12	SAG	17 Jul 1974	17:56	CAN	13 Jan 1975	03:03	AQU
20 Jan 1974	15:47	CAP	19 Jul 1974	17:42	LEO	15 Jan 1975	15:23	PIS
23 Jan 1974	04:49	AQU	21 Jul 1974	17:09	VIR	18 Jan 1975	04:03	ARI
25 Jan 1974	17:00	PIS	23 Jul 1974	18:18	LIB	20 Jan 1975	15:20	TAU
28 Jan 1974	03:31	ARI	25 Jul 1974	22:46	SCO	22 Jan 1975	23:21	GEM
30 Jan 1974	11:40	TAU	28 Jul 1974	06:59	SAG	25 Jan 1975	03:19	CAN
1 Feb 1974	16:52	GEM	30 Jul 1974	18:10	CAP	27 Jan 1975	03:59	LEO
3 Feb 1974	19:05	CAN	2 Aug 1974	06:46	AQU	29 Jan 1975	03:13	VIR
5 Feb 1974	19:11	LEO	4 Aug 1974	19:26	PIS	31 Jan 1975	03:14	LIB
7 Feb 1974	18:51	VIR	7 Aug 1974	07:14	ARI	2 Feb 1975	05:53	SCO
9 Feb 1974	20:10	LIB	9 Aug 1974	17:12	TAU	4 Feb 1975	12:11	SAG
12 Feb 1974	00:59	SCO	12 Aug 1974	00:13	GEM	6 Feb 1975	21:42	CAP
14 Feb 1974	10:01	SAG	14 Aug 1974	03:47	CAN	9 Feb 1975	09:16	AQU
16 Feb 1974	22:15	CAP	16 Aug 1974	04:26	LEO	11 Feb 1975	21:45	PIS
19 Feb 1974	11:20	AQU	18 Aug 1974	03:42	VIR	14 Feb 1975	10:21	ARI
21 Feb 1974	23:14	PIS	20 Aug 1974	03:45	LIB	16 Feb 1975	22:08	TAU
24 Feb 1974	09:11	ARI	22 Aug 1974	06:37	SCO	19 Feb 1975	07:34	GEM
26 Feb 1974	17:10	TAU	24 Aug 1974	13:35	SAG	21 Feb 1975	13:16	CAN
28 Feb 1974	23:09	GEM	27 Aug 1974	00:15	CAP	23 Feb 1975	15:12	LEO
3 Mar 1974	02:58	CAN	29 Aug 1974	12:52	AQU	25 Feb 1975	14:36	VIR
5 Mar 1974	04:48	LEO	1 Sep 1974	01:28	PIS	27 Feb 1975	13:39	LIB
7 Mar 1974	05:33	VIR	3 Sep 1974	12:57	ARI	1 Mar 1975	14:34	SCO
9 Mar 1974	06:51	LIB	5 Sep 1974	22:49	TAU	3 Mar 1975	19:05	SAG
11 Mar 1974	10:40	SCO	8 Sep 1974	06:35	GEM	6 Mar 1975	03:40	CAP
13 Mar 1974	18:19	SAG	10 Sep 1974	11:38	CAN	8 Mar 1975	15:09	AQU
16 Mar 1974	05:41	CAP	12 Sep 1974	13:53	LEO	11 Mar 1975	03:48	PIS
18 Mar 1974	18:38	AQU	14 Sep 1974	14:11	VIR	13 Mar 1975	16:18	ARI
21 Mar 1974	06:33	PIS	16 Sep 1974	14:17	LIB	16 Mar 1975	03:51	TAU
23 Mar 1974	16:01	ARI	18 Sep 1974	16:14	SCO	18 Mar 1975	13:42	GEM
25 Mar 1974	23:08	TAU	20 Sep 1974	21:47	SAG	20 Mar 1975	20:47	CAN
28 Mar 1974	04:32	GEM	23 Sep 1974	07:21	CAP	23 Mar 1975	00:29	LEO
30 Mar 1974	08:39	CAN	25 Sep 1974	19:38	AQU	25 Mar 1975	01:20	VIR
1 Apr 1974	11:40	LEO	28 Sep 1974	08:14	PIS	27 Mar 1975	00:51	LIB
3 Apr 1974	13:56	VIR	30 Sep 1974	19:25	ARI	29 Mar 1975	01:08	SCO
5 Apr 1974	16:22	LIB	3 Oct 1974	04:38	TAU	31 Mar 1975	04:10	SAG
7 Apr 1974	20:25	SCO	5 Oct 1974	11:59	GEM	2 Apr 1975	11:09	CAP
10 Apr 1974	03:27	SAG	7 Oct 1974	17:29	CAN	4 Apr 1975	21:45	AQU
12 Apr 1974	13:56	CAP	9 Oct 1974	21:02	LEO	7 Apr 1975	10:16	PIS
15 Apr 1974	02:33	AQU	11 Oct 1974	22:55	VIR	9 Apr 1975	22:43	ARI
17 Apr 1974	14:43	PIS	14 Oct 1974	00:11	LIB	12 Apr 1975	09:52	TAU
20 Apr 1974	00:18	ARI	16 Oct 1974	02:24	SCO	14 Apr 1975	19:13	GEM
22 Apr 1974	06:53	TAU	18 Oct 1974	07:14	SAG	17 Apr 1975	02:26	CAN
24 Apr 1974	11:10	GEM	20 Oct 1974	15:44	CAP	19 Apr 1975	07:13	LEO
26 Apr 1974	14:17	CAN	23 Oct 1974	03:20	AQU	21 Apr 1975	09:41	VIR
28 Apr 1974	17:03	LEO	25 Oct 1974	15:56	PIS	23 Apr 1975	10:41	LIB
30 Apr 1974	20:00	VIR	28 Oct 1974	03:12	ARI	25 Apr 1975	11:40	SCO
2 May 1974	23:39	LIB	30 Oct 1974	11:58	TAU	27 Apr 1975	14:20	SAG
5 May 1974	04:43	SCO	1 Nov 1974	18:22	GEM	29 Apr 1975	20:09	CAP
7 May 1974	12:06	SAG	3 Nov 1974	23:00	CAN	2 May 1975	05:33	AQU
9 May 1974	22:15	CAP	6 Nov 1974	02:29	LEO	4 May 1975	17:34	PIS
12 May 1974	10:34	AQU	8 Nov 1974	05:17	VIR	7 May 1975	06:02	ARI
14 May 1974	23:02	PIS	10 Nov 1974	07:58	LIB	9 May 1975	17:03	TAU
17 May 1974	09:18	ARI	12 Nov 1974	11:23	SCO	12 May 1975	01:43	GEM
19 May 1974	16:09	TAU	14 Nov 1974	16:39	SAG	14 May 1975	08:07	CAN
21 May 1974	19:53	GEM	17 Nov 1974	00:42	CAP	16 May 1975	12:37	LEO
23 May 1974	21:45	CAN	19 Nov 1974	11:39	AQU	18 May 1975	15:45	VIR
25 May 1974	23:12	LEO	22 Nov 1974	00:10	PIS	20 May 1975	18:04	LIB
28 May 1974	01:26	VIR	24 Nov 1974	11:57	ARI	22 May 1975	20:25	SCO
30 May 1974	05:15	LIB	26 Nov 1974	21:03	TAU	24 May 1975	23:52	SAG
1 Jun 1974	11:11	SCO	29 Nov 1974	02:57	GEM	27 May 1975	05:30	CAP
3 Jun 1974	19:21	SAG	1 Dec 1974	06:21	CAN	29 May 1975	14:10	AQU
6 Jun 1974	05:48	CAP	3 Dec 1974	08:31	LEO	1 Jun 1975	01:32	PIS
8 Jun 1974	18:01	AQU	5 Dec 1974	10:40	VIR	3 Jun 1975	14:00	ARI
11 Jun 1974	06:43	PIS	7 Dec 1974	13:42	LIB	6 Jun 1975	01:17	TAU
13 Jun 1974	17:52	ARI	9 Dec 1974	18:13	SCO	8 Jun 1975	09:48	GEM
16 Jun 1974	01:45	TAU	12 Dec 1974	00:35	SAG	10 Jun 1975	15:20	CAN
18 Jun 1974	05:58	GEM	14 Dec 1974	09:04	CAP	12 Jun 1975	18:45	LEO
20 Jun 1974	07:20	CAN	16 Dec 1974	19:48	AQU	14 Jun 1975	21:10	VIR
22 Jun 1974	07:29	LEO	19 Dec 1974	08:11	PIS	16 Jun 1975	23:41	LIB
24 Jun 1974	08:11	VIR	21 Dec 1974	20:34	ARI	19 Jun 1975	02:59	SCO
26 Jun 1974	10:58	LIB	24 Dec 1974	06:44	TAU	21 Jun 1975	07:34	SAG
28 Jun 1974	16:40	SCO	26 Dec 1974	13:14	GEM	23 Jun 1975	13:56	CAP
1 Jul 1974	01:21	SAG	28 Dec 1974	16:14	CAN	25 Jun 1975	22:33	AQU
3 Jul 1974	12:19	CAP	30 Dec 1974	17:04	LEO	28 Jun 1975	09:33	PIS
6 Jul 1974	00:41	AQU	1 Jan 1975	17:32	VIR	30 Jun 1975	22:01	ARI
8 Jul 1974	13:25	PIS	3 Jan 1975	19:21	LIB	3 Jul 1975	09:53	TAU
11 Jul 1974	01:09	ARI	5 Jan 1975	23:39	SCO	5 Jul 1975	18:58	GEM
13 Jul 1974	10:19	TAU	8 Jan 1975	06:39	SAG	8 Jul 1975	00:21	CAN

DATE	TIME	SIGN	DATE	TIME	SIGN	DATE	TIME	SIGN
10 Jul 1975	02:49	LEO	5 Jan 1976	11:35	PIS	3 Jul 1976	19:34	LIB
12 Jul 1975	03:55	VIR	7 Jan 1976	23:21	ARI	5 Jul 1976	22:33	SCO
14 Jul 1975	05:21	LIB	10 Jan 1976	12:08	TAU	8 Jul 1976	01:05	SAG
16 Jul 1975	08:23	SCO	12 Jan 1976	23:18	GEM	10 Jul 1976	03:49	CAP
18 Jul 1975	13:32	SAG	15 Jan 1976	06:59	CAN	12 Jul 1976	07:53	AQU
20 Jul 1975	20:46	CAP	17 Jan 1976	11:14	LEO	14 Jul 1976	14:36	PIS
23 Jul 1975	05:55	AQU	19 Jan 1976	13:24	VIR	17 Jul 1976	00:40	ARI
25 Jul 1975	16:58	PIS	21 Jan 1976	15:10	LIB	19 Jul 1976	13:11	TAU
28 Jul 1975	05:27	ARI	23 Jan 1976	17:47	SCO	22 Jul 1976	01:39	GEM
30 Jul 1975	17:53	TAU	25 Jan 1976	21:51	SAG	24 Jul 1976	11:38	CAN
2 Aug 1975	04:01	GEM	28 Jan 1976	03:24	CAP	26 Jul 1976	18:18	LEO
4 Aug 1975	10:15	CAN	30 Jan 1976	10:34	AQU	28 Jul 1976	22:22	VIR
6 Aug 1975	12:42	LEO	1 Feb 1976	19:46	PIS	31 Jul 1976	01:13	LIB
8 Aug 1975	12:53	VIR	4 Feb 1976	07:17	ARI	2 Aug 1976	03:55	SCO
10 Aug 1975	12:51	LIB	6 Feb 1976	20:12	TAU	4 Aug 1976	07:03	SAG
12 Aug 1975	14:30	SCO	9 Feb 1976	08:15	GEM	6 Aug 1976	10:54	CAP
14 Aug 1975	18:59	SAG	11 Feb 1976	16:58	CAN	8 Aug 1976	15:57	AQU
17 Aug 1975	02:25	CAP	13 Feb 1976	21:31	LEO	10 Aug 1976	23:01	PIS
19 Aug 1975	12:09	AQU	15 Feb 1976	22:58	VIR	13 Aug 1976	08:49	ARI
21 Aug 1975	23:32	PIS	17 Feb 1976	23:14	LIB	15 Aug 1976	21:05	TAU
24 Aug 1975	12:02	ARI	20 Feb 1976	00:14	SCO	18 Aug 1976	09:53	GEM
27 Aug 1975	00:44	TAU	22 Feb 1976	03:18	SAG	20 Aug 1976	20:32	CAN
29 Aug 1975	11:52	GEM	24 Feb 1976	08:54	CAP	23 Aug 1976	03:29	LEO
31 Aug 1975	19:34	CAN	26 Feb 1976	16:48	AQU	25 Aug 1976	07:03	VIR
2 Sep 1975	23:06	LEO	29 Feb 1976	02:41	PIS	27 Aug 1976	08:41	LIB
4 Sep 1975	23:28	VIR	2 Mar 1976	14:22	ARI	29 Aug 1976	10:05	SCO
6 Sep 1975	22:38	LIB	5 Mar 1976	03:17	TAU	31 Aug 1976	12:28	SAG
8 Sep 1975	22:46	SCO	7 Mar 1976	15:55	GEM	2 Sep 1976	16:29	CAP
11 Sep 1975	01:41	SAG	10 Mar 1976	01:57	CAN	4 Sep 1976	22:20	AQU
13 Sep 1975	08:11	CAP	12 Mar 1976	07:54	LEO	7 Sep 1976	06:11	PIS
15 Sep 1975	17:51	AQU	14 Mar 1976	09:57	VIR	9 Sep 1976	16:18	ARI
18 Sep 1975	05:31	PIS	16 Mar 1976	09:44	LIB	12 Sep 1976	04:30	TAU
20 Sep 1975	18:06	ARI	18 Mar 1976	09:18	SCO	14 Sep 1976	17:32	GEM
23 Sep 1975	06:43	TAU	20 Mar 1976	10:34	SAG	17 Sep 1976	05:06	CAN
25 Sep 1975	18:12	GEM	22 Mar 1976	14:49	CAP	19 Sep 1976	13:09	LEO
28 Sep 1975	03:05	CAN	24 Mar 1976	22:20	AQU	21 Sep 1976	17:15	VIR
30 Sep 1975	08:19	LEO	27 Mar 1976	08:34	PIS	23 Sep 1976	18:27	LIB
2 Oct 1975	10:02	VIR	29 Mar 1976	20:37	ARI	25 Sep 1976	18:33	SCO
4 Oct 1975	09:38	LIB	1 Apr 1976	09:33	TAU	27 Sep 1976	19:21	SAG
6 Oct 1975	09:09	SCO	3 Apr 1976	22:14	GEM	29 Sep 1976	22:14	CAP
8 Oct 1975	10:36	SAG	6 Apr 1976	09:05	CAN	2 Oct 1976	03:49	AQU
10 Oct 1975	15:29	CAP	8 Apr 1976	16:35	LEO	4 Oct 1976	12:10	PIS
13 Oct 1975	00:10	AQU	10 Apr 1976	20:14	VIR	6 Oct 1976	22:50	ARI
15 Oct 1975	11:40	PIS	12 Apr 1976	20:53	LIB	9 Oct 1976	11:11	TAU
18 Oct 1975	00:19	ARI	14 Apr 1976	20:14	SCO	12 Oct 1976	00:14	GEM
20 Oct 1975	12:42	TAU	16 Apr 1976	20:15	SAG	14 Oct 1976	12:22	CAN
22 Oct 1975	23:50	GEM	18 Apr 1976	22:44	CAP	16 Oct 1976	21:48	LEO
25 Oct 1975	08:56	CAN	21 Apr 1976	04:47	AQU	19 Oct 1976	03:23	VIR
27 Oct 1975	15:18	LEO	23 Apr 1976	14:28	PIS	21 Oct 1976	05:26	LIB
29 Oct 1975	18:46	VIR	26 Apr 1976	02:36	ARI	23 Oct 1976	05:16	SCO
31 Oct 1975	19:54	LIB	28 Apr 1976	15:37	TAU	25 Oct 1976	04:48	SAG
2 Nov 1975	20:07	SCO	1 May 1976	04:04	GEM	27 Oct 1976	05:55	CAP
4 Nov 1975	21:10	SAG	3 May 1976	14:52	CAN	29 Oct 1976	10:06	AQU
7 Nov 1975	00:46	CAP	5 May 1976	23:08	LEO	31 Oct 1976	17:53	PIS
9 Nov 1975	07:59	AQU	8 May 1976	04:20	VIR	3 Nov 1976	04:45	ARI
11 Nov 1975	18:41	PIS	10 May 1976	06:39	LIB	5 Nov 1976	17:22	TAU
14 Nov 1975	07:17	ARI	12 May 1976	07:02	SCO	8 Nov 1976	06:20	GEM
16 Nov 1975	19:37	TAU	14 May 1976	07:04	SAG	10 Nov 1976	18:27	CAN
19 Nov 1975	06:13	GEM	16 May 1976	08:32	CAP	13 Nov 1976	04:35	LEO
21 Nov 1975	14:35	CAN	18 May 1976	13:03	AQU	15 Nov 1976	11:44	VIR
23 Nov 1975	20:47	LEO	20 May 1976	21:27	PIS	17 Nov 1976	15:33	LIB
26 Nov 1975	01:03	VIR	23 May 1976	09:07	ARI	19 Nov 1976	16:31	SCO
28 Nov 1975	03:47	LIB	25 May 1976	22:06	TAU	21 Nov 1976	16:03	SAG
30 Nov 1975	05:36	SCO	28 May 1976	10:21	GEM	23 Nov 1976	16:03	CAP
2 Dec 1975	07:33	SAG	30 May 1976	20:38	CAN	25 Nov 1976	18:29	AQU
4 Dec 1975	10:59	CAP	2 Jun 1976	04:37	LEO	28 Nov 1976	00:48	PIS
6 Dec 1975	17:12	AQU	4 Jun 1976	10:20	VIR	30 Nov 1976	11:02	ARI
9 Dec 1975	02:52	PIS	6 Jun 1976	13:59	LIB	2 Dec 1976	23:41	TAU
11 Dec 1975	15:06	ARI	8 Jun 1976	15:57	SCO	5 Dec 1976	12:37	GEM
14 Dec 1975	03:38	TAU	10 Jun 1976	17:06	SAG	8 Dec 1976	00:20	CAN
16 Dec 1975	14:11	GEM	12 Jun 1976	18:45	CAP	10 Dec 1976	10:11	LEO
18 Dec 1975	21:48	CAN	14 Jun 1976	22:32	AQU	12 Dec 1976	17:54	VIR
21 Dec 1975	02:53	LEO	17 Jun 1976	05:43	PIS	14 Dec 1976	23:12	LIB
23 Dec 1975	06:27	VIR	19 Jun 1976	16:32	ARI	17 Dec 1976	02:00	SCO
25 Dec 1975	09:27	LIB	22 Jun 1976	05:21	TAU	19 Dec 1976	02:53	SAG
27 Dec 1975	12:27	SCO	24 Jun 1976	17:36	GEM	21 Dec 1976	03:11	CAP
29 Dec 1975	15:52	SAG	27 Jun 1976	03:28	CAN	23 Dec 1976	04:48	AQU
31 Dec 1975	20:16	CAP	29 Jun 1976	10:38	LEO	25 Dec 1976	09:37	PIS
3 Jan 1976	02:33	AQU	1 Jul 1976	15:45	VIR	27 Dec 1976	18:31	ARI

DATE	TIME	SIGN	DATE	TIME	SIGN	DATE	TIME	SIGN
30 Dec 1976	06:43	TAU	28 Jun 1977	13:01	SAG	25 Dec 1977	05:29	CAN
1 Jan 1977	19:42	GEM	30 Jun 1977	12:48	CAP	27 Dec 1977	17:51	LEO
4 Jan 1977	07:11	CAN	2 Jul 1977	12:57	AQU	30 Dec 1977	05:13	VIR
6 Jan 1977	16:20	LEO	4 Jul 1977	15:31	PIS	1 Jan 1978	14:30	LIB
8 Jan 1977	23:22	VIR	6 Jul 1977	22:04	ARI	3 Jan 1978	20:33	SCO
11 Jan 1977	04:47	LIB	9 Jul 1977	08:33	TAU	5 Jan 1978	23:02	SAG
13 Jan 1977	08:43	SCO	11 Jul 1977	21:14	GEM	7 Jan 1978	22:54	CAP
15 Jan 1977	11:17	SAG	14 Jul 1977	09:49	CAN	9 Jan 1978	22:05	AQU
17 Jan 1977	13:01	CAP	16 Jul 1977	20:50	LEO	11 Jan 1978	22:51	PIS
19 Jan 1977	15:12	AQU	19 Jul 1977	05:58	VIR	14 Jan 1978	03:05	ARI
21 Jan 1977	19:30	PIS	21 Jul 1977	13:08	LIB	16 Jan 1978	11:31	TAU
24 Jan 1977	03:20	ARI	23 Jul 1977	18:13	SCO	18 Jan 1978	23:06	GEM
26 Jan 1977	14:41	TAU	25 Jul 1977	21:03	SAG	21 Jan 1978	11:50	CAN
29 Jan 1977	03:36	GEM	27 Jul 1977	22:14	CAP	24 Jan 1978	00:01	LEO
31 Jan 1977	15:19	CAN	29 Jul 1977	23:04	AQU	26 Jan 1978	10:55	VIR
3 Feb 1977	00:10	LEO	1 Aug 1977	01:24	PIS	28 Jan 1978	20:07	LIB
5 Feb 1977	06:16	VIR	3 Aug 1977	06:54	ARI	31 Jan 1978	03:02	SCO
7 Feb 1977	10:35	LIB	5 Aug 1977	16:18	TAU	2 Feb 1978	07:12	SAG
9 Feb 1977	14:03	SCO	8 Aug 1977	04:29	GEM	4 Feb 1978	08:49	CAP
11 Feb 1977	17:10	SAG	10 Aug 1977	17:03	CAN	6 Feb 1978	09:04	AQU
13 Feb 1977	20:13	CAP	13 Aug 1977	03:56	LEO	8 Feb 1978	09:48	PIS
15 Feb 1977	23:45	AQU	15 Aug 1977	12:24	VIR	10 Feb 1978	12:57	ARI
18 Feb 1977	04:44	PIS	17 Aug 1977	18:48	LIB	12 Feb 1978	19:50	TAU
20 Feb 1977	12:23	ARI	19 Aug 1977	23:34	SCO	15 Feb 1978	06:24	GEM
22 Feb 1977	23:06	TAU	22 Aug 1977	03:02	SAG	17 Feb 1978	18:55	CAN
25 Feb 1977	11:49	GEM	24 Aug 1977	05:30	CAP	20 Feb 1978	07:09	LEO
28 Feb 1977	00:01	CAN	26 Aug 1977	07:40	AQU	22 Feb 1978	17:39	VIR
2 Mar 1977	09:23	LEO	28 Aug 1977	10:47	PIS	25 Feb 1978	02:02	LIB
4 Mar 1977	15:17	VIR	30 Aug 1977	16:11	ARI	27 Feb 1978	08:27	SCO
6 Mar 1977	18:34	LIB	2 Sep 1977	00:52	TAU	1 Mar 1978	13:01	SAG
8 Mar 1977	20:36	SCO	4 Sep 1977	12:27	GEM	3 Mar 1978	15:57	CAP
10 Mar 1977	22:42	SAG	7 Sep 1977	01:02	CAN	5 Mar 1978	17:50	AQU
13 Mar 1977	01:40	CAP	9 Sep 1977	12:12	LEO	7 Mar 1978	19:45	PIS
15 Mar 1977	05:59	AQU	11 Sep 1977	20:33	VIR	9 Mar 1978	23:09	ARI
17 Mar 1977	12:06	PIS	14 Sep 1977	02:06	LIB	12 Mar 1978	05:18	TAU
19 Mar 1977	20:23	ARI	16 Sep 1977	05:45	SCO	14 Mar 1978	14:48	GEM
22 Mar 1977	07:05	TAU	18 Sep 1977	08:28	SAG	17 Mar 1978	02:48	CAN
24 Mar 1977	19:38	GEM	20 Sep 1977	11:04	CAP	19 Mar 1978	15:11	LEO
27 Mar 1977	08:16	CAN	22 Sep 1977	14:12	AQU	22 Mar 1978	01:48	VIR
29 Mar 1977	18:40	LEO	24 Sep 1977	18:29	PIS	24 Mar 1978	09:40	LIB
1 Apr 1977	01:23	VIR	27 Sep 1977	00:41	ARI	26 Mar 1978	15:00	SCO
3 Apr 1977	04:38	LIB	29 Sep 1977	09:21	TAU	28 Mar 1978	18:37	SAG
5 Apr 1977	05:39	SCO	1 Oct 1977	20:33	GEM	30 Mar 1978	21:23	CAP
7 Apr 1977	06:08	SAG	4 Oct 1977	09:08	CAN	2 Apr 1978	00:05	AQU
9 Apr 1977	07:40	CAP	6 Oct 1977	20:56	LEO	4 Apr 1978	03:20	PIS
11 Apr 1977	11:24	AQU	9 Oct 1977	05:58	VIR	6 Apr 1978	07:51	ARI
13 Apr 1977	17:49	PIS	11 Oct 1977	11:28	LIB	8 Apr 1978	14:22	TAU
16 Apr 1977	02:52	ARI	13 Oct 1977	14:10	SCO	10 Apr 1978	23:28	GEM
18 Apr 1977	14:02	TAU	15 Oct 1977	15:27	SAG	13 Apr 1978	10:59	CAN
21 Apr 1977	02:37	GEM	17 Oct 1977	16:50	CAP	15 Apr 1978	23:29	LEO
23 Apr 1977	15:24	CAN	19 Oct 1977	19:36	AQU	18 Apr 1978	10:42	VIR
26 Apr 1977	02:42	LEO	22 Oct 1977	00:27	PIS	20 Apr 1978	18:52	LIB
28 Apr 1977	10:50	VIR	24 Oct 1977	07:34	ARI	22 Apr 1978	23:37	SCO
30 Apr 1977	15:11	LIB	26 Oct 1977	16:53	TAU	25 Apr 1978	01:59	SAG
2 May 1977	16:23	SCO	29 Oct 1977	04:07	GEM	27 Apr 1978	03:27	CAP
4 May 1977	15:58	SAG	31 Oct 1977	16:39	CAN	29 Apr 1978	05:27	AQU
6 May 1977	15:54	CAP	3 Nov 1977	05:02	LEO	1 May 1978	09:00	PIS
8 May 1977	17:59	AQU	5 Nov 1977	15:15	VIR	3 May 1978	14:27	ARI
10 May 1977	23:30	PIS	7 Nov 1977	21:49	LIB	5 May 1978	21:52	TAU
13 May 1977	08:29	ARI	10 Nov 1977	00:40	SCO	8 May 1978	07:18	GEM
15 May 1977	20:04	TAU	12 Nov 1977	01:03	SAG	10 May 1978	18:41	CAN
18 May 1977	08:50	GEM	14 Nov 1977	00:51	CAP	13 May 1978	07:16	LEO
20 May 1977	21:35	CAN	16 Nov 1977	02:00	AQU	15 May 1978	19:14	VIR
23 May 1977	09:12	LEO	18 Nov 1977	05:58	PIS	18 May 1978	04:23	LIB
25 May 1977	18:30	VIR	20 Nov 1977	13:13	ARI	20 May 1978	09:37	SCO
28 May 1977	00:26	LIB	22 Nov 1977	23:09	TAU	22 May 1978	11:30	SAG
30 May 1977	02:55	SCO	25 Nov 1977	10:48	GEM	24 May 1978	11:41	CAP
1 Jun 1977	02:53	SAG	27 Nov 1977	23:19	CAN	26 May 1978	12:10	AQU
3 Jun 1977	02:07	CAP	30 Nov 1977	11:52	LEO	28 May 1978	14:37	PIS
5 Jun 1977	02:44	AQU	2 Dec 1977	23:04	VIR	30 May 1978	19:52	ARI
7 Jun 1977	06:35	PIS	5 Dec 1977	07:16	LIB	2 Jun 1978	03:50	TAU
9 Jun 1977	14:35	ARI	7 Dec 1977	11:31	SCO	4 Jun 1978	13:53	GEM
12 Jun 1977	01:56	TAU	9 Dec 1977	12:20	SAG	7 Jun 1978	01:30	CAN
14 Jun 1977	14:49	GEM	11 Dec 1977	11:25	CAP	9 Jun 1978	14:07	LEO
17 Jun 1977	03:28	CAN	13 Dec 1977	11:00	AQU	12 Jun 1978	02:34	VIR
19 Jun 1977	14:52	LEO	15 Dec 1977	13:10	PIS	14 Jun 1978	12:54	LIB
22 Jun 1977	00:27	VIR	17 Dec 1977	19:11	ARI	16 Jun 1978	19:27	SCO
24 Jun 1977	07:34	LIB	20 Dec 1977	04:54	TAU	18 Jun 1978	21:59	SAG
26 Jun 1977	11:40	SCO	22 Dec 1977	16:51	GEM	20 Jun 1978	21:51	CAP

DATE	TIME	SIGN	DATE	TIME	SIGN	DATE	TIME	SIGN
22 Jun 1978	21:07	AQU	20 Dec 1978	04:34	VIR	17 Jun 1979	12:52	ARI
24 Jun 1978	21:57	PIS	22 Dec 1978	16:39	LIB	19 Jun 1979	17:18	TAU
27 Jun 1978	01:54	ARI	25 Dec 1978	01:30	SCO	21 Jun 1979	23:23	GEM
29 Jun 1978	09:21	TAU	27 Dec 1978	06:07	SAG	24 Jun 1979	07:24	CAN
1 Jul 1978	19:37	GEM	29 Dec 1978	07:15	CAP	26 Jun 1979	17:46	LEO
4 Jul 1978	07:33	CAN	31 Dec 1978	06:52	AQU	29 Jun 1979	06:13	VIR
6 Jul 1978	20:12	LEO	2 Jan 1979	07:08	PIS	1 Jul 1979	19:07	LIB
9 Jul 1978	08:44	VIR	4 Jan 1979	09:42	ARI	4 Jul 1979	05:57	SCO
11 Jul 1978	19:47	LIB	6 Jan 1979	15:18	TAU	6 Jul 1979	12:54	SAG
14 Jul 1978	03:45	SCO	8 Jan 1979	23:43	GEM	8 Jul 1979	16:06	CAP
16 Jul 1978	07:48	SAG	11 Jan 1979	10:14	CAN	10 Jul 1979	16:58	AQU
18 Jul 1978	08:32	CAP	13 Jan 1979	22:16	LEO	12 Jul 1979	17:22	PIS
20 Jul 1978	07:41	AQU	16 Jan 1979	11:09	VIR	14 Jul 1979	18:57	ARI
22 Jul 1978	07:26	PIS	18 Jan 1979	23:39	LIB	16 Jul 1979	22:43	TAU
24 Jul 1978	09:46	ARI	21 Jan 1979	09:49	SCO	19 Jul 1979	04:59	GEM
26 Jul 1978	15:51	TAU	23 Jan 1979	16:06	SAG	21 Jul 1979	13:40	CAN
29 Jul 1978	01:31	GEM	25 Jan 1979	18:27	CAP	24 Jul 1979	00:30	LEO
31 Jul 1978	13:28	CAN	27 Jan 1979	18:11	AQU	26 Jul 1979	13:01	VIR
3 Aug 1978	02:10	LEO	29 Jan 1979	17:25	PIS	29 Jul 1979	02:05	LIB
5 Aug 1978	14:28	VIR	31 Jan 1979	18:11	ARI	31 Jul 1979	13:45	SCO
8 Aug 1978	01:28	LIB	2 Feb 1979	22:04	TAU	2 Aug 1979	22:04	SAG
10 Aug 1978	10:10	SCO	5 Feb 1979	05:33	GEM	5 Aug 1979	02:21	CAP
12 Aug 1978	15:41	SAG	7 Feb 1979	16:05	CAN	7 Aug 1979	03:27	AQU
14 Aug 1978	18:02	CAP	10 Feb 1979	04:25	LEO	9 Aug 1979	03:05	PIS
16 Aug 1978	18:14	AQU	12 Feb 1979	17:17	VIR	11 Aug 1979	03:10	ARI
18 Aug 1978	18:04	PIS	15 Feb 1979	05:36	LIB	13 Aug 1979	05:21	TAU
20 Aug 1978	19:29	ARI	17 Feb 1979	16:11	SCO	15 Aug 1979	10:42	GEM
23 Aug 1978	00:06	TAU	19 Feb 1979	23:49	SAG	17 Aug 1979	19:17	CAN
25 Aug 1978	08:31	GEM	22 Feb 1979	03:59	CAP	20 Aug 1979	06:28	LEO
27 Aug 1978	19:59	CAN	24 Feb 1979	05:11	AQU	22 Aug 1979	19:11	VIR
30 Aug 1978	08:39	LEO	26 Feb 1979	04:52	PIS	25 Aug 1979	08:13	LIB
1 Sep 1978	20:45	VIR	28 Feb 1979	04:54	ARI	27 Aug 1979	20:11	SCO
4 Sep 1978	07:15	LIB	2 Mar 1979	07:09	TAU	30 Aug 1979	05:39	SAG
6 Sep 1978	15:37	SCO	4 Mar 1979	12:59	GEM	1 Sep 1979	11:32	CAP
8 Sep 1978	21:38	SAG	6 Mar 1979	22:34	CAN	3 Sep 1979	13:58	AQU
11 Sep 1978	01:18	CAP	9 Mar 1979	10:47	LEO	5 Sep 1979	14:02	PIS
13 Sep 1978	03:08	AQU	11 Mar 1979	23:42	VIR	7 Sep 1979	13:29	ARI
15 Sep 1978	04:09	PIS	14 Mar 1979	11:40	LIB	9 Sep 1979	14:13	TAU
17 Sep 1978	05:49	ARI	16 Mar 1979	21:48	SCO	11 Sep 1979	17:54	GEM
19 Sep 1978	09:43	TAU	19 Mar 1979	05:37	SAG	14 Sep 1979	01:27	CAN
21 Sep 1978	16:56	GEM	21 Mar 1979	10:55	CAP	16 Sep 1979	12:25	LEO
24 Sep 1978	03:31	CAN	23 Mar 1979	13:51	AQU	19 Sep 1979	01:15	VIR
26 Sep 1978	16:01	LEO	25 Mar 1979	15:04	PIS	21 Sep 1979	14:10	LIB
29 Sep 1978	04:10	VIR	27 Mar 1979	15:47	ARI	24 Sep 1979	01:53	SCO
1 Oct 1978	14:15	LIB	29 Mar 1979	17:36	TAU	26 Sep 1979	11:34	SAG
3 Oct 1978	21:47	SCO	31 Mar 1979	22:09	GEM	28 Sep 1979	18:39	CAP
6 Oct 1978	03:06	SAG	3 Apr 1979	06:23	CAN	30 Sep 1979	22:47	AQU
8 Oct 1978	06:52	CAP	5 Apr 1979	17:57	LEO	3 Oct 1979	00:22	PIS
10 Oct 1978	09:42	AQU	8 Apr 1979	06:51	VIR	5 Oct 1979	00:28	ARI
12 Oct 1978	12:12	PIS	10 Apr 1979	18:44	LIB	7 Oct 1979	00:45	TAU
14 Oct 1978	15:06	ARI	13 Apr 1979	04:15	SCO	9 Oct 1979	03:08	GEM
16 Oct 1978	19:22	TAU	15 Apr 1979	11:17	SAG	11 Oct 1979	09:10	CAN
19 Oct 1978	02:06	GEM	17 Apr 1979	16:22	CAP	13 Oct 1979	19:11	LEO
21 Oct 1978	11:53	CAN	19 Apr 1979	20:01	AQU	16 Oct 1979	07:51	VIR
24 Oct 1978	00:03	LEO	21 Apr 1979	22:40	PIS	18 Oct 1979	20:43	LIB
26 Oct 1978	12:31	VIR	24 Apr 1979	00:51	ARI	21 Oct 1979	08:01	SCO
28 Oct 1978	22:49	LIB	26 Apr 1979	03:27	TAU	23 Oct 1979	17:08	SAG
31 Oct 1978	05:52	SCO	28 Apr 1979	07:49	GEM	26 Oct 1979	00:10	CAP
2 Nov 1978	10:02	SAG	30 Apr 1979	15:12	CAN	28 Oct 1979	05:16	AQU
4 Nov 1978	12:40	CAP	3 May 1979	01:56	LEO	30 Oct 1979	08:28	PIS
6 Nov 1978	15:03	AQU	5 May 1979	14:41	VIR	1 Nov 1979	10:08	ARI
8 Nov 1978	18:05	PIS	8 May 1979	02:46	LIB	3 Nov 1979	11:16	TAU
10 Nov 1978	22:11	ARI	10 May 1979	12:08	SCO	5 Nov 1979	13:26	GEM
13 Nov 1978	03:35	TAU	12 May 1979	18:24	SAG	7 Nov 1979	18:23	CAN
15 Nov 1978	10:45	GEM	14 May 1979	22:25	CAP	10 Nov 1979	03:15	LEO
17 Nov 1978	20:16	CAN	17 May 1979	01:25	AQU	12 Nov 1979	15:20	VIR
20 Nov 1978	08:08	LEO	19 May 1979	04:18	PIS	15 Nov 1979	04:16	LIB
22 Nov 1978	20:56	VIR	21 May 1979	07:30	ARI	17 Nov 1979	15:28	SCO
25 Nov 1978	08:06	LIB	23 May 1979	11:20	TAU	19 Nov 1979	23:55	SAG
27 Nov 1978	15:37	SCO	25 May 1979	16:28	GEM	22 Nov 1979	06:01	CAP
29 Nov 1978	19:22	SAG	27 May 1979	23:51	CAN	24 Nov 1979	10:36	AQU
1 Dec 1978	20:43	CAP	30 May 1979	10:08	LEO	26 Nov 1979	14:16	PIS
3 Dec 1978	21:35	AQU	1 Jun 1979	22:40	VIR	28 Nov 1979	17:16	ARI
5 Dec 1978	23:37	PIS	4 Jun 1979	11:10	LIB	30 Nov 1979	19:54	TAU
8 Dec 1978	03:40	ARI	6 Jun 1979	21:03	SCO	2 Dec 1979	23:02	GEM
10 Dec 1978	09:50	TAU	9 Jun 1979	03:13	SAG	5 Dec 1979	04:02	CAN
12 Dec 1978	17:54	GEM	11 Jun 1979	06:23	CAP	7 Dec 1979	12:09	LEO
15 Dec 1978	03:50	CAN	13 Jun 1979	08:06	AQU	9 Dec 1979	23:33	VIR
17 Dec 1978	15:37	LEO	15 Jun 1979	09:56	PIS	12 Dec 1979	12:28	LIB

DATE	TIME	SIGN	DATE	TIME	SIGN	DATE	TIME	SIGN
15 Dec 1979	00:06	SCO	11 Jun 1980	07:22	GEM	8 Dec 1980	18:11	CAP
17 Dec 1979	08:35	SAG	13 Jun 1980	10:30	CAN	11 Dec 1980	02:35	AQU
19 Dec 1979	13:53	CAP	15 Jun 1980	16:22	LEO	13 Dec 1980	09:02	PIS
21 Dec 1979	17:12	AQU	18 Jun 1980	01:47	VIR	15 Dec 1980	13:20	ARI
23 Dec 1979	19:50	PIS	20 Jun 1980	13:55	LIB	17 Dec 1980	15:35	TAU
25 Dec 1979	22:40	ARI	23 Jun 1980	02:25	SCO	19 Dec 1980	16:39	GEM
28 Dec 1979	02:07	TAU	25 Jun 1980	13:00	SAG	21 Dec 1980	18:02	CAN
30 Dec 1979	06:32	GEM	27 Jun 1980	20:45	CAP	23 Dec 1980	21:34	LEO
1 Jan 1980	12:29	CAN	30 Jun 1980	02:03	AQU	26 Dec 1980	04:32	VIR
3 Jan 1980	20:47	LEO	2 Jul 1980	05:48	PIS	28 Dec 1980	15:05	LIB
6 Jan 1980	07:48	VIR	4 Jul 1980	08:46	ARI	31 Dec 1980	03:35	SCO
8 Jan 1980	20:37	LIB	6 Jul 1980	11:30	TAU	2 Jan 1981	15:41	SAG
11 Jan 1980	08:54	SCO	8 Jul 1980	14:33	GEM	5 Jan 1981	01:40	CAP
13 Jan 1980	18:16	SAG	10 Jul 1980	18:44	CAN	7 Jan 1981	09:11	AQU
15 Jan 1980	23:49	CAP	13 Jul 1980	01:03	LEO	9 Jan 1981	14:41	PIS
18 Jan 1980	02:24	AQU	15 Jul 1980	10:11	VIR	11 Jan 1981	18:43	ARI
20 Jan 1980	03:32	PIS	17 Jul 1980	21:55	LIB	13 Jan 1981	21:44	TAU
22 Jan 1980	04:51	ARI	20 Jul 1980	10:32	SCO	16 Jan 1981	00:17	GEM
24 Jan 1980	07:31	TAU	22 Jul 1980	21:41	SAG	18 Jan 1981	03:07	CAN
26 Jan 1980	12:11	GEM	25 Jul 1980	05:44	CAP	20 Jan 1981	07:21	LEO
28 Jan 1980	19:02	CAN	27 Jul 1980	10:33	AQU	22 Jan 1981	14:03	VIR
31 Jan 1980	04:08	LEO	29 Jul 1980	13:10	PIS	24 Jan 1981	23:45	LIB
2 Feb 1980	15:21	VIR	31 Jul 1980	14:53	ARI	27 Jan 1981	11:48	SCO
5 Feb 1980	04:04	LIB	2 Aug 1980	16:54	TAU	30 Jan 1981	00:10	SAG
7 Feb 1980	16:45	SCO	4 Aug 1980	20:10	GEM	1 Feb 1981	10:35	CAP
10 Feb 1980	03:18	SAG	7 Aug 1980	01:12	CAN	3 Feb 1981	17:54	AQU
12 Feb 1980	10:10	CAP	9 Aug 1980	08:23	LEO	5 Feb 1981	22:20	PIS
14 Feb 1980	13:18	AQU	11 Aug 1980	17:54	VIR	8 Feb 1981	01:01	ARI
16 Feb 1980	13:53	PIS	14 Aug 1980	05:32	LIB	10 Feb 1981	03:10	TAU
18 Feb 1980	13:42	ARI	16 Aug 1980	18:14	SCO	12 Feb 1981	05:50	GEM
20 Feb 1980	14:35	TAU	19 Aug 1980	06:07	SAG	14 Feb 1981	09:43	CAN
22 Feb 1980	17:58	GEM	21 Aug 1980	15:10	CAP	16 Feb 1981	15:10	LEO
25 Feb 1980	00:35	CAN	23 Aug 1980	20:31	AQU	18 Feb 1981	22:34	VIR
27 Feb 1980	10:10	LEO	25 Aug 1980	22:42	PIS	21 Feb 1981	08:12	LIB
29 Feb 1980	21:53	VIR	27 Aug 1980	23:10	ARI	23 Feb 1981	19:54	SCO
3 Mar 1980	10:39	LIB	29 Aug 1980	23:41	TAU	26 Feb 1981	08:28	SAG
5 Mar 1980	23:22	SCO	1 Sep 1980	01:50	GEM	28 Feb 1981	19:45	CAP
8 Mar 1980	10:37	SAG	3 Sep 1980	06:39	CAN	3 Mar 1981	03:49	AQU
10 Mar 1980	19:01	CAP	5 Sep 1980	14:22	LEO	5 Mar 1981	08:11	PIS
12 Mar 1980	23:43	AQU	8 Sep 1980	00:31	VIR	7 Mar 1981	09:47	ARI
15 Mar 1980	01:09	PIS	10 Sep 1980	12:22	LIB	9 Mar 1981	10:22	TAU
17 Mar 1980	00:40	ARI	13 Sep 1980	01:05	SCO	11 Mar 1981	11:42	GEM
19 Mar 1980	00:13	TAU	15 Sep 1980	13:27	SAG	13 Mar 1981	15:06	CAN
21 Mar 1980	01:48	GEM	17 Sep 1980	23:43	CAP	15 Mar 1981	21:03	LEO
23 Mar 1980	06:55	CAN	20 Sep 1980	06:30	AQU	18 Mar 1981	05:19	VIR
25 Mar 1980	15:58	LEO	22 Sep 1980	09:26	PIS	20 Mar 1981	15:30	LIB
28 Mar 1980	03:52	VIR	24 Sep 1980	09:36	ARI	23 Mar 1981	03:14	SCO
30 Mar 1980	16:48	LIB	26 Sep 1980	08:53	TAU	25 Mar 1981	15:50	SAG
2 Apr 1980	05:21	SCO	28 Sep 1980	09:21	GEM	28 Mar 1981	03:51	CAP
4 Apr 1980	16:34	SAG	30 Sep 1980	12:47	CAN	30 Mar 1981	13:14	AQU
7 Apr 1980	01:41	CAP	2 Oct 1980	19:57	LEO	1 Apr 1981	18:40	PIS
9 Apr 1980	07:58	AQU	5 Oct 1980	06:18	VIR	3 Apr 1981	20:24	ARI
11 Apr 1980	11:05	PIS	7 Oct 1980	18:30	LIB	5 Apr 1981	20:04	TAU
13 Apr 1980	11:39	ARI	10 Oct 1980	07:14	SCO	7 Apr 1981	19:47	GEM
15 Apr 1980	11:11	TAU	12 Oct 1980	19:37	SAG	9 Apr 1981	21:34	CAN
17 Apr 1980	11:42	GEM	15 Oct 1980	06:36	CAP	12 Apr 1981	02:37	LEO
19 Apr 1980	15:12	CAN	17 Oct 1980	14:52	AQU	14 Apr 1981	10:57	VIR
21 Apr 1980	22:52	LEO	19 Oct 1980	19:30	PIS	16 Apr 1981	21:38	LIB
24 Apr 1980	10:12	VIR	21 Oct 1980	20:42	ARI	19 Apr 1981	09:38	SCO
26 Apr 1980	23:09	LIB	23 Oct 1980	19:55	TAU	21 Apr 1981	22:14	SAG
29 Apr 1980	11:34	SCO	25 Oct 1980	19:17	GEM	24 Apr 1981	10:30	CAP
1 May 1980	22:21	SAG	27 Oct 1980	21:01	CAN	26 Apr 1981	20:55	AQU
4 May 1980	07:13	CAP	30 Oct 1980	02:39	LEO	29 Apr 1981	03:55	PIS
6 May 1980	14:02	AQU	1 Nov 1980	12:19	VIR	1 May 1981	06:56	ARI
8 May 1980	18:33	PIS	4 Nov 1980	00:31	LIB	3 May 1981	06:59	TAU
10 May 1980	20:43	ARI	6 Nov 1980	13:18	SCO	5 May 1981	06:00	GEM
12 May 1980	21:24	TAU	9 Nov 1980	01:25	SAG	7 May 1981	06:17	CAN
14 May 1980	22:08	GEM	11 Nov 1980	12:14	CAP	9 May 1981	09:41	LEO
17 May 1980	00:53	CAN	13 Nov 1980	21:09	AQU	11 May 1981	16:55	VIR
19 May 1980	07:14	LEO	16 Nov 1980	03:19	PIS	14 May 1981	03:24	LIB
21 May 1980	17:32	VIR	18 Nov 1980	06:21	ARI	16 May 1981	15:37	SCO
24 May 1980	06:10	LIB	20 Nov 1980	06:50	TAU	19 May 1981	04:13	SAG
26 May 1980	18:36	SCO	22 Nov 1980	06:27	GEM	21 May 1981	16:19	CAP
29 May 1980	05:04	SAG	24 Nov 1980	07:18	CAN	24 May 1981	02:59	AQU
31 May 1980	13:13	CAP	26 Nov 1980	11:24	LEO	26 May 1981	11:04	PIS
2 Jun 1980	19:29	AQU	28 Nov 1980	19:37	VIR	28 May 1981	15:42	ARI
5 Jun 1980	00:09	PIS	1 Dec 1980	07:13	LIB	30 May 1981	17:10	TAU
7 Jun 1980	03:22	ARI	3 Dec 1980	19:59	SCO	1 Jun 1981	16:48	GEM
9 Jun 1980	05:29	TAU	6 Dec 1980	07:57	SAG	3 Jun 1981	16:38	CAN

DATE	TIME	SIGN	DATE	TIME	SIGN	DATE	TIME	SIGN
5 Jun 1981	18:42	LEO	3 Dec 1981	17:15	PIS	31 May 1982	12:03	LIB
8 Jun 1981	00:26	VIR	5 Dec 1981	23:47	ARI	2 Jun 1982	21:12	SCO
10 Jun 1981	09:55	LIB	8 Dec 1981	02:30	TAU	5 Jun 1982	08:31	SAG
12 Jun 1981	21:54	SCO	10 Dec 1981	02:29	GEM	7 Jun 1982	21:11	CAP
15 Jun 1981	10:31	SAG	12 Dec 1981	01:40	CAN	10 Jun 1982	10:07	AQU
17 Jun 1981	22:20	CAP	14 Dec 1981	02:09	LEO	12 Jun 1982	21:43	PIS
20 Jun 1981	08:35	AQU	16 Dec 1981	05:38	VIR	15 Jun 1982	06:19	ARI
22 Jun 1981	16:43	PIS	18 Dec 1981	12:58	LIB	17 Jun 1982	11:05	TAU
24 Jun 1981	22:17	ARI	20 Dec 1981	23:39	SCO	19 Jun 1982	12:33	GEM
27 Jun 1981	01:15	TAU	23 Dec 1981	12:11	SAG	21 Jun 1982	12:12	CAN
29 Jun 1981	02:20	GEM	26 Dec 1981	00:58	CAP	23 Jun 1982	11:57	LEO
1 Jul 1981	02:57	CAN	28 Dec 1981	12:52	AQU	25 Jun 1982	13:37	VIR
3 Jul 1981	04:47	LEO	30 Dec 1981	22:59	PIS	27 Jun 1982	18:30	LIB
5 Jul 1981	09:27	VIR	2 Jan 1982	06:32	ARI	30 Jun 1982	03:02	SCO
7 Jul 1981	17:42	LIB	4 Jan 1982	11:01	TAU	2 Jul 1982	14:25	SAG
10 Jul 1981	05:01	SCO	6 Jan 1982	12:47	GEM	5 Jul 1982	03:14	CAP
12 Jul 1981	17:34	SAG	8 Jan 1982	13:01	CAN	7 Jul 1982	16:02	AQU
15 Jul 1981	05:19	CAP	10 Jan 1982	13:21	LEO	10 Jul 1982	03:34	PIS
17 Jul 1981	15:01	AQU	12 Jan 1982	15:37	VIR	12 Jul 1982	12:47	ARI
19 Jul 1981	22:24	PIS	14 Jan 1982	21:17	LIB	14 Jul 1982	18:59	TAU
22 Jul 1981	03:43	ARI	17 Jan 1982	06:46	SCO	16 Jul 1982	22:02	GEM
24 Jul 1981	07:18	TAU	19 Jan 1982	19:00	SAG	18 Jul 1982	22:45	CAN
26 Jul 1981	09:41	GEM	22 Jan 1982	07:50	CAP	20 Jul 1982	22:35	LEO
28 Jul 1981	11:41	CAN	24 Jan 1982	19:24	AQU	22 Jul 1982	23:21	VIR
30 Jul 1981	14:20	LEO	27 Jan 1982	04:48	PIS	25 Jul 1982	02:46	LIB
1 Aug 1981	18:54	VIR	29 Jan 1982	11:57	ARI	27 Jul 1982	09:59	SCO
4 Aug 1981	02:24	LIB	31 Jan 1982	17:03	TAU	29 Jul 1982	20:48	SAG
6 Aug 1981	12:58	SCO	2 Feb 1982	20:19	GEM	1 Aug 1982	09:35	CAP
9 Aug 1981	01:22	SAG	4 Feb 1982	22:17	CAN	3 Aug 1982	22:16	AQU
11 Aug 1981	13:19	CAP	6 Feb 1982	23:50	LEO	6 Aug 1982	09:22	PIS
13 Aug 1981	22:55	AQU	9 Feb 1982	02:15	VIR	8 Aug 1982	18:20	ARI
16 Aug 1981	05:34	PIS	11 Feb 1982	07:02	LIB	11 Aug 1982	00:59	TAU
18 Aug 1981	09:48	ARI	13 Feb 1982	15:16	SCO	13 Aug 1982	05:21	GEM
20 Aug 1981	12:43	TAU	16 Feb 1982	02:45	SAG	15 Aug 1982	07:40	CAN
22 Aug 1981	15:18	GEM	18 Feb 1982	15:35	CAP	17 Aug 1982	08:39	LEO
24 Aug 1981	18:16	CAN	21 Feb 1982	03:14	AQU	19 Aug 1982	09:40	VIR
26 Aug 1981	22:10	LEO	23 Feb 1982	12:07	PIS	21 Aug 1982	12:23	LIB
29 Aug 1981	03:32	VIR	25 Feb 1982	18:16	ARI	23 Aug 1982	18:20	SCO
31 Aug 1981	11:03	LIB	27 Feb 1982	22:31	TAU	26 Aug 1982	04:11	SAG
2 Sep 1981	21:10	SCO	2 Mar 1982	01:49	GEM	28 Aug 1982	16:41	CAP
5 Sep 1981	09:23	SAG	4 Mar 1982	04:48	CAN	31 Aug 1982	05:23	AQU
7 Sep 1981	21:47	CAP	6 Mar 1982	07:50	LEO	2 Sep 1982	16:10	PIS
10 Sep 1981	07:57	AQU	8 Mar 1982	11:27	VIR	5 Sep 1982	00:22	ARI
12 Sep 1981	14:32	PIS	10 Mar 1982	16:34	LIB	7 Sep 1982	06:26	TAU
14 Sep 1981	17:55	ARI	13 Mar 1982	00:17	SCO	9 Sep 1982	10:56	GEM
16 Sep 1981	19:30	TAU	15 Mar 1982	11:03	SAG	11 Sep 1982	14:17	CAN
18 Sep 1981	20:59	GEM	17 Mar 1982	23:46	CAP	13 Sep 1982	16:45	LEO
20 Sep 1981	23:40	CAN	20 Mar 1982	11:51	AQU	15 Sep 1982	18:57	VIR
23 Sep 1981	04:08	LEO	22 Mar 1982	21:00	PIS	17 Sep 1982	22:03	LIB
25 Sep 1981	10:29	VIR	25 Mar 1982	02:36	ARI	20 Sep 1982	03:33	SCO
27 Sep 1981	18:40	LIB	27 Mar 1982	05:39	TAU	22 Sep 1982	12:31	SAG
30 Sep 1981	04:52	SCO	29 Mar 1982	07:43	GEM	25 Sep 1982	00:31	CAP
2 Oct 1981	16:59	SAG	31 Mar 1982	10:09	CAN	27 Sep 1982	13:20	AQU
5 Oct 1981	05:48	CAP	2 Apr 1982	13:36	LEO	30 Sep 1982	00:17	PIS
7 Oct 1981	17:00	AQU	4 Apr 1982	18:18	VIR	2 Oct 1982	08:05	ARI
10 Oct 1981	00:30	PIS	7 Apr 1982	00:27	LIB	4 Oct 1982	13:08	TAU
12 Oct 1981	04:00	ARI	9 Apr 1982	08:33	SCO	6 Oct 1982	16:38	GEM
14 Oct 1981	04:42	TAU	11 Apr 1982	19:06	SAG	8 Oct 1982	19:39	CAN
16 Oct 1981	04:41	GEM	14 Apr 1982	07:41	CAP	10 Oct 1982	22:44	LEO
18 Oct 1981	05:52	CAN	16 Apr 1982	20:17	AQU	13 Oct 1982	02:09	VIR
20 Oct 1981	09:35	LEO	19 Apr 1982	06:19	PIS	15 Oct 1982	06:22	LIB
22 Oct 1981	16:05	VIR	21 Apr 1982	12:21	ARI	17 Oct 1982	12:21	SCO
25 Oct 1981	00:57	LIB	23 Apr 1982	14:58	TAU	19 Oct 1982	21:03	SAG
27 Oct 1981	11:38	SCO	25 Apr 1982	15:48	GEM	22 Oct 1982	08:38	CAP
29 Oct 1981	23:48	SAG	27 Apr 1982	16:43	CAN	24 Oct 1982	21:35	AQU
1 Nov 1981	12:45	CAP	29 Apr 1982	19:09	LEO	27 Oct 1982	09:11	PIS
4 Nov 1981	00:49	AQU	1 May 1982	23:45	VIR	29 Oct 1982	17:24	ARI
6 Nov 1981	09:50	PIS	4 May 1982	06:32	LIB	31 Oct 1982	22:02	TAU
8 Nov 1981	14:37	ARI	6 May 1982	15:24	SCO	3 Nov 1982	00:22	GEM
10 Nov 1981	15:43	TAU	9 May 1982	02:17	SAG	5 Nov 1982	01:58	CAN
12 Nov 1981	14:59	GEM	11 May 1982	14:49	CAP	7 Nov 1982	04:10	LEO
14 Nov 1981	14:37	CAN	14 May 1982	03:43	AQU	9 Nov 1982	07:40	VIR
16 Nov 1981	16:33	LEO	16 May 1982	14:45	PIS	11 Nov 1982	12:46	LIB
18 Nov 1981	21:53	VIR	18 May 1982	22:02	ARI	13 Nov 1982	19:42	SCO
21 Nov 1981	06:32	LIB	21 May 1982	01:20	TAU	16 Nov 1982	04:51	SAG
23 Nov 1981	17:36	SCO	23 May 1982	01:54	GEM	18 Nov 1982	16:21	CAP
26 Nov 1981	06:00	SAG	25 May 1982	01:38	CAN	21 Nov 1982	05:20	AQU
28 Nov 1981	18:52	CAP	27 May 1982	02:27	LEO	23 Nov 1982	17:42	PIS
1 Dec 1981	07:08	AQU	29 May 1982	05:43	VIR	26 Nov 1982	03:05	ARI

DATE	TIME	SIGN	DATE	TIME	SIGN	DATE	TIME	SIGN
28 Nov 1982	08:30	TAU	26 May 1983	09:27	SAG	22 Nov 1983	21:10	CAN
30 Nov 1982	10:34	GEM	28 May 1983	19:06	CAP	25 Nov 1983	00:19	LEO
2 Dec 1982	10:57	CAN	31 May 1983	06:59	AQU	27 Nov 1983	03:01	VIR
4 Dec 1982	11:26	LEO	2 Jun 1983	19:41	PIS	29 Nov 1983	05:56	LIB
6 Dec 1982	13:33	VIR	5 Jun 1983	06:58	ARI	1 Dec 1983	09:41	SCO
8 Dec 1982	18:10	LIB	7 Jun 1983	15:03	TAU	3 Dec 1983	14:56	SAG
11 Dec 1982	01:35	SCO	9 Jun 1983	19:36	GEM	5 Dec 1983	22:28	CAP
13 Dec 1982	11:27	SAG	11 Jun 1983	21:31	CAN	8 Dec 1983	08:39	AQU
15 Dec 1982	23:15	CAP	13 Jun 1983	22:21	LEO	10 Dec 1983	20:52	PIS
18 Dec 1982	12:12	AQU	15 Jun 1983	23:38	VIR	13 Dec 1983	09:16	ARI
21 Dec 1982	00:55	PIS	18 Jun 1983	02:37	LIB	15 Dec 1983	19:32	TAU
23 Dec 1982	11:32	ARI	20 Jun 1983	07:59	SCO	18 Dec 1983	02:22	GEM
25 Dec 1982	18:36	TAU	22 Jun 1983	15:55	SAG	20 Dec 1983	06:02	CAN
27 Dec 1982	21:47	GEM	25 Jun 1983	02:08	CAP	22 Dec 1983	07:43	LEO
29 Dec 1982	22:11	CAN	27 Jun 1983	14:06	AQU	24 Dec 1983	09:01	VIR
31 Dec 1982	21:33	LEO	30 Jun 1983	02:51	PIS	26 Dec 1983	11:19	LIB
2 Jan 1983	21:50	VIR	2 Jul 1983	14:46	ARI	28 Dec 1983	15:27	SCO
5 Jan 1983	00:45	LIB	5 Jul 1983	00:03	TAU	30 Dec 1983	21:44	SAG
7 Jan 1983	07:16	SCO	7 Jul 1983	05:40	GEM	2 Jan 1984	06:07	CAP
9 Jan 1983	17:13	SAG	9 Jul 1983	07:49	CAN	4 Jan 1984	16:30	AQU
12 Jan 1983	05:25	CAP	11 Jul 1983	07:53	LEO	7 Jan 1984	04:34	PIS
14 Jan 1983	18:26	AQU	13 Jul 1983	07:43	VIR	9 Jan 1984	17:15	ARI
17 Jan 1983	07:02	PIS	15 Jul 1983	09:10	LIB	12 Jan 1984	04:35	TAU
19 Jan 1983	18:07	ARI	17 Jul 1983	13:39	SCO	14 Jan 1984	12:38	GEM
22 Jan 1983	02:34	TAU	19 Jul 1983	21:32	SAG	16 Jan 1984	16:46	CAN
24 Jan 1983	07:39	GEM	22 Jul 1983	08:11	CAP	18 Jan 1984	17:49	LEO
26 Jan 1983	09:27	CAN	24 Jul 1983	20:26	AQU	20 Jan 1984	17:35	VIR
28 Jan 1983	09:09	LEO	27 Jul 1983	09:11	PIS	22 Jan 1984	18:06	LIB
30 Jan 1983	08:35	VIR	29 Jul 1983	21:20	ARI	24 Jan 1984	21:04	SCO
1 Feb 1983	09:48	LIB	1 Aug 1983	07:36	TAU	27 Jan 1984	03:13	SAG
3 Feb 1983	14:33	SCO	3 Aug 1983	14:41	GEM	29 Jan 1984	12:12	CAP
5 Feb 1983	23:29	SAG	5 Aug 1983	18:08	CAN	31 Jan 1984	23:11	AQU
8 Feb 1983	11:33	CAP	7 Aug 1983	18:36	LEO	3 Feb 1984	11:21	PIS
11 Feb 1983	00:40	AQU	9 Aug 1983	17:48	VIR	6 Feb 1984	00:03	ARI
13 Feb 1983	13:01	PIS	11 Aug 1983	17:51	LIB	8 Feb 1984	12:04	TAU
15 Feb 1983	23:45	ARI	13 Aug 1983	20:44	SCO	10 Feb 1984	21:38	GEM
18 Feb 1983	08:29	TAU	16 Aug 1983	03:34	SAG	13 Feb 1984	03:19	CAN
20 Feb 1983	14:50	GEM	18 Aug 1983	13:59	CAP	15 Feb 1984	05:08	LEO
22 Feb 1983	18:30	CAN	21 Aug 1983	02:25	AQU	17 Feb 1984	04:31	VIR
24 Feb 1983	19:46	LEO	23 Aug 1983	15:09	PIS	19 Feb 1984	03:39	LIB
26 Feb 1983	19:49	VIR	26 Aug 1983	03:07	ARI	21 Feb 1984	04:44	SCO
28 Feb 1983	20:30	LIB	28 Aug 1983	13:37	TAU	23 Feb 1984	09:23	SAG
2 Mar 1983	23:52	SCO	30 Aug 1983	21:47	GEM	25 Feb 1984	17:49	CAP
5 Mar 1983	07:15	SAG	2 Sep 1983	02:51	CAN	28 Feb 1984	05:02	AQU
7 Mar 1983	18:29	CAP	4 Sep 1983	04:46	LEO	1 Mar 1984	17:29	PIS
10 Mar 1983	07:29	AQU	6 Sep 1983	04:35	VIR	4 Mar 1984	06:06	ARI
12 Mar 1983	19:46	PIS	8 Sep 1983	04:13	LIB	6 Mar 1984	18:08	TAU
15 Mar 1983	06:00	ARI	10 Sep 1983	05:49	SCO	9 Mar 1984	04:29	GEM
17 Mar 1983	14:03	TAU	12 Sep 1983	11:09	SAG	11 Mar 1984	11:46	CAN
19 Mar 1983	20:19	GEM	14 Sep 1983	20:34	CAP	13 Mar 1984	15:19	LEO
22 Mar 1983	00:51	CAN	17 Sep 1983	08:45	AQU	15 Mar 1984	15:46	VIR
24 Mar 1983	03:42	LEO	19 Sep 1983	21:29	PIS	17 Mar 1984	14:51	LIB
26 Mar 1983	05:17	VIR	22 Sep 1983	09:09	ARI	19 Mar 1984	14:49	SCO
28 Mar 1983	06:48	LIB	24 Sep 1983	19:12	TAU	21 Mar 1984	17:41	SAG
30 Mar 1983	09:57	SCO	27 Sep 1983	03:23	GEM	24 Mar 1984	00:37	CAP
1 Apr 1983	16:20	SAG	29 Sep 1983	09:23	CAN	26 Mar 1984	11:09	AQU
4 Apr 1983	02:30	CAP	1 Oct 1983	12:53	LEO	28 Mar 1984	23:37	PIS
6 Apr 1983	15:06	AQU	3 Oct 1983	14:14	VIR	31 Mar 1984	12:13	ARI
9 Apr 1983	03:29	PIS	5 Oct 1983	14:41	LIB	2 Apr 1984	23:54	TAU
11 Apr 1983	13:36	ARI	7 Oct 1983	16:06	SCO	5 Apr 1984	10:03	GEM
13 Apr 1983	20:58	TAU	9 Oct 1983	20:21	SAG	7 Apr 1984	17:59	CAN
16 Apr 1983	02:14	GEM	12 Oct 1983	04:30	CAP	9 Apr 1984	23:00	LEO
18 Apr 1983	06:13	CAN	14 Oct 1983	16:00	AQU	12 Apr 1984	01:10	VIR
20 Apr 1983	09:26	LEO	17 Oct 1983	04:41	PIS	14 Apr 1984	01:29	LIB
22 Apr 1983	12:11	VIR	19 Oct 1983	16:18	ARI	16 Apr 1984	01:41	SCO
24 Apr 1983	15:03	LIB	22 Oct 1983	01:46	TAU	18 Apr 1984	03:44	SAG
26 Apr 1983	19:04	SCO	24 Oct 1983	09:09	GEM	20 Apr 1984	09:11	CAP
29 Apr 1983	01:29	SAG	26 Oct 1983	14:46	CAN	22 Apr 1984	18:27	AQU
1 May 1983	11:01	CAP	28 Oct 1983	18:50	LEO	25 Apr 1984	06:26	PIS
3 May 1983	23:09	AQU	30 Oct 1983	21:32	VIR	27 Apr 1984	19:02	ARI
6 May 1983	11:42	PIS	1 Nov 1983	23:30	LIB	30 Apr 1984	06:30	TAU
8 May 1983	22:15	ARI	4 Nov 1983	01:53	SCO	2 May 1984	16:01	GEM
11 May 1983	05:35	TAU	6 Nov 1983	06:08	SAG	4 May 1984	23:25	CAN
13 May 1983	10:02	GEM	8 Nov 1983	13:32	CAP	7 May 1984	04:42	LEO
15 May 1983	12:47	CAN	11 Nov 1983	00:10	AQU	9 May 1984	08:01	VIR
17 May 1983	15:00	LEO	13 Nov 1983	12:40	PIS	11 May 1984	09:53	LIB
19 May 1983	17:36	VIR	16 Nov 1983	00:35	ARI	13 May 1984	11:22	SCO
21 May 1983	21:11	LIB	18 Nov 1983	10:05	TAU	15 May 1984	13:50	SAG
24 May 1983	02:17	SCO	20 Nov 1983	16:44	GEM	17 May 1984	18:43	CAP

DATE	TIME	SIGN	DATE	TIME	SIGN	DATE	TIME	SIGN
20 May 1984	02:56	AQU	16 Nov 1984	17:07	VIR	14 May 1985	22:25	ARI
22 May 1984	14:08	PIS	18 Nov 1984	19:29	LIB	17 May 1985	11:23	TAU
25 May 1984	02:39	ARI	20 Nov 1984	20:30	SCO	20 May 1985	00:00	GEM
27 May 1984	14:12	TAU	22 Nov 1984	21:34	SAG	22 May 1985	11:03	CAN
29 May 1984	23:21	GEM	25 Nov 1984	00:18	CAP	24 May 1985	19:53	LEO
1 Jun 1984	05:53	CAN	27 Nov 1984	06:05	AQU	27 May 1985	02:05	VIR
3 Jun 1984	10:18	LEO	29 Nov 1984	15:33	PIS	29 May 1985	05:40	LIB
5 Jun 1984	13:26	VIR	2 Dec 1984	03:42	ARI	31 May 1985	07:07	SCO
7 Jun 1984	16:03	LIB	4 Dec 1984	16:20	TAU	2 Jun 1985	07:33	SAG
9 Jun 1984	18:48	SCO	7 Dec 1984	03:23	CAN	4 Jun 1985	08:34	CAP
11 Jun 1984	22:26	SAG	9 Dec 1984	11:55	CAN	6 Jun 1985	11:53	AQU
14 Jun 1984	03:48	CAP	11 Dec 1984	18:08	LEO	8 Jun 1985	18:46	PIS
16 Jun 1984	11:41	AQU	13 Dec 1984	22:34	VIR	11 Jun 1985	05:24	ARI
18 Jun 1984	22:18	PIS	16 Dec 1984	01:51	LIB	13 Jun 1985	18:11	TAU
21 Jun 1984	10:40	ARI	18 Dec 1984	04:27	SCO	16 Jun 1985	06:45	GEM
23 Jun 1984	22:37	TAU	20 Dec 1984	06:58	SAG	18 Jun 1985	17:21	CAN
26 Jun 1984	08:03	GEM	22 Dec 1984	10:21	CAP	21 Jun 1985	01:31	LEO
28 Jun 1984	14:08	CAN	24 Dec 1984	15:47	AQU	23 Jun 1985	07:32	VIR
30 Jun 1984	17.23	LEO	27 Dec 1984	00:19	PIS	25 Jun 1985	11:46	LIB
2 Jul 1984	19:27	VIR	29 Dec 1984	11:49	ARI	27 Jun 1985	14:36	SCO
4 Jul 1984	21:26	LIB	1 Jan 1985	00:35	TAU	29 Jun 1985	16:30	SAG
7 Jul 1984	00:28	SCO	3 Jan 1985	11:59	GEM	1 Jul 1985	18:22	CAP
9 Jul 1984	05:03	SAG	5 Jan 1985	20:16	CAN	3 Jul 1985	21:36	AQU
11 Jul 1984	11:23	CAP	8 Jan 1985	01:27	LEO	6 Jul 1985	03:40	PIS
13 Jul 1984	19:41	AQU	10 Jan 1985	04:39	VIR	8 Jul 1985	13:21	ARI
16 Jul 1984	06:10	PIS	12 Jan 1985	07:13	LIB	11 Jul 1985	01:44	TAU
18 Jul 1984	18:25	ARI	14 Jan 1985	10:07	SCO	13 Jul 1985	14:22	GEM
21 Jul 1984	06:52	TAU	16 Jan 1985	13:48	SAG	16 Jul 1985	00:53	CAN
23 Jul 1984	17:09	GEM	18 Jan 1985	18:28	CAP	18 Jul 1985	08:24	LEO
25 Jul 1984	23:42	CAN	21 Jan 1985	00:38	AQU	20 Jul 1985	13:28	VIR
28 Jul 1984	02:40	LEO	23 Jan 1985	09:02	PIS	22 Jul 1985	17:09	LIB
30 Jul 1984	03:28	VIR	25 Jan 1985	20:05	ARI	24 Jul 1985	20:15	SCO
1 Aug 1984	04:03	LIB	28 Jan 1985	08:53	TAU	26 Jul 1985	23:12	SAG
3 Aug 1984	06:03	SCO	30 Jan 1985	20:59	GEM	29 Jul 1985	02:21	CAP
5 Aug 1984	10:30	SAG	2 Feb 1985	05:58	CAN	31 Jul 1985	06:25	AQU
7 Aug 1984	17:24	CAP	4 Feb 1985	11:00	LEO	2 Aug 1985	12:34	PIS
10 Aug 1984	02:25	AQU	6 Feb 1985	13:08	VIR	4 Aug 1985	21:43	ARI
12 Aug 1984	13:13	PIS	8 Feb 1985	14:10	LIB	7 Aug 1985	09:41	TAU
15 Aug 1984	01:28	ARI	10 Feb 1985	15:49	SCO	9 Aug 1985	22:30	GEM
17 Aug 1984	14:12	TAU	12 Feb 1985	19:08	SAG	12 Aug 1985	09:27	CAN
20 Aug 1984	01:30	GEM	15 Feb 1985	00:27	CAP	14 Aug 1985	16:56	LEO
22 Aug 1984	09:18	CAN	17 Feb 1985	07:36	AQU	16 Aug 1985	21:14	VIR
24 Aug 1984	12:58	LEO	19 Feb 1985	16:38	PIS	18 Aug 1985	23:43	LIB
26 Aug 1984	13:31	VIR	22 Feb 1985	03:42	ARI	21 Aug 1985	01:51	SCO
28 Aug 1984	12:57	LIB	24 Feb 1985	16:27	TAU	23 Aug 1985	04:36	SAG
30 Aug 1984	13:24	SCO	27 Feb 1985	05:10	GEM	25 Aug 1985	08:24	CAP
1 Sep 1984	16:30	SAG	1 Mar 1985	15:22	CAN	27 Aug 1985	13:31	AQU
3 Sep 1984	22:55	CAP	3 Mar 1985	21:26	LEO	29 Aug 1985	20:25	PIS
6 Sep 1984	08:11	AQU	5 Mar 1985	23:41	VIR	1 Sep 1985	05:41	ARI
8 Sep 1984	19:24	PIS	7 Mar 1985	23:47	LIB	3 Sep 1985	17:27	TAU
11 Sep 1984	07:46	ARI	9 Mar 1985	23:47	SCO	6 Sep 1985	06:26	GEM
13 Sep 1984	20:32	TAU	12 Mar 1985	01:29	SAG	8 Sep 1985	18:10	CAN
16 Sep 1984	08:25	GEM	14 Mar 1985	05:54	CAP	11 Sep 1985	02:26	LEO
18 Sep 1984	17:35	CAN	16 Mar 1985	13:11	AQU	13 Sep 1985	06:52	VIR
20 Sep 1984	22:47	LEO	18 Mar 1985	22:50	PIS	15 Sep 1985	08:33	LIB
23 Sep 1984	00:17	VIR	21 Mar 1985	10:20	ARI	17 Sep 1985	09:17	SCO
24 Sep 1984	23:40	LIB	23 Mar 1985	23:06	TAU	19 Sep 1985	10:41	SAG
26 Sep 1984	23:04	SCO	26 Mar 1985	12:01	GEM	21 Sep 1985	13:49	CAP
29 Sep 1984	00:33	SAG	28 Mar 1985	23:12	CAN	23 Sep 1985	19:11	AQU
1 Oct 1984	05:27	CAP	31 Mar 1985	06:51	LEO	26 Sep 1985	02:50	PIS
3 Oct 1984	14:03	AQU	2 Apr 1985	10:23	VIR	28 Sep 1985	12:43	ARI
6 Oct 1984	01:19	PIS	4 Apr 1985	10:53	LIB	1 Oct 1985	00:35	TAU
8 Oct 1984	13:50	ARI	6 Apr 1985	10:10	SCO	3 Oct 1985	13:36	GEM
11 Oct 1984	02:27	TAU	8 Apr 1985	10:18	SAG	6 Oct 1985	01:58	CAN
13 Oct 1984	14:13	GEM	10 Apr 1985	12:58	CAP	8 Oct 1985	11:32	LEO
15 Oct 1984	23:58	CAN	12 Apr 1985	19:04	AQU	10 Oct 1985	17:09	VIR
18 Oct 1984	06:40	LEO	15 Apr 1985	04:30	PIS	12 Oct 1985	19:11	LIB
20 Oct 1984	09:54	VIR	17 Apr 1985	16:18	ARI	14 Oct 1985	19:12	SCO
22 Oct 1984	10:31	LIB	20 Apr 1985	05:12	TAU	16 Oct 1985	19:05	SAG
24 Oct 1984	10:08	SCO	22 Apr 1985	18:00	GEM	18 Oct 1985	20:35	CAP
26 Oct 1984	10:44	SAG	25 Apr 1985	05:25	CAN	21 Oct 1985	00:55	AQU
28 Oct 1984	14:05	CAP	27 Apr 1985	14:08	LEO	23 Oct 1985	08:27	PIS
30 Oct 1984	21:14	AQU	29 Apr 1985	19:23	VIR	25 Oct 1985	18:47	ARI
2 Nov 1984	07:49	PIS	1 May 1985	21:21	LIB	28 Oct 1985	06:59	TAU
4 Nov 1984	20:20	ARI	3 May 1985	21:16	SCO	30 Oct 1985	19:58	GEM
7 Nov 1984	08:52	TAU	5 May 1985	20:56	SAG	2 Nov 1985	08:30	CAN
9 Nov 1984	20:09	GEM	7 May 1985	22:12	CAP	4 Nov 1985	19:03	LEO
12 Nov 1984	05:31	CAN	10 May 1985	02:38	AQU	7 Nov 1985	02:17	VIR
14 Nov 1984	12:32	LEO	12 May 1985	10:56	PIS	9 Nov 1985	05:51	LIB

DATE	TIME	SIGN	DATE	TIME	SIGN	DATE	TIME	SIGN
11 Nov 1985	06:30	SCO	9 May 1986	22:25	GEM	5 Nov 1986	15:48	CAP
13 Nov 1985	05:52	SAG	12 May 1986	11:17	CAN	7 Nov 1986	17:28	AQU
15 Nov 1985	05:53	CAP	14 May 1986	23:14	LEO	9 Nov 1986	21:30	PIS
17 Nov 1985	08:26	AQU	17 May 1986	08:44	VIR	12 Nov 1986	04:14	ARI
19 Nov 1985	14:43	PIS	19 May 1986	14:39	LIB	14 Nov 1986	13:24	TAU
22 Nov 1985	00:43	ARI	21 May 1986	17:01	SCO	17 Nov 1986	00:26	GEM
24 Nov 1985	13:06	TAU	23 May 1986	16:56	SAG	19 Nov 1986	12:45	CAN
27 Nov 1985	02:07	GEM	25 May 1986	16:15	CAP	22 Nov 1986	01:24	LEO
29 Nov 1985	14:22	CAN	27 May 1986	17:00	AQU	24 Nov 1986	12:44	VIR
2 Dec 1985	00:58	LEO	29 May 1986	20:55	PIS	26 Nov 1986	20:57	LIB
4 Dec 1985	09:13	VIR	1 Jun 1986	04:43	ARI	29 Nov 1986	01:11	SCO
6 Dec 1985	14:32	LIB	3 Jun 1986	15:45	TAU	1 Dec 1986	02:07	SAG
8 Dec 1985	16:56	SCO	6 Jun 1986	04:26	GEM	3 Dec 1986	01:28	CAP
10 Dec 1985	17:13	SAG	8 Jun 1986	17:15	CAN	5 Dec 1986	01:23	AQU
12 Dec 1985	16:59	CAP	11 Jun 1986	05:11	LEO	7 Dec 1986	03:49	PIS
14 Dec 1985	18:14	AQU	13 Jun 1986	15:17	VIR	9 Dec 1986	09:49	ARI
16 Dec 1985	22:51	PIS	15 Jun 1986	22:36	LIB	11 Dec 1986	19:10	TAU
19 Dec 1985	07:36	ARI	18 Jun 1986	02:35	SCO	14 Dec 1986	06:41	GEM
21 Dec 1985	19:40	TAU	20 Jun 1986	03:35	SAG	16 Dec 1986	19:09	CAN
24 Dec 1985	08:44	GEM	22 Jun 1986	02:59	CAP	19 Dec 1986	07:43	LEO
26 Dec 1985	20:43	CAN	24 Jun 1986	02:50	AQU	21 Dec 1986	19:30	VIR
29 Dec 1985	06:44	LEO	26 Jun 1986	05:12	PIS	24 Dec 1986	05:04	LIB
31 Dec 1985	14:42	VIR	28 Jun 1986	11:35	ARI	26 Dec 1986	11:04	SCO
2 Jan 1986	20:44	LIB	30 Jun 1986	21:54	TAU	28 Dec 1986	13:18	SAG
5 Jan 1986	00:43	SCO	3 Jul 1986	10:31	GEM	30 Dec 1986	12:53	CAP
7 Jan 1986	02:46	SAG	5 Jul 1986	23:18	CAN	1 Jan 1987	11:54	AQU
9 Jan 1986	03:41	CAP	8 Jul 1986	10:55	LEO	3 Jan 1987	12:37	PIS
11 Jan 1986	05:01	AQU	10 Jul 1986	20:49	VIR	5 Jan 1987	16:51	ARI
13 Jan 1986	08:39	PIS	13 Jul 1986	04:39	LIB	8 Jan 1987	01:13	TAU
15 Jan 1986	16:03	ARI	15 Jul 1986	09:57	SCO	10 Jan 1987	12:39	GEM
18 Jan 1986	03:13	TAU	17 Jul 1986	12:33	SAG	13 Jan 1987	01:18	CAN
20 Jan 1986	16:11	GEM	19 Jul 1986	13:09	CAP	15 Jan 1987	13:44	LEO
23 Jan 1986	04:14	CAN	21 Jul 1986	13:18	AQU	18 Jan 1987	01:14	VIR
25 Jan 1986	13:46	LEO	23 Jul 1986	14:59	PIS	20 Jan 1987	11:08	LIB
27 Jan 1986	20:50	VIR	25 Jul 1986	20:03	ARI	22 Jan 1987	18:30	SCO
30 Jan 1986	02:09	LIB	28 Jul 1986	05:11	TAU	24 Jan 1987	22:34	SAG
1 Feb 1986	06:19	SCO	30 Jul 1986	17:19	GEM	26 Jan 1987	23:41	CAP
3 Feb 1986	09:31	SAG	2 Aug 1986	06:03	CAN	28 Jan 1987	23:17	AQU
5 Feb 1986	12:01	CAP	4 Aug 1986	17:26	LEO	30 Jan 1987	23:25	PIS
7 Feb 1986	14:35	AQU	7 Aug 1986	02:43	VIR	2 Feb 1987	02:10	ARI
9 Feb 1986	18:32	PIS	9 Aug 1986	10:03	LIB	4 Feb 1987	08:53	TAU
12 Feb 1986	01:21	ARI	11 Aug 1986	15:35	SCO	6 Feb 1987	19:23	GEM
14 Feb 1986	11:38	TAU	13 Aug 1986	19:16	SAG	9 Feb 1987	07:55	CAN
17 Feb 1986	00:16	GEM	15 Aug 1986	21:22	CAP	11 Feb 1987	20:20	LEO
19 Feb 1986	12:38	CAN	17 Aug 1986	22:44	AQU	14 Feb 1987	07:25	VIR
21 Feb 1986	22:23	LEO	20 Aug 1986	00:52	PIS	16 Feb 1987	16:44	LIB
24 Feb 1986	04:57	VIR	22 Aug 1986	05:27	ARI	19 Feb 1987	00:03	SCO
26 Feb 1986	09:06	LIB	24 Aug 1986	13:37	TAU	21 Feb 1987	05:08	SAG
28 Feb 1986	12:05	SCO	27 Aug 1986	01:00	GEM	23 Feb 1987	07:56	CAP
2 Mar 1986	14:51	SAG	29 Aug 1986	13:39	CAN	25 Feb 1987	09:08	AQU
4 Mar 1986	17:55	CAP	1 Sep 1986	01:07	LEO	27 Feb 1987	10:07	PIS
6 Mar 1986	21:42	AQU	3 Sep 1986	10:04	VIR	1 Mar 1987	12:37	ARI
9 Mar 1986	02:48	PIS	5 Sep 1986	16:33	LIB	3 Mar 1987	18:11	TAU
11 Mar 1986	10:04	ARI	7 Sep 1986	21:11	SCO	6 Mar 1987	03:26	GEM
13 Mar 1986	20:04	TAU	10 Sep 1986	00:39	SAG	8 Mar 1987	15:24	CAN
16 Mar 1986	08:22	GEM	12 Sep 1986	03:27	CAP	11 Mar 1987	03:54	LEO
18 Mar 1986	21:03	CAN	14 Sep 1986	06:06	AQU	13 Mar 1987	14:54	VIR
21 Mar 1986	07:37	LEO	16 Sep 1986	09:27	PIS	15 Mar 1987	23:33	LIB
23 Mar 1986	14:38	VIR	18 Sep 1986	14:34	ARI	18 Mar 1987	05:56	SCO
25 Mar 1986	18:22	LIB	20 Sep 1986	22:26	TAU	20 Mar 1987	10:31	SAG
27 Mar 1986	20:05	SCO	23 Sep 1986	09:13	GEM	22 Mar 1987	13:48	CAP
29 Mar 1986	21:20	SAG	25 Sep 1986	21:44	CAN	24 Mar 1987	16:18	AQU
31 Mar 1986	23:25	CAP	28 Sep 1986	09:38	LEO	26 Mar 1987	18:45	PIS
3 Apr 1986	03:11	AQU	30 Sep 1986	18:57	VIR	28 Mar 1987	22:12	ARI
5 Apr 1986	09:04	PIS	3 Oct 1986	01:01	LIB	31 Mar 1987	03:46	TAU
7 Apr 1986	17:12	ARI	5 Oct 1986	04:34	SCO	2 Apr 1987	12:17	GEM
10 Apr 1986	03:36	TAU	7 Oct 1986	06:47	SAG	4 Apr 1987	23:33	CAN
12 Apr 1986	15:50	GEM	9 Oct 1986	08:52	CAP	7 Apr 1987	12:03	LEO
15 Apr 1986	04:41	CAN	11 Oct 1986	11:45	AQU	9 Apr 1987	23:27	VIR
17 Apr 1986	16:09	LEO	13 Oct 1986	16:03	PIS	12 Apr 1987	08:04	LIB
20 Apr 1986	00:22	VIR	15 Oct 1986	22:13	ARI	14 Apr 1987	13:39	SCO
22 Apr 1986	04:49	LIB	18 Oct 1986	06:35	TAU	16 Apr 1987	17:01	SAG
24 Apr 1986	06:15	SCO	20 Oct 1986	17:15	GEM	18 Apr 1987	19:20	CAP
26 Apr 1986	06:16	SAG	23 Oct 1986	05:37	CAN	20 Apr 1987	21:45	AQU
28 Apr 1986	06:40	CAP	25 Oct 1986	18:02	LEO	23 Apr 1987	01:02	PIS
30 Apr 1986	09:06	AQU	28 Oct 1986	04:19	VIR	25 Apr 1987	05:40	ARI
2 May 1986	14:31	PIS	30 Oct 1986	11:03	LIB	27 Apr 1987	12:06	TAU
4 May 1986	23:01	ARI	1 Nov 1986	14:18	SCO	29 Apr 1987	20:43	GEM
7 May 1986	09:59	TAU	3 Nov 1986	15:18	SAG	2 May 1987	07:39	CAN

DATE	TIME	SIGN
4 May 1987	20:06	LEO
7 May 1987	08:06	VIR
9 May 1987	17:28	LIB
11 May 1987	23:07	SCO
14 May 1987	01:40	SAG
16 May 1987	02:36	CAP
18 May 1987	03:42	AQU
20 May 1987	06:24	PIS
22 May 1987	11:23	ARI
24 May 1987	18:39	TAU
27 May 1987	03:55	GEM
29 May 1987	14:59	CAN
1 Jun 1987	03:25	LEO
3 Jun 1987	15:55	VIR
6 Jun 1987	02:23	LIB
8 Jun 1987	09:05	SCO
10 Jun 1987	11:51	SAG
12 Jun 1987	12:04	CAP
14 Jun 1987	11:45	AQU
16 Jun 1987	12:55	PIS
18 Jun 1987	16:56	ARI
21 Jun 1987	00:09	TAU
23 Jun 1987	09:54	GEM
25 Jun 1987	21:22	CAN
28 Jun 1987	09:52	LEO
30 Jun 1987	22:33	VIR
3 Jul 1987	09:53	LIB
5 Jul 1987	18:02	SCO
7 Jul 1987	22:03	SAG
9 Jul 1987	22:42	CAP
11 Jul 1987	21:49	AQU
13 Jul 1987	21:36	PIS
16 Jul 1987	00:01	ARI
18 Jul 1987	06:04	TAU
20 Jul 1987	15:33	GEM
23 Jul 1987	03:13	CAN
25 Jul 1987	15:49	LEO
28 Jul 1987	04:25	VIR
30 Jul 1987	15:59	LIB
2 Aug 1987	01:08	SCO
4 Aug 1987	06:46	SAG
6 Aug 1987	08:50	CAP
8 Aug 1987	08:36	AQU
10 Aug 1987	08:01	PIS
12 Aug 1987	09:10	ARI
14 Aug 1987	13:39	TAU
16 Aug 1987	21:59	GEM
19 Aug 1987	09:19	CAN
21 Aug 1987	21:57	LEO
24 Aug 1987	10:22	VIR
26 Aug 1987	21:34	LIB
29 Aug 1987	06:48	SCO
31 Aug 1987	13:22	SAG
2 Sep 1987	17:03	CAP
4 Sep 1987	18:21	AQU
6 Sep 1987	18:36	PIS
8 Sep 1987	19:34	ARI
10 Sep 1987	22:58	TAU
13 Sep 1987	05:54	GEM
15 Sep 1987	16:22	CAN
18 Sep 1987	04:50	LEO
20 Sep 1987	17:12	VIR
23 Sep 1987	03:57	LIB
25 Sep 1987	12:29	SCO
27 Sep 1987	18:48	SAG
29 Sep 1987	23:07	CAP
2 Oct 1987	01:50	AQU
4 Oct 1987	03:39	PIS
6 Oct 1987	05:34	ARI
8 Oct 1987	08:58	TAU
10 Oct 1987	15:04	GEM
13 Oct 1987	00:31	CAN
15 Oct 1987	12:34	LEO
18 Oct 1987	01:05	VIR
20 Oct 1987	11:48	LIB
22 Oct 1987	19:41	SCO
25 Oct 1987	00:56	SAG
27 Oct 1987	04:32	CAP
29 Oct 1987	07:26	AQU

DATE	TIME	SIGN
31 Oct 1987	10:19	PIS
2 Nov 1987	13:40	ARI
4 Nov 1987	18:01	TAU
7 Nov 1987	00:16	GEM
9 Nov 1987	09:10	CAN
11 Nov 1987	20:45	LEO
14 Nov 1987	09:28	VIR
16 Nov 1987	20:47	LIB
19 Nov 1987	04:46	SCO
21 Nov 1987	09:15	SAG
23 Nov 1987	11:31	CAP
25 Nov 1987	13:12	AQU
27 Nov 1987	15:40	PIS
29 Nov 1987	19:36	ARI
2 Dec 1987	01:06	TAU
4 Dec 1987	08:13	GEM
6 Dec 1987	17:20	CAN
9 Dec 1987	04:40	LEO
11 Dec 1987	17:30	VIR
14 Dec 1987	05:39	LIB
16 Dec 1987	14:39	SCO
18 Dec 1987	19:32	SAG
20 Dec 1987	21:07	CAP
22 Dec 1987	21:20	AQU
24 Dec 1987	22:10	PIS
27 Dec 1987	01:06	ARI
29 Dec 1987	06:36	TAU
31 Dec 1987	14:29	GEM
3 Jan 1988	00:17	CAN
5 Jan 1988	11:47	LEO
8 Jan 1988	00:35	VIR
10 Jan 1988	13:16	LIB
12 Jan 1988	23:37	SCO
15 Jan 1988	05:58	SAG
17 Jan 1988	08:14	CAP
19 Jan 1988	08:01	AQU
21 Jan 1988	07:26	PIS
23 Jan 1988	08:31	ARI
25 Jan 1988	12:37	TAU
27 Jan 1988	20:02	GEM
30 Jan 1988	06:11	CAN
1 Feb 1988	18:05	LEO
4 Feb 1988	06:54	VIR
6 Feb 1988	19:35	LIB
9 Feb 1988	06:41	SCO
11 Feb 1988	14:34	SAG
13 Feb 1988	18:36	CAP
15 Feb 1988	19:24	AQU
17 Feb 1988	18:43	PIS
19 Feb 1988	18:35	ARI
21 Feb 1988	20:51	TAU
24 Feb 1988	02:43	GEM
26 Feb 1988	12:12	CAN
29 Feb 1988	00:12	LEO
2 Mar 1988	13:06	VIR
5 Mar 1988	01:31	LIB
7 Mar 1988	12:26	SCO
9 Mar 1988	20:57	SAG
12 Mar 1988	02:30	CAP
14 Mar 1988	05:07	AQU
16 Mar 1988	05:41	PIS
18 Mar 1988	05:45	ARI
20 Mar 1988	07:05	TAU
22 Mar 1988	11:22	GEM
24 Mar 1988	19:27	CAN
27 Mar 1988	06:53	LEO
29 Mar 1988	19:48	VIR
1 Apr 1988	08:04	LIB
3 Apr 1988	18:25	SCO
6 Apr 1988	02:28	SAG
8 Apr 1988	08:18	CAP
10 Apr 1988	12:09	AQU
12 Apr 1988	14:23	PIS
14 Apr 1988	15:46	ARI
16 Apr 1988	17:31	TAU
18 Apr 1988	21:10	GEM
21 Apr 1988	04:05	CAN
23 Apr 1988	14:34	LEO
26 Apr 1988	03:15	VIR

DATE	TIME	SIGN
28 Apr 1988	15:36	LIB
1 May 1988	01:38	SCO
3 May 1988	08:51	SAG
5 May 1988	13:53	CAP
7 May 1988	17:36	AQU
9 May 1988	20:38	PIS
11 May 1988	23:23	ARI
14 May 1988	02:22	TAU
16 May 1988	06:31	GEM
18 May 1988	13:06	CAN
20 May 1988	22:52	LEO
23 May 1988	11:12	VIR
25 May 1988	23:48	LIB
28 May 1988	10:05	SCO
30 May 1988	16:56	SAG
1 Jun 1988	20:58	CAP
3 Jun 1988	23:33	AQU
6 Jun 1988	02:00	PIS
8 Jun 1988	05:03	ARI
10 Jun 1988	09:02	TAU
12 Jun 1988	14:14	GEM
14 Jun 1988	21:19	CAN
17 Jun 1988	06:57	LEO
19 Jun 1988	19:03	VIR
22 Jun 1988	07:56	LIB
24 Jun 1988	18:57	SCO
27 Jun 1988	02:16	SAG
29 Jun 1988	05:59	CAP
1 Jul 1988	07:29	AQU
3 Jul 1988	08:33	PIS
5 Jul 1988	10:37	ARI
7 Jul 1988	14:27	TAU
9 Jul 1988	20:16	GEM
12 Jul 1988	04:08	CAN
14 Jul 1988	14:11	LEO
17 Jul 1988	02:17	VIR
19 Jul 1988	15:21	LIB
22 Jul 1988	03:12	SCO
24 Jul 1988	11:40	SAG
26 Jul 1988	16:06	CAP
28 Jul 1988	17:24	AQU
30 Jul 1988	17:22	PIS
1 Aug 1988	17:53	ARI
3 Aug 1988	20:24	TAU
6 Aug 1988	01:43	GEM
8 Aug 1988	09:52	CAN
10 Aug 1988	20:26	LEO
13 Aug 1988	08:45	VIR
15 Aug 1988	21:51	LIB
18 Aug 1988	10:10	SCO
20 Aug 1988	19:53	SAG
23 Aug 1988	01:47	CAP
25 Aug 1988	04:04	AQU
27 Aug 1988	04:00	PIS
29 Aug 1988	03:29	ARI
31 Aug 1988	04:22	TAU
2 Sep 1988	08:11	GEM
4 Sep 1988	15:37	CAN
7 Sep 1988	02:14	LEO
9 Sep 1988	14:47	VIR
12 Sep 1988	03:50	LIB
14 Sep 1988	16:06	SCO
17 Sep 1988	02:24	SAG
19 Sep 1988	09:43	CAP
21 Sep 1988	13:41	AQU
23 Sep 1988	14:50	PIS
25 Sep 1988	14:29	ARI
27 Sep 1988	14:29	TAU
29 Sep 1988	16:43	GEM
1 Oct 1988	22:39	CAN
4 Oct 1988	08:31	LEO
6 Oct 1988	21:01	VIR
9 Oct 1988	10:03	LIB
11 Oct 1988	21:57	SCO
14 Oct 1988	07:57	SAG
16 Oct 1988	15:43	CAP
18 Oct 1988	21:04	AQU
20 Oct 1988	23:57	PIS
23 Oct 1988	00:58	ARI

DATE	TIME	SIGN	DATE	TIME	SIGN	DATE	TIME	SIGN
25 Oct 1988	01:22	TAU	23 Apr 1989	12:37	SAG	19 Oct 1989	11:10	CAN
27 Oct 1988	02:56	GEM	25 Apr 1989	22:14	CAP	21 Oct 1989	16:47	LEO
29 Oct 1988	07:28	CAN	28 Apr 1989	05:32	AQU	24 Oct 1989	02:15	VIR
31 Oct 1988	16:03	LEO	30 Apr 1989	10:02	PIS	26 Oct 1989	14:11	LIB
3 Nov 1988	04:01	VIR	2 May 1989	11:49	ARI	29 Oct 1989	02:55	SCO
5 Nov 1988	17:03	LIB	4 May 1989	11:54	TAU	31 Oct 1989	15:22	SAG
8 Nov 1988	04:45	SCO	6 May 1989	12:04	GEM	3 Nov 1989	02:45	CAP
10 Nov 1988	14:04	SAG	8 May 1989	14:20	CAN	5 Nov 1989	12:08	AQU
12 Nov 1988	21:11	CAP	10 May 1989	20:23	LEO	7 Nov 1989	18:24	PIS
15 Nov 1988	02:35	AQU	13 May 1989	06:30	VIR	9 Nov 1989	21:07	ARI
17 Nov 1988	06:33	PIS	15 May 1989	19:07	LIB	11 Nov 1989	21:08	TAU
19 Nov 1988	09:12	ARI	18 May 1989	07:47	SCO	13 Nov 1989	20:19	GEM
21 Nov 1988	11:01	TAU	20 May 1989	18:51	SAG	15 Nov 1989	20:52	CAN
23 Nov 1988	13:12	GEM	23 May 1989	03:53	CAP	18 Nov 1989	00:47	LEO
25 Nov 1988	17:19	CAN	25 May 1989	11:00	AQU	20 Nov 1989	08:55	VIR
28 Nov 1988	00:52	LEO	27 May 1989	16:12	PIS	22 Nov 1989	20:25	LIB
30 Nov 1988	12:00	VIR	29 May 1989	19:25	ARI	25 Nov 1989	09:12	SCO
3 Dec 1988	00:55	LIB	31 May 1989	20:59	TAU	27 Nov 1989	21:29	SAG
5 Dec 1988	12:50	SCO	2 Jun 1989	22:02	GEM	30 Nov 1989	08:25	CAP
7 Dec 1988	21:54	SAG	5 Jun 1989	00:18	CAN	2 Dec 1989	17:41	AQU
10 Dec 1988	04:06	CAP	7 Jun 1989	05:28	LEO	5 Dec 1989	00:46	PIS
12 Dec 1988	08:25	AQU	9 Jun 1989	14:30	VIR	7 Dec 1989	05:11	ARI
14 Dec 1988	11:52	PIS	12 Jun 1989	02:31	LIB	9 Dec 1989	06:58	TAU
16 Dec 1988	15:03	ARI	14 Jun 1989	15:10	SCO	11 Dec 1989	07:14	GEM
18 Dec 1988	18:10	TAU	17 Jun 1989	02:11	SAG	13 Dec 1989	07:49	CAN
20 Dec 1988	21:43	GEM	19 Jun 1989	10:40	CAP	15 Dec 1989	10:42	LEO
23 Dec 1988	02:35	CAN	21 Jun 1989	16:56	AQU	17 Dec 1989	17:19	VIR
25 Dec 1988	09:58	LEO	23 Jun 1989	21:35	PIS	20 Dec 1989	03:45	LIB
27 Dec 1988	20:27	VIR	26 Jun 1989	01:05	ARI	22 Dec 1989	16:18	SCO
30 Dec 1988	09:09	LIB	28 Jun 1989	03:44	TAU	25 Dec 1989	04:36	SAG
1 Jan 1989	21:32	SCO	30 Jun 1989	06:08	GEM	27 Dec 1989	15:09	CAP
4 Jan 1989	07:11	SAG	2 Jul 1989	09:19	CAN	29 Dec 1989	23:36	AQU
6 Jan 1989	13:12	CAP	4 Jul 1989	14:38	LEO	1 Jan 1990	06:10	PIS
8 Jan 1989	16:30	AQU	6 Jul 1989	23:05	VIR	3 Jan 1990	10:55	ARI
10 Jan 1989	18:30	PIS	9 Jul 1989	10:30	LIB	5 Jan 1990	14:03	TAU
12 Jan 1989	20:35	ARI	11 Jul 1989	23:08	SCO	7 Jan 1990	16:01	GEM
14 Jan 1989	23:36	TAU	14 Jul 1989	10:30	SAG	9 Jan 1990	17:51	CAN
17 Jan 1989	03:56	GEM	16 Jul 1989	19:00	CAP	11 Jan 1990	21:03	LEO
19 Jan 1989	09:57	CAN	19 Jul 1989	00:34	AQU	14 Jan 1990	02:58	VIR
21 Jan 1989	18:02	LEO	21 Jul 1989	04:06	PIS	16 Jan 1990	12:18	LIB
24 Jan 1989	04:32	VIR	23 Jul 1989	06:40	ARI	19 Jan 1990	00:16	SCO
26 Jan 1989	17:01	LIB	25 Jul 1989	09:10	TAU	21 Jan 1990	12:43	SAG
29 Jan 1989	05:48	SCO	27 Jul 1989	12:15	GEM	23 Jan 1990	23:26	CAP
31 Jan 1989	16:29	SAG	29 Jul 1989	16:31	CAN	26 Jan 1990	07:24	AQU
2 Feb 1989	23:28	CAP	31 Jul 1989	22:41	LEO	28 Jan 1990	12:49	PIS
5 Feb 1989	02:50	AQU	3 Aug 1989	07:19	VIR	30 Jan 1990	16:33	ARI
7 Feb 1989	03:51	PIS	5 Aug 1989	18:28	LIB	1 Feb 1990	19:27	TAU
9 Feb 1989	04:17	ARI	8 Aug 1989	07:04	SCO	3 Feb 1990	22:12	GEM
11 Feb 1989	05:44	TAU	10 Aug 1989	19:01	SAG	6 Feb 1990	01:27	CAN
13 Feb 1989	09:23	GEM	13 Aug 1989	04:15	CAP	8 Feb 1990	05:51	LEO
15 Feb 1989	15:40	CAN	15 Aug 1989	09:57	AQU	10 Feb 1990	12:13	VIR
18 Feb 1989	00:33	LEO	17 Aug 1989	12:44	PIS	12 Feb 1990	21:09	LIB
20 Feb 1989	11:34	VIR	19 Aug 1989	13:58	ARI	15 Feb 1990	08:34	SCO
23 Feb 1989	00:04	LIB	21 Aug 1989	15:10	TAU	17 Feb 1990	21:06	SAG
25 Feb 1989	12:56	SCO	23 Aug 1989	17:38	GEM	20 Feb 1990	08:29	CAP
28 Feb 1989	00:28	SAG	25 Aug 1989	22:13	CAN	22 Feb 1990	16:51	AQU
2 Mar 1989	08:56	CAP	28 Aug 1989	05:11	LEO	24 Feb 1990	21:48	PIS
4 Mar 1989	13:35	AQU	30 Aug 1989	14:29	VIR	27 Feb 1990	00:15	ARI
6 Mar 1989	14:58	PIS	2 Sep 1989	01:47	LIB	1 Mar 1990	01:42	TAU
8 Mar 1989	14:36	ARI	4 Sep 1989	14:23	SCO	3 Mar 1990	03:37	GEM
10 Mar 1989	14:25	TAU	7 Sep 1989	02:50	SAG	5 Mar 1990	07:02	CAN
12 Mar 1989	16:16	GEM	9 Sep 1989	13:11	CAP	7 Mar 1990	12:25	LEO
14 Mar 1989	21:28	CAN	11 Sep 1989	20:00	AQU	9 Mar 1990	19:47	VIR
17 Mar 1989	06:12	LEO	13 Sep 1989	23:06	PIS	12 Mar 1990	05:08	LIB
19 Mar 1989	17:39	VIR	15 Sep 1989	23:37	ARI	14 Mar 1990	16:25	SCO
22 Mar 1989	06:23	LIB	17 Sep 1989	23:22	TAU	17 Mar 1990	04:56	SAG
24 Mar 1989	19:10	SCO	20 Sep 1989	00:16	GEM	19 Mar 1990	17:01	CAP
27 Mar 1989	06:53	SAG	22 Sep 1989	03:51	CAN	22 Mar 1990	02:29	AQU
29 Mar 1989	16:24	CAP	24 Sep 1989	10:45	LEO	24 Mar 1990	08:07	PIS
31 Mar 1989	22:43	AQU	26 Sep 1989	20:32	VIR	26 Mar 1990	10:14	ARI
3 Apr 1989	01:35	PIS	29 Sep 1989	08:14	LIB	28 Mar 1990	10:26	TAU
5 Apr 1989	01:50	ARI	1 Oct 1989	20:52	SCO	30 Mar 1990	10:42	GEM
7 Apr 1989	01:07	TAU	4 Oct 1989	09:28	SAG	1 Apr 1990	12:50	CAN
9 Apr 1989	01:32	GEM	6 Oct 1989	20:44	CAP	3 Apr 1990	17:49	LEO
11 Apr 1989	04:58	CAN	9 Oct 1989	05:06	AQU	6 Apr 1990	01:42	VIR
13 Apr 1989	12:32	LEO	11 Oct 1989	09:36	PIS	8 Apr 1990	11:44	LIB
15 Apr 1989	23:39	VIR	13 Oct 1989	10:40	ARI	10 Apr 1990	23:17	SCO
18 Apr 1989	12:31	LIB	15 Oct 1989	09:52	TAU	13 Apr 1990	11:47	SAG
21 Apr 1989	01:12	SCO	17 Oct 1989	09:19	GEM	16 Apr 1990	00:14	CAP

DATE	TIME	SIGN	DATE	TIME	SIGN	DATE	TIME	SIGN
18 Apr 1990	10:51	AQU	14 Oct 1990	07:20	VIR	13 Apr 1991	01:48	ARI
20 Apr 1990	17:56	PIS	16 Oct 1990	15:26	LIB	15 Apr 1991	05:05	TAU
22 Apr 1990	20:57	ARI	19 Oct 1990	01:24	SCO	17 Apr 1991	06:41	GEM
24 Apr 1990	21:02	TAU	21 Oct 1990	13:09	SAG	19 Apr 1991	08:17	CAN
26 Apr 1990	20:12	GEM	24 Oct 1990	02:02	CAP	21 Apr 1991	11:04	LEO
28 Apr 1990	20:39	CAN	26 Oct 1990	14:13	AQU	23 Apr 1991	15:29	VIR
1 May 1990	00:09	LEO	28 Oct 1990	23:20	PIS	25 Apr 1991	21:36	LIB
3 May 1990	07:18	VIR	31 Oct 1990	04:13	ARI	28 Apr 1991	05:33	SCO
5 May 1990	17:28	LIB	2 Nov 1990	05:31	TAU	30 Apr 1991	15:42	SAG
8 May 1990	05:22	SCO	4 Nov 1990	05:05	GEM	3 May 1991	03:54	CAP
10 May 1990	17:56	SAG	6 Nov 1990	05:07	CAN	5 May 1991	16:50	AQU
13 May 1990	06:20	CAP	8 Nov 1990	07:24	LEO	8 May 1991	04:03	PIS
15 May 1990	17:29	AQU	10 Nov 1990	12:49	VIR	10 May 1991	11:33	ARI
18 May 1990	01:52	PIS	12 Nov 1990	21:08	LIB	12 May 1991	15:06	TAU
20 May 1990	06:31	ARI	15 Nov 1990	07:39	SCO	14 May 1991	16:01	GEM
22 May 1990	07:41	TAU	17 Nov 1990	19:39	SAG	16 May 1991	16:13	CAN
24 May 1990	06:59	GEM	20 Nov 1990	08:31	CAP	18 May 1991	17:30	LEO
26 May 1990	06:33	CAN	22 Nov 1990	21:06	AQU	20 May 1991	21:00	VIR
28 May 1990	08:30	LEO	25 Nov 1990	07:31	PIS	23 May 1991	03:08	LIB
30 May 1990	14:08	VIR	27 Nov 1990	14:04	ARI	25 May 1991	11:41	SCO
1 Jun 1990	23:31	LIB	29 Nov 1990	16:36	TAU	27 May 1991	22:21	SAG
4 Jun 1990	11:21	SCO	1 Dec 1990	16:22	GEM	30 May 1991	10:40	CAP
6 Jun 1990	23:59	SAG	3 Dec 1990	15:27	CAN	1 Jun 1991	23:41	AQU
9 Jun 1990	12:11	CAP	5 Dec 1990	16:00	LEO	4 Jun 1991	11:35	PIS
11 Jun 1990	23:08	AQU	7 Dec 1990	19:39	VIR	6 Jun 1991	20:24	ARI
14 Jun 1990	07:59	PIS	10 Dec 1990	03:00	LIB	9 Jun 1991	01:11	TAU
16 Jun 1990	13:53	ARI	12 Dec 1990	13:28	SCO	11 Jun 1991	02:35	GEM
18 Jun 1990	16:42	TAU	15 Dec 1990	01:43	SAG	13 Jun 1991	02:16	CAN
20 Jun 1990	17:14	GEM	17 Dec 1990	14:34	CAP	15 Jun 1991	02:11	LEO
22 Jun 1990	17:09	CAN	20 Dec 1990	02:58	AQU	17 Jun 1991	04:03	VIR
24 Jun 1990	18:24	LEO	22 Dec 1990	13:46	PIS	19 Jun 1991	09:02	LIB
26 Jun 1990	22:43	VIR	24 Dec 1990	21:43	ARI	21 Jun 1991	17:18	SCO
29 Jun 1990	06:47	LIB	27 Dec 1990	02:07	TAU	24 Jun 1991	04:16	SAG
1 Jul 1990	18:00	SCO	29 Dec 1990	03:25	GEM	26 Jun 1991	16:49	CAP
4 Jul 1990	06:35	SAG	31 Dec 1990	03:02	CAN	29 Jun 1991	05:47	AQU
6 Jul 1990	18:39	CAP	2 Jan 1991	02:54	LEO	1 Jul 1991	17:50	PIS
9 Jul 1990	05:06	AQU	4 Jan 1991	04:57	VIR	4 Jul 1991	03:32	ARI
11 Jul 1990	13:28	PIS	6 Jan 1991	10:34	LIB	6 Jul 1991	09:50	TAU
13 Jul 1990	19:35	ARI	8 Jan 1991	19:59	SCO	8 Jul 1991	12:40	GEM
15 Jul 1990	23:27	TAU	11 Jan 1991	08:06	SAG	10 Jul 1991	13:02	CAN
18 Jul 1990	01:31	GEM	13 Jan 1991	20:59	CAP	12 Jul 1991	12:35	LEO
20 Jul 1990	02:43	CAN	16 Jan 1991	09:03	AQU	14 Jul 1991	13:12	VIR
22 Jul 1990	04:28	LEO	18 Jan 1991	19:22	PIS	16 Jul 1991	16:34	LIB
24 Jul 1990	08:18	VIR	21 Jan 1991	03:26	ARI	18 Jul 1991	23:41	SCO
26 Jul 1990	15:19	LIB	23 Jan 1991	08:59	TAU	21 Jul 1991	10:17	SAG
29 Jul 1990	01:39	SCO	25 Jan 1991	12:05	GEM	23 Jul 1991	22:55	CAP
31 Jul 1990	13:59	SAG	27 Jan 1991	13:22	CAN	26 Jul 1991	11:48	AQU
3 Aug 1990	02:07	CAP	29 Jan 1991	14:03	LEO	28 Jul 1991	23:33	PIS
5 Aug 1990	12:18	AQU	31 Jan 1991	15:44	VIR	31 Jul 1991	09:19	ARI
7 Aug 1990	19:53	PIS	2 Feb 1991	20:02	LIB	2 Aug 1991	16:31	TAU
10 Aug 1990	01:12	ARI	5 Feb 1991	04:01	SCO	4 Aug 1991	20:53	GEM
12 Aug 1990	04:54	TAU	7 Feb 1991	15:23	SAG	6 Aug 1991	22:46	CAN
14 Aug 1990	07:41	GEM	10 Feb 1991	04:15	CAP	8 Aug 1991	23:09	LEO
16 Aug 1990	10:12	CAN	12 Feb 1991	16:16	AQU	10 Aug 1991	23:35	VIR
18 Aug 1990	13:11	LEO	15 Feb 1991	01:57	PIS	13 Aug 1991	01:53	LIB
20 Aug 1990	17:33	VIR	17 Feb 1991	09:10	ARI	15 Aug 1991	07:34	SCO
23 Aug 1990	00:17	LIB	19 Feb 1991	14:23	TAU	17 Aug 1991	17:10	SAG
25 Aug 1990	09:56	SCO	21 Feb 1991	18:10	GEM	20 Aug 1991	05:34	CAP
27 Aug 1990	21:57	SAG	23 Feb 1991	20:56	CAN	22 Aug 1991	18:26	AQU
30 Aug 1990	10:22	CAP	25 Feb 1991	23:12	LEO	25 Aug 1991	05:51	PIS
1 Sep 1990	20:50	AQU	28 Feb 1991	01:50	VIR	27 Aug 1991	15:00	ARI
4 Sep 1990	04:04	PIS	2 Mar 1991	06:03	LIB	29 Aug 1991	21:58	TAU
6 Sep 1990	08:22	ARI	4 Mar 1991	13:09	SCO	1 Sep 1991	03:01	GEM
8 Sep 1990	10:55	TAU	6 Mar 1991	23:35	SAG	3 Sep 1991	06:19	CAN
10 Sep 1990	13:04	GEM	9 Mar 1991	12:13	CAP	5 Sep 1991	08:12	LEO
12 Sep 1990	15:52	CAN	12 Mar 1991	00:29	AQU	7 Sep 1991	09:35	VIR
14 Sep 1990	19:52	LEO	14 Mar 1991	10:09	PIS	9 Sep 1991	11:52	LIB
17 Sep 1990	01:19	VIR	16 Mar 1991	16:37	ARI	11 Sep 1991	16:42	SCO
19 Sep 1990	08:34	LIB	18 Mar 1991	20:40	TAU	14 Sep 1991	01:15	SAG
21 Sep 1990	18:05	SCO	20 Mar 1991	23:36	GEM	16 Sep 1991	13:03	CAP
24 Sep 1990	05:52	SAG	23 Mar 1991	02:27	CAN	19 Sep 1991	01:57	AQU
26 Sep 1990	18:36	CAP	25 Mar 1991	05:43	LEO	21 Sep 1991	13:19	PIS
29 Sep 1990	05:53	AQU	27 Mar 1991	09:41	VIR	23 Sep 1991	21:54	ARI
1 Oct 1990	13:40	PIS	29 Mar 1991	14:49	LIB	26 Sep 1991	03:58	TAU
3 Oct 1990	17:41	ARI	31 Mar 1991	22:01	SCO	28 Sep 1991	08:25	GEM
5 Oct 1990	19:05	TAU	3 Apr 1991	07:59	SAG	30 Sep 1991	11:57	CAN
7 Oct 1990	19:47	GEM	5 Apr 1991	20:19	CAP	2 Oct 1991	14:58	LEO
9 Oct 1990	21:30	CAN	8 Apr 1991	08:58	AQU	4 Oct 1991	17:44	VIR
12 Oct 1990	01:17	LEO	10 Apr 1991	19:17	PIS	6 Oct 1991	21:00	LIB

DATE	TIME	SIGN	DATE	TIME	SIGN	DATE	TIME	SIGN
9 Oct 1991	02:00	SCO	6 Apr 1992	17:32	GEM	2 Oct 1992	17:29	CAP
11 Oct 1991	09:58	SAG	8 Apr 1992	22:17	CAN	5 Oct 1992	04:52	AQU
13 Oct 1991	21:10	CAP	11 Apr 1992	01:45	LEO	7 Oct 1992	17:37	PIS
16 Oct 1991	10:04	AQU	13 Apr 1992	04:08	VIR	10 Oct 1992	05:35	ARI
18 Oct 1991	21:51	PIS	15 Apr 1992	06:10	LIB	12 Oct 1992	15:47	TAU
21 Oct 1991	06:32	ARI	17 Apr 1992	09:10	SCO	15 Oct 1992	00:07	GEM
23 Oct 1991	11:54	TAU	19 Apr 1992	14:41	SAG	17 Oct 1992	06:35	CAN
25 Oct 1991	15:08	GEM	21 Apr 1992	23:41	CAP	19 Oct 1992	11:00	LEO
27 Oct 1991	17:36	CAN	24 Apr 1992	11:38	AQU	21 Oct 1992	13:26	VIR
29 Oct 1991	20:20	LEO	27 Apr 1992	00:19	PIS	23 Oct 1992	14:39	LIB
31 Oct 1991	23:46	VIR	29 Apr 1992	11:12	ARI	25 Oct 1992	16:04	SCO
3 Nov 1991	04:12	LIB	1 May 1992	19:08	TAU	27 Oct 1992	19:29	SAG
5 Nov 1991	10:09	SCO	4 May 1992	00:27	GEM	30 Oct 1992	02:18	CAP
7 Nov 1991	18:21	SAG	6 May 1992	04:09	CAN	1 Nov 1992	12:43	AQU
10 Nov 1991	05:16	CAP	8 May 1992	07:07	LEO	4 Nov 1992	01:12	PIS
12 Nov 1991	18:06	AQU	10 May 1992	09:56	VIR	6 Nov 1992	13:18	ARI
15 Nov 1991	06:33	PIS	12 May 1992	13:05	LIB	8 Nov 1992	23:18	TAU
17 Nov 1991	16:06	ARI	14 May 1992	17:15	SCO	11 Nov 1992	06:49	GEM
19 Nov 1991	21:47	TAU	16 May 1992	23:22	SAG	13 Nov 1992	12:18	CAN
22 Nov 1991	00:21	GEM	19 May 1992	08:13	CAP	15 Nov 1992	16:22	LEO
24 Nov 1991	01:25	CAN	21 May 1992	19:43	AQU	17 Nov 1992	19:27	VIR
26 Nov 1991	02:37	LEO	24 May 1992	08:24	PIS	19 Nov 1992	22:02	LIB
28 Nov 1991	05:12	VIR	26 May 1992	19:51	ARI	22 Nov 1992	00:52	SCO
30 Nov 1991	09:47	LIB	29 May 1992	04:15	TAU	24 Nov 1992	05:01	SAG
2 Dec 1991	16:33	SCO	31 May 1992	09:18	GEM	26 Nov 1992	11:39	CAP
5 Dec 1991	01:32	SAG	2 Jun 1992	11:57	CAN	28 Nov 1992	21:19	AQU
7 Dec 1991	12:41	CAP	4 Jun 1992	13:34	LEO	1 Dec 1992	09:23	PIS
10 Dec 1991	01:26	AQU	6 Jun 1992	15:28	VIR	3 Dec 1992	21:48	ARI
12 Dec 1991	14:18	PIS	8 Jun 1992	18:33	LIB	6 Dec 1992	08:15	TAU
15 Dec 1991	01:05	ARI	10 Jun 1992	23:27	SCO	8 Dec 1992	15:35	GEM
17 Dec 1991	08:08	TAU	13 Jun 1992	06:28	SAG	10 Dec 1992	20:04	CAN
19 Dec 1991	11:20	GEM	15 Jun 1992	15:50	CAP	12 Dec 1992	22:46	LEO
21 Dec 1991	11:54	CAN	18 Jun 1992	03:19	AQU	15 Dec 1992	00:56	VIR
23 Dec 1991	11:38	LEO	20 Jun 1992	15:59	PIS	17 Dec 1992	03:33	LIB
25 Dec 1991	12:24	VIR	23 Jun 1992	04:02	ARI	19 Dec 1992	07:19	SCO
27 Dec 1991	15:38	LIB	25 Jun 1992	13:27	TAU	21 Dec 1992	12:43	SAG
29 Dec 1991	22:04	SCO	27 Jun 1992	19:13	GEM	23 Dec 1992	20:04	CAP
1 Jan 1992	07:30	SAG	29 Jun 1992	21:41	CAN	26 Dec 1992	05:43	AQU
3 Jan 1992	19:09	CAP	1 Jul 1992	22:14	LEO	28 Dec 1992	17:27	PIS
6 Jan 1992	07:59	AQU	3 Jul 1992	22:37	VIR	31 Dec 1992	06:06	ARI
8 Jan 1992	20:51	PIS	6 Jul 1992	00:28	LIB	2 Jan 1993	17:29	TAU
11 Jan 1992	08:21	ARI	8 Jul 1992	04:53	SCO	5 Jan 1993	01:40	GEM
13 Jan 1992	16:59	TAU	10 Jul 1992	12:18	SAG	7 Jan 1993	06:10	CAN
15 Jan 1992	21:53	GEM	12 Jul 1992	22:16	CAP	9 Jan 1993	07:49	LEO
17 Jan 1992	23:25	CAN	15 Jul 1992	10:02	AQU	11 Jan 1993	08:20	VIR
19 Jan 1992	22:56	LEO	17 Jul 1992	22:44	PIS	13 Jan 1993	09:30	LIB
21 Jan 1992	22:22	VIR	20 Jul 1992	11:06	ARI	15 Jan 1993	12:42	SCO
23 Jan 1992	23:43	LIB	22 Jul 1992	21:34	TAU	17 Jan 1993	18:30	SAG
26 Jan 1992	04:32	SCO	25 Jul 1992	04:43	GEM	20 Jan 1993	02:46	CAP
28 Jan 1992	13:20	SAG	27 Jul 1992	08:07	CAN	22 Jan 1993	13:00	AQU
31 Jan 1992	01:07	CAP	29 Jul 1992	08:38	LEO	25 Jan 1993	00:47	PIS
2 Feb 1992	14:08	AQU	31 Jul 1992	08:01	VIR	27 Jan 1993	13:27	ARI
5 Feb 1992	02:50	PIS	2 Aug 1992	08:17	LIB	30 Jan 1993	01:36	TAU
7 Feb 1992	14:14	ARI	4 Aug 1992	11:17	SCO	1 Feb 1993	11:13	GEM
9 Feb 1992	23:34	TAU	6 Aug 1992	17:56	SAG	3 Feb 1993	16:55	CAN
12 Feb 1992	06:07	GEM	9 Aug 1992	04:00	CAP	5 Feb 1993	18:50	LEO
14 Feb 1992	09:29	CAN	11 Aug 1992	16:06	AQU	7 Feb 1993	18:28	VIR
16 Feb 1992	10:14	LEO	14 Aug 1992	04:50	PIS	9 Feb 1993	17:58	LIB
18 Feb 1992	09:46	VIR	16 Aug 1992	17:11	ARI	11 Feb 1993	19:23	SCO
20 Feb 1992	10:05	LIB	19 Aug 1992	04:09	TAU	14 Feb 1993	00:08	SAG
22 Feb 1992	13:12	SCO	21 Aug 1992	12:34	GEM	16 Feb 1993	08:20	CAP
24 Feb 1992	20:26	SAG	23 Aug 1992	17:36	CAN	18 Feb 1993	19:05	AQU
27 Feb 1992	07:33	CAP	25 Aug 1992	19:14	LEO	21 Feb 1993	07:11	PIS
29 Feb 1992	20:33	AQU	27 Aug 1992	18:46	VIR	23 Feb 1993	19:50	ARI
3 Mar 1992	09:10	PIS	29 Aug 1992	18:10	LIB	26 Feb 1993	08:11	TAU
5 Mar 1992	20:06	ARI	31 Aug 1992	19:39	SCO	28 Feb 1993	18:51	GEM
8 Mar 1992	05:04	TAU	3 Sep 1992	00:51	SAG	3 Mar 1993	02:14	CAN
10 Mar 1992	12:02	GEM	5 Sep 1992	10:06	CAP	5 Mar 1993	05:40	LEO
12 Mar 1992	16:49	CAN	7 Sep 1992	22:08	AQU	7 Mar 1993	05:52	VIR
14 Mar 1992	19:20	LEO	10 Sep 1992	10:55	PIS	9 Mar 1993	04:46	LIB
16 Mar 1992	20:13	VIR	12 Sep 1992	23:01	ARI	11 Mar 1993	04:40	SCO
18 Mar 1992	20:55	LIB	15 Sep 1992	09:46	TAU	13 Mar 1993	07:34	SAG
20 Mar 1992	23:21	SCO	17 Sep 1992	18:39	GEM	15 Mar 1993	14:28	CAP
23 Mar 1992	05:13	SAG	20 Sep 1992	00:57	CAN	18 Mar 1993	00:52	AQU
25 Mar 1992	15:09	CAP	22 Sep 1992	04:18	LEO	20 Mar 1993	13:10	PIS
28 Mar 1992	03:44	AQU	24 Sep 1992	05:07	VIR	23 Mar 1993	01:51	ARI
30 Mar 1992	16:22	PIS	26 Sep 1992	04:55	LIB	25 Mar 1993	13:58	TAU
2 Apr 1992	03:03	ARI	28 Sep 1992	05:44	SCO	28 Mar 1993	00:47	GEM
4 Apr 1992	11:17	TAU	30 Sep 1992	09:34	SAG	30 Mar 1993	09:13	CAN

DATE	TIME	SIGN	DATE	TIME	SIGN	DATE	TIME	SIGN
1 Apr 1993	14:20	LEO	27 Sep 1993	15:13	PIS	27 Mar 1994	00:45	LIB
3 Apr 1993	16:09	VIR	30 Sep 1993	03:28	ARI	29 Mar 1994	00:15	SCO
5 Apr 1993	15:54	LIB	2 Oct 1993	16:13	TAU	31 Mar 1994	00:42	SAG
7 Apr 1993	15:32	SCO	5 Oct 1993	04:26	GEM	2 Apr 1994	03:38	CAP
9 Apr 1993	17:09	SAG	7 Oct 1993	14:41	CAN	4 Apr 1994	09:46	AQU
11 Apr 1993	22:25	CAP	9 Oct 1993	21:32	LEO	6 Apr 1994	18:51	PIS
14 Apr 1993	07:36	AQU	12 Oct 1993	00:34	VIR	9 Apr 1994	06:08	ARI
16 Apr 1993	19:32	PIS	14 Oct 1993	00:46	LIB	11 Apr 1994	18:47	TAU
19 Apr 1993	08:14	ARI	16 Oct 1993	00:01	SCO	14 Apr 1994	07:47	GEM
21 Apr 1993	20:07	TAU	18 Oct 1993	00:24	SAG	16 Apr 1994	19:40	CAN
24 Apr 1993	06:26	GEM	20 Oct 1993	03:42	CAP	19 Apr 1994	04:44	LEO
26 Apr 1993	14:44	CAN	22 Oct 1993	10:50	AQU	21 Apr 1994	09:56	VIR
28 Apr 1993	20:38	LEO	24 Oct 1993	21:17	PIS	23 Apr 1994	11:39	LIB
30 Apr 1993	23:58	VIR	27 Oct 1993	09:39	ARI	25 Apr 1994	11:18	SCO
3 May 1993	01:19	LIB	29 Oct 1993	22:19	TAU	27 Apr 1994	10:48	SAG
5 May 1993	01:57	SCO	1 Nov 1993	10:12	GEM	29 Apr 1994	12:06	CAP
7 May 1993	03:35	SAG	3 Nov 1993	20:23	CAN	1 May 1994	16:34	AQU
9 May 1993	07:51	CAP	6 Nov 1993	04:05	LEO	4 May 1994	00:47	PIS
11 May 1993	15:44	AQU	8 Nov 1993	08:46	VIR	6 May 1994	12:01	ARI
14 May 1993	02:50	PIS	10 Nov 1993	10:41	LIB	9 May 1994	00:50	TAU
16 May 1993	15:23	ARI	12 Nov 1993	10:59	SCO	11 May 1994	13:43	GEM
19 May 1993	03:15	TAU	14 Nov 1993	11:21	SAG	14 May 1994	01:26	CAN
21 May 1993	13:06	GEM	16 Nov 1993	13:35	CAP	16 May 1994	10:57	LEO
23 May 1993	20:37	CAN	18 Nov 1993	19:08	AQU	18 May 1994	17:30	VIR
26 May 1993	02:02	LEO	21 Nov 1993	04:27	PIS	20 May 1994	20:53	LIB
28 May 1993	05:46	VIR	23 Nov 1993	16:30	ARI	22 May 1994	21:50	SCO
30 May 1993	08:17	LIB	26 Nov 1993	05:13	TAU	24 May 1994	21:43	SAG
1 Jun 1993	10:22	SCO	28 Nov 1993	16:47	GEM	26 May 1994	22:17	CAP
3 Jun 1993	13:01	SAG	1 Dec 1993	02:16	CAN	29 May 1994	01:20	AQU
5 Jun 1993	17:26	CAP	3 Dec 1993	09:32	LEO	31 May 1994	08:03	PIS
8 Jun 1993	00:40	AQU	5 Dec 1993	14:42	VIR	2 Jun 1994	18:31	ARI
10 Jun 1993	10:57	PIS	7 Dec 1993	18:03	LIB	5 Jun 1994	07:13	TAU
12 Jun 1993	23:13	ARI	9 Dec 1993	20:04	SCO	7 Jun 1994	20:02	GEM
15 Jun 1993	11:18	TAU	11 Dec 1993	21:39	SAG	10 Jun 1994	07:21	CAN
17 Jun 1993	21:10	GEM	14 Dec 1993	00:06	CAP	12 Jun 1994	16:28	LEO
20 Jun 1993	04:04	CAN	16 Dec 1993	04:51	AQU	14 Jun 1994	23:15	VIR
22 Jun 1993	08:25	LEO	18 Dec 1993	12:59	PIS	17 Jun 1994	03:47	LIB
24 Jun 1993	11:17	VIR	21 Dec 1993	00:19	ARI	19 Jun 1994	06:19	SCO
26 Jun 1993	13:45	LIB	23 Dec 1993	13:04	TAU	21 Jun 1994	07:32	SAG
28 Jun 1993	16:37	SCO	26 Dec 1993	00:44	GEM	23 Jun 1994	08:37	CAP
30 Jun 1993	20:28	SAG	28 Dec 1993	09:45	CAN	25 Jun 1994	11:10	AQU
3 Jul 1993	01:49	CAP	30 Dec 1993	15:58	LEO	27 Jun 1994	16:44	PIS
5 Jul 1993	09:14	AQU	1 Jan 1994	20:14	VIR	30 Jun 1994	02:07	ARI
7 Jul 1993	19:09	PIS	3 Jan 1994	23:30	LIB	2 Jul 1994	14:23	TAU
10 Jul 1993	07:11	ARI	6 Jan 1994	02:28	SCO	5 Jul 1994	03:11	GEM
12 Jul 1993	19:36	TAU	8 Jan 1994	05:33	SAG	7 Jul 1994	14:16	CAN
15 Jul 1993	06:06	GEM	10 Jan 1994	09:16	CAP	9 Jul 1994	22:42	LEO
17 Jul 1993	13:06	CAN	12 Jan 1994	14:25	AQU	12 Jul 1994	04:47	VIR
19 Jul 1993	16:46	LEO	14 Jan 1994	22:04	PIS	14 Jul 1994	09:14	LIB
21 Jul 1993	18:23	VIR	17 Jan 1994	08:42	ARI	16 Jul 1994	12:34	SCO
23 Jul 1993	19:39	LIB	19 Jan 1994	21:21	TAU	18 Jul 1994	15:09	SAG
25 Jul 1993	22:00	SCO	22 Jan 1994	09:33	GEM	20 Jul 1994	17:30	CAP
28 Jul 1993	02:13	SAG	24 Jan 1994	18:54	CAN	22 Jul 1994	20:38	AQU
30 Jul 1993	08:26	CAP	27 Jan 1994	00:36	LEO	25 Jul 1994	01:57	PIS
1 Aug 1993	16:36	AQU	29 Jan 1994	03:38	VIR	27 Jul 1994	10:31	ARI
4 Aug 1993	02:43	PIS	31 Jan 1994	05:33	LIB	29 Jul 1994	22:13	TAU
6 Aug 1993	14:39	ARI	2 Feb 1994	07:49	SCO	1 Aug 1994	11:04	GEM
9 Aug 1993	03:22	TAU	4 Feb 1994	11:14	SAG	3 Aug 1994	22:21	CAN
11 Aug 1993	14:45	GEM	6 Feb 1994	16:01	CAP	6 Aug 1994	06:30	LEO
13 Aug 1993	22:44	CAN	8 Feb 1994	22:17	AQU	8 Aug 1994	11:41	VIR
16 Aug 1993	02:42	LEO	11 Feb 1994	06:22	PIS	10 Aug 1994	15:06	LIB
18 Aug 1993	03:40	VIR	13 Feb 1994	16:49	ARI	12 Aug 1994	17:55	SCO
20 Aug 1993	03:35	LIB	16 Feb 1994	05:19	TAU	14 Aug 1994	20:53	SAG
22 Aug 1993	04:27	SCO	18 Feb 1994	18:05	GEM	17 Aug 1994	00:18	CAP
24 Aug 1993	07:45	SAG	21 Feb 1994	04:26	CAN	19 Aug 1994	04:33	AQU
26 Aug 1993	13:58	CAP	23 Feb 1994	10:46	LEO	21 Aug 1994	10:28	PIS
28 Aug 1993	22:42	AQU	25 Feb 1994	13:26	VIR	23 Aug 1994	18:54	ARI
31 Aug 1993	09:18	PIS	27 Feb 1994	14:05	LIB	26 Aug 1994	06:13	TAU
2 Sep 1993	21:20	ARI	1 Mar 1994	14:43	SCO	28 Aug 1994	19:07	GEM
5 Sep 1993	10:09	TAU	3 Mar 1994	16:53	SAG	31 Aug 1994	06:59	CAN
7 Sep 1993	22:15	GEM	5 Mar 1994	21:24	CAP	2 Sep 1994	15:36	LEO
10 Sep 1993	07:35	CAN	8 Mar 1994	04:15	AQU	4 Sep 1994	20:32	VIR
12 Sep 1993	12:49	LEO	10 Mar 1994	13:09	PIS	6 Sep 1994	22:56	LIB
14 Sep 1993	14:19	VIR	12 Mar 1994	23:59	ARI	9 Sep 1994	00:25	SCO
16 Sep 1993	13:43	LIB	15 Mar 1994	12:27	TAU	11 Sep 1994	02:25	SAG
18 Sep 1993	13:15	SCO	18 Mar 1994	01:28	GEM	13 Sep 1994	05:44	CAP
20 Sep 1993	14:54	SAG	20 Mar 1994	12:52	CAN	15 Sep 1994	10:42	AQU
22 Sep 1993	19:54	CAP	22 Mar 1994	20:37	LEO	17 Sep 1994	17:31	PIS
25 Sep 1993	04:19	AQU	25 Mar 1994	00:12	VIR	20 Sep 1994	02:30	ARI

DATE	TIME	SIGN	DATE	TIME	SIGN	DATE	TIME	SIGN
22 Sep 1994	13:47	TAU	21 Mar 1995	12:57	SAG	17 Sep 1995	10:15	CAN
25 Sep 1994	02:41	GEM	23 Mar 1995	15:31	CAP	19 Sep 1995	22:18	LEO
27 Sep 1994	15:11	CAN	25 Mar 1995	19:09	AQU	22 Sep 1995	08:00	VIR
30 Sep 1994	00:53	LEO	28 Mar 1995	00:18	PIS	24 Sep 1995	14:48	LIB
2 Oct 1994	06:39	VIR	30 Mar 1995	07:25	ARI	26 Sep 1995	19:19	SCO
4 Oct 1994	08:55	LIB	1 Apr 1995	16:58	TAU	28 Sep 1995	22:30	SAG
6 Oct 1994	09:21	SCO	4 Apr 1995	04:49	GEM	1 Oct 1995	01:10	CAP
8 Oct 1994	09:47	SAG	6 Apr 1995	17:39	CAN	3 Oct 1995	03:59	AQU
10 Oct 1994	11:44	CAP	9 Apr 1995	05:15	LEO	5 Oct 1995	07:35	PIS
12 Oct 1994	16:09	AQU	11 Apr 1995	13:37	VIR	7 Oct 1995	12:42	ARI
14 Oct 1994	23:18	PIS	13 Apr 1995	18:19	LIB	9 Oct 1995	20:05	TAU
17 Oct 1994	08:56	ARI	15 Apr 1995	20:12	SCO	12 Oct 1995	06:09	GEM
19 Oct 1994	20:34	TAU	17 Apr 1995	20:51	SAG	14 Oct 1995	18:19	CAN
22 Oct 1994	09:27	GEM	19 Apr 1995	21:54	CAP	17 Oct 1995	06:46	LEO
24 Oct 1994	22:14	CAN	22 Apr 1995	00:38	AQU	19 Oct 1995	17:11	VIR
27 Oct 1994	09:03	LEO	24 Apr 1995	05:50	PIS	22 Oct 1995	00:13	LIB
29 Oct 1994	16:20	VIR	26 Apr 1995	13:41	ARI	24 Oct 1995	04:06	SCO
31 Oct 1994	19:45	LIB	28 Apr 1995	23:53	TAU	26 Oct 1995	05:56	SAG
2 Nov 1994	20:19	SCO	1 May 1995	11:53	GEM	28 Oct 1995	07:14	CAP
4 Nov 1994	19:46	SAG	4 May 1995	00:44	CAN	30 Oct 1995	09:23	AQU
6 Nov 1994	20:02	CAP	6 May 1995	12:54	LEO	1 Nov 1995	13:18	PIS
8 Nov 1994	22:49	AQU	8 May 1995	22:32	VIR	3 Nov 1995	19:20	ARI
11 Nov 1994	05:04	PIS	11 May 1995	04:29	LIB	6 Nov 1995	03:35	TAU
13 Nov 1994	14:44	ARI	13 May 1995	06:52	SCO	8 Nov 1995	13:54	GEM
16 Nov 1994	02:44	TAU	15 May 1995	06:58	SAG	11 Nov 1995	01:56	CAN
18 Nov 1994	15:41	GEM	17 May 1995	06:35	CAP	13 Nov 1995	14:36	LEO
21 Nov 1994	04:20	CAN	19 May 1995	07:39	AQU	16 Nov 1995	02:01	VIR
23 Nov 1994	15:32	LEO	21 May 1995	11:41	PIS	18 Nov 1995	10:16	LIB
26 Nov 1994	00:07	VIR	23 May 1995	19:13	ARI	20 Nov 1995	14:39	SCO
28 Nov 1994	05:21	LIB	26 May 1995	05:46	TAU	22 Nov 1995	15:55	SAG
30 Nov 1994	07:21	SCO	28 May 1995	18:06	GEM	24 Nov 1995	15:48	CAP
2 Dec 1994	07:12	SAG	31 May 1995	06:59	CAN	26 Nov 1995	16:15	AQU
4 Dec 1994	06:42	CAP	2 Jun 1995	19:16	LEO	28 Nov 1995	18:59	PIS
6 Dec 1994	07:52	AQU	5 Jun 1995	05:45	VIR	1 Dec 1995	00:51	ARI
8 Dec 1994	12:25	PIS	7 Jun 1995	13:11	LIB	3 Dec 1995	09:40	TAU
10 Dec 1994	21:04	ARI	9 Jun 1995	17:02	SCO	5 Dec 1995	20:34	GEM
13 Dec 1994	08:56	TAU	11 Jun 1995	17:49	SAG	8 Dec 1995	08:44	CAN
15 Dec 1994	21:59	GEM	13 Jun 1995	17:04	CAP	10 Dec 1995	21:24	LEO
18 Dec 1994	10:24	CAN	15 Jun 1995	16:52	AQU	13 Dec 1995	09:25	VIR
20 Dec 1994	21:12	LEO	17 Jun 1995	19:13	PIS	15 Dec 1995	19:08	LIB
23 Dec 1994	06:00	VIR	20 Jun 1995	01:30	ARI	18 Dec 1995	01:05	SCO
25 Dec 1994	12:26	LIB	22 Jun 1995	11:36	TAU	20 Dec 1995	03:12	SAG
27 Dec 1994	16:16	SCO	25 Jun 1995	00:02	GEM	22 Dec 1995	02:45	CAP
29 Dec 1994	17:45	SAG	27 Jun 1995	12:55	CAN	24 Dec 1995	01:52	AQU
31 Dec 1994	17:57	CAP	30 Jun 1995	01:01	LEO	26 Dec 1995	02:45	PIS
2 Jan 1995	18:38	AQU	2 Jul 1995	11:34	VIR	28 Dec 1995	07:06	ARI
4 Jan 1995	21:50	PIS	4 Jul 1995	19:54	LIB	30 Dec 1995	15:21	TAU
7 Jan 1995	04:56	ARI	7 Jul 1995	01:17	SCO	2 Jan 1996	02:29	GEM
9 Jan 1995	15:58	TAU	9 Jul 1995	03:36	SAG	4 Jan 1996	14:55	CAN
12 Jan 1995	04:57	GEM	11 Jul 1995	03:43	CAP	7 Jan 1996	03:30	LEO
14 Jan 1995	17:19	CAN	13 Jul 1995	03:21	AQU	9 Jan 1996	15:28	VIR
17 Jan 1995	03:35	LEO	15 Jul 1995	04:37	PIS	12 Jan 1996	01:54	LIB
19 Jan 1995	11:38	VIR	17 Jul 1995	09:24	ARI	14 Jan 1996	09:28	SCO
21 Jan 1995	17:53	LIB	19 Jul 1995	18:20	TAU	16 Jan 1996	13:23	SAG
23 Jan 1995	22:31	SCO	22 Jul 1995	06:23	GEM	18 Jan 1996	14:06	CAP
26 Jan 1995	01:35	SAG	24 Jul 1995	19:15	CAN	20 Jan 1996	13:14	AQU
28 Jan 1995	03:26	CAP	27 Jul 1995	07:06	LEO	22 Jan 1996	13:02	PIS
30 Jan 1995	05:03	AQU	29 Jul 1995	17:11	VIR	24 Jan 1996	15:37	ARI
1 Feb 1995	08:05	PIS	1 Aug 1995	01:22	LIB	26 Jan 1996	22:17	TAU
3 Feb 1995	14:13	ARI	3 Aug 1995	07:28	SCO	29 Jan 1996	08:42	GEM
6 Feb 1995	00:09	TAU	5 Aug 1995	11:13	SAG	31 Jan 1996	21:10	CAN
8 Feb 1995	12:43	GEM	7 Aug 1995	12:51	CAP	3 Feb 1996	09:45	LEO
11 Feb 1995	01:16	CAN	9 Aug 1995	13:27	AQU	5 Feb 1996	21:21	VIR
13 Feb 1995	11:30	LEO	11 Aug 1995	14:46	PIS	8 Feb 1996	07:29	LIB
15 Feb 1995	18:51	VIR	13 Aug 1995	18:40	ARI	10 Feb 1996	15:34	SCO
17 Feb 1995	23:59	LIB	16 Aug 1995	02:26	TAU	12 Feb 1996	20:57	SAG
20 Feb 1995	03:54	SCO	18 Aug 1995	13:40	GEM	14 Feb 1996	23:28	CAP
22 Feb 1995	07:12	SAG	21 Aug 1995	02:23	CAN	16 Feb 1996	23:59	AQU
24 Feb 1995	10:10	CAP	23 Aug 1995	14:11	LEO	19 Feb 1996	00:09	PIS
26 Feb 1995	13:49	AQU	25 Aug 1995	23:49	VIR	21 Feb 1996	01:59	ARI
28 Feb 1995	17:15	PIS	28 Aug 1995	07:14	LIB	23 Feb 1996	07:08	TAU
2 Mar 1995	23:30	ARI	30 Aug 1995	12:50	SCO	25 Feb 1996	16:14	GEM
5 Mar 1995	08:50	TAU	1 Sep 1995	16:56	SAG	28 Feb 1996	04:10	CAN
7 Mar 1995	20:55	GEM	3 Sep 1995	19:44	CAP	1 Mar 1996	16:46	LEO
10 Mar 1995	09:39	CAN	5 Sep 1995	21:47	AQU	4 Mar 1996	04:12	VIR
12 Mar 1995	20:27	LEO	8 Sep 1995	00:08	PIS	6 Mar 1996	13:39	LIB
15 Mar 1995	03:53	VIR	10 Sep 1995	04:14	ARI	8 Mar 1996	21:04	SCO
17 Mar 1995	08:17	LIB	12 Sep 1995	11:22	TAU	11 Mar 1996	02:31	SAG
19 Mar 1995	10:51	SCO	14 Sep 1995	21:48	GEM	13 Mar 1996	06:07	CAP

DATE	TIME	SIGN	DATE	TIME	SIGN	DATE	TIME	SIGN
15 Mar 1996	08:14	AQU	11 Sep 1996	06:28	VIR	9 Mar 1997	19:32	ARI
17 Mar 1996	09:50	PIS	13 Sep 1996	17:50	LIB	11 Mar 1997	20:38	TAU
19 Mar 1996	12:16	ARI	16 Sep 1996	03:19	SCO	14 Mar 1997	00:49	GEM
21 Mar 1996	16:58	TAU	18 Sep 1996	10:29	SAG	16 Mar 1997	08:51	CAN
24 Mar 1996	01:00	GEM	20 Sep 1996	15:11	CAP	18 Mar 1997	20:08	LEO
26 Mar 1996	12:06	CAN	22 Sep 1996	17:39	AQU	21 Mar 1997	08:59	VIR
29 Mar 1996	00:36	LEO	24 Sep 1996	18:42	PIS	23 Mar 1997	21:34	LIB
31 Mar 1996	12:13	VIR	26 Sep 1996	19:45	ARI	26 Mar 1997	08:41	SCO
2 Apr 1996	21:25	LIB	28 Sep 1996	22:24	TAU	28 Mar 1997	17:39	SAG
5 Apr 1996	03:56	SCO	1 Oct 1996	04:02	GEM	31 Mar 1997	00:05	CAP
7 Apr 1996	08:21	SAG	3 Oct 1996	13:15	CAN	2 Apr 1997	03:58	AQU
9 Apr 1996	11:29	CAP	6 Oct 1996	01:11	LEO	4 Apr 1997	05:41	PIS
11 Apr 1996	14:09	AQU	8 Oct 1996	13:48	VIR	6 Apr 1997	06:18	ARI
13 Apr 1996	16:59	PIS	11 Oct 1996	00:59	LIB	8 Apr 1997	07:20	TAU
15 Apr 1996	20:42	ARI	13 Oct 1996	09:44	SCO	10 Apr 1997	10:29	GEM
18 Apr 1996	02:06	TAU	15 Oct 1996	16:06	SAG	12 Apr 1997	17:03	CAN
20 Apr 1996	09:54	GEM	17 Oct 1996	20:36	CAP	15 Apr 1997	03:22	LEO
22 Apr 1996	20:25	CAN	19 Oct 1996	23:50	AQU	17 Apr 1997	16:00	VIR
25 Apr 1996	08:44	LEO	22 Oct 1996	02:21	PIS	20 Apr 1997	04:36	LIB
27 Apr 1996	20:48	VIR	24 Oct 1996	04:50	ARI	22 Apr 1997	15:18	SCO
30 Apr 1996	06:26	LIB	26 Oct 1996	08:11	TAU	24 Apr 1997	23:31	SAG
2 May 1996	12:41	SCO	28 Oct 1996	13:35	GEM	27 Apr 1997	05:32	CAP
4 May 1996	16:04	SAG	30 Oct 1996	21:57	CAN	29 Apr 1997	09:49	AQU
6 May 1996	17:53	CAP	2 Nov 1996	09:16	LEO	1 May 1997	12:49	PIS
8 May 1996	19:38	AQU	4 Nov 1996	21:56	VIR	3 May 1997	14:58	ARI
10 May 1996	22:29	PIS	7 Nov 1996	09:27	LIB	5 May 1997	17:04	TAU
13 May 1996	03:00	ARI	9 Nov 1996	18:01	SCO	7 May 1997	20:21	GEM
15 May 1996	09:25	TAU	11 Nov 1996	23:25	SAG	10 May 1997	02:13	CAN
17 May 1996	17:47	GEM	14 Nov 1996	02:43	CAP	12 May 1997	11:33	LEO
20 May 1996	04:16	CAN	16 Nov 1996	05:13	AQU	14 May 1997	23:43	VIR
22 May 1996	16:27	LEO	18 Nov 1996	07:59	PIS	17 May 1997	12:26	LIB
25 May 1996	04:58	VIR	20 Nov 1996	11:34	ARI	19 May 1997	23:10	SCO
27 May 1996	15:32	LIB	22 Nov 1996	16:12	TAU	22 May 1997	06:50	SAG
29 May 1996	22:29	SCO	24 Nov 1996	22:20	GEM	24 May 1997	11:50	CAP
1 Jun 1996	01:41	SAG	27 Nov 1996	06:37	CAN	26 May 1997	15:19	AQU
3 Jun 1996	02:28	CAP	29 Nov 1996	17:29	LEO	28 May 1997	18:17	PIS
5 Jun 1996	02:44	AQU	2 Dec 1996	06:10	VIR	30 May 1997	21:17	ARI
7 Jun 1996	04:19	PIS	4 Dec 1996	18:23	LIB	2 Jun 1997	00:39	TAU
9 Jun 1996	08:23	ARI	7 Dec 1996	03:37	SCO	4 Jun 1997	04:54	GEM
11 Jun 1996	15:11	TAU	9 Dec 1996	08:57	SAG	6 Jun 1997	11:02	CAN
14 Jun 1996	00:16	GEM	11 Dec 1996	11:13	CAP	8 Jun 1997	19:58	LEO
16 Jun 1996	11:08	CAN	13 Dec 1996	12:14	AQU	11 Jun 1997	07:43	VIR
18 Jun 1996	23:21	LEO	15 Dec 1996	13:44	PIS	13 Jun 1997	20:34	LIB
21 Jun 1996	12:06	VIR	17 Dec 1996	16:55	ARI	16 Jun 1997	07:50	SCO
23 Jun 1996	23:36	LIB	19 Dec 1996	22:10	TAU	18 Jun 1997	15:38	SAG
26 Jun 1996	07:52	SCO	22 Dec 1996	05:17	GEM	20 Jun 1997	20:01	CAP
28 Jun 1996	11:59	SAG	24 Dec 1996	14:14	CAN	22 Jun 1997	22:20	AQU
30 Jun 1996	12:46	CAP	27 Dec 1996	01:09	LEO	25 Jun 1997	00:09	PIS
2 Jul 1996	12:05	AQU	29 Dec 1996	13:44	VIR	27 Jun 1997	02:38	ARI
4 Jul 1996	12:07	PIS	1 Jan 1997	02:31	LIB	29 Jun 1997	06:23	TAU
6 Jul 1996	14:42	ARI	3 Jan 1997	13:00	SCO	1 Jul 1997	11:35	GEM
8 Jul 1996	20:44	TAU	5 Jan 1997	19:26	SAG	3 Jul 1997	18:32	CAN
11 Jul 1996	05:52	GEM	7 Jan 1997	21:53	CAP	6 Jul 1997	03:45	LEO
13 Jul 1996	17:07	CAN	9 Jan 1997	21:59	AQU	8 Jul 1997	15:21	VIR
16 Jul 1996	05:31	LEO	11 Jan 1997	21:51	PIS	11 Jul 1997	04:20	LIB
18 Jul 1996	18:16	VIR	13 Jan 1997	23:22	ARI	13 Jul 1997	16:19	SCO
21 Jul 1996	06:13	LIB	16 Jan 1997	03:40	TAU	16 Jul 1997	01:00	SAG
23 Jul 1996	15:41	SCO	18 Jan 1997	10:53	GEM	18 Jul 1997	05:45	CAP
25 Jul 1996	21:22	SAG	20 Jan 1997	20:28	CAN	20 Jul 1997	07:28	AQU
27 Jul 1996	23:16	CAP	23 Jan 1997	07:49	LEO	22 Jul 1997	07:59	PIS
29 Jul 1996	22:47	AQU	25 Jan 1997	20:26	VIR	24 Jul 1997	09:03	ARI
31 Jul 1996	22:01	PIS	28 Jan 1997	09:20	LIB	26 Jul 1997	11:54	TAU
2 Aug 1996	23:06	ARI	30 Jan 1997	20:47	SCO	28 Jul 1997	17:04	GEM
5 Aug 1996	03:34	TAU	2 Feb 1997	04:50	SAG	31 Jul 1997	00:38	CAN
7 Aug 1996	11:49	GEM	4 Feb 1997	08:43	CAP	2 Aug 1997	10:27	LEO
9 Aug 1996	22:57	CAN	6 Feb 1997	09:20	AQU	4 Aug 1997	22:15	VIR
12 Aug 1996	11:28	LEO	8 Feb 1997	08:33	PIS	7 Aug 1997	11:16	LIB
15 Aug 1996	00:06	VIR	10 Feb 1997	08:29	ARI	9 Aug 1997	23:49	SCO
17 Aug 1996	11:54	LIB	12 Feb 1997	10:57	TAU	12 Aug 1997	09:43	SAG
19 Aug 1996	21:49	SCO	14 Feb 1997	16:53	GEM	14 Aug 1997	15:41	CAP
22 Aug 1996	04:47	SAG	17 Feb 1997	02:13	CAN	16 Aug 1997	17:58	AQU
24 Aug 1996	08:21	CAP	19 Feb 1997	13:52	LEO	18 Aug 1997	18:00	PIS
26 Aug 1996	09:09	AQU	22 Feb 1997	02:38	VIR	20 Aug 1997	17:44	ARI
28 Aug 1996	08:48	PIS	24 Feb 1997	15:22	LIB	22 Aug 1997	18:57	TAU
30 Aug 1996	09:15	ARI	27 Feb 1997	02:56	SCO	24 Aug 1997	22:57	GEM
1 Sep 1996	12:20	TAU	1 Mar 1997	11:59	SAG	27 Aug 1997	06:10	CAN
3 Sep 1996	19:08	GEM	3 Mar 1997	17:38	CAP	29 Aug 1997	16:18	LEO
6 Sep 1996	05:29	CAN	5 Mar 1997	19:53	AQU	1 Sep 1997	04:26	VIR
8 Sep 1996	17:53	LEO	7 Mar 1997	19:56	PIS	3 Sep 1997	17:29	LIB

DATE	TIME	SIGN	DATE	TIME	SIGN	DATE	TIME	SIGN
6 Sep 1997	06:09	SCO	4 Mar 1998	07:15	GEM	1 Sep 1998	02:21	CAP
8 Sep 1997	16:53	SAG	6 Mar 1998	12:27	CAN	3 Sep 1998	09:19	AQU
11 Sep 1997	00:21	CAP	8 Mar 1998	20:46	LEO	5 Sep 1998	12:46	PIS
13 Sep 1997	04:09	AQU	11 Mar 1998	07:35	VIR	7 Sep 1998	13:52	ARI
15 Sep 1997	04:58	PIS	13 Mar 1998	19:57	LIB	9 Sep 1998	14:16	TAU
17 Sep 1997	04:24	ARI	16 Mar 1998	08:50	SCO	11 Sep 1998	15:40	GEM
19 Sep 1997	04:21	TAU	18 Mar 1998	20:55	SAG	13 Sep 1998	19:20	CAN
21 Sep 1997	06:38	GEM	21 Mar 1998	06:43	CAP	16 Sep 1998	01:48	LEO
23 Sep 1997	12:34	CAN	23 Mar 1998	13:00	AQU	18 Sep 1998	10:52	VIR
25 Sep 1997	22:13	LEO	25 Mar 1998	15:41	PIS	20 Sep 1998	21:57	LIB
28 Sep 1997	10:27	VIR	27 Mar 1998	15:48	ARI	23 Sep 1998	10:21	SCO
30 Sep 1997	23:31	LIB	29 Mar 1998	15:06	TAU	25 Sep 1998	23:04	SAG
3 Oct 1997	11:56	SCO	31 Mar 1998	15:38	GEM	28 Sep 1998	10:29	CAP
5 Oct 1997	22:41	SAG	2 Apr 1998	19:09	CAN	30 Sep 1998	18:52	AQU
8 Oct 1997	07:03	CAP	5 Apr 1998	02:36	LEO	2 Oct 1998	23:21	PIS
10 Oct 1997	12:27	AQU	7 Apr 1998	13:25	VIR	5 Oct 1998	00:31	ARI
12 Oct 1997	14:58	PIS	10 Apr 1998	02:04	LIB	6 Oct 1998	23:57	TAU
14 Oct 1997	15:24	ARI	12 Apr 1998	14:55	SCO	8 Oct 1998	23:44	GEM
16 Oct 1997	15:16	TAU	15 Apr 1998	02:51	SAG	11 Oct 1998	01:49	CAN
18 Oct 1997	16:26	GEM	17 Apr 1998	13:04	CAP	13 Oct 1998	07:25	LEO
20 Oct 1997	20:46	CAN	19 Apr 1998	20:40	AQU	15 Oct 1998	16:32	VIR
23 Oct 1997	05:10	LEO	22 Apr 1998	01:04	PIS	18 Oct 1998	04:02	LIB
25 Oct 1997	16:59	VIR	24 Apr 1998	02:29	ARI	20 Oct 1998	16:36	SCO
28 Oct 1997	06:04	LIB	26 Apr 1998	02:08	TAU	23 Oct 1998	05:15	SAG
30 Oct 1997	18:15	SCO	28 Apr 1998	01:56	GEM	25 Oct 1998	17:04	CAP
2 Nov 1997	04:26	SAG	30 Apr 1998	03:57	CAN	28 Oct 1998	02:43	AQU
4 Nov 1997	12:29	CAP	2 May 1998	09:50	LEO	30 Oct 1998	08:57	PIS
6 Nov 1997	18:33	AQU	4 May 1998	19:47	VIR	1 Nov 1998	11:25	ARI
8 Nov 1997	22:33	PIS	7 May 1998	08:18	LIB	3 Nov 1998	11:11	TAU
11 Nov 1997	00:42	ARI	9 May 1998	21:09	SCO	5 Nov 1998	10:11	GEM
13 Nov 1997	01:44	TAU	12 May 1998	08:47	SAG	7 Nov 1998	10:40	CAN
15 Nov 1997	03:05	GEM	14 May 1998	18:38	CAP	9 Nov 1998	14:34	LEO
17 Nov 1997	06:32	CAN	17 May 1998	02:29	AQU	11 Nov 1998	22:37	VIR
19 Nov 1997	13:39	LEO	19 May 1998	08:02	PIS	14 Nov 1998	09:57	LIB
22 Nov 1997	00:33	VIR	21 May 1998	11:04	ARI	16 Nov 1998	22:40	SCO
24 Nov 1997	13:29	LIB	23 May 1998	12:05	TAU	19 Nov 1998	11:12	SAG
27 Nov 1997	01:42	SCO	25 May 1998	12:25	GEM	21 Nov 1998	22:44	CAP
29 Nov 1997	11:27	SAG	27 May 1998	13:59	CAN	24 Nov 1998	08:42	AQU
1 Dec 1997	18:38	CAP	29 May 1998	18:38	LEO	26 Nov 1998	16:13	PIS
3 Dec 1997	23:57	AQU	1 Jun 1998	03:21	VIR	28 Nov 1998	20:32	ARI
6 Dec 1997	04:06	PIS	3 Jun 1998	15:17	LIB	30 Nov 1998	21:51	TAU
8 Dec 1997	07:23	ARI	6 Jun 1998	04:05	SCO	2 Dec 1998	21:29	GEM
10 Dec 1997	09:59	TAU	8 Jun 1998	15:33	SAG	4 Dec 1998	21:28	CAN
12 Dec 1997	12:35	GEM	11 Jun 1998	00:49	CAP	6 Dec 1998	23:56	LEO
14 Dec 1997	16:25	CAN	13 Jun 1998	08:02	AQU	9 Dec 1998	06:21	VIR
16 Dec 1997	22:58	LEO	15 Jun 1998	13:30	PIS	11 Dec 1998	16:43	LIB
19 Dec 1997	09:00	VIR	17 Jun 1998	17:22	ARI	14 Dec 1998	05:16	SCO
21 Dec 1997	21:34	LIB	19 Jun 1998	19:47	TAU	16 Dec 1998	17:47	SAG
24 Dec 1997	10:06	SCO	21 Jun 1998	21:26	GEM	19 Dec 1998	04:54	CAP
26 Dec 1997	20:06	SAG	23 Jun 1998	23:39	CAN	21 Dec 1998	14:16	AQU
29 Dec 1997	02:47	CAP	26 Jun 1998	04:04	LEO	23 Dec 1998	21:44	PIS
31 Dec 1997	06:58	AQU	28 Jun 1998	11:55	VIR	26 Dec 1998	03:02	ARI
2 Jan 1998	09:55	PIS	30 Jun 1998	23:05	LIB	28 Dec 1998	06:04	TAU
4 Jan 1998	12:43	ARI	3 Jul 1998	11:44	SCO	30 Dec 1998	07:21	GEM
6 Jan 1998	15:52	TAU	5 Jul 1998	23:22	SAG	1 Jan 1999	08:15	CAN
8 Jan 1998	19:42	GEM	8 Jul 1998	08:26	CAP	3 Jan 1999	10:31	LEO
11 Jan 1998	00:43	CAN	10 Jul 1998	14:51	AQU	5 Jan 1999	15:49	VIR
13 Jan 1998	07:45	LEO	12 Jul 1998	19:22	PIS	8 Jan 1999	00:53	LIB
15 Jan 1998	17:31	VIR	14 Jul 1998	22:44	ARI	10 Jan 1999	12:48	SCO
18 Jan 1998	05:44	LIB	17 Jul 1998	01:33	TAU	13 Jan 1999	01:22	SAG
20 Jan 1998	18:34	SCO	19 Jul 1998	04:18	GEM	15 Jan 1999	12:27	CAP
23 Jan 1998	05:24	SAG	21 Jul 1998	07:43	CAN	17 Jan 1999	21:10	AQU
25 Jan 1998	12:37	CAP	23 Jul 1998	12:49	LEO	20 Jan 1999	03:39	PIS
27 Jan 1998	16:26	AQU	25 Jul 1998	20:34	VIR	22 Jan 1999	08:24	ARI
29 Jan 1998	18:08	PIS	28 Jul 1998	07:14	LIB	24 Jan 1999	11:51	TAU
31 Jan 1998	19:20	ARI	30 Jul 1998	19:44	SCO	26 Jan 1999	14:29	GEM
2 Feb 1998	21:25	TAU	2 Aug 1998	07:47	SAG	28 Jan 1999	16:56	CAN
5 Feb 1998	01:10	GEM	4 Aug 1998	17:17	CAP	30 Jan 1999	20:16	LEO
7 Feb 1998	06:57	CAN	6 Aug 1998	23:29	AQU	2 Feb 1999	01:38	VIR
9 Feb 1998	14:57	LEO	9 Aug 1998	03:03	PIS	4 Feb 1999	09:56	LIB
12 Feb 1998	01:10	VIR	11 Aug 1998	05:10	ARI	6 Feb 1999	21:06	SCO
14 Feb 1998	13:17	LIB	13 Aug 1998	07:04	TAU	9 Feb 1999	09:37	SAG
17 Feb 1998	02:12	SCO	15 Aug 1998	09:46	GEM	11 Feb 1999	21:09	CAP
19 Feb 1998	13:55	SAG	17 Aug 1998	13:55	CAN	14 Feb 1999	05:56	AQU
21 Feb 1998	22:28	CAP	19 Aug 1998	20:00	LEO	16 Feb 1999	11:38	PIS
24 Feb 1998	03:09	AQU	22 Aug 1998	04:21	VIR	18 Feb 1999	15:05	ARI
26 Feb 1998	04:41	PIS	24 Aug 1998	15:02	LIB	20 Feb 1999	17:28	TAU
28 Feb 1998	04:41	ARI	27 Aug 1998	03:25	SCO	22 Feb 1999	19:53	GEM
2 Mar 1998	05:00	TAU	29 Aug 1998	15:54	SAG	24 Feb 1999	23:09	CAN

DATE	TIME	SIGN	DATE	TIME	SIGN	DATE	TIME	SIGN
27 Feb 1999	03:44	LEO	26 Aug 1999	17:49	PIS	21 Feb 2000	19:21	LIB
1 Mar 1999	10:05	VIR	28 Aug 1999	23:08	ARI	24 Feb 2000	01:58	SCO
3 Mar 1999	18:34	LIB	31 Aug 1999	02:40	TAU	26 Feb 2000	12:10	SAG
6 Mar 1999	05:22	SCO	2 Sep 1999	05:24	GEM	29 Feb 2000	00:45	CAP
8 Mar 1999	17:45	SAG	4 Sep 1999	08:09	CAN	2 Mar 2000	13:13	AQU
11 Mar 1999	05:53	CAP	6 Sep 1999	11:29	LEO	4 Mar 2000	23:28	PIS
13 Mar 1999	15:31	AQU	8 Sep 1999	15:56	VIR	7 Mar 2000	06:53	ARI
15 Mar 1999	21:29	PIS	10 Sep 1999	22:16	LIB	9 Mar 2000	12:00	TAU
18 Mar 1999	00:11	ARI	13 Sep 1999	07:08	SCO	11 Mar 2000	15:45	GEM
20 Mar 1999	01:08	TAU	15 Sep 1999	18:34	SAG	13 Mar 2000	18:51	CAN
22 Mar 1999	02:05	GEM	18 Sep 1999	07:13	CAP	15 Mar 2000	21:43	LEO
24 Mar 1999	04:33	CAN	20 Sep 1999	18:37	AQU	18 Mar 2000	00:48	VIR
26 Mar 1999	09:22	LEO	23 Sep 1999	02:50	PIS	20 Mar 2000	04:57	LIB
28 Mar 1999	16:34	VIR	25 Sep 1999	07:33	ARI	22 Mar 2000	11:18	SCO
31 Mar 1999	01:49	LIB	27 Sep 1999	09:50	TAU	24 Mar 2000	20:43	SAG
2 Apr 1999	12:48	SCO	29 Sep 1999	11:21	GEM	27 Mar 2000	08:50	CAP
5 Apr 1999	01:07	SAG	1 Oct 1999	13:31	CAN	29 Mar 2000	21:33	AQU
7 Apr 1999	13:38	CAP	3 Oct 1999	17:13	LEO	1 Apr 2000	08:11	PIS
10 Apr 1999	00:23	AQU	5 Oct 1999	22:40	VIR	3 Apr 2000	15:20	ARI
12 Apr 1999	07:33	PIS	8 Oct 1999	05:51	LIB	5 Apr 2000	19:28	TAU
14 Apr 1999	10:44	ARI	10 Oct 1999	15:01	SCO	7 Apr 2000	21:58	GEM
16 Apr 1999	11:06	TAU	13 Oct 1999	02:18	SAG	10 Apr 2000	00:16	CAN
18 Apr 1999	10:39	GEM	15 Oct 1999	15:03	CAP	12 Apr 2000	03:16	LEO
20 Apr 1999	11:28	CAN	18 Oct 1999	03:16	AQU	14 Apr 2000	07:18	VIR
22 Apr 1999	15:06	LEO	20 Oct 1999	12:31	PIS	16 Apr 2000	12:36	LIB
24 Apr 1999	22:04	VIR	22 Oct 1999	17:41	ARI	18 Apr 2000	19:35	SCO
27 Apr 1999	07:46	LIB	24 Oct 1999	19:24	TAU	21 Apr 2000	04:57	SAG
29 Apr 1999	19:12	SCO	26 Oct 1999	19:33	GEM	23 Apr 2000	16:47	CAP
2 May 1999	07:36	SAG	28 Oct 1999	20:09	CAN	26 Apr 2000	05:41	AQU
4 May 1999	20:11	CAP	30 Oct 1999	22:48	LEO	28 Apr 2000	17:05	PIS
7 May 1999	07:39	AQU	2 Nov 1999	04:07	VIR	1 May 2000	00:53	ARI
9 May 1999	16:15	PIS	4 Nov 1999	11:57	LIB	3 May 2000	04:53	TAU
11 May 1999	20:51	ARI	6 Nov 1999	21:46	SCO	5 May 2000	06:23	GEM
13 May 1999	21:55	TAU	9 Nov 1999	09:15	SAG	7 May 2000	07:13	CAN
15 May 1999	21:07	GEM	11 Nov 1999	22:00	CAP	9 May 2000	09:01	LEO
17 May 1999	20:40	CAN	14 Nov 1999	10:44	AQU	11 May 2000	12:41	VIR
19 May 1999	22:38	LEO	16 Nov 1999	21:19	PIS	13 May 2000	18:27	LIB
22 May 1999	04:15	VIR	19 Nov 1999	03:56	ARI	16 May 2000	02:16	SCO
24 May 1999	13:29	LIB	21 Nov 1999	06:25	TAU	18 May 2000	12:09	SAG
27 May 1999	01:05	SCO	23 Nov 1999	06:13	GEM	21 May 2000	00:01	CAP
29 May 1999	13:37	SAG	25 Nov 1999	05:28	CAN	23 May 2000	12:59	AQU
1 Jun 1999	02:05	CAP	27 Nov 1999	06:18	LEO	26 May 2000	01:06	PIS
3 Jun 1999	13:36	AQU	29 Nov 1999	10:12	VIR	28 May 2000	10:06	ARI
5 Jun 1999	22:59	PIS	1 Dec 1999	17:29	LIB	30 May 2000	15:00	TAU
8 Jun 1999	05:07	ARI	4 Dec 1999	03:35	SCO	1 Jun 2000	16:33	GEM
10 Jun 1999	07:42	TAU	6 Dec 1999	15:27	SAG	3 Jun 2000	16:29	CAN
12 Jun 1999	07:48	GEM	9 Dec 1999	04:13	CAP	5 Jun 2000	16:45	LEO
14 Jun 1999	07:14	CAN	11 Dec 1999	16:58	AQU	7 Jun 2000	18:57	VIR
16 Jun 1999	08:07	LEO	14 Dec 1999	04:17	PIS	9 Jun 2000	23:59	LIB
18 Jun 1999	12:13	VIR	16 Dec 1999	12:28	ARI	12 Jun 2000	07:55	SCO
20 Jun 1999	20:10	LIB	18 Dec 1999	16:44	TAU	14 Jun 2000	18:17	SAG
23 Jun 1999	07:18	SCO	20 Dec 1999	17:38	GEM	17 Jun 2000	06:26	CAP
25 Jun 1999	19:50	SAG	22 Dec 1999	16:52	CAN	19 Jun 2000	19:25	AQU
28 Jun 1999	08:11	CAP	24 Dec 1999	16:32	LEO	22 Jun 2000	07:51	PIS
30 Jun 1999	19:19	AQU	26 Dec 1999	18:34	VIR	24 Jun 2000	17:55	ARI
3 Jul 1999	04:34	PIS	29 Dec 1999	00:15	LIB	27 Jun 2000	00:17	TAU
5 Jul 1999	11:20	ARI	31 Dec 1999	09:37	SCO	29 Jun 2000	02:58	GEM
7 Jul 1999	15:21	TAU	2 Jan 2000	21:31	SAG	1 Jul 2000	03:09	CAN
9 Jul 1999	16:59	GEM	5 Jan 2000	10:23	CAP	3 Jul 2000	02:38	LEO
11 Jul 1999	17:27	CAN	7 Jan 2000	22:52	AQU	5 Jul 2000	03:19	VIR
13 Jul 1999	18:25	LEO	10 Jan 2000	09:58	PIS	7 Jul 2000	06:46	LIB
15 Jul 1999	21:39	VIR	12 Jan 2000	18:48	ARI	9 Jul 2000	13:49	SCO
18 Jul 1999	04:19	LIB	15 Jan 2000	00:36	TAU	12 Jul 2000	00:06	SAG
20 Jul 1999	14:30	SCO	17 Jan 2000	03:24	GEM	14 Jul 2000	12:27	CAP
23 Jul 1999	02:48	SAG	19 Jan 2000	04:00	CAN	17 Jul 2000	01:26	AQU
25 Jul 1999	15:07	CAP	21 Jan 2000	03:58	LEO	19 Jul 2000	13:43	PIS
28 Jul 1999	01:53	AQU	23 Jan 2000	05:07	VIR	22 Jul 2000	00:08	ARI
30 Jul 1999	10:26	PIS	25 Jan 2000	09:10	LIB	24 Jul 2000	07:42	TAU
1 Aug 1999	16:46	ARI	27 Jan 2000	17:01	SCO	26 Jul 2000	12:00	GEM
3 Aug 1999	21:08	TAU	30 Jan 2000	04:17	SAG	28 Jul 2000	13:28	CAN
5 Aug 1999	23:56	GEM	1 Feb 2000	17:09	CAP	30 Jul 2000	13:23	LEO
8 Aug 1999	01:52	CAN	4 Feb 2000	05:30	AQU	1 Aug 2000	13:27	VIR
10 Aug 1999	03:55	LEO	6 Feb 2000	16:01	PIS	3 Aug 2000	15:32	LIB
12 Aug 1999	07:21	VIR	9 Feb 2000	00:16	ARI	5 Aug 2000	21:05	SCO
14 Aug 1999	13:24	LIB	11 Feb 2000	06:20	TAU	8 Aug 2000	06:30	SAG
16 Aug 1999	22:40	SCO	13 Feb 2000	10:22	GEM	10 Aug 2000	18:43	CAP
19 Aug 1999	10:31	SAG	15 Feb 2000	12:44	CAN	13 Aug 2000	07:42	AQU
21 Aug 1999	22:58	CAP	17 Feb 2000	14:11	LEO	15 Aug 2000	19:40	PIS
24 Aug 1999	09:48	AQU	19 Feb 2000	15:53	VIR	18 Aug 2000	05:43	ARI

Appendix 235

DATE	TIME	SIGN
20 Aug 2000	13:29	TAU
22 Aug 2000	18:54	GEM
24 Aug 2000	21:58	CAN
26 Aug 2000	23:16	LEO
28 Aug 2000	23:55	VIR
31 Aug 2000	01:33	LIB
2 Sep 2000	05:54	SCO
4 Sep 2000	14:09	SAG
7 Sep 2000	01:47	CAP
9 Sep 2000	14:44	AQU
12 Sep 2000	02:33	PIS
14 Sep 2000	11:59	ARI
16 Sep 2000	19:04	TAU
19 Sep 2000	00:21	GEM
21 Sep 2000	04:15	CAN
23 Sep 2000	06:59	LEO
25 Sep 2000	09:01	VIR
27 Sep 2000	11:22	LIB
29 Sep 2000	15:30	SCO
1 Oct 2000	22:50	SAG
4 Oct 2000	09:42	CAP
6 Oct 2000	22:32	AQU
9 Oct 2000	10:35	PIS
11 Oct 2000	19:50	ARI
14 Oct 2000	02:05	TAU
16 Oct 2000	06:18	GEM
18 Oct 2000	09:36	CAN
20 Oct 2000	12:42	LEO
22 Oct 2000	15:52	VIR
24 Oct 2000	19:29	LIB
27 Oct 2000	00:24	SCO
29 Oct 2000	07:40	SAG
31 Oct 2000	18:01	CAP
3 Nov 2000	06:40	AQU
5 Nov 2000	19:12	PIS
8 Nov 2000	05:01	ARI
10 Nov 2000	11:10	TAU
12 Nov 2000	14:26	GEM
14 Nov 2000	16:20	CAN
16 Nov 2000	18:18	LEO
18 Nov 2000	21:15	VIR
21 Nov 2000	01:35	LIB
23 Nov 2000	07:33	SCO
25 Nov 2000	15:33	SAG
28 Nov 2000	01:57	CAP
30 Nov 2000	14:26	AQU
3 Dec 2000	03:22	PIS
5 Dec 2000	14:16	ARI
7 Dec 2000	21:25	TAU
10 Dec 2000	00:49	GEM
12 Dec 2000	01:48	CAN
14 Dec 2000	02:08	LEO
16 Dec 2000	03:30	VIR
18 Dec 2000	07:01	LIB
20 Dec 2000	13:12	SCO
22 Dec 2000	21:57	SAG
25 Dec 2000	08:53	CAP
27 Dec 2000	21:25	AQU
30 Dec 2000	10:26	PIS
1 Jan 2001	22:13	ARI
4 Jan 2001	06:56	TAU
6 Jan 2001	11:42	GEM
8 Jan 2001	13:07	CAN
10 Jan 2001	12:43	LEO
12 Jan 2001	12:26	VIR
14 Jan 2001	14:06	LIB
16 Jan 2001	19:02	SCO
19 Jan 2001	03:36	SAG
21 Jan 2001	14:56	CAP
24 Jan 2001	03:43	AQU
26 Jan 2001	16:38	PIS
29 Jan 2001	04:34	ARI
31 Jan 2001	14:20	TAU
2 Feb 2001	20:54	GEM
4 Feb 2001	23:58	CAN
7 Feb 2001	00:20	LEO
8 Feb 2001	23:35	VIR
10 Feb 2001	23:47	LIB
13 Feb 2001	02:52	SCO

DATE	TIME	SIGN
15 Feb 2001	10:03	SAG
17 Feb 2001	20:59	CAP
20 Feb 2001	09:53	AQU
22 Feb 2001	22:44	PIS
25 Feb 2001	10:19	ARI
27 Feb 2001	20:05	TAU
2 Mar 2001	03:35	GEM
4 Mar 2001	08:23	CAN
6 Mar 2001	10:28	LEO
8 Mar 2001	10:43	VIR
10 Mar 2001	10:47	LIB
12 Mar 2001	12:43	SCO
14 Mar 2001	18:16	SAG
17 Mar 2001	04:02	CAP
19 Mar 2001	16:36	AQU
22 Mar 2001	05:27	PIS
24 Mar 2001	16:43	ARI
27 Mar 2001	01:49	TAU
29 Mar 2001	09:00	GEM
31 Mar 2001	14:22	CAN
2 Apr 2001	17:53	LEO
4 Apr 2001	19:46	VIR
6 Apr 2001	20:57	LIB
8 Apr 2001	23:02	SCO
11 Apr 2001	03:47	SAG
13 Apr 2001	12:21	CAP
16 Apr 2001	00:11	AQU
18 Apr 2001	12:59	PIS
21 Apr 2001	00:16	ARI
23 Apr 2001	08:55	TAU
25 Apr 2001	15:10	GEM
27 Apr 2001	19:49	CAN
29 Apr 2001	23:24	LEO
2 May 2001	02:15	VIR
4 May 2001	04:49	LIB
6 May 2001	08:00	SCO
8 May 2001	13:05	SAG
10 May 2001	21:10	CAP
13 May 2001	08:20	AQU
15 May 2001	21:00	PIS
18 May 2001	08:40	ARI
20 May 2001	17:29	TAU
22 May 2001	23:10	GEM
25 May 2001	02:42	CAN
27 May 2001	05:11	LEO
29 May 2001	07:37	VIR
31 May 2001	10:41	LIB
2 Jun 2001	14:56	SCO
4 Jun 2001	20:58	SAG
7 Jun 2001	05:23	CAP
9 Jun 2001	16:19	AQU
12 Jun 2001	04:53	PIS
14 Jun 2001	17:02	ARI
17 Jun 2001	02:37	TAU
19 Jun 2001	08:41	GEM
21 Jun 2001	11:39	CAN
23 Jun 2001	12:54	LEO
25 Jun 2001	13:57	VIR
27 Jun 2001	16:11	LIB
29 Jun 2001	20:28	SCO
2 Jul 2001	03:13	SAG
4 Jul 2001	12:22	CAP
6 Jul 2001	23:33	AQU
9 Jul 2001	12:04	PIS
12 Jul 2001	00:35	ARI
14 Jul 2001	11:11	TAU
16 Jul 2001	18:25	GEM
18 Jul 2001	21:54	CAN
20 Jul 2001	22:42	LEO
22 Jul 2001	22:28	VIR
24 Jul 2001	23:08	LIB
27 Jul 2001	02:17	SCO
29 Jul 2001	08:44	SAG
31 Jul 2001	18:15	CAP
3 Aug 2001	05:53	AQU
5 Aug 2001	18:30	PIS
8 Aug 2001	07:04	ARI
10 Aug 2001	18:22	TAU
13 Aug 2001	02:57	GEM

DATE	TIME	SIGN
15 Aug 2001	07:53	CAN
17 Aug 2001	09:24	LEO
19 Aug 2001	08:52	VIR
21 Aug 2001	08:19	LIB
23 Aug 2001	09:51	SCO
25 Aug 2001	15:00	SAG
28 Aug 2001	00:02	CAP
30 Aug 2001	11:47	AQU
2 Sep 2001	00:31	PIS
4 Sep 2001	12:57	ARI
7 Sep 2001	00:17	TAU
9 Sep 2001	09:39	GEM
11 Sep 2001	16:08	CAN
13 Sep 2001	19:15	LEO
15 Sep 2001	19:39	VIR
17 Sep 2001	18:59	LIB
19 Sep 2001	19:27	SCO
21 Sep 2001	23:03	SAG
24 Sep 2001	06:48	CAP
26 Sep 2001	18:04	AQU
29 Sep 2001	06:49	PIS
1 Oct 2001	19:07	ARI
4 Oct 2001	06:00	TAU
6 Oct 2001	15:11	GEM
8 Oct 2001	22:18	CAN
11 Oct 2001	02:53	LEO
13 Oct 2001	04:57	VIR
15 Oct 2001	05:26	LIB
17 Oct 2001	06:02	SCO
19 Oct 2001	08:47	SAG
21 Oct 2001	15:12	CAP
24 Oct 2001	01:26	AQU
26 Oct 2001	13:55	PIS
29 Oct 2001	02:14	ARI
31 Oct 2001	12:46	TAU
2 Nov 2001	21:11	GEM
5 Nov 2001	03:43	CAN
7 Nov 2001	08:33	LEO
9 Nov 2001	11:48	VIR
11 Nov 2001	13:52	LIB
13 Nov 2001	15:44	SCO
15 Nov 2001	18:51	SAG
18 Nov 2001	00:40	CAP
20 Nov 2001	09:55	AQU
22 Nov 2001	21:52	PIS
25 Nov 2001	10:20	ARI
27 Nov 2001	21:04	TAU
30 Nov 2001	05:03	GEM
2 Dec 2001	10:29	CAN
4 Dec 2001	14:15	LEO
6 Dec 2001	17:10	VIR
8 Dec 2001	19:56	LIB
10 Dec 2001	23:09	SCO
13 Dec 2001	03:30	SAG
15 Dec 2001	09:48	CAP
17 Dec 2001	18:42	AQU
20 Dec 2001	06:09	PIS
22 Dec 2001	18:45	ARI
25 Dec 2001	06:12	TAU
27 Dec 2001	14:37	GEM
29 Dec 2001	19:39	CAN
31 Dec 2001	22:08	LEO
2 Jan 2002	23:34	VIR
5 Jan 2002	01:24	LIB
7 Jan 2002	04:41	SCO
9 Jan 2002	09:58	SAG
11 Jan 2002	17:18	CAP
14 Jan 2002	02:41	AQU
16 Jan 2002	14:00	PIS
19 Jan 2002	02:34	ARI
21 Jan 2002	14:46	TAU
24 Jan 2002	00:26	GEM
26 Jan 2002	06:16	CAN
28 Jan 2002	08:30	LEO
30 Jan 2002	08:39	VIR
1 Feb 2002	08:44	LIB
3 Feb 2002	10:36	SCO
5 Feb 2002	15:21	SAG
7 Feb 2002	23:09	CAP

DATE	TIME	SIGN	DATE	TIME	SIGN	DATE	TIME	SIGN
10 Feb 2002	09:14	AQU	9 Aug 2002	18:02	VIR	5 Feb 2003	05:44	ARI
12 Feb 2002	20:52	PIS	11 Aug 2002	18:37	LIB	7 Feb 2003	17:59	TAU
15 Feb 2002	09:25	ARI	13 Aug 2002	20:00	SCO	10 Feb 2003	06:44	GEM
17 Feb 2002	21:57	TAU	15 Aug 2002	23:26	SAG	12 Feb 2003	17:18	CAN
20 Feb 2002	08:49	GEM	18 Aug 2002	05:15	CAP	15 Feb 2003	00:02	LEO
22 Feb 2002	16:15	CAN	20 Aug 2002	13:16	AQU	17 Feb 2003	03:21	VIR
24 Feb 2002	19:35	LEO	22 Aug 2002	23:11	PIS	19 Feb 2003	04:47	LIB
26 Feb 2002	19:46	VIR	25 Aug 2002	10:47	ARI	21 Feb 2003	06:09	SCO
28 Feb 2002	18:46	LIB	27 Aug 2002	23:31	TAU	23 Feb 2003	08:46	SAG
2 Mar 2002	18:51	SCO	30 Aug 2002	11:44	GEM	25 Feb 2003	13:11	CAP
4 Mar 2002	21:55	SAG	1 Sep 2002	21:12	CAN	27 Feb 2003	19:24	AQU
7 Mar 2002	04:47	CAP	4 Sep 2002	02:35	LEO	2 Mar 2003	03:26	PIS
9 Mar 2002	14:56	AQU	6 Sep 2002	04:15	VIR	4 Mar 2003	13:30	ARI
12 Mar 2002	02:56	PIS	8 Sep 2002	03:56	LIB	7 Mar 2003	01:36	TAU
14 Mar 2002	15:33	ARI	10 Sep 2002	03:48	SCO	9 Mar 2003	14:37	GEM
17 Mar 2002	04:00	TAU	12 Sep 2002	05:44	SAG	12 Mar 2003	02:10	CAN
19 Mar 2002	15:19	GEM	14 Sep 2002	10:48	CAP	14 Mar 2003	10:04	LEO
22 Mar 2002	00:04	CAN	16 Sep 2002	18:54	AQU	16 Mar 2003	13:51	VIR
24 Mar 2002	05:12	LEO	19 Sep 2002	05:17	PIS	18 Mar 2003	14:42	LIB
26 Mar 2002	06:43	VIR	21 Sep 2002	17:10	ARI	20 Mar 2003	14:38	SCO
28 Mar 2002	06:03	LIB	24 Sep 2002	05:54	TAU	22 Mar 2003	15:33	SAG
30 Mar 2002	05:21	SCO	26 Sep 2002	18:26	GEM	24 Mar 2003	18:48	CAP
1 Apr 2002	06:48	SAG	29 Sep 2002	05:01	CAN	27 Mar 2003	00:51	AQU
3 Apr 2002	11:59	CAP	1 Oct 2002	11:56	LEO	29 Mar 2003	09:26	PIS
5 Apr 2002	21:07	AQU	3 Oct 2002	14:51	VIR	31 Mar 2003	20:04	ARI
8 Apr 2002	08:57	PIS	5 Oct 2002	14:50	LIB	3 Apr 2003	08:20	TAU
10 Apr 2002	21:40	ARI	7 Oct 2002	13:57	SCO	5 Apr 2003	21:23	GEM
13 Apr 2002	09:54	TAU	9 Oct 2002	14:21	SAG	8 Apr 2003	09:35	CAN
15 Apr 2002	20:55	GEM	11 Oct 2002	17:44	CAP	10 Apr 2003	18:53	LEO
18 Apr 2002	06:00	CAN	14 Oct 2002	00:52	AQU	13 Apr 2003	00:05	VIR
20 Apr 2002	12:19	LEO	16 Oct 2002	11:07	PIS	15 Apr 2003	01:40	LIB
22 Apr 2002	15:33	VIR	18 Oct 2002	23:13	ARI	17 Apr 2003	01:15	SCO
24 Apr 2002	16:21	LIB	21 Oct 2002	11:56	TAU	19 Apr 2003	00:52	SAG
26 Apr 2002	16:15	SCO	24 Oct 2002	00:16	GEM	21 Apr 2003	02:21	CAP
28 Apr 2002	17:12	SAG	26 Oct 2002	11:09	CAN	23 Apr 2003	06:58	AQU
30 Apr 2002	21:03	CAP	28 Oct 2002	19:19	LEO	25 Apr 2003	15:02	PIS
3 May 2002	04:43	AQU	30 Oct 2002	23:57	VIR	28 Apr 2003	01:54	ARI
5 May 2002	15:46	PIS	2 Nov 2002	01:27	LIB	30 Apr 2003	14:26	TAU
8 May 2002	04:22	ARI	4 Nov 2002	01:10	SCO	3 May 2003	03:27	GEM
10 May 2002	16:31	TAU	6 Nov 2002	01:02	SAG	5 May 2003	15:41	CAN
13 May 2002	03:03	GEM	8 Nov 2002	02:59	CAP	8 May 2003	01:45	LEO
15 May 2002	11:32	CAN	10 Nov 2002	08:27	AQU	10 May 2003	08:29	VIR
17 May 2002	17:52	LEO	12 Nov 2002	17:41	PIS	12 May 2003	11:41	LIB
19 May 2002	21:59	VIR	15 Nov 2002	05:37	ARI	14 May 2003	12:13	SCO
22 May 2002	00:18	LIB	17 Nov 2002	18:23	TAU	16 May 2003	11:42	SAG
24 May 2002	01:38	SCO	20 Nov 2002	06:24	GEM	18 May 2003	12:04	CAP
26 May 2002	03:20	SAG	22 Nov 2002	16:47	CAN	20 May 2003	15:01	AQU
28 May 2002	06:54	CAP	25 Nov 2002	00:58	LEO	22 May 2003	21:42	PIS
30 May 2002	13:35	AQU	27 Nov 2002	06:41	VIR	25 May 2003	07:58	ARI
1 Jun 2002	23:37	PIS	29 Nov 2002	09:53	LIB	27 May 2003	20:32	TAU
4 Jun 2002	11:51	ARI	1 Dec 2002	11:14	SCO	30 May 2003	09:31	GEM
7 Jun 2002	00:05	TAU	3 Dec 2002	11:58	SAG	1 Jun 2003	21:26	CAN
9 Jun 2002	10:28	GEM	5 Dec 2002	13:39	CAP	4 Jun 2003	07:24	LEO
11 Jun 2002	18:14	CAN	7 Dec 2002	17:53	AQU	6 Jun 2003	14:49	VIR
13 Jun 2002	23:38	LEO	10 Dec 2002	01:46	PIS	8 Jun 2003	19:29	LIB
16 Jun 2002	03:23	VIR	12 Dec 2002	12:58	ARI	10 Jun 2003	21:38	SCO
18 Jun 2002	06:10	LIB	15 Dec 2002	01:42	TAU	12 Jun 2003	22:12	SAG
20 Jun 2002	08:42	SCO	17 Dec 2002	13:42	GEM	14 Jun 2003	22:38	CAP
22 Jun 2002	11:42	SAG	19 Dec 2002	23:28	CAN	17 Jun 2003	00:42	AQU
24 Jun 2002	16:01	CAP	22 Dec 2002	06:48	LEO	19 Jun 2003	05:56	PIS
26 Jun 2002	22:36	AQU	24 Dec 2002	12:04	VIR	21 Jun 2003	15:06	ARI
29 Jun 2002	08:00	PIS	26 Dec 2002	15:52	LIB	24 Jun 2003	03:15	TAU
1 Jul 2002	19:49	ARI	28 Dec 2002	18:41	SCO	26 Jun 2003	16:12	GEM
4 Jul 2002	08:15	TAU	30 Dec 2002	21:01	SAG	29 Jun 2003	03:51	CAN
6 Jul 2002	19:00	GEM	1 Jan 2003	23:43	CAP	1 Jul 2003	13:12	LEO
9 Jul 2002	02:35	CAN	4 Jan 2003	03:56	AQU	3 Jul 2003	20:15	VIR
11 Jul 2002	07:07	LEO	6 Jan 2003	10:57	PIS	6 Jul 2003	01:19	LIB
13 Jul 2002	09:40	VIR	8 Jan 2003	21:15	ARI	8 Jul 2003	04:43	SCO
15 Jul 2002	11:39	LIB	11 Jan 2003	09:47	TAU	10 Jul 2003	06:48	SAG
17 Jul 2002	14:13	SCO	13 Jan 2003	22:06	GEM	12 Jul 2003	08:20	CAP
19 Jul 2002	18:01	SAG	16 Jan 2003	07:55	CAN	14 Jul 2003	10:38	AQU
21 Jul 2002	23:26	CAP	18 Jan 2003	14:28	LEO	16 Jul 2003	15:14	PIS
24 Jul 2002	06:39	AQU	20 Jan 2003	18:31	VIR	18 Jul 2003	23:20	ARI
26 Jul 2002	16:04	PIS	22 Jan 2003	21:22	LIB	21 Jul 2003	10:48	TAU
29 Jul 2002	03:38	ARI	25 Jan 2003	00:08	SCO	23 Jul 2003	23:41	GEM
31 Jul 2002	16:16	TAU	27 Jan 2003	03:25	SAG	26 Jul 2003	11:21	CAN
3 Aug 2002	03:45	GEM	29 Jan 2003	07:29	CAP	28 Jul 2003	20:15	LEO
5 Aug 2002	12:00	CAN	31 Jan 2003	12:44	AQU	31 Jul 2003	02:26	VIR
7 Aug 2002	16:26	LEO	2 Feb 2003	19:54	PIS	2 Aug 2003	06:47	LIB

DATE	TIME	SIGN
4 Aug 2003	10:12	SCO
6 Aug 2003	13:10	SAG
8 Aug 2003	16:02	CAP
10 Aug 2003	19:23	AQU
13 Aug 2003	00:19	PIS
15 Aug 2003	08:00	ARI
17 Aug 2003	18:52	TAU
20 Aug 2003	07:40	GEM
22 Aug 2003	19:43	CAN
25 Aug 2003	04:47	LEO
27 Aug 2003	10:25	VIR
29 Aug 2003	13:40	LIB
31 Aug 2003	15:59	SCO
2 Sep 2003	18:31	SAG
4 Sep 2003	21:51	CAP
7 Sep 2003	02:14	AQU
9 Sep 2003	08:07	PIS
11 Sep 2003	16:09	ARI
14 Sep 2003	02:50	TAU
16 Sep 2003	15:31	GEM
19 Sep 2003	04:06	CAN
21 Sep 2003	14:01	LEO
23 Sep 2003	20:03	VIR
25 Sep 2003	22:48	LIB
27 Sep 2003	23:52	SCO
30 Sep 2003	00:57	SAG
2 Oct 2003	03:21	CAP
4 Oct 2003	07:45	AQU
6 Oct 2003	14:20	PIS
8 Oct 2003	23:08	ARI
11 Oct 2003	10:05	TAU
13 Oct 2003	22:44	GEM
16 Oct 2003	11:40	CAN
18 Oct 2003	22:40	LEO
21 Oct 2003	06:01	VIR
23 Oct 2003	09:25	LIB
25 Oct 2003	10:08	SCO
27 Oct 2003	09:55	SAG
29 Oct 2003	10:37	CAP
31 Oct 2003	13:42	AQU
2 Nov 2003	19:52	PIS
5 Nov 2003	05:02	ARI
7 Nov 2003	16:29	TAU
10 Nov 2003	05:14	GEM
12 Nov 2003	18:09	CAN
15 Nov 2003	05:48	LEO
17 Nov 2003	14:35	VIR
19 Nov 2003	19:41	LIB
21 Nov 2003	21:22	SCO
23 Nov 2003	21:02	SAG
25 Nov 2003	20:31	CAP
27 Nov 2003	21:49	AQU
30 Nov 2003	02:26	PIS
2 Dec 2003	10:56	ARI
4 Dec 2003	22:30	TAU
7 Dec 2003	11:26	GEM
10 Dec 2003	00:10	CAN
12 Dec 2003	11:39	LEO
14 Dec 2003	21:05	VIR
17 Dec 2003	03:45	LIB
19 Dec 2003	07:19	SCO
21 Dec 2003	08:15	SAG
23 Dec 2003	07:55	CAP
25 Dec 2003	08:13	AQU
27 Dec 2003	11:11	PIS
29 Dec 2003	18:08	ARI
1 Jan 2004	05:01	TAU
3 Jan 2004	17:58	GEM
6 Jan 2004	06:38	CAN
8 Jan 2004	17:37	LEO
11 Jan 2004	02:36	VIR
13 Jan 2004	09:37	LIB
15 Jan 2004	14:31	SCO
17 Jan 2004	17:17	SAG
19 Jan 2004	18:23	CAP
21 Jan 2004	19:10	AQU
23 Jan 2004	21:29	PIS
26 Jan 2004	03:06	ARI
28 Jan 2004	12:46	TAU

DATE	TIME	SIGN
31 Jan 2004	01:18	GEM
2 Feb 2004	14:02	CAN
5 Feb 2004	00:48	LEO
7 Feb 2004	09:02	VIR
9 Feb 2004	15:12	LIB
11 Feb 2004	19:57	SCO
13 Feb 2004	23:34	SAG
16 Feb 2004	02:13	CAP
18 Feb 2004	04:27	AQU
20 Feb 2004	07:26	PIS
22 Feb 2004	12:46	ARI
24 Feb 2004	21:30	TAU
27 Feb 2004	09:22	GEM
29 Feb 2004	22:11	CAN
3 Mar 2004	09:16	LEO
5 Mar 2004	17:17	VIR
7 Mar 2004	22:29	LIB
10 Mar 2004	02:02	SCO
12 Mar 2004	04:56	SAG
14 Mar 2004	07:51	CAP
16 Mar 2004	11:10	AQU
18 Mar 2004	15:26	PIS
20 Mar 2004	21:29	ARI
23 Mar 2004	06:09	TAU
25 Mar 2004	17:34	GEM
28 Mar 2004	06:23	CAN
30 Mar 2004	18:07	LEO
2 Apr 2004	02:44	VIR
4 Apr 2004	07:51	LIB
6 Apr 2004	10:23	SCO
8 Apr 2004	11:50	SAG
10 Apr 2004	13:33	CAP
12 Apr 2004	16:32	AQU
14 Apr 2004	21:24	PIS
17 Apr 2004	04:24	ARI
19 Apr 2004	13:43	TAU
22 Apr 2004	01:10	GEM
24 Apr 2004	13:55	CAN
27 Apr 2004	02:13	LEO
29 Apr 2004	11:58	VIR
1 May 2004	18:02	LIB
3 May 2004	20:37	SCO
5 May 2004	21:07	SAG
7 May 2004	21:16	CAP
9 May 2004	22:47	AQU
12 May 2004	02:52	PIS
14 May 2004	10:03	ARI
16 May 2004	19:57	TAU
19 May 2004	07:47	GEM
21 May 2004	20:34	CAN
24 May 2004	09:06	LEO
26 May 2004	19:51	VIR
29 May 2004	03:21	LIB
31 May 2004	07:07	SCO
2 Jun 2004	07:51	SAG
4 Jun 2004	07:12	CAP
6 Jun 2004	07:09	AQU
8 Jun 2004	09:39	PIS
10 Jun 2004	15:49	ARI
13 Jun 2004	01:37	TAU
15 Jun 2004	13:44	GEM
18 Jun 2004	02:36	CAN
20 Jun 2004	15:04	LEO
23 Jun 2004	02:09	VIR
25 Jun 2004	10:48	LIB
27 Jun 2004	16:11	SCO
29 Jun 2004	18:15	SAG
1 Jul 2004	18:01	CAP
3 Jul 2004	17:21	AQU
5 Jul 2004	18:26	PIS
7 Jul 2004	23:04	ARI
10 Jul 2004	07:50	TAU
12 Jul 2004	19:44	GEM
15 Jul 2004	08:40	CAN
17 Jul 2004	20:55	LEO
20 Jul 2004	07:43	VIR
22 Jul 2004	16:38	LIB
24 Jul 2004	23:07	SCO
27 Jul 2004	02:46	SAG

DATE	TIME	SIGN
29 Jul 2004	03:56	CAP
31 Jul 2004	03:54	AQU
2 Aug 2004	04:34	PIS
4 Aug 2004	08:00	ARI
6 Aug 2004	15:26	TAU
9 Aug 2004	02:33	GEM
11 Aug 2004	15:19	CAN
14 Aug 2004	03:29	LEO
16 Aug 2004	13:48	VIR
18 Aug 2004	22:08	LIB
21 Aug 2004	04:36	SCO
23 Aug 2004	09:07	SAG
25 Aug 2004	11:45	CAP
27 Aug 2004	13:07	AQU
29 Aug 2004	14:33	PIS
31 Aug 2004	17:45	ARI
3 Sep 2004	00:16	TAU
5 Sep 2004	10:25	GEM
7 Sep 2004	22:50	CAN
10 Sep 2004	11:04	LEO
12 Sep 2004	21:15	VIR
15 Sep 2004	04:53	LIB
17 Sep 2004	10:24	SCO
19 Sep 2004	14:29	SAG
21 Sep 2004	17:35	CAP
23 Sep 2004	20:09	AQU
25 Sep 2004	22:55	PIS
28 Sep 2004	02:57	ARI
30 Sep 2004	09:24	TAU
2 Oct 2004	18:54	GEM
5 Oct 2004	06:54	CAN
7 Oct 2004	19:22	LEO
10 Oct 2004	06:00	VIR
12 Oct 2004	13:30	LIB
14 Oct 2004	18:10	SCO
16 Oct 2004	20:57	SAG
18 Oct 2004	23:06	CAP
21 Oct 2004	01:37	AQU
23 Oct 2004	05:13	PIS
25 Oct 2004	10:25	ARI
27 Oct 2004	17:37	TAU
30 Oct 2004	03:11	GEM
1 Nov 2004	14:53	CAN
4 Nov 2004	03:31	LEO
6 Nov 2004	14:59	VIR
8 Nov 2004	23:21	LIB
11 Nov 2004	04:04	SCO
13 Nov 2004	05:56	SAG
15 Nov 2004	06:32	CAP
17 Nov 2004	07:38	AQU
19 Nov 2004	10:38	PIS
21 Nov 2004	16:11	ARI
24 Nov 2004	00:16	TAU
26 Nov 2004	10:25	GEM
28 Nov 2004	22:10	CAN
1 Dec 2004	10:49	LEO
3 Dec 2004	22:59	VIR
6 Dec 2004	08:45	LIB
8 Dec 2004	14:42	SCO
10 Dec 2004	16:53	SAG
12 Dec 2004	16:41	CAP
14 Dec 2004	16:10	AQU
16 Dec 2004	17:23	PIS
18 Dec 2004	21:53	ARI
21 Dec 2004	05:52	TAU
23 Dec 2004	16:32	GEM
26 Dec 2004	04:37	CAN
28 Dec 2004	17:13	LEO
31 Dec 2004	05:32	VIR
2 Jan 2005	16:18	LIB
4 Jan 2005	23:57	SCO
7 Jan 2005	03:43	SAG
9 Jan 2005	04:10	CAP
11 Jan 2005	03:06	AQU
13 Jan 2005	02:51	PIS
15 Jan 2005	05:26	ARI
17 Jan 2005	12:07	TAU
19 Jan 2005	22:24	GEM
22 Jan 2005	10:42	CAN

DATE	TIME	SIGN	DATE	TIME	SIGN	DATE	TIME	SIGN
24 Jan 2005	23:20	LEO	23 Jul 2005	12:12	PIS	19 Jan 2006	22:48	LIB
27 Jan 2005	11:23	VIR	25 Jul 2005	13:23	ARI	22 Jan 2006	10:27	SCO
29 Jan 2005	22:11	LIB	27 Jul 2005	17:54	TAU	24 Jan 2006	18:37	SAG
1 Feb 2005	06:50	SCO	30 Jul 2005	02:02	GEM	26 Jan 2006	22:29	CAP
3 Feb 2005	12:19	SAG	1 Aug 2005	12:52	CAN	28 Jan 2006	23:08	AQU
5 Feb 2005	14:31	CAP	4 Aug 2005	01:09	LEO	30 Jan 2006	22:32	PIS
7 Feb 2005	14:26	AQU	6 Aug 2005	13:53	VIR	1 Feb 2006	22:46	ARI
9 Feb 2005	13:59	PIS	9 Aug 2005	02:07	LIB	4 Feb 2006	01:32	TAU
11 Feb 2005	15:22	ARI	11 Aug 2005	12:33	SCO	6 Feb 2006	07:32	GEM
13 Feb 2005	20:18	TAU	13 Aug 2005	19:46	SAG	8 Feb 2006	16:33	CAN
16 Feb 2005	05:18	GEM	15 Aug 2005	23:11	CAP	11 Feb 2006	03:44	LEO
18 Feb 2005	17:12	CAN	17 Aug 2005	23:37	AQU	13 Feb 2006	16:13	VIR
21 Feb 2005	05:54	LEO	19 Aug 2005	22:52	PIS	16 Feb 2006	05:08	LIB
23 Feb 2005	17:43	VIR	21 Aug 2005	23:02	ARI	18 Feb 2006	17:10	SCO
26 Feb 2005	03:58	LIB	24 Aug 2005	01:58	TAU	21 Feb 2006	02:36	SAG
28 Feb 2005	12:19	SCO	26 Aug 2005	08:43	GEM	23 Feb 2006	08:14	CAP
2 Mar 2005	18:29	SAG	28 Aug 2005	18:56	CAN	25 Feb 2006	10:13	AQU
4 Mar 2005	22:10	CAP	31 Aug 2005	07:14	LEO	27 Feb 2006	09:55	PIS
6 Mar 2005	23:48	AQU	2 Sep 2005	19:55	VIR	1 Mar 2006	09:19	ARI
9 Mar 2005	00:32	PIS	5 Sep 2005	07:51	LIB	3 Mar 2006	10:23	TAU
11 Mar 2005	02:03	ARI	7 Sep 2005	18:09	SCO	5 Mar 2006	14:38	GEM
13 Mar 2005	06:04	TAU	10 Sep 2005	02:01	SAG	7 Mar 2006	22:38	CAN
15 Mar 2005	13:45	GEM	12 Sep 2005	06:56	CAP	10 Mar 2006	09:42	LEO
18 Mar 2005	00:44	CAN	14 Sep 2005	09:01	AQU	12 Mar 2006	22:23	VIR
20 Mar 2005	13:16	LEO	16 Sep 2005	09:24	PIS	15 Mar 2006	11:12	LIB
23 Mar 2005	01:09	VIR	18 Sep 2005	09:43	ARI	17 Mar 2006	22:58	SCO
25 Mar 2005	10:58	LIB	20 Sep 2005	11:48	TAU	20 Mar 2006	08:42	SAG
27 Mar 2005	18:28	SCO	22 Sep 2005	17:06	GEM	22 Mar 2006	15:35	CAP
29 Mar 2005	23:55	SAG	25 Sep 2005	02:11	CAN	24 Mar 2006	19:20	AQU
1 Apr 2005	03:47	CAP	27 Sep 2005	14:02	LEO	26 Mar 2006	20:32	PIS
3 Apr 2005	06:30	AQU	30 Sep 2005	02:43	VIR	28 Mar 2006	20:30	ARI
5 Apr 2005	08:45	PIS	2 Oct 2005	14:23	LIB	30 Mar 2006	21:01	TAU
7 Apr 2005	11:28	ARI	5 Oct 2005	00:02	SCO	1 Apr 2006	23:50	GEM
9 Apr 2005	15:50	TAU	7 Oct 2005	07:27	SAG	4 Apr 2006	06:14	CAN
11 Apr 2005	22:55	GEM	9 Oct 2005	12:42	CAP	6 Apr 2006	16:25	LEO
14 Apr 2005	09:03	CAN	11 Oct 2005	16:04	AQU	9 Apr 2006	04:58	VIR
16 Apr 2005	21:17	LEO	13 Oct 2005	18:05	PIS	11 Apr 2006	17:46	LIB
19 Apr 2005	09:26	VIR	15 Oct 2005	19:39	ARI	14 Apr 2006	05:08	SCO
21 Apr 2005	19:26	LIB	17 Oct 2005	22:04	TAU	16 Apr 2006	14:18	SAG
24 Apr 2005	02:24	SCO	20 Oct 2005	02:45	GEM	18 Apr 2006	21:12	CAP
26 Apr 2005	06:45	SAG	22 Oct 2005	10:41	CAN	21 Apr 2006	01:54	AQU
28 Apr 2005	09:32	CAP	24 Oct 2005	21:48	LEO	23 Apr 2006	04:42	PIS
30 Apr 2005	11:53	AQU	27 Oct 2005	10:27	VIR	25 Apr 2006	06:11	ARI
2 May 2005	14:42	PIS	29 Oct 2005	22:14	LIB	27 Apr 2006	07:26	TAU
4 May 2005	18:35	ARI	1 Nov 2005	07:28	SCO	29 Apr 2006	09:58	GEM
7 May 2005	00:01	TAU	3 Nov 2005	13:54	SAG	1 May 2006	15:18	CAN
9 May 2005	07:28	GEM	5 Nov 2005	18:16	CAP	4 May 2006	00:18	LEO
11 May 2005	17:20	CAN	7 Nov 2005	21:30	AQU	6 May 2006	12:20	VIR
14 May 2005	05:17	LEO	10 Nov 2005	00:22	PIS	9 May 2006	01:09	LIB
16 May 2005	17:46	VIR	12 Nov 2005	03:22	ARI	11 May 2006	12:23	SCO
19 May 2005	04:29	LIB	14 Nov 2005	07:02	TAU	13 May 2006	20:55	SAG
21 May 2005	11:47	SCO	16 Nov 2005	12:10	GEM	16 May 2006	02:58	CAP
23 May 2005	15:37	SAG	18 Nov 2005	19:42	CAN	18 May 2006	07:18	AQU
25 May 2005	17:10	CAP	21 Nov 2005	06:09	LEO	20 May 2006	10:38	PIS
27 May 2005	18:09	AQU	23 Nov 2005	18:41	VIR	22 May 2006	13:23	ARI
29 May 2005	20:09	PIS	26 Nov 2005	06:57	LIB	24 May 2006	16:00	TAU
1 Jun 2005	00:08	ARI	28 Nov 2005	16:32	SCO	26 May 2006	19:19	GEM
3 Jun 2005	06:19	TAU	30 Nov 2005	22:31	SAG	29 May 2006	00:34	CAN
5 Jun 2005	14:36	GEM	3 Dec 2005	01:41	CAP	31 May 2006	08:52	LEO
8 Jun 2005	00:46	CAN	5 Dec 2005	03:35	AQU	2 Jun 2006	20:17	VIR
10 Jun 2005	12:39	LEO	7 Dec 2005	05:44	PIS	5 Jun 2006	09:07	LIB
13 Jun 2005	01:21	VIR	9 Dec 2005	09:02	ARI	7 Jun 2006	20:40	SCO
15 Jun 2005	12:57	LIB	11 Dec 2005	13:46	TAU	10 Jun 2006	05:04	SAG
17 Jun 2005	21:22	SCO	13 Dec 2005	19:59	GEM	12 Jun 2006	10:18	CAP
20 Jun 2005	01:43	SAG	16 Dec 2005	04:01	CAN	14 Jun 2006	13:31	AQU
22 Jun 2005	02:51	CAP	18 Dec 2005	14:18	LEO	16 Jun 2006	16:05	PIS
24 Jun 2005	02:36	AQU	21 Dec 2005	02:38	VIR	18 Jun 2006	18:53	ARI
26 Jun 2005	03:03	PIS	23 Dec 2005	15:25	LIB	20 Jun 2006	22:22	TAU
28 Jun 2005	05:51	ARI	26 Dec 2005	02:02	SCO	23 Jun 2006	02:49	GEM
30 Jun 2005	11:45	TAU	28 Dec 2005	08:42	SAG	25 Jun 2006	08:48	CAN
2 Jul 2005	20:25	GEM	30 Dec 2005	11:34	CAP	27 Jun 2006	17:08	LEO
5 Jul 2005	07:07	CAN	1 Jan 2006	12:14	AQU	30 Jun 2006	04:14	VIR
7 Jul 2005	19:10	LEO	3 Jan 2006	12:44	PIS	2 Jul 2006	17:05	LIB
10 Jul 2005	07:57	VIR	5 Jan 2006	14:44	ARI	5 Jul 2006	05:12	SCO
12 Jul 2005	20:08	LIB	7 Jan 2006	19:09	TAU	7 Jul 2006	14:12	SAG
15 Jul 2005	05:50	SCO	10 Jan 2006	01:58	GEM	9 Jul 2006	19:24	CAP
17 Jul 2005	11:33	SAG	12 Jan 2006	10:50	CAN	11 Jul 2006	21:45	AQU
19 Jul 2005	13:24	CAP	14 Jan 2006	21:30	LEO	13 Jul 2006	22:59	PIS
21 Jul 2005	12:54	AQU	17 Jan 2006	09:48	VIR	16 Jul 2006	00:39	ARI

DATE	TIME	SIGN	DATE	TIME	SIGN	DATE	TIME	SIGN
18 Jul 2006	03:44	TAU	14 Jan 2007	18:10	SAG	12 Jul 2007	22:39	CAN
20 Jul 2006	08:38	GEM	17 Jan 2007	01:47	CAP	15 Jul 2007	02:44	LEO
22 Jul 2006	15:28	CAN	19 Jan 2007	06:15	AQU	17 Jul 2007	09:40	VIR
25 Jul 2006	00:25	LEO	21 Jan 2007	08:47	PIS	19 Jul 2007	19:53	LIB
27 Jul 2006	11:36	VIR	23 Jan 2007	10:52	ARI	22 Jul 2007	08:17	SCO
30 Jul 2006	00:27	LIB	25 Jan 2007	13:28	TAU	24 Jul 2007	20:28	SAG
1 Aug 2006	13:06	SCO	27 Jan 2007	17:09	GEM	27 Jul 2007	06:21	CAP
3 Aug 2006	23:11	SAG	29 Jan 2007	22:16	CAN	29 Jul 2007	13:12	AQU
6 Aug 2006	05:19	CAP	1 Feb 2007	05:14	LEO	31 Jul 2007	17:40	PIS
8 Aug 2006	07:46	AQU	3 Feb 2007	14:34	VIR	2 Aug 2007	20:42	ARI
10 Aug 2006	08:10	PIS	6 Feb 2007	02:15	LIB	4 Aug 2007	23:15	TAU
12 Aug 2006	08:21	ARI	8 Feb 2007	15:09	SCO	7 Aug 2007	02:01	GEM
14 Aug 2006	10:00	TAU	11 Feb 2007	03:00	SAG	9 Aug 2007	05:35	CAN
16 Aug 2006	14:07	GEM	13 Feb 2007	11:40	CAP	11 Aug 2007	10:42	LEO
18 Aug 2006	21:03	CAN	15 Feb 2007	16:33	AQU	13 Aug 2007	18:02	VIR
21 Aug 2006	06:33	LEO	17 Feb 2007	18:29	PIS	16 Aug 2007	04:04	LIB
23 Aug 2006	18:07	VIR	19 Feb 2007	19:05	ARI	18 Aug 2007	16:13	SCO
26 Aug 2006	07:01	LIB	21 Feb 2007	20:03	TAU	21 Aug 2007	04:43	SAG
28 Aug 2006	19:55	SCO	23 Feb 2007	22:42	GEM	23 Aug 2007	15:18	CAP
31 Aug 2006	06:59	SAG	26 Feb 2007	03:48	CAN	25 Aug 2007	22:33	AQU
2 Sep 2006	14:33	CAP	28 Feb 2007	11:30	LEO	28 Aug 2007	02:33	PIS
4 Sep 2006	18:14	AQU	2 Mar 2007	21:32	VIR	30 Aug 2007	04:24	ARI
6 Sep 2006	18:56	PIS	5 Mar 2007	09:25	LIB	1 Sep 2007	05:35	TAU
8 Sep 2006	18:22	ARI	7 Mar 2007	22:16	SCO	3 Sep 2007	07:29	GEM
10 Sep 2006	18:29	TAU	10 Mar 2007	10:36	SAG	5 Sep 2007	11:08	CAN
12 Sep 2006	20:59	GEM	12 Mar 2007	20:33	CAP	7 Sep 2007	16:59	LEO
15 Sep 2006	02:54	CAN	15 Mar 2007	02:50	AQU	10 Sep 2007	01:10	VIR
17 Sep 2006	12:15	LEO	17 Mar 2007	05:29	PIS	12 Sep 2007	11:31	LIB
20 Sep 2006	00:07	VIR	19 Mar 2007	05:41	ARI	14 Sep 2007	23:36	SCO
22 Sep 2006	13:06	LIB	21 Mar 2007	05:15	TAU	17 Sep 2007	12:20	SAG
25 Sep 2006	01:53	SCO	23 Mar 2007	06:06	GEM	19 Sep 2007	23:50	CAP
27 Sep 2006	13:15	SAG	25 Mar 2007	09:49	CAN	22 Sep 2007	08:17	AQU
29 Sep 2006	21:59	CAP	27 Mar 2007	17:04	LEO	24 Sep 2007	12:53	PIS
2 Oct 2006	03:23	AQU	30 Mar 2007	03:27	VIR	26 Sep 2007	14:21	ARI
4 Oct 2006	05:32	PIS	1 Apr 2007	15:43	LIB	28 Sep 2007	14:16	TAU
6 Oct 2006	05:31	ARI	4 Apr 2007	04:35	SCO	30 Sep 2007	14:34	GEM
8 Oct 2006	05:04	TAU	6 Apr 2007	16:56	SAG	2 Oct 2007	16:57	CAN
10 Oct 2006	06:06	GEM	9 Apr 2007	03:35	CAP	4 Oct 2007	22:27	LEO
12 Oct 2006	10:22	CAN	11 Apr 2007	11:21	AQU	7 Oct 2007	07:03	VIR
14 Oct 2006	18:38	LEO	13 Apr 2007	15:37	PIS	9 Oct 2007	17:57	LIB
17 Oct 2006	06:15	VIR	15 Apr 2007	16:46	ARI	12 Oct 2007	06:13	SCO
19 Oct 2006	19:19	LIB	17 Apr 2007	16:10	TAU	14 Oct 2007	18:58	SAG
22 Oct 2006	07:53	SCO	19 Apr 2007	15:51	GEM	17 Oct 2007	07:02	CAP
24 Oct 2006	18:52	SAG	21 Apr 2007	17:49	CAN	19 Oct 2007	16:51	AQU
27 Oct 2006	03:46	CAP	23 Apr 2007	23:39	LEO	21 Oct 2007	23:00	PIS
29 Oct 2006	10:15	AQU	26 Apr 2007	09:24	VIR	24 Oct 2007	01:22	ARI
31 Oct 2006	14:09	PIS	28 Apr 2007	21:44	LIB	26 Oct 2007	01:06	TAU
2 Nov 2006	15:45	ARI	1 May 2007	10:40	SCO	28 Oct 2007	00:11	GEM
4 Nov 2006	16:04	TAU	3 May 2007	22:47	SAG	30 Oct 2007	00:50	CAN
6 Nov 2006	16:46	GEM	6 May 2007	09:20	CAP	1 Nov 2007	04:48	LEO
8 Nov 2006	19:46	CAN	8 May 2007	17:47	AQU	3 Nov 2007	12:45	VIR
11 Nov 2006	02:35	LEO	10 May 2007	23:30	PIS	5 Nov 2007	23:47	LIB
13 Nov 2006	13:19	VIR	13 May 2007	02:17	ARI	8 Nov 2007	12:18	SCO
16 Nov 2006	02:14	LIB	15 May 2007	02:47	TAU	11 Nov 2007	00:58	SAG
18 Nov 2006	14:45	SCO	17 May 2007	02:34	GEM	13 Nov 2007	12:59	CAP
21 Nov 2006	01:14	SAG	19 May 2007	03:38	CAN	15 Nov 2007	23:28	AQU
23 Nov 2006	09:24	CAP	21 May 2007	07:57	LEO	18 Nov 2007	07:13	PIS
25 Nov 2006	15:40	AQU	23 May 2007	16:26	VIR	20 Nov 2007	11:22	ARI
27 Nov 2006	20:20	PIS	26 May 2007	04:16	LIB	22 Nov 2007	12:17	TAU
29 Nov 2006	23:29	ARI	28 May 2007	17:11	SCO	24 Nov 2007	11:29	GEM
2 Dec 2006	01:25	TAU	31 May 2007	05:06	SAG	26 Nov 2007	11:07	CAN
4 Dec 2006	03:05	GEM	2 Jun 2007	15:08	CAP	28 Nov 2007	13:24	LEO
6 Dec 2006	06:00	CAN	4 Jun 2007	23:14	AQU	30 Nov 2007	19:44	VIR
8 Dec 2006	11:53	LEO	7 Jun 2007	05:23	PIS	3 Dec 2007	06:00	LIB
10 Dec 2006	21:31	VIR	9 Jun 2007	09:25	ARI	5 Dec 2007	18:30	SCO
13 Dec 2006	10:00	LIB	11 Jun 2007	11:28	TAU	8 Dec 2007	07:10	SAG
15 Dec 2006	22:41	SCO	13 Jun 2007	12:23	GEM	10 Dec 2007	18:50	CAP
18 Dec 2006	09:09	SAG	15 Jun 2007	13:45	CAN	13 Dec 2007	05:00	AQU
20 Dec 2006	16:38	CAP	17 Jun 2007	17:24	LEO	15 Dec 2007	13:13	PIS
22 Dec 2006	21:48	AQU	20 Jun 2007	00:46	VIR	17 Dec 2007	18:52	ARI
25 Dec 2006	01:42	PIS	22 Jun 2007	11:43	LIB	19 Dec 2007	21:37	TAU
27 Dec 2006	05:03	ARI	25 Jun 2007	00:26	SCO	21 Dec 2007	22:13	GEM
29 Dec 2006	08:08	TAU	27 Jun 2007	12:22	SAG	23 Dec 2007	22:18	CAN
31 Dec 2006	11:16	GEM	29 Jun 2007	22:03	CAP	25 Dec 2007	23:53	LEO
2 Jan 2007	15:14	CAN	2 Jul 2007	05:23	AQU	28 Dec 2007	04:44	VIR
4 Jan 2007	21:14	LEO	4 Jul 2007	10:51	PIS	30 Dec 2007	13:38	LIB
7 Jan 2007	06:18	VIR	6 Jul 2007	14:56	ARI	2 Jan 2008	01:32	SCO
9 Jan 2007	18:14	LIB	8 Jul 2007	17:53	TAU	4 Jan 2008	14:12	SAG
12 Jan 2007	07:07	SCO	10 Jul 2007	20:09	GEM	7 Jan 2008	01:42	CAP

DATE	TIME	SIGN	DATE	TIME	SIGN	DATE	TIME	SIGN
9 Jan 2008	11:12	AQU	6 Jul 2008	11:04	VIR	3 Jan 2009	09:48	ARI
11 Jan 2008	18:43	PIS	8 Jul 2008	17:31	LIB	5 Jan 2009	15:44	TAU
14 Jan 2008	00:22	ARI	11 Jul 2008	03:35	SCO	7 Jan 2009	18:11	GEM
16 Jan 2008	04:12	TAU	13 Jul 2008	15:49	SAG	9 Jan 2009	18:13	CAN
18 Jan 2008	06:29	GEM	16 Jul 2008	04:19	CAP	11 Jan 2009	17:40	LEO
20 Jan 2008	08:04	CAN	18 Jul 2008	15:39	AQU	13 Jan 2009	18:32	VIR
22 Jan 2008	10:20	LEO	21 Jul 2008	01:06	PIS	15 Jan 2009	22:31	LIB
24 Jan 2008	14:48	VIR	23 Jul 2008	08:21	ARI	18 Jan 2009	06:20	SCO
26 Jan 2008	22:35	LIB	25 Jul 2008	13:13	TAU	20 Jan 2009	17:29	SAG
29 Jan 2008	09:35	SCO	27 Jul 2008	15:54	GEM	23 Jan 2009	06:17	CAP
31 Jan 2008	22:07	SAG	29 Jul 2008	17:11	CAN	25 Jan 2009	18:56	AQU
3 Feb 2008	09:51	CAP	31 Jul 2008	18:21	LEO	28 Jan 2009	06:11	PIS
5 Feb 2008	19:09	AQU	2 Aug 2008	20:59	VIR	30 Jan 2009	15:24	ARI
8 Feb 2008	01:45	PIS	5 Aug 2008	02:28	LIB	1 Feb 2009	22:07	TAU
10 Feb 2008	06:17	ARI	7 Aug 2008	11:26	SCO	4 Feb 2009	02:13	GEM
12 Feb 2008	09:33	TAU	9 Aug 2008	23:10	SAG	6 Feb 2009	04:05	CAN
14 Feb 2008	12:19	GEM	12 Aug 2008	11:41	CAP	8 Feb 2009	04:43	LEO
16 Feb 2008	15:11	CAN	14 Aug 2008	22:55	AQU	10 Feb 2009	05:38	VIR
18 Feb 2008	18:51	LEO	17 Aug 2008	07:45	PIS	12 Feb 2009	08:33	LIB
21 Feb 2008	00:07	VIR	19 Aug 2008	14:09	ARI	14 Feb 2009	14:51	SCO
23 Feb 2008	07:44	LIB	21 Aug 2008	18:37	TAU	17 Feb 2009	00:53	SAG
25 Feb 2008	18:05	SCO	23 Aug 2008	21:47	GEM	19 Feb 2009	13:25	CAP
28 Feb 2008	06:22	SAG	26 Aug 2008	00:18	CAN	22 Feb 2009	02:05	AQU
1 Mar 2008	18:32	CAP	28 Aug 2008	02:50	LEO	24 Feb 2009	12:58	PIS
4 Mar 2008	04:23	AQU	30 Aug 2008	06:18	VIR	26 Feb 2009	21:22	ARI
6 Mar 2008	10:51	PIS	1 Sep 2008	11:45	LIB	1 Mar 2009	03:32	TAU
8 Mar 2008	14:22	ARI	3 Sep 2008	20:02	SCO	3 Mar 2009	07:58	GEM
10 Mar 2008	16:13	TAU	6 Sep 2008	07:10	SAG	5 Mar 2009	11:06	CAN
12 Mar 2008	17:54	GEM	8 Sep 2008	19:44	CAP	7 Mar 2009	13:24	LEO
14 Mar 2008	20:37	CAN	11 Sep 2008	07:19	AQU	9 Mar 2009	15:34	VIR
17 Mar 2008	01:04	LEO	13 Sep 2008	16:03	PIS	11 Mar 2009	18:45	LIB
19 Mar 2008	07:25	VIR	15 Sep 2008	21:38	ARI	14 Mar 2009	00:23	SCO
21 Mar 2008	15:45	LIB	18 Sep 2008	00:56	TAU	16 Mar 2009	09:22	SAG
24 Mar 2008	02:06	SCO	20 Sep 2008	03:16	GEM	18 Mar 2009	21:18	CAP
26 Mar 2008	14:10	SAG	22 Sep 2008	05:48	CAN	21 Mar 2009	10:05	AQU
29 Mar 2008	02:42	CAP	24 Sep 2008	09:13	LEO	23 Mar 2009	21:07	PIS
31 Mar 2008	13:32	AQU	26 Sep 2008	13:52	VIR	26 Mar 2009	05:02	ARI
2 Apr 2008	20:53	PIS	28 Sep 2008	20:05	LIB	28 Mar 2009	10:08	TAU
5 Apr 2008	00:25	ARI	1 Oct 2008	04:26	SCO	30 Mar 2009	13:35	GEM
7 Apr 2008	01:19	TAU	3 Oct 2008	15:14	SAG	1 Apr 2009	16:30	CAN
9 Apr 2008	01:27	GEM	6 Oct 2008	03:48	CAP	3 Apr 2009	19:32	LEO
11 Apr 2008	02:43	CAN	8 Oct 2008	16:02	AQU	5 Apr 2009	23:01	VIR
13 Apr 2008	06:28	LEO	11 Oct 2008	01:29	PIS	8 Apr 2009	03:22	LIB
15 Apr 2008	13:07	VIR	13 Oct 2008	07:06	ARI	10 Apr 2009	09:23	SCO
17 Apr 2008	22:10	LIB	15 Oct 2008	09:30	TAU	12 Apr 2009	18:00	SAG
20 Apr 2008	09:00	SCO	17 Oct 2008	10:25	GEM	15 Apr 2009	05:27	CAP
22 Apr 2008	21:07	SAG	19 Oct 2008	11:40	CAN	17 Apr 2009	18:18	AQU
25 Apr 2008	09:46	CAP	21 Oct 2008	14:35	LEO	20 Apr 2009	05:54	PIS
27 Apr 2008	21:26	AQU	23 Oct 2008	19:40	VIR	22 Apr 2009	14:07	ARI
30 Apr 2008	06:10	PIS	26 Oct 2008	02:47	LIB	24 Apr 2009	18:45	TAU
2 May 2008	10:49	ARI	28 Oct 2008	11:47	SCO	26 Apr 2009	21:01	GEM
4 May 2008	11:56	TAU	30 Oct 2008	22:41	SAG	28 Apr 2009	22:38	CAN
6 May 2008	11:17	GEM	2 Nov 2008	11:13	CAP	1 May 2009	00:56	LEO
8 May 2008	11:02	CAN	5 Nov 2008	00:00	AQU	3 May 2009	04:36	VIR
10 May 2008	13:11	LEO	7 Nov 2008	10:41	PIS	5 May 2009	09:51	LIB
12 May 2008	18:48	VIR	9 Nov 2008	17:25	ARI	7 May 2009	16:47	SCO
15 May 2008	03:46	LIB	11 Nov 2008	20:04	TAU	10 May 2009	01:49	SAG
17 May 2008	14:59	SCO	13 Nov 2008	20:11	GEM	12 May 2009	13:09	CAP
20 May 2008	03:18	SAG	15 Nov 2008	19:52	CAN	15 May 2009	02:00	AQU
22 May 2008	15:55	CAP	17 Nov 2008	21:08	LEO	17 May 2009	14:15	PIS
25 May 2008	03:51	AQU	20 Nov 2008	01:13	VIR	19 May 2009	23:28	ARI
27 May 2008	13:37	PIS	22 Nov 2008	08:20	LIB	22 May 2009	04:39	TAU
29 May 2008	19:51	ARI	24 Nov 2008	17:53	SCO	24 May 2009	06:33	GEM
31 May 2008	22:17	TAU	27 Nov 2008	05:13	SAG	26 May 2009	06:57	CAN
2 Jun 2008	22:05	GEM	29 Nov 2008	17:47	CAP	28 May 2009	07:44	LEO
4 Jun 2008	21:16	CAN	2 Dec 2008	06:44	AQU	30 May 2009	10:18	VIR
6 Jun 2008	22:01	LEO	4 Dec 2008	18:22	PIS	1 Jun 2009	15:17	LIB
9 Jun 2008	02:02	VIR	7 Dec 2008	02:42	ARI	3 Jun 2009	22:44	SCO
11 Jun 2008	09:55	LIB	9 Dec 2008	06:51	TAU	6 Jun 2009	08:23	SAG
13 Jun 2008	20:52	SCO	11 Dec 2008	07:32	GEM	8 Jun 2009	19:59	CAP
16 Jun 2008	09:19	SAG	13 Dec 2008	06:39	CAN	11 Jun 2009	08:52	AQU
18 Jun 2008	21:51	CAP	15 Dec 2008	06:22	LEO	13 Jun 2009	21:31	PIS
21 Jun 2008	09:32	AQU	17 Dec 2008	08:36	VIR	16 Jun 2009	07:50	ARI
23 Jun 2008	19:31	PIS	19 Dec 2008	14:23	LIB	18 Jun 2009	14:18	TAU
26 Jun 2008	02:47	ARI	21 Dec 2008	23:37	SCO	20 Jun 2009	16:59	GEM
28 Jun 2008	06:49	TAU	24 Dec 2008	11:12	SAG	22 Jun 2009	17:11	CAN
30 Jun 2008	08:02	GEM	26 Dec 2008	23:55	CAP	24 Jun 2009	16:50	LEO
2 Jul 2008	07:52	CAN	29 Dec 2008	12:42	AQU	26 Jun 2009	17:46	VIR
4 Jul 2008	08:15	LEO	1 Jan 2009	00:26	PIS	28 Jun 2009	21:25	LIB

DATE	TIME	SIGN
1 Jul 2009	04:18	SCO
3 Jul 2009	14:11	SAG
6 Jul 2009	02:07	CAP
8 Jul 2009	15:03	AQU
11 Jul 2009	03:43	PIS
13 Jul 2009	14:38	ARI
15 Jul 2009	22:28	TAU
18 Jul 2009	02:40	GEM
20 Jul 2009	03:50	CAN
22 Jul 2009	03:27	LEO
24 Jul 2009	03:23	VIR
26 Jul 2009	05:25	LIB
28 Jul 2009	10:56	SCO
30 Jul 2009	20:10	SAG
2 Aug 2009	08:08	CAP
4 Aug 2009	21:07	AQU
7 Aug 2009	09:33	PIS
9 Aug 2009	20:22	ARI
12 Aug 2009	04:49	TAU
14 Aug 2009	10:24	GEM
16 Aug 2009	13:11	CAN
18 Aug 2009	13:56	LEO
20 Aug 2009	14:00	VIR
22 Aug 2009	15:12	LIB
24 Aug 2009	19:16	SCO
27 Aug 2009	03:16	SAG
29 Aug 2009	14:44	CAP
1 Sep 2009	03:42	AQU
3 Sep 2009	15:57	PIS
6 Sep 2009	02:13	ARI
8 Sep 2009	10:16	TAU
10 Sep 2009	16:16	GEM
12 Sep 2009	20:18	CAN
14 Sep 2009	22:38	LEO
16 Sep 2009	23:55	VIR
19 Sep 2009	01:26	LIB
21 Sep 2009	04:52	SCO
23 Sep 2009	11:43	SAG
25 Sep 2009	22:19	CAP
28 Sep 2009	11:06	AQU
30 Sep 2009	23:24	PIS
3 Oct 2009	09:19	ARI
5 Oct 2009	16:32	TAU
7 Oct 2009	21:45	GEM
10 Oct 2009	01:47	CAN
12 Oct 2009	05:02	LEO
14 Oct 2009	07:45	VIR
16 Oct 2009	10:29	LIB
18 Oct 2009	14:23	SCO
20 Oct 2009	20:49	SAG
23 Oct 2009	06:39	CAP
25 Oct 2009	19:07	AQU
28 Oct 2009	07:44	PIS
30 Oct 2009	17:56	ARI
2 Nov 2009	00:43	TAU
4 Nov 2009	04:52	GEM
6 Nov 2009	07:42	CAN
8 Nov 2009	10:22	LEO
10 Nov 2009	13:30	VIR
12 Nov 2009	17:22	LIB
14 Nov 2009	22:24	SCO
17 Nov 2009	05:21	SAG
19 Nov 2009	15:01	CAP
22 Nov 2009	03:10	AQU
24 Nov 2009	16:07	PIS
27 Nov 2009	03:09	ARI
29 Nov 2009	10:32	TAU
1 Dec 2009	14:22	GEM
3 Dec 2009	16:00	CAN
5 Dec 2009	17:06	LEO
7 Dec 2009	19:05	VIR
9 Dec 2009	22:47	LIB
12 Dec 2009	04:31	SCO
14 Dec 2009	12:25	SAG
16 Dec 2009	22:32	CAP
19 Dec 2009	10:38	AQU
21 Dec 2009	23:41	PIS
24 Dec 2009	11:38	ARI
26 Dec 2009	20:24	TAU

DATE	TIME	SIGN
29 Dec 2009	01:11	GEM
31 Dec 2009	02:44	CAN
2 Jan 2010	02:40	LEO
4 Jan 2010	02:52	VIR
6 Jan 2010	04:58	LIB
8 Jan 2010	10:00	SCO
10 Jan 2010	18:09	SAG
13 Jan 2010	04:53	CAP
15 Jan 2010	17:16	AQU
18 Jan 2010	06:16	PIS
20 Jan 2010	18:35	ARI
23 Jan 2010	04:38	TAU
25 Jan 2010	11:09	GEM
27 Jan 2010	14:00	CAN
29 Jan 2010	14:09	LEO
31 Jan 2010	13:23	VIR
2 Feb 2010	13:42	LIB
4 Feb 2010	16:55	SCO
7 Feb 2010	00:04	SAG
9 Feb 2010	10:43	CAP
11 Feb 2010	23:23	AQU
14 Feb 2010	12:22	PIS
17 Feb 2010	00:29	ARI
19 Feb 2010	10:54	TAU
21 Feb 2010	18:46	GEM
23 Feb 2010	23:27	CAN
26 Feb 2010	01:07	LEO
28 Feb 2010	00:52	VIR
2 Mar 2010	00:31	LIB
4 Mar 2010	02:12	SCO
6 Mar 2010	07:36	SAG
8 Mar 2010	17:13	CAP
11 Mar 2010	05:42	AQU
13 Mar 2010	18:43	PIS
16 Mar 2010	06:31	ARI
18 Mar 2010	16:28	TAU
21 Mar 2010	00:27	GEM
23 Mar 2010	06:15	CAN
25 Mar 2010	09:37	LEO
27 Mar 2010	10:56	VIR
29 Mar 2010	11:21	LIB
31 Mar 2010	12:41	SCO
2 Apr 2010	16:52	SAG
5 Apr 2010	01:07	CAP
7 Apr 2010	12:50	AQU
10 Apr 2010	01:47	PIS
12 Apr 2010	13:30	ARI
14 Apr 2010	22:53	TAU
17 Apr 2010	06:07	GEM
19 Apr 2010	11:38	CAN
21 Apr 2010	15:41	LEO
23 Apr 2010	18:23	VIR
25 Apr 2010	20:16	LIB
27 Apr 2010	22:29	SCO
30 Apr 2010	02:36	SAG
2 May 2010	10:00	CAP
4 May 2010	20:51	AQU
7 May 2010	09:33	PIS
9 May 2010	21:28	ARI
12 May 2010	06:47	TAU
14 May 2010	13:16	GEM
16 May 2010	17:45	CAN
18 May 2010	21:05	LEO
20 May 2010	23:58	VIR
23 May 2010	02:49	LIB
25 May 2010	06:16	SCO
27 May 2010	11:16	SAG
29 May 2010	18:44	CAP
1 Jun 2010	05:07	AQU
3 Jun 2010	17:33	PIS
6 Jun 2010	05:49	ARI
8 Jun 2010	15:39	TAU
10 Jun 2010	22:09	GEM
13 Jun 2010	01:49	CAN
15 Jun 2010	03:53	LEO
17 Jun 2010	05:40	VIR
19 Jun 2010	08:13	LIB
21 Jun 2010	12:14	SCO
23 Jun 2010	18:09	SAG

DATE	TIME	SIGN
26 Jun 2010	02:21	CAP
28 Jun 2010	12:52	AQU
1 Jul 2010	01:09	PIS
3 Jul 2010	13:43	ARI
6 Jul 2010	00:27	TAU
8 Jul 2010	07:49	GEM
10 Jul 2010	11:36	CAN
12 Jul 2010	12:52	LEO
14 Jul 2010	13:15	VIR
16 Jul 2010	14:24	LIB
18 Jul 2010	17:41	SCO
20 Jul 2010	23:49	SAG
23 Jul 2010	08:38	CAP
25 Jul 2010	19:37	AQU
28 Jul 2010	07:59	PIS
30 Jul 2010	20:41	ARI
2 Aug 2010	08:12	TAU
4 Aug 2010	16:53	GEM
6 Aug 2010	21:48	CAN
8 Aug 2010	23:21	LEO
10 Aug 2010	23:00	VIR
12 Aug 2010	22:43	LIB
15 Aug 2010	00:27	SCO
17 Aug 2010	05:33	SAG
19 Aug 2010	14:17	CAP
22 Aug 2010	01:37	AQU
24 Aug 2010	14:10	PIS
27 Aug 2010	02:48	ARI
29 Aug 2010	14:34	TAU
1 Sep 2010	00:17	GEM
3 Sep 2010	06:49	CAN
5 Sep 2010	09:43	LEO
7 Sep 2010	09:52	VIR
9 Sep 2010	09:00	LIB
11 Sep 2010	09:21	SCO
13 Sep 2010	12:53	SAG
15 Sep 2010	20:30	CAP
18 Sep 2010	07:34	AQU
20 Sep 2010	20:14	PIS
23 Sep 2010	08:46	ARI
25 Sep 2010	20:16	TAU
28 Sep 2010	06:10	GEM
30 Sep 2010	13:44	CAN
2 Oct 2010	18:20	LEO
4 Oct 2010	19:59	VIR
6 Oct 2010	19:51	LIB
8 Oct 2010	19:52	SCO
10 Oct 2010	22:09	SAG
13 Oct 2010	04:17	CAP
15 Oct 2010	14:24	AQU
18 Oct 2010	02:51	PIS
20 Oct 2010	15:22	ARI
23 Oct 2010	02:28	TAU
25 Oct 2010	11:46	GEM
27 Oct 2010	19:13	CAN
30 Oct 2010	00:37	LEO
1 Nov 2010	03:50	VIR
3 Nov 2010	05:18	LIB
5 Nov 2010	06:15	SCO
7 Nov 2010	08:28	SAG
9 Nov 2010	13:37	CAP
11 Nov 2010	22:32	AQU
14 Nov 2010	10:24	PIS
16 Nov 2010	22:57	ARI
19 Nov 2010	10:03	TAU
21 Nov 2010	18:45	GEM
24 Nov 2010	01:13	CAN
26 Nov 2010	06:00	LEO
28 Nov 2010	09:33	VIR
30 Nov 2010	12:14	LIB
2 Dec 2010	14:43	SCO
4 Dec 2010	17:58	SAG
6 Dec 2010	23:16	CAP
9 Dec 2010	07:30	AQU
11 Dec 2010	18:40	PIS
14 Dec 2010	07:14	ARI
16 Dec 2010	18:48	TAU
19 Dec 2010	03:36	GEM
21 Dec 2010	09:21	CAN

DATE	TIME	SIGN	DATE	TIME	SIGN	DATE	TIME	SIGN
23 Dec 2010	12:49	LEO	20 Jun 2011	20:45	PIS	18 Dec 2011	08:05	LIB
25 Dec 2010	15:13	VIR	23 Jun 2011	08:23	ARI	20 Dec 2011	10:32	SCO
27 Dec 2010	17:37	LIB	25 Jun 2011	20:52	TAU	22 Dec 2011	12:02	SAG
29 Dec 2010	20:49	SCO	28 Jun 2011	07:55	GEM	24 Dec 2011	13:47	CAP
1 Jan 2011	01:21	SAG	30 Jun 2011	16:12	CAN	26 Dec 2011	17:14	AQU
3 Jan 2011	07:38	CAP	2 Jul 2011	21:41	LEO	28 Dec 2011	23:46	PIS
5 Jan 2011	16:07	AQU	5 Jul 2011	01:14	VIR	31 Dec 2011	09:48	ARI
8 Jan 2011	02:56	PIS	7 Jul 2011	03:53	LIB	2 Jan 2012	22:15	TAU
10 Jan 2011	15:23	ARI	9 Jul 2011	06:31	SCO	5 Jan 2012	10:43	GEM
13 Jan 2011	03:36	TAU	11 Jul 2011	09:46	SAG	7 Jan 2012	21:04	CAN
15 Jan 2011	13:21	GEM	13 Jul 2011	14:13	CAP	10 Jan 2012	04:34	LEO
17 Jan 2011	19:27	CAN	15 Jul 2011	20:30	AQU	12 Jan 2012	09:43	VIR
19 Jan 2011	22:14	LEO	18 Jul 2011	05:12	PIS	14 Jan 2012	13:27	LIB
21 Jan 2011	23:09	VIR	20 Jul 2011	16:25	ARI	16 Jan 2012	16:33	SCO
23 Jan 2011	23:59	LIB	23 Jul 2011	04:57	TAU	18 Jan 2012	19:28	SAG
26 Jan 2011	02:16	SCO	25 Jul 2011	16:33	GEM	20 Jan 2012	22:40	CAP
28 Jan 2011	06:54	SAG	28 Jul 2011	01:09	CAN	23 Jan 2012	02:53	AQU
30 Jan 2011	14:04	CAP	30 Jul 2011	06:15	LEO	25 Jan 2012	09:11	PIS
1 Feb 2011	23:21	AQU	1 Aug 2011	08:40	VIR	27 Jan 2012	18:27	ARI
4 Feb 2011	10:24	PIS	3 Aug 2011	10:04	LIB	30 Jan 2012	06:28	TAU
6 Feb 2011	22:45	ARI	5 Aug 2011	11:57	SCO	1 Feb 2012	19:14	GEM
9 Feb 2011	11:21	TAU	7 Aug 2011	15:21	SAG	4 Feb 2012	06:03	CAN
11 Feb 2011	22:19	GEM	9 Aug 2011	20:37	CAP	6 Feb 2012	13:22	LEO
14 Feb 2011	05:48	CAN	12 Aug 2011	03:47	AQU	8 Feb 2012	17:32	VIR
16 Feb 2011	09:12	LEO	14 Aug 2011	12:54	PIS	10 Feb 2012	19:53	LIB
18 Feb 2011	09:38	VIR	17 Aug 2011	00:01	ARI	12 Feb 2012	22:01	SCO
20 Feb 2011	09:00	LIB	19 Aug 2011	12:35	TAU	15 Feb 2012	00:56	SAG
22 Feb 2011	09:29	SCO	22 Aug 2011	00:51	GEM	17 Feb 2012	05:03	CAP
24 Feb 2011	12:46	SAG	24 Aug 2011	10:29	CAN	19 Feb 2012	10:28	AQU
26 Feb 2011	19:31	CAP	26 Aug 2011	16:07	LEO	21 Feb 2012	17:31	PIS
1 Mar 2011	05:14	AQU	28 Aug 2011	18:12	VIR	24 Feb 2012	02:48	ARI
3 Mar 2011	16:46	PIS	30 Aug 2011	18:25	LIB	26 Feb 2012	14:29	TAU
6 Mar 2011	05:13	ARI	1 Sep 2011	18:47	SCO	29 Feb 2012	03:26	GEM
8 Mar 2011	17:51	TAU	3 Sep 2011	21:04	SAG	2 Mar 2012	15:07	CAN
11 Mar 2011	05:30	GEM	6 Sep 2011	02:04	CAP	4 Mar 2012	23:15	LEO
13 Mar 2011	14:28	CAN	8 Sep 2011	09:42	AQU	7 Mar 2012	03:25	VIR
15 Mar 2011	19:31	LEO	10 Sep 2011	19:26	PIS	9 Mar 2012	04:49	LIB
17 Mar 2011	20:52	VIR	13 Sep 2011	06:49	ARI	11 Mar 2012	05:23	SCO
19 Mar 2011	20:02	LIB	15 Sep 2011	19:24	TAU	13 Mar 2012	06:53	SAG
21 Mar 2011	19:16	SCO	18 Sep 2011	08:05	GEM	15 Mar 2012	10:24	CAP
23 Mar 2011	20:46	SAG	20 Sep 2011	18:52	CAN	17 Mar 2012	16:11	AQU
26 Mar 2011	01:58	CAP	23 Sep 2011	01:53	LEO	20 Mar 2012	00:05	PIS
28 Mar 2011	11:00	AQU	25 Sep 2011	04:48	VIR	22 Mar 2012	09:57	ARI
30 Mar 2011	22:38	PIS	27 Sep 2011	04:50	LIB	24 Mar 2012	21:43	TAU
2 Apr 2011	11:15	ARI	29 Sep 2011	04:05	SCO	27 Mar 2012	10:42	GEM
4 Apr 2011	23:45	TAU	1 Oct 2011	04:41	SAG	29 Mar 2012	23:06	CAN
7 Apr 2011	11:20	GEM	3 Oct 2011	08:16	CAP	1 Apr 2012	08:34	LEO
9 Apr 2011	21:00	CAN	5 Oct 2011	15:18	AQU	3 Apr 2012	13:51	VIR
12 Apr 2011	03:35	LEO	8 Oct 2011	01:13	PIS	5 Apr 2012	15:31	LIB
14 Apr 2011	06:39	VIR	10 Oct 2011	12:57	ARI	7 Apr 2012	15:17	SCO
16 Apr 2011	06:58	LIB	13 Oct 2011	01:34	TAU	9 Apr 2012	15:12	SAG
18 Apr 2011	06:18	SCO	15 Oct 2011	14:14	GEM	11 Apr 2012	17:01	CAP
20 Apr 2011	06:49	SAG	18 Oct 2011	01:36	CAN	13 Apr 2012	21:48	AQU
22 Apr 2011	10:25	CAP	20 Oct 2011	10:04	LEO	16 Apr 2012	05:37	PIS
24 Apr 2011	17:58	AQU	22 Oct 2011	14:39	VIR	18 Apr 2012	15:58	ARI
27 Apr 2011	04:57	PIS	24 Oct 2011	15:48	LIB	21 Apr 2012	04:05	TAU
29 Apr 2011	17:33	ARI	26 Oct 2011	15:08	SCO	23 Apr 2012	17:04	GEM
2 May 2011	05:58	TAU	28 Oct 2011	14:45	SAG	26 Apr 2012	05:41	CAN
4 May 2011	17:08	GEM	30 Oct 2011	16:39	CAP	28 Apr 2012	16:09	LEO
7 May 2011	02:30	CAN	1 Nov 2011	22:08	AQU	30 Apr 2012	23:00	VIR
9 May 2011	09:34	LEO	4 Nov 2011	07:17	PIS	3 May 2012	02:02	LIB
11 May 2011	13:57	VIR	6 Nov 2011	19:01	ARI	5 May 2012	02:18	SCO
13 May 2011	15:55	LIB	9 Nov 2011	07:45	TAU	7 May 2012	01:39	SAG
15 May 2011	16:31	SCO	11 Nov 2011	20:09	GEM	9 May 2012	02:00	CAP
17 May 2011	17:22	SAG	14 Nov 2011	07:18	CAN	11 May 2012	05:02	AQU
19 May 2011	20:16	CAP	16 Nov 2011	16:16	LEO	13 May 2012	11:42	PIS
22 May 2011	02:32	AQU	18 Nov 2011	22:17	VIR	15 May 2012	21:45	ARI
24 May 2011	12:24	PIS	21 Nov 2011	01:15	LIB	18 May 2012	10:03	TAU
27 May 2011	00:36	ARI	23 Nov 2011	01:57	SCO	20 May 2012	23:04	GEM
29 May 2011	13:01	TAU	25 Nov 2011	01:57	SAG	23 May 2012	11:30	CAN
31 May 2011	23:55	GEM	27 Nov 2011	03:05	CAP	25 May 2012	22:10	LEO
3 Jun 2011	08:35	CAN	29 Nov 2011	07:01	AQU	28 May 2012	06:05	VIR
5 Jun 2011	15:02	LEO	1 Dec 2011	14:46	PIS	30 May 2012	10:44	LIB
7 Jun 2011	19:32	VIR	4 Dec 2011	01:51	ARI	1 Jun 2012	12:30	SCO
9 Jun 2011	22:30	LIB	6 Dec 2011	14:34	TAU	3 Jun 2012	12:32	SAG
12 Jun 2011	00:33	SCO	9 Dec 2011	02:51	GEM	5 Jun 2012	12:31	CAP
14 Jun 2011	02:38	SAG	11 Dec 2011	13:24	CAN	7 Jun 2012	14:17	AQU
16 Jun 2011	05:58	CAP	13 Dec 2011	21:47	LEO	9 Jun 2012	19:22	PIS
18 Jun 2011	11:48	AQU	16 Dec 2011	03:57	VIR	12 Jun 2012	04:21	ARI

DATE	TIME	SIGN
14 Jun 2012	16:21	TAU
17 Jun 2012	05:23	GEM
19 Jun 2012	17:33	CAN
22 Jun 2012	03:46	LEO
24 Jun 2012	11:41	VIR
26 Jun 2012	17:14	LIB
28 Jun 2012	20:31	SCO
30 Jun 2012	22:03	SAG
2 Jul 2012	22:51	CAP
5 Jul 2012	00:26	AQU
7 Jul 2012	04:29	PIS
9 Jul 2012	12:14	ARI
11 Jul 2012	23:30	TAU
14 Jul 2012	12:25	GEM
17 Jul 2012	00:30	CAN
19 Jul 2012	10:12	LEO
21 Jul 2012	17:23	VIR
23 Jul 2012	22:37	LIB
26 Jul 2012	02:28	SCO
28 Jul 2012	05:17	SAG
30 Jul 2012	07:29	CAP
1 Aug 2012	09:56	AQU
3 Aug 2012	13:58	PIS
5 Aug 2012	20:59	ARI
8 Aug 2012	07:27	TAU
10 Aug 2012	20:10	GEM
13 Aug 2012	08:26	CAN
15 Aug 2012	18:04	LEO
18 Aug 2012	00:32	VIR
20 Aug 2012	04:44	LIB
22 Aug 2012	07:53	SCO
24 Aug 2012	10:49	SAG
26 Aug 2012	13:58	CAP
28 Aug 2012	17:38	AQU
30 Aug 2012	22:31	PIS
2 Sep 2012	05:37	ARI
4 Sep 2012	15:41	TAU
7 Sep 2012	04:09	GEM
9 Sep 2012	16:48	CAN
12 Sep 2012	02:59	LEO
14 Sep 2012	09:29	VIR
16 Sep 2012	12:54	LIB
18 Sep 2012	14:45	SCO
20 Sep 2012	16:33	SAG
22 Sep 2012	19:20	CAP
24 Sep 2012	23:32	AQU
27 Sep 2012	05:23	PIS
29 Sep 2012	13:14	ARI
1 Oct 2012	23:26	TAU
4 Oct 2012	11:46	GEM
7 Oct 2012	00:44	CAN
9 Oct 2012	11:53	LEO
11 Oct 2012	19:22	VIR
13 Oct 2012	23:00	LIB
16 Oct 2012	00:05	SCO
18 Oct 2012	00:26	SAG
20 Oct 2012	01:41	CAP
22 Oct 2012	05:02	AQU
24 Oct 2012	11:00	PIS
26 Oct 2012	19:31	ARI
29 Oct 2012	06:15	TAU
31 Oct 2012	18:40	GEM
3 Nov 2012	07:42	CAN
5 Nov 2012	19:38	LEO
8 Nov 2012	04:33	VIR
10 Nov 2012	09:33	LIB
12 Nov 2012	11:09	SCO
14 Nov 2012	10:51	SAG
16 Nov 2012	10:36	CAP
18 Nov 2012	12:11	AQU
20 Nov 2012	16:55	PIS
23 Nov 2012	01:12	ARI
25 Nov 2012	12:18	TAU
28 Nov 2012	00:58	GEM
30 Nov 2012	13:54	CAN
3 Dec 2012	01:56	LEO
5 Dec 2012	11:50	VIR
7 Dec 2012	18:34	LIB
9 Dec 2012	21:49	SCO
11 Dec 2012	22:20	SAG
13 Dec 2012	21:42	CAP
15 Dec 2012	21:53	AQU
18 Dec 2012	00:49	PIS
20 Dec 2012	07:43	ARI
22 Dec 2012	18:24	TAU
25 Dec 2012	07:13	GEM
27 Dec 2012	20:05	CAN
30 Dec 2012	07:44	LEO
1 Jan 2013	17:34	VIR
4 Jan 2013	01:09	LIB
6 Jan 2013	06:08	SCO
8 Jan 2013	08:27	SAG
10 Jan 2013	08:54	CAP
12 Jan 2013	09:01	AQU
14 Jan 2013	10:50	PIS
16 Jan 2013	16:07	ARI
19 Jan 2013	01:36	TAU
21 Jan 2013	14:04	GEM
24 Jan 2013	02:59	CAN
26 Jan 2013	14:19	LEO
28 Jan 2013	23:26	VIR
31 Jan 2013	06:35	LIB
2 Feb 2013	12:00	SCO
4 Feb 2013	15:44	SAG
6 Feb 2013	17:54	CAP
8 Feb 2013	19:16	AQU
10 Feb 2013	21:20	PIS
13 Feb 2013	01:52	ARI
15 Feb 2013	10:08	TAU
17 Feb 2013	21:49	GEM
20 Feb 2013	10:44	CAN
22 Feb 2013	22:10	LEO
25 Feb 2013	06:51	VIR
27 Feb 2013	13:00	LIB
1 Mar 2013	17:33	SCO
3 Mar 2013	21:10	SAG
6 Mar 2013	00:13	CAP
8 Mar 2013	03:01	AQU
10 Mar 2013	06:18	PIS
12 Mar 2013	11:17	ARI
14 Mar 2013	19:08	TAU
17 Mar 2013	06:08	GEM
19 Mar 2013	18:54	CAN
22 Mar 2013	06:49	LEO
24 Mar 2013	15:48	VIR
26 Mar 2013	21:30	LIB
29 Mar 2013	00:52	SCO
31 Mar 2013	03:12	SAG
2 Apr 2013	05:35	CAP
4 Apr 2013	08:41	AQU
6 Apr 2013	13:00	PIS
8 Apr 2013	19:02	ARI
11 Apr 2013	03:22	TAU
13 Apr 2013	14:12	GEM
16 Apr 2013	02:49	CAN
18 Apr 2013	15:12	LEO
21 Apr 2013	01:06	VIR
23 Apr 2013	07:23	LIB
25 Apr 2013	10:24	SCO
27 Apr 2013	11:31	SAG
29 Apr 2013	12:21	CAP
1 May 2013	14:20	AQU
3 May 2013	18:25	PIS
6 May 2013	01:03	ARI
8 May 2013	10:09	TAU
10 May 2013	21:21	GEM
13 May 2013	09:56	CAN
15 May 2013	22:36	LEO
18 May 2013	09:31	VIR
20 May 2013	17:06	LIB
22 May 2013	20:53	SCO
24 May 2013	21:48	SAG
26 May 2013	21:28	CAP
28 May 2013	21:48	AQU
31 May 2013	00:31	PIS
2 Jun 2013	06:33	ARI
4 Jun 2013	15:53	TAU
7 Jun 2013	03:31	GEM
9 Jun 2013	16:15	CAN
12 Jun 2013	04:57	LEO
14 Jun 2013	16:25	VIR
17 Jun 2013	01:17	LIB
19 Jun 2013	06:37	SCO
21 Jun 2013	08:29	SAG
23 Jun 2013	08:08	CAP
25 Jun 2013	07:26	AQU
27 Jun 2013	08:32	PIS
29 Jun 2013	13:07	ARI
1 Jul 2013	21:43	TAU
4 Jul 2013	09:21	GEM
6 Jul 2013	22:13	CAN
9 Jul 2013	10:47	LEO
11 Jul 2013	22:11	VIR
14 Jul 2013	07:39	LIB
16 Jul 2013	14:22	SCO
18 Jul 2013	17:53	SAG
20 Jul 2013	18:38	CAP
22 Jul 2013	18:06	AQU
24 Jul 2013	18:22	PIS
26 Jul 2013	21:30	ARI
29 Jul 2013	04:43	TAU
31 Jul 2013	15:41	GEM
3 Aug 2013	04:29	CAN
5 Aug 2013	16:57	LEO
8 Aug 2013	03:56	VIR
10 Aug 2013	13:07	LIB
12 Aug 2013	20:16	SCO
15 Aug 2013	01:03	SAG
17 Aug 2013	03:24	CAP
19 Aug 2013	04:06	AQU
21 Aug 2013	04:43	PIS
23 Aug 2013	07:13	ARI
25 Aug 2013	13:14	TAU
27 Aug 2013	23:08	GEM
30 Aug 2013	11:32	CAN
1 Sep 2013	23:59	LEO
4 Sep 2013	10:42	VIR
6 Sep 2013	19:11	LIB
9 Sep 2013	01:43	SCO
11 Sep 2013	06:35	SAG
13 Sep 2013	09:55	CAP
15 Sep 2013	12:04	AQU
17 Sep 2013	13:58	PIS
19 Sep 2013	16:57	ARI
21 Sep 2013	22:34	TAU
24 Sep 2013	07:34	GEM
26 Sep 2013	19:24	CAN
29 Sep 2013	07:56	LEO
1 Oct 2013	18:51	VIR
4 Oct 2013	02:58	LIB
6 Oct 2013	08:31	SCO
8 Oct 2013	12:20	SAG
10 Oct 2013	15:16	CAP
12 Oct 2013	17:59	AQU
14 Oct 2013	21:05	PIS
17 Oct 2013	01:18	ARI
19 Oct 2013	07:26	TAU
21 Oct 2013	16:14	GEM
24 Oct 2013	03:35	CAN
26 Oct 2013	16:11	LEO
29 Oct 2013	03:43	VIR
31 Oct 2013	12:20	LIB
2 Nov 2013	17:34	SCO
4 Nov 2013	20:13	SAG
6 Nov 2013	21:43	CAP
8 Nov 2013	23:29	AQU
11 Nov 2013	02:36	PIS
13 Nov 2013	07:39	ARI
15 Nov 2013	14:49	TAU
18 Nov 2013	00:07	GEM
20 Nov 2013	11:23	CAN
22 Nov 2013	23:56	LEO
25 Nov 2013	12:09	VIR
27 Nov 2013	21:58	LIB
30 Nov 2013	04:01	SCO
2 Dec 2013	06:30	SAG
4 Dec 2013	06:49	CAP

DATE	TIME	SIGN	DATE	TIME	SIGN	DATE	TIME	SIGN
6 Dec 2013	06:53	AQU	4 Jun 2014	14:19	VIR	1 Dec 2014	01:13	ARI
8 Dec 2013	08:34	PIS	7 Jun 2014	01:59	LIB	3 Dec 2014	05:14	TAU
10 Dec 2013	13:06	ARI	9 Jun 2014	10:36	SCO	5 Dec 2014	10:28	GEM
12 Dec 2013	20:40	TAU	11 Jun 2014	15:21	SAG	7 Dec 2014	17:34	CAN
15 Dec 2013	06:40	GEM	13 Jun 2014	17:04	CAP	10 Dec 2014	03:14	LEO
17 Dec 2013	18:16	CAN	15 Jun 2014	17:27	AQU	12 Dec 2014	15:18	VIR
20 Dec 2013	06:47	LEO	17 Jun 2014	18:25	PIS	15 Dec 2014	04:04	LIB
22 Dec 2013	19:18	VIR	19 Jun 2014	21:26	ARI	17 Dec 2014	14:50	SCO
25 Dec 2013	06:16	LIB	22 Jun 2014	03:03	TAU	19 Dec 2014	21:53	SAG
27 Dec 2013	13:56	SCO	24 Jun 2014	11:05	GEM	22 Dec 2014	01:23	CAP
29 Dec 2013	17:36	SAG	26 Jun 2014	21:05	CAN	24 Dec 2014	02:51	AQU
31 Dec 2013	18:00	CAP	29 Jun 2014	08:42	LEO	26 Dec 2014	04:06	PIS
2 Jan 2014	17:02	AQU	1 Jul 2014	21:23	VIR	28 Dec 2014	06:35	ARI
4 Jan 2014	16:58	PIS	4 Jul 2014	09:41	LIB	30 Dec 2014	10:56	TAU
6 Jan 2014	19:45	ARI	6 Jul 2014	19:32	SCO	1 Jan 2015	17:08	GEM
9 Jan 2014	02:24	TAU	9 Jul 2014	01:22	SAG	4 Jan 2015	01:07	CAN
11 Jan 2014	12:26	GEM	11 Jul 2014	03:23	CAP	6 Jan 2015	11:03	LEO
14 Jan 2014	00:24	CAN	13 Jul 2014	03:06	AQU	8 Jan 2015	22:57	VIR
16 Jan 2014	13:00	LEO	15 Jul 2014	02:49	PIS	11 Jan 2015	11:55	LIB
19 Jan 2014	01:22	VIR	17 Jul 2014	04:07	ARI	13 Jan 2015	23:42	SCO
21 Jan 2014	12:42	LIB	19 Jul 2014	08:43	TAU	16 Jan 2015	07:59	SAG
23 Jan 2014	21:42	SCO	21 Jul 2014	16:36	GEM	18 Jan 2015	12:02	CAP
26 Jan 2014	03:11	SAG	24 Jul 2014	02:59	CAN	20 Jan 2015	12:58	AQU
28 Jan 2014	05:03	CAP	26 Jul 2014	14:54	LEO	22 Jan 2015	12:47	PIS
30 Jan 2014	04:32	AQU	29 Jul 2014	03:36	VIR	24 Jan 2015	13:32	ARI
1 Feb 2014	03:44	PIS	31 Jul 2014	16:08	LIB	26 Jan 2015	16:37	TAU
3 Feb 2014	04:54	ARI	3 Aug 2014	02:55	SCO	28 Jan 2015	22:36	GEM
5 Feb 2014	09:47	TAU	5 Aug 2014	10:16	SAG	31 Jan 2015	07:08	CAN
7 Feb 2014	18:43	GEM	7 Aug 2014	13:36	CAP	2 Feb 2015	17:40	LEO
10 Feb 2014	06:32	CAN	9 Aug 2014	13:51	AQU	5 Feb 2015	05:45	VIR
12 Feb 2014	19:14	LEO	11 Aug 2014	12:55	PIS	7 Feb 2015	18:43	LIB
15 Feb 2014	07:25	VIR	13 Aug 2014	13:01	ARI	10 Feb 2015	07:04	SCO
17 Feb 2014	18:22	LIB	15 Aug 2014	15:58	TAU	12 Feb 2015	16:45	SAG
20 Feb 2014	03:32	SCO	17 Aug 2014	22:41	GEM	14 Feb 2015	22:22	CAP
22 Feb 2014	10:10	SAG	20 Aug 2014	08:45	CAN	17 Feb 2015	00:11	AQU
24 Feb 2014	13:49	CAP	22 Aug 2014	20:49	LEO	18 Feb 2015	23:47	PIS
26 Feb 2014	14:54	AQU	25 Aug 2014	09:32	VIR	20 Feb 2015	23:13	ARI
28 Feb 2014	14:52	PIS	27 Aug 2014	21:53	LIB	23 Feb 2015	00:29	TAU
2 Mar 2014	15:40	ARI	30 Aug 2014	08:51	SCO	25 Feb 2015	04:53	GEM
4 Mar 2014	19:12	TAU	1 Sep 2014	17:16	SAG	27 Feb 2015	12:50	CAN
7 Mar 2014	02:38	GEM	3 Sep 2014	22:13	CAP	1 Mar 2015	23:34	LEO
9 Mar 2014	13:33	CAN	5 Sep 2014	23:57	AQU	4 Mar 2015	11:57	VIR
12 Mar 2014	02:08	LEO	7 Sep 2014	23:46	PIS	7 Mar 2015	00:51	LIB
14 Mar 2014	14:16	VIR	9 Sep 2014	23:33	ARI	9 Mar 2015	13:08	SCO
17 Mar 2014	00:44	LIB	12 Sep 2014	01:17	TAU	11 Mar 2015	23:29	SAG
19 Mar 2014	09:12	SCO	14 Sep 2014	06:25	GEM	14 Mar 2015	06:39	CAP
21 Mar 2014	15:38	SAG	16 Sep 2014	15:24	CAN	16 Mar 2015	10:12	AQU
23 Mar 2014	20:02	CAP	19 Sep 2014	03:09	LEO	18 Mar 2015	10:56	PIS
25 Mar 2014	22:38	AQU	21 Sep 2014	15:53	VIR	20 Mar 2015	10:28	ARI
28 Mar 2014	00:10	PIS	24 Sep 2014	03:58	LIB	22 Mar 2015	10:40	TAU
30 Mar 2014	01:53	ARI	26 Sep 2014	14:28	SCO	24 Mar 2015	13:23	GEM
1 Apr 2014	05:20	TAU	28 Sep 2014	22:49	SAG	26 Mar 2015	19:45	CAN
3 Apr 2014	11:48	GEM	1 Oct 2014	04:40	CAP	29 Mar 2015	05:47	LEO
5 Apr 2014	21:39	CAN	3 Oct 2014	07:59	AQU	31 Mar 2015	18:11	VIR
8 Apr 2014	09:49	LEO	5 Oct 2014	09:23	PIS	3 Apr 2015	07:07	LIB
10 Apr 2014	22:06	VIR	7 Oct 2014	10:06	ARI	5 Apr 2015	19:03	SCO
13 Apr 2014	08:32	LIB	9 Oct 2014	11:44	TAU	8 Apr 2015	05:07	SAG
15 Apr 2014	16:19	SCO	11 Oct 2014	15:51	GEM	10 Apr 2015	12:45	CAP
17 Apr 2014	21:42	SAG	13 Oct 2014	23:30	CAN	12 Apr 2015	17:43	AQU
20 Apr 2014	01:27	CAP	16 Oct 2014	10:29	LEO	14 Apr 2015	20:11	PIS
22 Apr 2014	04:17	AQU	18 Oct 2014	23:07	VIR	16 Apr 2015	20:59	ARI
24 Apr 2014	06:54	PIS	21 Oct 2014	11:10	LIB	18 Apr 2015	21:31	TAU
26 Apr 2014	10:00	ARI	23 Oct 2014	21:08	SCO	20 Apr 2015	23:28	GEM
28 Apr 2014	14:23	TAU	26 Oct 2014	04:39	SAG	23 Apr 2015	04:25	CAN
30 Apr 2014	20:56	GEM	28 Oct 2014	10:02	CAP	25 Apr 2015	13:13	LEO
3 May 2014	06:12	CAN	30 Oct 2014	13:51	AQU	28 Apr 2015	01:07	VIR
5 May 2014	17:55	LEO	1 Nov 2014	16:36	PIS	30 Apr 2015	14:02	LIB
8 May 2014	06:23	VIR	3 Nov 2014	18:53	ARI	3 May 2015	01:46	SCO
10 May 2014	17:18	LIB	5 Nov 2014	21:33	TAU	5 May 2015	11:11	SAG
13 May 2014	01:05	SCO	8 Nov 2014	01:45	GEM	7 May 2015	18:15	CAP
15 May 2014	05:43	SAG	10 Nov 2014	08:38	CAN	9 May 2015	23:21	AQU
17 May 2014	08:11	CAP	12 Nov 2014	18:44	LEO	12 May 2015	02:52	PIS
19 May 2014	09:57	AQU	15 Nov 2014	07:07	VIR	14 May 2015	05:13	ARI
21 May 2014	12:18	PIS	17 Nov 2014	19:29	LIB	16 May 2015	07:02	TAU
23 May 2014	16:01	ARI	20 Nov 2014	05:30	SCO	18 May 2015	09:27	GEM
25 May 2014	21:27	TAU	22 Nov 2014	12:17	SAG	20 May 2015	13:56	CAN
28 May 2014	04:47	GEM	24 Nov 2014	16:30	CAP	22 May 2015	21:42	LEO
30 May 2014	14:13	CAN	26 Nov 2014	19:22	AQU	25 May 2015	08:51	VIR
2 Jun 2014	01:43	LEO	28 Nov 2014	22:03	PIS	27 May 2015	21:41	LIB

DATE	TIME	SIGN	DATE	TIME	SIGN	DATE	TIME	SIGN
30 May 2015	09:32	SCO	25 Nov 2015	17:15	GEM	24 May 2016	05:33	CAP
1 Jun 2015	18:38	SAG	27 Nov 2015	19:26	CAN	26 May 2016	14:25	AQU
4 Jun 2015	00:49	CAP	30 Nov 2015	00:48	LEO	28 May 2016	21:04	PIS
6 Jun 2015	05:01	AQU	2 Dec 2015	10:09	VIR	31 May 2016	01:07	ARI
8 Jun 2015	08:15	PIS	4 Dec 2015	22:33	LIB	2 Jun 2016	02:45	TAU
10 Jun 2015	11:13	ARI	7 Dec 2015	11:24	SCO	4 Jun 2016	03:01	GEM
12 Jun 2015	14:15	TAU	9 Dec 2015	22:23	SAG	6 Jun 2016	03:41	CAN
14 Jun 2015	17:50	GEM	12 Dec 2015	06:46	CAP	8 Jun 2016	06:47	LEO
16 Jun 2015	22:51	CAN	14 Dec 2015	12:57	AQU	10 Jun 2016	13:46	VIR
19 Jun 2015	06:22	LEO	16 Dec 2015	17:44	PIS	13 Jun 2016	00:33	LIB
21 Jun 2015	16:58	VIR	18 Dec 2015	21:25	ARI	15 Jun 2016	13:17	SCO
24 Jun 2015	05:40	LIB	21 Dec 2015	00:12	TAU	18 Jun 2016	01:33	SAG
26 Jun 2015	17:56	SCO	23 Dec 2015	02:30	GEM	20 Jun 2016	11:53	CAP
29 Jun 2015	03:20	SAG	25 Dec 2015	05:26	CAN	22 Jun 2016	20:07	AQU
1 Jul 2015	09:09	CAP	27 Dec 2015	10:31	LEO	25 Jun 2016	02:29	PIS
3 Jul 2015	12:20	AQU	29 Dec 2015	18:58	VIR	27 Jun 2016	07:07	ARI
5 Jul 2015	14:22	PIS	1 Jan 2016	06:40	LIB	29 Jun 2016	10:02	TAU
7 Jul 2015	16:37	ARI	3 Jan 2016	19:35	SCO	1 Jul 2016	11:44	GEM
9 Jul 2015	19:49	TAU	6 Jan 2016	06:55	SAG	3 Jul 2016	13:20	CAN
12 Jul 2015	00:16	GEM	8 Jan 2016	15:05	CAP	5 Jul 2016	16:28	LEO
14 Jul 2015	06:13	CAN	10 Jan 2016	20:21	AQU	7 Jul 2016	22:41	VIR
16 Jul 2015	14:15	LEO	12 Jan 2016	23:52	PIS	10 Jul 2016	08:32	LIB
19 Jul 2015	00:47	VIR	15 Jan 2016	02:48	ARI	12 Jul 2016	20:51	SCO
21 Jul 2015	13:22	LIB	17 Jan 2016	05:47	TAU	15 Jul 2016	09:13	SAG
24 Jul 2015	02:06	SCO	19 Jan 2016	09:12	GEM	17 Jul 2016	19:32	CAP
26 Jul 2015	12:22	SAG	21 Jan 2016	13:28	CAN	20 Jul 2016	03:09	AQU
28 Jul 2015	18:46	CAP	23 Jan 2016	19:20	LEO	22 Jul 2016	08:34	PIS
30 Jul 2015	21:39	AQU	26 Jan 2016	03:46	VIR	24 Jul 2016	12:32	ARI
1 Aug 2015	22:35	PIS	28 Jan 2016	14:59	LIB	26 Jul 2016	15:37	TAU
3 Aug 2015	23:24	ARI	31 Jan 2016	03:49	SCO	28 Jul 2016	18:16	GEM
6 Aug 2015	01:29	TAU	2 Feb 2016	15:48	SAG	30 Jul 2016	21:08	CAN
8 Aug 2015	05:39	GEM	5 Feb 2016	00:42	CAP	2 Aug 2016	01:12	LEO
10 Aug 2015	12:08	CAN	7 Feb 2016	05:58	AQU	4 Aug 2016	07:34	VIR
12 Aug 2015	20:52	LEO	9 Feb 2016	08:30	PIS	6 Aug 2016	16:56	LIB
15 Aug 2015	07:45	VIR	11 Feb 2016	09:54	ARI	9 Aug 2016	04:51	SCO
17 Aug 2015	20:22	LIB	13 Feb 2016	11:35	TAU	11 Aug 2016	17:23	SAG
20 Aug 2015	09:23	SCO	15 Feb 2016	14:34	GEM	14 Aug 2016	04:10	CAP
22 Aug 2015	20:39	SAG	17 Feb 2016	19:23	CAN	16 Aug 2016	11:50	AQU
25 Aug 2015	04:20	CAP	20 Feb 2016	02:17	LEO	18 Aug 2016	16:33	PIS
27 Aug 2015	08:02	AQU	22 Feb 2016	11:24	VIR	20 Aug 2016	19:18	ARI
29 Aug 2015	08:50	PIS	24 Feb 2016	22:41	LIB	22 Aug 2016	21:19	TAU
31 Aug 2015	08:32	ARI	27 Feb 2016	11:25	SCO	24 Aug 2016	23:39	GEM
2 Sep 2015	09:02	TAU	29 Feb 2016	23:54	SAG	27 Aug 2016	03:06	CAN
4 Sep 2015	11:48	GEM	3 Mar 2016	09:59	CAP	29 Aug 2016	08:11	LEO
6 Sep 2015	17:39	CAN	5 Mar 2016	16:21	AQU	31 Aug 2016	15:22	VIR
9 Sep 2015	02:36	LEO	7 Mar 2016	19:07	PIS	3 Sep 2016	00:55	LIB
11 Sep 2015	13:55	VIR	9 Mar 2016	19:39	ARI	5 Sep 2016	12:38	SCO
14 Sep 2015	02:40	LIB	11 Mar 2016	19:43	TAU	8 Sep 2016	01:19	SAG
16 Sep 2015	15:42	SCO	13 Mar 2016	21:04	GEM	10 Sep 2016	12:53	CAP
19 Sep 2015	03:30	SAG	16 Mar 2016	00:57	CAN	12 Sep 2016	21:27	AQU
21 Sep 2015	12:31	CAP	18 Mar 2016	07:54	LEO	15 Sep 2016	02:21	PIS
23 Sep 2015	17:50	AQU	20 Mar 2016	17:38	VIR	17 Sep 2016	04:21	ARI
25 Sep 2015	19:42	PIS	23 Mar 2016	05:23	LIB	19 Sep 2016	04:57	TAU
27 Sep 2015	19:28	ARI	25 Mar 2016	18:08	SCO	21 Sep 2016	05:52	GEM
29 Sep 2015	18:56	TAU	28 Mar 2016	06:45	SAG	23 Sep 2016	08:33	CAN
1 Oct 2015	20:03	GEM	30 Mar 2016	17:44	CAP	25 Sep 2016	13:48	LEO
4 Oct 2015	00:23	CAN	2 Apr 2016	01:35	AQU	27 Sep 2016	21:43	VIR
6 Oct 2015	08:31	LEO	4 Apr 2016	05:45	PIS	30 Sep 2016	07:52	LIB
8 Oct 2015	19:50	VIR	6 Apr 2016	06:45	ARI	2 Oct 2016	19:42	SCO
11 Oct 2015	08:45	LIB	8 Apr 2016	06:10	TAU	5 Oct 2016	08:25	SAG
13 Oct 2015	21:37	SCO	10 Apr 2016	05:58	GEM	7 Oct 2016	20:39	CAP
16 Oct 2015	09:17	SAG	12 Apr 2016	08:07	CAN	10 Oct 2016	06:32	AQU
18 Oct 2015	18:51	CAP	14 Apr 2016	13:53	LEO	12 Oct 2016	12:41	PIS
21 Oct 2015	01:36	AQU	16 Apr 2016	23:23	VIR	14 Oct 2016	15:06	ARI
23 Oct 2015	05:17	PIS	19 Apr 2016	11:23	LIB	16 Oct 2016	15:03	TAU
25 Oct 2015	06:21	ARI	22 Apr 2016	00:17	SCO	18 Oct 2016	14:30	GEM
27 Oct 2015	06:07	TAU	24 Apr 2016	12:45	SAG	20 Oct 2016	15:28	CAN
29 Oct 2015	06:24	GEM	26 Apr 2016	23:53	CAP	22 Oct 2016	19:34	LEO
31 Oct 2015	09:10	CAN	29 Apr 2016	08:45	AQU	25 Oct 2016	03:16	VIR
2 Nov 2015	15:48	LEO	1 May 2016	14:32	PIS	27 Oct 2016	13:50	LIB
5 Nov 2015	02:22	VIR	3 May 2016	17:03	ARI	30 Oct 2016	02:00	SCO
7 Nov 2015	15:13	LIB	5 May 2016	17:09	TAU	1 Nov 2016	14:42	SAG
10 Nov 2015	04:01	SCO	7 May 2016	16:34	GEM	4 Nov 2016	03:04	CAP
12 Nov 2015	15:13	SAG	9 May 2016	17:23	CAN	6 Nov 2016	13:54	AQU
15 Nov 2015	00:20	CAP	11 May 2016	21:32	LEO	8 Nov 2016	21:43	PIS
17 Nov 2015	07:23	AQU	14 May 2016	05:51	VIR	11 Nov 2016	01:42	ARI
19 Nov 2015	12:20	PIS	16 May 2016	17:32	LIB	13 Nov 2016	02:22	TAU
21 Nov 2015	15:11	ARI	19 May 2016	06:29	SCO	15 Nov 2016	01:22	GEM
23 Nov 2015	16:25	TAU	21 May 2016	18:47	SAG	17 Nov 2016	00:57	CAN

DATE	TIME	SIGN	DATE	TIME	SIGN	DATE	TIME	SIGN
19 Nov 2016	03:15	LEO	19 May 2017	03:50	PIS	13 Nov 2017	23:26	LIB
21 Nov 2016	09:34	VIR	21 May 2017	10:08	ARI	16 Nov 2017	08:18	SCO
23 Nov 2016	19:42	LIB	23 May 2017	12:31	TAU	18 Nov 2017	18:58	SAG
26 Nov 2016	08:01	SCO	25 May 2017	12:14	GEM	21 Nov 2017	07:13	CAP
28 Nov 2016	20:45	SAG	27 May 2017	11:24	CAN	23 Nov 2017	20:13	AQU
1 Dec 2016	08:51	CAP	29 May 2017	12:13	LEO	26 Nov 2017	08:02	PIS
3 Dec 2016	19:43	AQU	31 May 2017	16:16	VIR	28 Nov 2017	16:29	ARI
6 Dec 2016	04:30	PIS	3 Jun 2017	00:04	LIB	30 Nov 2017	20:36	TAU
8 Dec 2016	10:14	ARI	5 Jun 2017	10:46	SCO	2 Dec 2017	21:20	GEM
10 Dec 2016	12:39	TAU	7 Jun 2017	22:59	SAG	4 Dec 2017	20:36	CAN
12 Dec 2016	12:40	GEM	10 Jun 2017	11:35	CAP	6 Dec 2017	20:37	LEO
14 Dec 2016	12:09	CAN	12 Jun 2017	23:43	AQU	8 Dec 2017	23:09	VIR
16 Dec 2016	13:15	LEO	15 Jun 2017	10:16	PIS	11 Dec 2017	05:00	LIB
18 Dec 2016	17:51	VIR	17 Jun 2017	17:54	ARI	13 Dec 2017	13:58	SCO
21 Dec 2016	02:40	LIB	19 Jun 2017	21:51	TAU	16 Dec 2017	01:07	SAG
23 Dec 2016	14:32	SCO	21 Jun 2017	22:43	GEM	18 Dec 2017	13:33	CAP
26 Dec 2016	03:18	SAG	23 Jun 2017	22:06	CAN	21 Dec 2017	02:28	AQU
28 Dec 2016	15:11	CAP	25 Jun 2017	22:07	LEO	23 Dec 2017	14:40	PIS
31 Dec 2016	01:27	AQU	28 Jun 2017	00:42	VIR	26 Dec 2017	00:25	ARI
2 Jan 2017	09:56	PIS	30 Jun 2017	07:02	LIB	28 Dec 2017	06:22	TAU
4 Jan 2017	16:18	ARI	2 Jul 2017	16:59	SCO	30 Dec 2017	08:29	GEM
6 Jan 2017	20:17	TAU	5 Jul 2017	05:07	SAG	1 Jan 2018	08:09	CAN
8 Jan 2017	22:05	GEM	7 Jul 2017	17:44	CAP	3 Jan 2018	07:22	LEO
10 Jan 2017	22:48	CAN	10 Jul 2017	05:34	AQU	5 Jan 2018	08:12	VIR
13 Jan 2017	00:08	LEO	12 Jul 2017	15:50	PIS	7 Jan 2018	12:15	LIB
15 Jan 2017	03:52	VIR	14 Jul 2017	23:50	ARI	9 Jan 2018	20:05	SCO
17 Jan 2017	11:16	LIB	17 Jul 2017	05:03	TAU	12 Jan 2018	07:04	SAG
19 Jan 2017	22:09	SCO	19 Jul 2017	07:30	GEM	14 Jan 2018	19:41	CAP
22 Jan 2017	10:44	SAG	21 Jul 2017	08:09	CAN	17 Jan 2018	08:31	AQU
24 Jan 2017	22:42	CAP	23 Jul 2017	08:33	LEO	19 Jan 2018	20:25	PIS
27 Jan 2017	08:35	AQU	25 Jul 2017	10:33	VIR	22 Jan 2018	06:26	ARI
29 Jan 2017	16:09	PIS	27 Jul 2017	15:37	LIB	24 Jan 2018	13:38	TAU
31 Jan 2017	21:45	ARI	30 Jul 2017	00:23	SCO	26 Jan 2018	17:39	GEM
3 Feb 2017	01:49	TAU	1 Aug 2017	12:01	SAG	28 Jan 2018	18:56	CAN
5 Feb 2017	04:43	GEM	4 Aug 2017	00:36	CAP	30 Jan 2018	18:52	LEO
7 Feb 2017	07:02	CAN	6 Aug 2017	12:14	AQU	1 Feb 2018	19:12	VIR
9 Feb 2017	09:41	LEO	8 Aug 2017	21:54	PIS	3 Feb 2018	21:48	LIB
11 Feb 2017	13:52	VIR	11 Aug 2017	05:21	ARI	6 Feb 2018	03:56	SCO
13 Feb 2017	20:43	LIB	13 Aug 2017	10:38	TAU	8 Feb 2018	13:53	SAG
16 Feb 2017	06:40	SCO	15 Aug 2017	14:05	GEM	11 Feb 2018	02:20	CAP
18 Feb 2017	18:51	SAG	17 Aug 2017	16:12	CAN	13 Feb 2018	15:10	AQU
21 Feb 2017	07:07	CAP	19 Aug 2017	17:54	LEO	16 Feb 2018	02:40	PIS
23 Feb 2017	17:16	AQU	21 Aug 2017	20:25	VIR	18 Feb 2018	12:03	ARI
26 Feb 2017	00:23	PIS	24 Aug 2017	01:05	LIB	20 Feb 2018	19:11	TAU
28 Feb 2017	04:51	ARI	26 Aug 2017	08:53	SCO	23 Feb 2018	00:06	GEM
2 Mar 2017	07:42	TAU	28 Aug 2017	19:47	SAG	25 Feb 2018	03:05	CAN
4 Mar 2017	10:05	GEM	31 Aug 2017	08:17	CAP	27 Feb 2018	04:41	LEO
6 Mar 2017	12:54	CAN	2 Sep 2017	20:05	AQU	1 Mar 2018	05:57	VIR
8 Mar 2017	16:45	LEO	5 Sep 2017	05:27	PIS	3 Mar 2018	08:20	LIB
10 Mar 2017	22:07	VIR	7 Sep 2017	12:00	ARI	5 Mar 2018	13:23	SCO
13 Mar 2017	05:27	LIB	9 Sep 2017	16:22	TAU	7 Mar 2018	22:03	SAG
15 Mar 2017	15:10	SCO	11 Sep 2017	19:28	GEM	10 Mar 2018	09:51	CAP
18 Mar 2017	02:59	SAG	13 Sep 2017	22:12	CAN	12 Mar 2018	22:43	AQU
20 Mar 2017	15:30	CAP	16 Sep 2017	01:08	LEO	15 Mar 2018	10:10	PIS
23 Mar 2017	02:27	AQU	18 Sep 2017	04:52	VIR	17 Mar 2018	18:56	ARI
25 Mar 2017	10:04	PIS	20 Sep 2017	10:06	LIB	20 Mar 2018	01:05	TAU
27 Mar 2017	14:09	ARI	22 Sep 2017	17:39	SCO	22 Mar 2018	05:29	GEM
29 Mar 2017	15:47	TAU	25 Sep 2017	04:00	SAG	24 Mar 2018	08:52	CAN
31 Mar 2017	16:40	GEM	27 Sep 2017	16:23	CAP	26 Mar 2018	11:44	LEO
2 Apr 2017	18:26	CAN	30 Sep 2017	04:39	AQU	28 Mar 2018	14:30	VIR
4 Apr 2017	22:13	LEO	2 Oct 2017	14:24	PIS	30 Mar 2018	17:51	LIB
7 Apr 2017	04:19	VIR	4 Oct 2017	20:38	ARI	1 Apr 2018	22:58	SCO
9 Apr 2017	12:34	LIB	6 Oct 2017	23:54	TAU	4 Apr 2018	06:54	SAG
11 Apr 2017	22:41	SCO	9 Oct 2017	01:44	GEM	6 Apr 2018	18:00	CAP
14 Apr 2017	10:26	SAG	11 Oct 2017	03:38	CAN	9 Apr 2018	06:49	AQU
16 Apr 2017	23:03	CAP	13 Oct 2017	06:41	LEO	11 Apr 2018	18:39	PIS
19 Apr 2017	10:50	AQU	15 Oct 2017	11:19	VIR	14 Apr 2018	03:24	ARI
21 Apr 2017	19:41	PIS	17 Oct 2017	17:34	LIB	16 Apr 2018	08:50	TAU
24 Apr 2017	00:30	ARI	20 Oct 2017	01:41	SCO	18 Apr 2018	12:01	GEM
26 Apr 2017	01:55	TAU	22 Oct 2017	11:57	SAG	20 Apr 2018	14:26	CAN
28 Apr 2017	01:38	GEM	25 Oct 2017	00:12	CAP	22 Apr 2018	17:08	LEO
30 Apr 2017	01:48	CAN	27 Oct 2017	12:57	AQU	24 Apr 2018	20:40	VIR
2 May 2017	04:12	LEO	29 Oct 2017	23:44	PIS	27 Apr 2018	01:12	LIB
4 May 2017	09:47	VIR	1 Nov 2017	06:41	ARI	29 Apr 2018	07:11	SCO
6 May 2017	18:19	LIB	3 Nov 2017	09:44	TAU	1 May 2018	15:19	SAG
9 May 2017	05:00	SCO	5 Nov 2017	10:25	GEM	4 May 2018	02:06	CAP
11 May 2017	16:59	SAG	7 Nov 2017	10:44	CAN	6 May 2018	14:48	AQU
14 May 2017	05:37	CAP	9 Nov 2017	12:29	LEO	9 May 2018	03:09	PIS
16 May 2017	17:49	AQU	11 Nov 2017	16:41	VIR	11 May 2018	12:38	ARI

DATE	TIME	SIGN
13 May 2018	18:14	TAU
15 May 2018	20:42	GEM
17 May 2018	21:47	CAN
19 May 2018	23:10	LEO
22 May 2018	02:03	VIR
24 May 2018	06:51	LIB
26 May 2018	13:39	SCO
28 May 2018	22:29	SAG
31 May 2018	09:26	CAP
2 Jun 2018	22:06	AQU
5 Jun 2018	10:52	PIS
7 Jun 2018	21:24	ARI
10 Jun 2018	04:02	TAU
12 Jun 2018	06:52	GEM
14 Jun 2018	07:19	CAN
16 Jun 2018	07:20	LEO
18 Jun 2018	08:40	VIR
20 Jun 2018	12:30	LIB
22 Jun 2018	19:10	SCO
25 Jun 2018	04:29	SAG
27 Jun 2018	15:52	CAP
30 Jun 2018	04:36	AQU
2 Jul 2018	17:30	PIS
5 Jul 2018	04:48	ARI
7 Jul 2018	12:49	TAU
9 Jul 2018	16:57	GEM
11 Jul 2018	17:58	CAN
13 Jul 2018	17:30	LEO
15 Jul 2018	17:30	VIR
17 Jul 2018	19:42	LIB
20 Jul 2018	01:13	SCO
22 Jul 2018	10:12	SAG
24 Jul 2018	21:48	CAP
27 Jul 2018	10:40	AQU
29 Jul 2018	23:27	PIS
1 Aug 2018	10:53	ARI
3 Aug 2018	19:49	TAU
6 Aug 2018	01:30	GEM
8 Aug 2018	03:59	CAN
10 Aug 2018	04:17	LEO
12 Aug 2018	03:58	VIR
14 Aug 2018	04:57	LIB
16 Aug 2018	08:54	SCO
18 Aug 2018	16:45	SAG
21 Aug 2018	04:00	CAP
23 Aug 2018	16:55	AQU
26 Aug 2018	05:31	PIS
28 Aug 2018	16:34	ARI
31 Aug 2018	01:29	TAU
2 Sep 2018	08:00	GEM
4 Sep 2018	12:02	CAN
6 Sep 2018	13:53	LEO
8 Sep 2018	14:28	VIR
10 Sep 2018	15:20	LIB
12 Sep 2018	18:14	SCO
15 Sep 2018	00:46	SAG
17 Sep 2018	11:07	CAP
19 Sep 2018	23:51	AQU
22 Sep 2018	12:25	PIS
24 Sep 2018	23:02	ARI
27 Sep 2018	07:14	TAU
29 Sep 2018	13:25	GEM
1 Oct 2018	18:00	CAN
3 Oct 2018	21:11	LEO
5 Oct 2018	23:18	VIR
8 Oct 2018	01:10	LIB
10 Oct 2018	04:09	SCO
12 Oct 2018	09:53	SAG
14 Oct 2018	19:16	CAP
17 Oct 2018	07:35	AQU
19 Oct 2018	20:19	PIS
22 Oct 2018	06:57	ARI
24 Oct 2018	14:32	TAU
26 Oct 2018	19:40	GEM
28 Oct 2018	23:26	CAN
31 Oct 2018	02:41	LEO
2 Nov 2018	05:47	VIR
4 Nov 2018	09:00	LIB
6 Nov 2018	13:02	SCO

DATE	TIME	SIGN
8 Nov 2018	18:59	SAG
11 Nov 2018	03:54	CAP
13 Nov 2018	15:45	AQU
16 Nov 2018	04:40	PIS
18 Nov 2018	15:54	ARI
20 Nov 2018	23:41	TAU
23 Nov 2018	04:09	GEM
25 Nov 2018	06:37	CAN
27 Nov 2018	08:34	LEO
29 Nov 2018	11:07	VIR
1 Dec 2018	14:48	LIB
3 Dec 2018	19:54	SCO
6 Dec 2018	02:49	SAG
8 Dec 2018	12:01	CAP
10 Dec 2018	23:39	AQU
13 Dec 2018	12:39	PIS
16 Dec 2018	00:42	ARI
18 Dec 2018	09:35	TAU
20 Dec 2018	14:33	GEM
22 Dec 2018	16:27	CAN
24 Dec 2018	16:58	LEO
26 Dec 2018	17:49	VIR
28 Dec 2018	20:23	LIB
31 Dec 2018	01:23	SCO
2 Jan 2019	08:58	SAG
4 Jan 2019	18:54	CAP
7 Jan 2019	06:45	AQU
9 Jan 2019	19:43	PIS
12 Jan 2019	08:17	ARI
14 Jan 2019	18:30	TAU
17 Jan 2019	00:58	GEM
19 Jan 2019	03:42	CAN
21 Jan 2019	03:53	LEO
23 Jan 2019	03:22	VIR
25 Jan 2019	04:02	LIB
27 Jan 2019	07:30	SCO
29 Jan 2019	14:33	SAG
1 Feb 2019	00:47	CAP
3 Feb 2019	13:02	AQU
6 Feb 2019	02:01	PIS
8 Feb 2019	14:33	ARI
11 Feb 2019	01:27	TAU
13 Feb 2019	09:30	GEM
15 Feb 2019	14:01	CAN
17 Feb 2019	15:20	LEO
19 Feb 2019	14:46	VIR
21 Feb 2019	14:17	LIB
23 Feb 2019	15:56	SCO
25 Feb 2019	21:20	SAG
28 Feb 2019	06:48	CAP
2 Mar 2019	19:05	AQU
5 Mar 2019	08:10	PIS
7 Mar 2019	20:26	ARI
10 Mar 2019	07:09	TAU
12 Mar 2019	15:47	GEM
14 Mar 2019	21:47	CAN
17 Mar 2019	00:55	LEO
19 Mar 2019	01:40	VIR
21 Mar 2019	01:28	LIB
23 Mar 2019	02:17	SCO
25 Mar 2019	06:05	SAG
27 Mar 2019	14:08	CAP
30 Mar 2019	01:45	AQU
1 Apr 2019	14:47	PIS
4 Apr 2019	02:55	ARI
6 Apr 2019	13:05	TAU
8 Apr 2019	21:14	GEM
11 Apr 2019	03:30	CAN
13 Apr 2019	07:49	LEO
15 Apr 2019	10:13	VIR
17 Apr 2019	11:21	LIB
19 Apr 2019	12:41	SCO
21 Apr 2019	15:59	SAG
23 Apr 2019	22:51	CAP
26 Apr 2019	09:27	AQU
28 Apr 2019	22:10	PIS
1 May 2019	10:22	ARI
3 May 2019	20:17	TAU
6 May 2019	03:39	GEM

DATE	TIME	SIGN
8 May 2019	09:05	CAN
10 May 2019	13:13	LEO
12 May 2019	16:21	VIR
14 May 2019	18:50	LIB
16 May 2019	21:25	SCO
19 May 2019	01:21	SAG
21 May 2019	07:56	CAP
23 May 2019	17:48	AQU
26 May 2019	06:07	PIS
28 May 2019	18:31	ARI
31 May 2019	04:42	TAU
2 Jun 2019	11:46	GEM
4 Jun 2019	16:16	CAN
6 Jun 2019	19:15	LEO
8 Jun 2019	21:44	VIR
11 Jun 2019	00:29	LIB
13 Jun 2019	04:02	SCO
15 Jun 2019	09:03	SAG
17 Jun 2019	16:13	CAP
20 Jun 2019	02:00	AQU
22 Jun 2019	14:01	PIS
25 Jun 2019	02:36	ARI
27 Jun 2019	13:30	TAU
29 Jun 2019	21:07	GEM
2 Jul 2019	01:22	CAN
4 Jul 2019	03:18	LEO
6 Jul 2019	04:24	VIR
8 Jul 2019	06:06	LIB
10 Jul 2019	09:29	SCO
12 Jul 2019	15:05	SAG
14 Jul 2019	23:05	CAP
17 Jul 2019	09:18	AQU
19 Jul 2019	21:18	PIS
22 Jul 2019	10:01	ARI
24 Jul 2019	21:41	TAU
27 Jul 2019	06:28	GEM
29 Jul 2019	11:29	CAN
31 Jul 2019	13:17	LEO
2 Aug 2019	13:20	VIR
4 Aug 2019	13:30	LIB
6 Aug 2019	15:31	SCO
8 Aug 2019	20:35	SAG
11 Aug 2019	04:50	CAP
13 Aug 2019	15:35	AQU
16 Aug 2019	03:49	PIS
18 Aug 2019	16:32	ARI
21 Aug 2019	04:36	TAU
23 Aug 2019	14:32	GEM
25 Aug 2019	21:03	CAN
27 Aug 2019	23:51	LEO
29 Aug 2019	23:56	VIR
31 Aug 2019	23:08	LIB
2 Sep 2019	23:35	SCO
5 Sep 2019	03:08	SAG
7 Sep 2019	10:37	CAP
9 Sep 2019	21:23	AQU
12 Sep 2019	09:51	PIS
14 Sep 2019	22:31	ARI
17 Sep 2019	10:30	TAU
19 Sep 2019	20:56	GEM
22 Sep 2019	04:49	CAN
24 Sep 2019	09:17	LEO
26 Sep 2019	10:35	VIR
28 Sep 2019	10:02	LIB
30 Sep 2019	09:42	SCO
2 Oct 2019	11:45	SAG
4 Oct 2019	17:43	CAP
7 Oct 2019	03:42	AQU
9 Oct 2019	16:04	PIS
12 Oct 2019	04:45	ARI
14 Oct 2019	16:23	TAU
17 Oct 2019	02:29	GEM
19 Oct 2019	10:41	CAN
21 Oct 2019	16:27	LEO
23 Oct 2019	19:28	VIR
25 Oct 2019	20:19	LIB
27 Oct 2019	20:29	SCO
29 Oct 2019	21:59	SAG
1 Nov 2019	02:39	CAP

DATE	TIME	SIGN
3 Nov 2019	11:20	AQU
5 Nov 2019	23:07	PIS
8 Nov 2019	11:47	ARI
10 Nov 2019	23:16	TAU
13 Nov 2019	08:44	GEM
15 Nov 2019	16:14	CAN
17 Nov 2019	21:56	LEO
20 Nov 2019	01:53	VIR
22 Nov 2019	04:19	LIB
24 Nov 2019	05:57	SCO
26 Nov 2019	08:11	SAG
28 Nov 2019	12:33	CAP
30 Nov 2019	20:13	AQU
3 Dec 2019	07:10	PIS
5 Dec 2019	19:43	ARI
8 Dec 2019	07:28	TAU
10 Dec 2019	16:46	GEM
12 Dec 2019	23:22	CAN
15 Dec 2019	03:55	LEO
17 Dec 2019	07:15	VIR
19 Dec 2019	10:04	LIB
21 Dec 2019	12:57	SCO
23 Dec 2019	16:34	SAG
25 Dec 2019	21:45	CAP
28 Dec 2019	05:20	AQU
30 Dec 2019	15:41	PIS

DATE	TIME	SIGN

DATE	TIME	SIGN

Index

Zambezi Publishing Ltd

We hope you have enjoyed reading this book. The Zambezi range of books includes titles by top level, internationally acknowledged authors on fresh, thought-provoking viewpoints in your favourite subjects. A common thread with all our books is the easy accessibility of content; we have no sleep-inducing tomes, just down-to-earth, easily digestible, credible books.

~~~~~~

Please visit our website (www.zampub.com) to browse our full range of Lifestyle and Mind, Body & Spirit titles, and to discover what might spark your interest next...

~~~~~~

Please note:-
Our books are available from good bookshops throughout the UK, but nowadays, no bookshop can hope to carry in stock more than a fraction of the books published each year (over 200,000 new titles were published in the UK last year!). However, most UK bookshops can order and supply our titles swiftly, in no more than a few days (within the UK).

You can also find all our books on amazon.co.uk, other UK internet bookshops, and many are also on amazon.com; sometimes under different titles and ISBNs. Look for the author's name.

Our website (www.zampub.com) also carries and sells our whole range, direct to you. If you prefer not to use the Internet for book purchases, you are welcome to contact us direct (our address is at the front of this book, and on our website) for pricing and payment methods.

Lightning Source UK Ltd.
Milton Keynes UK
UKOW031018050412

190225UK00001B/11/P